Ownership Structure and Corporate Performance

European University Studies

Europäische Hochschulschriften

Publications Universitaires Européennes

Series V	**Economics and Management**
Reihe V	Volks- und Betriebswirtschaft
Série V	Sciences économiques

Volume/Band **3442**

Katinka Wölfer

Ownership Structure and Corporate Performance

A Panel Data Analysis for the German Market

PL ACADEMIC RESEARCH

Bibliographic Information published by the Deutsche Nationalbibliothek
The Deutsche Nationalbibliothek lists this publication in the Deutsche Nationalbibliografie; detailed bibliographic data is available in the internet at http://dnb.d-nb.de.

Zugl.: EBS Universität für Wirtschaft und Recht, Univ., Diss., 2015

D 1540
ISSN 0721-7339
ISBN 978-3-631-66715-6 (Print)
E-ISBN 978-3-653-06275-5 (E-Book)
DOI 10.3726/ 978-3-653-06275-5

PL Academic Research is an Imprint of Peter Lang GmbH.
Peter Lang – Frankfurt am Main · Bern · Bruxelles · New York · Oxford · Warszawa · Wien

This publication has been peer reviewed.

www.peterlang.com

Preface

This dissertation was written during my time as a doctoral candidate at the Endowed Chair of Corporate Finance and Capital Markets at the EBS Universität für Wirtschaft und Recht, Oestrich-Winkel/Wiesbaden, Germany. Throughout this dissertation process, I was supported by several people. At this point, I would like to express my sincere thanks.

I owe special thanks to my academic supervisor Professor Ulrich Hommel, Ph.D., who continually facilitated my research project and academic development, and to my second advisor Professor Ansgar Richter, Ph.D., whose guidance and relentless advice were a great help in writing this dissertation. I am also grateful to the team members and alumni of the Endowed Chair for the friendly and cooperative working atmosphere and the support provided for my dissertation.

My research also benefited from valuable discussions at the American Finance Association Annual Meeting in Atlanta, United States, the European Institute for Advanced Studies in Management Workshop on Family Firms Management Research in Jönköping, Sweden, the seminar on data management and panel data models at the Universidad de Salamanca, Spain, and various workshops at the EBS Universität für Wirtschaft und Recht as well as the Universität St. Gallen, Switzerland.

A special thank you goes to my fiancé who dedicated much time and thought to proofreading my manuscript at various stages and who has always been a source of great strength to me.

Finally, I would like to express my deepest gratitude to my parents, grandparents and grandaunt for their love, unfailing encouragement and support during this project and throughout my whole life. This dissertation is dedicated to them.

Katinka Wölfer

Summary of Contents

Table of Contents

List of Figures

List of Tables

List of Abbreviations

2SLS	Two-stage least squares
3SLS	Three-stage least squares
4SLS	Four-stage least squares
AIC	Akaike's information criterion
AktG	Aktiengesetz
BaFin	Bundesanstalt für Finanzdienstleistungsaufsicht
CDAX	Composite DAX
CFR	Cash flow rights
DAX	Deutscher Aktienindex
DCGK	Deutscher Corporate Governance Kodex
DrittelbG	Drittelbeteiligungsgesetz
EBIT(DA)	Earnings before interest and taxes (and depreciation and amortization)
FD	First-difference
FE	Fixed effects
GLS	Generalized least squares
GMM	Generalized method of moments
HGB	Handelsgesetzbuch
IFRS	International Financial Reporting Standards
IV	Instrumental variable
IZEF	Iterative Zellner efficient estimator
JIVE	Jacknife IV
KWG	Gesetz über das Kreditwesen
LIML	Limited information ML
LM	Lagrange multiplier
LSDV	Least-squares dummy-variable
MDAX	Mid-cap DAX
MitbestG	Mitbestimmungsgesetz

ML	Maximum likelihood
MTB	Market-to-book value
OLS	Ordinary least squares
PP&E	Property, plant & equipment
PSC	Power subscale
RE	Random effects
ROA	Return on assets
ROE	Return on equity
ROS	Return on sales
Root MSE	Root mean square error
SDAX	Small-cap DAX
SIC	Standard industry classification
TecDAX	Technology DAX
VR	Voting rights
WLS	Weighted least squares
WpHG	Wertpapierhandelsgesetz
WpÜG	Wertpapiererwerbs- und Übernahmegesetz

List of Symbols

-l1, -l2, -l3	Annexes to ownership concentration variables to denote the value of a variable lagged by one, two or three years, respectively
α_i	Time-invariant component of the error term (firm-fixed effects)
BANK	Aggregated control rights in the hands of commercial banks
BANK(dummy)	Binary variable, which takes the value of 1 if the largest owner is a commercial bank and 0 otherwise
BLOCK	Fraction of control rights held in blocks of 5% or more
BOARD	Aggregated control rights in the hands of members of the supervisory board
BOARD(dummy)	Binary variable, which takes the value of 1 if the largest owner is a member of the supervisory board and 0 otherwise
CAPX	Capital expenditures
CB	Cubed value of a variable
CORP	Aggregated control rights in the hands of nonfinancial companies
CORP(dummy)	Binary variable, which takes the value of 1 if the largest owner is a nonfinancial company and 0 otherwise
DCORP	Aggregated control rights in the hands of domestic, nonfinancial companies
DCORP(dummy)	Binary variable, which takes the value of 1 if the largest owner is a domestic, nonfinancial company and 0 otherwise
DEBT	Debt level
DFINAN	Aggregated control rights in the hands of domestic financial institutions
DFINAN(dummy)	Binary variable, which takes the value of 1 if the largest owner is a domestic financial institution and 0 otherwise
ε_{it}	Random component of the error term (idiosyncratic error)
FCOPR	Aggregated control rights in the hands of foreign, nonfinancial companies
FCORP(dummy)	Binary variable, which takes the value of 1 if the largest owner is a foreign, nonfinancial company and 0 otherwise
FFINAN	Aggregated control rights in the hands of foreign financial institutions

FFINAN(dummy)	Binary variable, which takes the value of 1 if the largest owner is a foreign financial institution and 0 otherwise
FINAN	Aggregated control rights in the hands of financial institutions
FINAN(dummy)	Binary variable, which takes the value of 1 if the largest owner is a financial institution and 0 otherwise
g, h	Largest owner(s)
GOV	Aggregated control rights in the hands of national government, local authorities, or government agencies
GOV(dummy)	Binary variable, which takes the value of 1 if the largest owner is a national government, local authority or government agency and 0 otherwise
GRO	Sales growth, year to year
HHI	Herfindahl-Hirschmann-Index
i	Index for observational units (sample companies)
I	Number of sample companies
INSIDER	Aggregated control rights in the hands of insiders
INSIDER(dummy)	Binary variable, which takes the value of 1 if the largest owner is an insider and 0 otherwise
j	Number of instruments
k	Number of regressors
K	Number of knots
K_1	Set of exogenous variables ($\boldsymbol{x}'_{1it}$)
m	Number of endogenous variables
MGMT	Aggregated control rights in the hands of members of the management
MGMT(dummy)	Binary variable, which takes the value of 1 if the largest owner is a member of the management and 0 otherwise
N	Number of observations
OWN1	Control rights held by the largest shareholder
OWN12 (OWN123)	Aggregated control rights of the two (three) largest shareholders
OWN1/OWN2	Ratio of the control rights held by the largest shareholder and the second largest shareholder

PRIVATE	Aggregated control rights in the hands of private investors with no executive involvement in the company
PRIVATE(dummy)	Binary variable, which takes the value of 1 if the largest owner is a private investor with no executive function and 0 otherwise
Q	Tobin's Q
r	Rejection rate
R^2	R-squared (-within, -between, -overall)
RDX	Investments in R&D
REV	Annual revenues
RISK1 (RISK2)	Beta of a firm's equity measured over a 1-year (3-year) period (weekly)
RISK3 (RISK4, RISK5)	Beta of a firm's equity measured over a 1-year (3-year, 5-year) period (monthly)
ROA	Return on assets
ROE	Return on equity
s, t	Indices for time periods
SQ	Squared value of a variable
t_i	Position of knots
T	Number of time periods
T_{ij}	Tolerance of variable i on variable j
TA	Total assets
u_{it}	Error term, $u_{it} = \alpha_i + \varepsilon_{it}$
VIF	Variance inflation factor
x_i	Spline variable
$\boldsymbol{x}'_{it}$ ($\boldsymbol{x}'_{1it}$)	Vector of independent (exogenous) variables
$\boldsymbol{x}'_{2it}$	Vector of instrumental variables
v_{it}	Error term in the first-stage equation of a 2SLS model
y_{it} (y_{1it})	Dependent variable
$\boldsymbol{y}'_{2it}$	Vector of endogenous variables
$\boldsymbol{z}'_{it}$	Instrument vector, $\boldsymbol{z}'_{it} = [\boldsymbol{x}'_{1it}\ \boldsymbol{x}'_{2it}]$

1 Introduction

1.1 Motivation and Objectives

The term *ownership* conceptually refers to two formal rights: the right to control the firm and the right to claim the firm's residual earnings (Hansmann, 1988). Formal control does not necessarily mean effective control as formal control generally involves only the right to elect the firm's supervisory board and to vote directly on a few fundamental matters, such as, for example, amendments to the statutes, dividend payouts, or a merger or dissolution of the firm. If shareholders are too numerous and too dispersed, it might not be possible to exercise even these limited control rights meaningfully, with the result that managers possess substantial autonomy. This raises the concern that managers might use their power to pursue own interests, oblivious to the welfare of the owners. Berle and Means (1932) investigated the issue of separating ownership from control and provided an early statement of the principal-agent problem: Those who control a corporation "can serve their own pockets better by profiting at the expense of the company than by making profits for it" (p. 122). Since Jensen and Meckling (1976) picked up the debate and developed a formal concept of the principal-agent conflict between shareholders and managers, a whole branch of research has evolved investigating the issue of separating control from ownership and its resulting impact on corporate performance.

Various arguments have been put forward supporting the notion that the structure of ownership will have significant implications for the performance of the firm. For example, it has been suggested that concentrated ownership may contribute to the solution of agency conflicts in large companies because large shareholders have an interest in value maximization and also possess enough voting control to put pressure on the management and have their interests respected (Shleifer & Vishny, 1997). However, there may be costs of large investors as well. The fundamental problem is that large investors represent their own interests, which need not coincide with the interests of other investors (and other stakeholders) in the firm. As a consequence, large investors might be incentivized to secure private benefits and thereby redistribute wealth from others (Barclay & Holderness, 1989). Yet another view on the relation between ownership and performance is raised by Demsetz (1983) who argues that ownership is an endogenous variable and that ownership structure has no equilibrium effect because this would imply that profit-seeking owners could gain by rearranging their portfolio.

Based on theoretical considerations, it is uncertain as to whether large shareholders contribute to the solution of agency problems, exacerbate them or even have no effect at all. A wealth of empirical research has been conducted, but evidence is mixed and does not provide unambiguous results. Most studies use single equation regression models to explore the relation between ownership concentration and performance and find a positive (e.g., Thomsen & Pedersen, 2000) or insignificant effect (e.g., Hill & Snell, 1988; Holderness & Sheehan, 1988; Pedersen & Thomsen, 1999), although some studies identify a negative effect (e.g., Konijn, Kräussl, & Lucas, 2001). More recent contributions accept the view voiced by Demsetz (1983) that ownership is an endogenous variable and that this needs to be taken into account when estimating its effect on performance. These studies apply simultaneous equation models and mainly find the effects of ownership structure to be insignificant (e.g., Demsetz & Lehn, 1985; Demsetz & Villalonga, 2001; Weiss & Hilger, 2012). However, most studies that use data from the German market provide evidence of a positive effect of ownership concentration on performance even when addressing endogeneity of ownership (e.g., Edwards & Weichenrieder, 2004; Gugler & Weigand, 2003), although some studies find contradicting evidence of a negative effect (e.g., Lehman & Weigand, 2000). As the ongoing debate on ownership concentration and performance has, so far, largely produced inconclusive results, the question remains whether concentrated ownership does significantly affect performance.

While most research treats large owners as a homogenous group with a singular interest on maximizing shareholder value, a complimentary area of investigation suggests that the identity of large owners is an equally important but often neglected dimension of ownership structure with important implications for corporate performance. Accordingly, it has been argued that the commitment of owners and their willingness to engage in monitoring activities or alternatively to exploit private benefits may crucially depend on their identity (e.g., Thomsen & Pedersen, 2000). This suggests that simply examining ownership structure in terms of the distribution of shares does not provide a full account of the story.

A great deal of research has been carried out, which focuses on the effect on performance of ownership in the hands of insiders (e.g., Hermalin & Weisbach, 1991; McConnell & Servaes, 1990; Morck, Shleifer, & Vishny, 1988), financial investors (e.g., Bushee, 1998; Brickley, Lease, & Smith, 1988; Chung, Firth, & Kim, 2002), commercial banks (e.g., Cable, 1985; Gorton & Schmid, 2000; Morck, Nakamura, & Shivdasani, 2000) or the government (e.g., Atkinson & Halvorsen, 1986; Megginson, Nash, & van Randenborgh, 1994; Meyer, 1975), whereas little attention has been devoted to the impact of ownership held by nonfinancial corporations or private investors. To the best of knowledge, only five empirical studies have sought to incorporate the entirety of owner identity groups into the empirical investigation of the effect of ownership structure on performance (Edwards & Nibler, 2000; Edwards & Weichenrieder, 2004; Lehmann & Weigand, 2000; Pedersen & Thomsen, 2003, and Thomsen & Pedersen, 2000). This is largely due to the extraordinary data requirements concerning the size and identity of all shareholder parties in a firm. Another reason is that research mainly relies on U.S. or U.K. evidence, which is – partly due to legal restrictions – characterized by the dominance of institutional and insider shareholders, whereas there is considerable variation in owner identity in Continental Europe where ownership is typically also concentrated in the hands of families, nonfinancial corporations, banks or the government (Fohlin, 2005). As a consequence, still little is known about the impact of the various groups of large shareholders on corporate performance. For this reason, the empirical analyses in this dissertation classify shareholders as individuals, insiders, corporations, financial investors, commercial banks and government entities. The investigation of a broad basis of shareholder identities fills a gap in literature and aims to contribute to a more thorough understanding of the relation between ownership structure and corporate performance.

Another contribution to the literature on ownership and performance is the estimation of nonlinear effects of ownership concentration using restricted cubic splines. Most previous empirical studies estimate linear relations, with only few studies also modeling quadratic, cubic or piecewise-linear model shapes. However, when underlying mechanisms are not known, cubic spline functions offer a much better way to model nonlinear relations because they can assume virtually any shape and hence provide greater flexibility for fitting data. As a result, cubic splines are much less likely to be biased than quadratics or other polynominals, or (piecewise-) linear regressions. To the best of knowledge, this approach is a novelty in the field of ownership and performance and has not been applied before.

A further improvement of the quality of findings stems from the construction of a panel data set, which captures not only variation across companies but also variation over time. In contrast to many studies that focus only on a certain number of large firms, the data set used in this dissertation consists of almost all companies listed at the Frankfurt Stock Exchange and hence reflects the overall German equity market. Furthermore, data are collected for the five consecutive years 2005-09 and hence cover all major phases of an economic cycle. This should lead to an improvement of data quality compared with many studies that are based on a snapshot of only one or few observation years. Due to the large number of 2,118 observations (489 corporations), the data set is rich in content and should therefore produce an increased precision in estimation.

Lastly, another advantage of the data sample is the use of German data. As emphasized, existing empirical evidence mainly refers to the US or UK. However, ownership structures in Anglo-American countries are much more dispersed than in Continental Europe, which is characterized by a higher ownership concentration (Organisation for Economic Co-operation and Development, 2014). As a consequence, studies based on data collected in the US or UK might yield good results for firms with low levels of ownership concentration but are less suitable for analyses of concentrated firms because they cannot provide a large enough sample of those firms. German firms hence appear to be a promising research object, making the results also applicable to other Continental European countries.

Combining the improved conceptual approach of investigating both ownership concentration and identity with the advanced methodological design and the advantageous data sample sheds new light on the relation between ownership structure and performance. The empirical results indicate that ownership concentration has a generally positive effect on capital market performance. However, the effect is nonlinear with a negative effect at low levels of ownership concentration, a positive but bell-shaped effect at medium levels, and again a positive effect at high levels of ownership concentration. Moreover, the analyses reveal that the identity of large owners matters for this relation. That is, the positive performance effect at medium to high levels of ownership concentration is driven by the relative dominance of large financial institutions and intercorporate owners who are documented to have a positive impact on corporate performance. In contrast, the negative performance effect at low levels of ownership concentration is attributed to the value-decreasing impact of small ownership in the hands of insiders (in particular managers), individual investors and government agencies. The effect of bank ownership is insignificant. A major conclusion to arise from this dissertation is therefore that the relation between ownership concentration and corporate performance can be explained to a large degree by the distinction between various owner identities that have different implications for firm performance and, at the same time, diverge in their preferences for ownership in particular size brackets. This implies that ownership concentration effects should rather be interpreted as owner identity effects.

1.2 Outline

This dissertation consists of seven parts: Chapter 1 explains the motivation and objectives of the research and outlines the structure of the work.

Chapter 2 introduces the subject and examines the characteristics of ownership and performance. This will form the basis for the selection of variables for the empirical analyses. First, the chapter elaborates on the construct of ownership concentration and presents the universe of possible measures and their usage in the relevant literature. Second, the various types of owners and their relevance in the German context as well as means of measurement are examined. Finally, measures of corporate performance are explained and compared.

The third chapter builds the theoretical framework of the relation between ownership and performance. As the discussion is mainly grounded in the fundamental conflict between managers and owners, the chapter first elaborates on agency theory, its consequences and the role of ownership structure as a mechanism to overcome shareholder-management conflicts. The chapter then concentrates on the concepts of ownership concentration and owner identity and develops hypotheses regarding the link between ownership and performance.

Existing literature is reviewed in Chapter 4. The major conclusion is that simply examining ownership in terms of the percentage of shares owned by the largest shareholder does not provide a full account of the story. Instead, there is a need to incorporate the identity of owner groups into the analysis, assuming that various motivations and abilities of different types of shareholders may result in their distinctive effectiveness to influence corporate value. The literature review is summarized in a table of more than 60 papers in Appendix A.1.

Chapter 5 develops the research design for the subsequent empirical analyses by describing the data, outlining the model and introducing the econometric approach.

The sixth chapter presents the empirical analyses. First, the chapter examines the effects of ownership concentration. Second, the impact of owner identity is investigated. Finally, the two effects are conflated to a combined model in order to capture the effect of ownership concentration as a function of the identity of owners. The chapter closes with a summary and discussion of results.

Finally, Chapter 7 concludes the dissertation, derives implications for public policy and corporate decision makers, and gives an outlook on future research directions.

2 Characteristics of Ownership Structure and Performance

2.1 Introduction

To introduce the subject, the following chapter takes a close look on the characteristics of ownership structure and performance and discusses general aspects as well as means of measurement. This will form the basis for the selection of variables for the empirical analyses. First, the concept of ownership structure is examined. Ownership is commonly considered a multidimensional construct, which cannot be mirrored by a single variable and instead is characterized by the two dimensions ownership concentration and owner identity: Ownership concentration renders quantitative information on ownership, whereas owner identity reveals qualitative information about the type of shareholder. Sections 2.2 and 2.3 elaborate on these two dimensions of ownership. The subsequent Section 2.4 then discusses various measures of performance and their appropriateness for empirical studies on the effect of corporate ownership structure.

2.2 Concentration of Ownership

Central to the concept of ownership is the definition and measurement of ownership concentration. This is by far the most widely researched dimension of ownership.

2.2.1 Preliminary Considerations

Shares represent a fraction of ownership in a corporation and normally endow the owner with a cash flow right (CFR) and a voting right (VR).[1] The former represents a claim on part of the corporation's earnings and (residual) assets, which entitles the owner to receive dividends. The latter provides the owner with the right to vote at annual shareholders' meetings. Ideally, a share reflects both a cash flow and a voting right. However, control rights can be separated from cash flow rights in two ways.

---

1 The denotations *voting right* and *control right* are used synonymously.

First, a company can issue dual classes of shares, which differ in terms of their relative proportion of control rights and dividend entitlements: Common shares (*Stammaktien*) entitle the owner to receive a dividend and also carry a voting right (one-share-one-vote principle). In contrast, preferred shares (*Vorzugsaktien*) have no voting right but provide the owner with a preferred dividend entitlement. As a consequence, measures of ownership concentration relying solely on cash flow rights rather than on control rights might not necessarily mirror a shareholder's actual control power.

Second, a separation of cash flow and control rights can arise as a result of complex ownership structures such as (multiple) control chains, pyramiding, or crossholdings. Companies form a control chain if firm A directly controls firm B, which in turn controls firm C. In a multiple control chain, the control over a company is executed via several parallel control chains. Pyramiding is a special case of control chains in which every shareholding in the chain has to hold a minimum of control. Crossholding exists if a company directly or indirectly controls its own shares – for example, firm A holds a stake in firm B, which, in turn has a stake in firm A.[2] Following La Porta, Lopez-de-Silanes, and Shleifer (1999), cash flow rights across all levels of shareholdings are calculated by multiplying all percentage shareholdings in a chain, whereas control rights correspond to the lowest percentage shareholding in a chain (weakest-link rule).[3] As a consequence, cash flow rights can deviate from control rights.

The majority of ownership performance studies use control rights as the main ownership variable, while only very few studies refer to cash flow rights (e.g., Kaserer & Moldenhauer, 2008). Some papers include the ratio of control rights divided by cash flow rights as an additional control variable in order to account for the potential divergence of cash flow and control rights (e.g., Chen, 2012).

In the light of complex ownership structures, the question arises at which level ownership should be measured. The vast majority of ownership and performance studies measure

---

[2] Control enhancing mechanisms are not very common in Germany. According to a survey conducted by Institutional Shareholder Services (2007) as part of a larger study commissioned by the European Commission, crossholdings used to be very strong in Germany, but the number of crossholdings as well as their importance is constantly decreasing (see the discussion in Section 3.4.3). Crossholdings are infrequent in all European countries today. Pyramid structures are a more common phenomenon in the EU. The study identifies 18% of the companies in the EU-wide sample using pyramids. In Germany, pyramiding is comparably less frequent (13%).

[3] See Jaskiewicz (2006, p. 29-33), for an exemplary calculation of cash flow and control rights.

shareholdings only on the first level, that is, only the direct ownership of shares of the considered company. Few studies argue for an incorporation of further levels of ownership in order to gain a fair picture of the ultimate owner and hence backtrack up to three levels of owners (e.g., Gorton & Schmid, 2000; Groß, 2007). However, this approach imposes extraordinary high data requirements.

2.2.2 Ownership Concentration Measures

Measures of ownership concentration can be divided into two groups: categorical and continuous measures. Table 2.1 summarizes the most frequently used measures.

2.2.2.1 Categorical Concentration Measures

Most of the early empirical literature on ownership and performance differentiates between owner controlled and management controlled firms, based on ownership percentage criteria.[4] Accordingly, firms are classified as owner controlled if a dominant stockholder owns a specified fraction of the shares and as management controlled if ownership is so disperse that no single shareholders can effectively control the firm.[5] However, because there is no general consensus about the critical control stake, the applied thresholds vary through the different studies from 5% to 50% (e.g., Berle & Means, 1932; Larner, 1966). In order to circumvent the problem of defining one exact threshold and the resulting fuzziness of the classification, later studies use two thresholds and omit companies within the undefined middle range from the analysis in order to capture only companies that can clearly be defined as either owner or management controlled (e.g., Sorensen, 1974). Other studies include the unused but potentially valuable information of the omitted middle range of concentrations by classifying different levels of ownership concentration by more than two categories and differentiate, for example, between management controlled, weakly owner controlled, and strongly owner controlled firms (e.g., Palmer, 1973).

Categorical ownership concentration variables are simple to use but loose potentially valuable information on the ownership structure. Moreover, one of the major problems of the interpretation of the results is the use of different fixed rules to define control categories. In

4 See Short (1994) for a review of the early literature on ownership and performance.

5 This appears misleading from a today's point of view because the variable mirrors only general ownership concentration and not managerial ownership.

order to overcome these shortfalls, more recent studies utilize continuous variables such as shareholder concentration measures.

2.2.2.2 Continuous Concentration Measures

Continuous ownership concentration ratios are defined as percentage of share ownership by the largest or a group of largest shareholders. The majority of Continental European studies refer to the existence and power of a controlling shareholder. Ownership concentration is therefore typically measured as the percentage share of the largest shareholder (e.g., Çitak, 2007; Edwards & Weichenrieder, 2004; Groß, 2007; Pedersen & Thomsen, 1999). Nevertheless, a shareholder's power depends not only on his own share size but also on the holdings of other owners and hence referring solely to the share of the largest owner obviously fails to take into account the control power of other shareholders. Especially in Anglo-American studies, it is common practice to extend the concentration measure to further shareholders by using the aggregated share of the *g*-th largest shareholders. The number of shareholders included in the ratio varies with the most important ones being the three largest (e.g., Kirchmaier & Grant, 2005), the five largest (e.g., Welch, 2003), the 10 largest (e.g., Leech & Leahy, 1991), and the 20 largest (e.g., Demsetz & Lehn, 1985) shareholders. A similar measure is the percentage of shares held in blocks of 5% (e.g., Gedajlovic & Shapiro, 1998; Kaserer & Moldenhauer, 2008). The large number of shareholders considered in Anglo-American studies reflects the relatively high stock market dispersion in these countries as in more dispersed markets alliances of shareholders might be needed to exploit potential benefits from blockholdings. However, measures of ownership concentration that cumulate the holdings of a group of largest shareholders might not always yield reliable results. For example, if ownership is held by one dominating shareholder together with a multitude of atomistic shareholders, an increase in the second largest owner's share size would be interpreted as an increase in ownership concentration, whereas, in reality, the opposite is true.

In order to consider the case of more than one large owner, Overland, Mavruk, and Sjögren (2012) propose to calculate the ratio of the shareholdings of the largest and the second largest owner (or a group of owners following the largest owner). Accordingly, concentration increases with the size of the largest shareholder but decreases if the combined size of other large shareholders increases.

Concentration indices, such as the Herfindahl-Hirschman-Index, measure the symmetry of share size over all shareholders. It is calculated as the sum of the squared percentages of ownership shares. The measure takes into account all owners, thereby drawing a precise picture of ownership dispersion. The value increases with rising inequality of shares among stockholders and decreases with an increasing number of stockholders. However, concentration indices do not say anything about the control ability of the largest shareholder(s) and are therefore typically used only as an additional measure of ownership concentration (e.g., Bøhren & Ødegaard, 2006; Lehmann & Weigand, 2000; Mínguez-Vera & Martín-Ugedo, 2007).

Table 2.1: Common Ownership Concentration Measures

Ownership concentration	Comment
(a) Categorical ownership measures	
One threshold	Separation of concentrated and dispersed firms by a critical control stake
Two thresholds	Separation of concentrated and dispersed firms by two thresholds, with unused middle range
Two and more thresholds	Classification of different ownership concentration levels by more than two categories
(b) Continuous ownership measures	
Own(g)	Aggregated percentage share of the g-th largest owner(s), with $g \geq 1$
Own(g)/own(h)	Ratio of the percentage share of the g-th largest and the h-largest owner (or a group of owners following the largest owner), with $h \geq 2$
Block	Percentage of shares held in blocks, for example, of 5%
HHI	Herfindahl-Hirschman-Index, calculated as the sum of the squared percentages of ownership shares

2.3 Identity of Owners

Measures of ownership concentration can be extended by the additional information of the owners' identity in order to reflect the concentration of stockholdings in the hands of particular types of shareholders.

2.3.1 Preliminary Considerations

Early research in financial economics was simply concerned with examining the impact of ownership concentration and made no attempt to identify the party owning a particular block of shares. Most studies thereby treated owners as a homogenous group, implicitly assuming they all share the same goal of maximizing shareholder value. In contrast, an increasing number of works in organization theory suggest that the identity of owners reveals important information because owner types can be characterized by differing motivations and behavior, which might have important implications for corporate strategy and performance. If ownership of the firm is distributed across different types of owners, the identities of these owners will likely affect the priorities they give to pursuing shareholder value management versus other goals (see Section 3.4). It is therefore of great relevance to develop a framework that gives close attention to the various aspects of the different types of owners.

Owner identity can be captured by measuring the aggregated sum of shares held by all shareholders belonging to the same identity group, assuming no difference in the utility function and the behavior of shareholders with different stake sizes (e.g., Baert & Vennet, 2009; Dittmann, Maug, & Schneider, 2010; Renneboog, 2000). Another method to capture owner identity is to create dummy variables that delineate the identity of certain owners, for example, the largest shareholder (e.g., Mínguez-Vera & Martín-Ugedo, 2007; Thomsen & Pedersen, 2000). Finally, an alternative approach is to measure the aggregated share of the g-th largest shareholder and, at the same time, classify him by owner identity (e.g., Thomsen & Pedersen, 2000). Table 2.2 summarizes the most frequently used measures.

Table 2.2: Common Owner Identity Measures

Owner identity	Comment
Own($identity$)	Percentage of shares held by all shareholders belonging to the same owner type
Dummy($g\_identity$)	Dummy variables referring to the owner type of the g-th largest shareholder, with $g \geq 1$
Own($g\_identity$)	Percentage of shares held by the g-th largest shareholder by owner type, with $g \geq 1$

After having examined various methods to apply the concept of owner identity in practice, the next step is to categorize ownership groups.

2.3.2 Owner Typology

Types of owners typically include individual investors, insiders, corporations, financial investors, commercial banks, and government entities. The various types of owners and their relevance in the German context are examined in the following subsections.

2.3.2.1 Individual Investors

Individual investors buy and sell securities for their personal account and not for another company or organization. They are further characterized by no executive involvement in the firm (otherwise, they would classify as insiders).[6] As of 2014, only 4.1m Germans hold direct stakes in corporations (Deutsches Aktieninstitut, 2015).[7] This relates to 6.4% of the population.[8] Although this is an increase by 1.0m since the end of the 1980s and by 0.5m since the bottom of the financial crisis in 2009, the number of private investors decreased by 2.1m compared with the record high in 2000.[9] About one fourth of private investors hold stocks in the company they are employed at. This is typically the result of employee stock ownership programs in which companies provide their employees with an ownership interest as part of the compensation, often at a preferential price. These shares are usually subject to a lockup period, and owners are relatively inflexible to quickly sell out.

Individual investors often hold relatively small stakes and therefore have limited influence at annual shareholders' meetings. Small shareholders hence often bundle their voting power through shareholders' associations, which are independent organizations representing the interests of private shareholders.[10] Alternatively, small investors might authorize depository

---

6 Kaserer and Moldenhauer (2008) use the term *outside individuals* to describe individuals with no executive function in the company.

7 Statistically, private investors are older than 40 years, well-educated, and have an above-average income (Deutsches Aktieninstitut, 2015).

8 Another 4.3m Germans are invested in stock funds. This results in a total number of 8.4m Germans, or 13.1% of the population, directly or indirectly holding corporate shares (these numbers also include individual investors with an executive function in the company, namely, insiders).

9 Deutsches Aktieninstitut (2015) attributes the deficient attractiveness of private share ownership to the German tax system, which discriminates share returns compared with returns from fixed-income securities, a generally insufficient economic education of the population, and inadequate advisory on the part of commercial banks.

10 According to a 2013 survey of 38,127 private investors of Deutsche Post DHL, 11% of the respondents attend annual shareholders' meetings in person, 39% authorize a third party, and 13% are planning either one option. An interesting fact is that 36% of private investors forfeit their control rights (Pellens & Schmidt, 2014).

banks to vote on their behalf. Investors can issue explicit voting instructions, otherwise, banks are bound to exercise the assigned control rights in the best interest of the delegating shareholders (§135 AktG). The main justification for proxy votes is to guarantee a certain level of attendance at annual shareholders' meetings and hence to avoid random majorities. Nevertheless, proxies are highly controversial because they allow banks a significant level of influence, even without owning stock themselves. In addition, depository banks that also have a credit relation with the company might be accused of prioritizing their own interests as debtholders over their mandate to represent shareholders' interests.[11]

The low level of household ownership may (partly) serve as explanation for the particularly high ownership concentration in Germany compared with other countries, where private investors' participation in the stock market is much higher (Dufey & Hommel, 1997). A study on investor attitudes across Europe finds that German investors are the most risk-averse and are very likely to be financially cautious, whereas British investors show the highest affinity towards stocks (TNS Infratest, 2002). 15% of the population in the UK directly or indirectly own shares, as of 2005 (Grout, Megginson, & Zalewska, 2009).[12] In the US, individual stock ownership is even higher.[13] According to the most recent annual economy and finance survey conducted by Gallup (2013), 52% of American households hold individual stocks, stock mutual funds, or stocks in their 401(k) pension plan, or individual retirement account. Individual stock ownership in the US is currently at the lowest level since 1999 (58%) and has continuously trended downward since 2007 (65%) when the global financial and economic crisis began.

2.3.2.2 Insiders

The definition of insiders varies in literature. Houmes, Boylan, and Dickins (2009), for example, focus only on CEO ownership. However, most studies apply a broader definition and

---

11 See Baums and von Randow (1995) for an in-depth examination of conflicts of interest on the part of depositary banks. See also, for example, Brickwell (2001) for a critical discussion of the influence of commercial banks on industrial companies in Germany.

12 Information on individual investors in the UK is hardly available because the majority of shares is held in nominee accounts, which makes it difficult to identify owners. See ShareSoc UK Individual Shareholder Society (n.d.) on the difficulties to obtain statistics on the UK stock market and its investors.

13 Guiso, Haliassos, and Jappelli (2003) attribute the difference in individual stockholdings between Europe (especially Germany) and the US to the much greater development of mutual funds and pension funds in the US, which significantly lowers participation costs.

define all members of the board as insiders (e.g., Cho, 1998; McConnell & Servaes, 1990; Morck et al., 1988). Studies in Continental European countries with a two-tier system typically classify both members of the management board (*Vorstand*) and of the supervisory board (*Aufsichtsrat*) as insiders and use these measures either separately or in combination (e.g., Groß, 2007). Some studies also treat the family of board members as insiders (e.g., Short & Keasey, 1999; Seifert, Gonenc, & Wright, 2005). In addition, Kaserer and Moldenhauer (2008) define a third category of quasi-insiders in which they classify all former management and supervisory board members as they argue that former insiders with large ownership stakes often still exert considerable influence on the company without being officially in charge.

Insiders typically own an equity fraction as a result of equity-based compensation in the form of (restricted) stocks, stock options, or stock appreciation rights. However, German corporations use equity-based compensation only to a limited degree. Rapp, Schaller, and Wolff (2011) identify 37% of the corporations listed in the German *prime standard* in 2006 as providing stock-based compensation to their executives. In companies offering equity-based pay to executives, this form of compensation accounts, on average, for 23% of total remuneration. According to the study, large, R&D intensive corporations with a diffuse ownership structure are more likely to employ share-based compensation plans. This shows that equity-based compensation is primarily used in companies that are characterized by high complexity and information asymmetries. In comparison with other European countries, the proportion of equity-based compensation of total remuneration in German corporations is far below average. Conyon, Fernandes, Ferreira, Matos, and Murphy (2013) analyze the compensation composition in companies with sales exceeding €100m in 2008 and find that CEOs of European companies receive, on average, 19% of their compensation in form of equity-based pay, whereas CEOs of German companies receive only 9% of their pay in form of equity (the low average might also be due to the fact that only a relatively small number of German firms does offer equity-based compensation at all). In Anglo-American economies, the ideology of creating shareholder value is a key element of corporate governance. In the belief that stock ownership helps align the interest of executives with those of the company's shareholders, almost all *Fortune 500* companies employ stock-based executive compensation plans to boost management's equity ownership in their companies. According to a survey by Tovar and Newbury (2010), 95% of the Fortune 500 companies award annual or recurring equity grants to directors. On average, the equity component corresponds to 52% of executives' total compensation.

Insider ownership does also occur (or accumulate) if insiders trade stocks. However, because management and board members regularly acquire knowledge of price-sensitive, nonpublic information in the course of their work, they render themselves liable to prosecution if they trade on their inside knowledge. Insiders must therefore notify dealings in their own company's shares to the issuer and to the Federal Financial Supervisory Authority (*Bundesanstalt für Finanzdienstleistungsaufsicht*, BaFin). At the same time, companies are obliged to promptly (*ad hoc*) publish new information of which the public is not aware if this information has the potential to influence the price of the company's stock or other financial instruments (WpHG §15, §15a). In an analysis of 2,657 legal insider transactions reported to the BaFin in the period 2002-05, Dymke and Walter (2008) find that trading activity differs significantly between groups of insiders. Accordingly, they reveal that supervisory board members and family members of both management and board members are more active in trading on inside information than executive managers because the former are probably least closely watched by the regulator. In 2013, the BaFin investigated 42 new cases of possibly illegal insider trading (previous year: 26) and reported 35 cases involving 99 individuals to the public prosecution authority. The investigated cases were mainly related to inside information on M&A transactions, earnings reports, and insolvencies (Bundesanstalt für Finanzdienstleistungsaufsicht, 2014). Insider trading is likewise prohibited in other countries within the EU.[14] The prosecution of insider trading also has a high priority in the US. In 2014, the U.S. Securities and Exchange Commission filed 52 (previous year: 44; 2008: 61) cases of insider trading actions (U.S. Securities and Exchange Commission, 2015).

Insider ownership can also be the result of the election of shareholders to the supervisory board. The main function of the supervisory board is the control of management. In German publicly listed companies, the stockholders' meeting elects 50% of the members of the supervisory board if the company has more than 2,000 employees (MitbestG §7) or two third of the board members if the company has less than 2,000 but more than 500 employees

[14] In 2014, the EU adopted legislation harmonizes criminal sanctions for insider dealing. All EU member states agreed to introduce a common definition of insider trading as well as a common set of criminal sanctions including fines and imprisonment of at least four years for serious cases of market manipulation and insider dealing (European Commission, 2014).

(DrittelbG §4).[15] The stockholders' meeting can either nominate independent third parties as board members (share ownership is no prerequisite) or representatives of the company's shareholders.[16] It is also common for major shareholders to negotiate amendments to the articles of association that allow them to directly appoint board members.[17] However, in order to guarantee that boards are truly able to exercise efficient monitoring, the *German Corporate Governance Codex* follows the Anglo-American standard and recommends a "sufficient number" of independent board members (DCGK §5.4.2).

Special Case: Family Ownership

A special case of insider ownership is family ownership.[18] Although family businesses are considered to be a significant and important part of the German economy, family business research has existed only since the 1970s, and is still in its infancy.[19] Until now, there is no generally accepted and consistent theory to explain why and how family businesses differ from publicly held companies. The very basic problem even concerns defining the term *family business*.[20] Some researchers rely on the self-reported assessment of family businesses (e.g., Birley, 2001) or try to capture the family culture within an organization (e.g., Björnberg & Nicholson, 2007), but most definition and classification approaches focus on the family's involvement in the business. It is generally accepted that a family's involvement in the business materially influences the firm's goals, strategies and structure and should thus be used in order

---

15 The remaining seats are given to representatives of employees.

16 Shareholders owning more than 10% of the company's voting shares have to declare within 20 days of exceeding the 10%-threshold whether they strive for a position in the supervisory board (WpHG §27a).

17 AktG §101 limits the number of board members to be appointed by a major shareholder to 1/3 of the total number of seats to be elected by the stockholders' meeting.

18 Ng (2005) finds a correlation of 0.978 between managerial ownership and family shareholdings for Hong Kong companies and consequently uses the percentage of shares held by directors in the firm as a proxy for family ownership. For the U.S. market, where the corporate structure is not as family concentrated as in Hong Kong, Demsetz and Villalonga (2001) identify a correlation of 0.67. See also Kaserer and Moldenhauer (2008).

19 Parts of the section on family ownership were derived from Wölfer (2010).

20 Family businesses are often placed on a par with so-called *Mittelstand* businesses. Although there is a great overlap between the two, they differ in a way that the term Mittelstand refers to businesses that, according to the Institut für Mittelstandsforschung, generate annual revenues of €2m to €50m and provide jobs for 10 to 500 employees, whereas family businesses are characterized by a substantial family influence. See Picot (2008) for a detailed discussion.

to distinguish family businesses from nonfamily ones.[21] Most researchers therefore concentrate on a combination of the components of a family's involvement in the business: ownership percentage (e.g., Lansberg, Perrow, & Rogolsky, 1988), presence of family members in the management and/or on the supervisory board (e.g., Handler, 1989), and transgenerational succession (e.g., Churchill & Hatten, 1987).[22] Lansberg et al. (1988), for example, define a family business as an entity in which the members of a family have legal control over ownership. For Daily and Dollinger (1992), at least two relatives of the owner must serve as managers in order to classify the business as a family business. In contrast, Klein (2000) equally includes family ownership and the presence of family members in the management as well as on the board in her definition of family businesses. Practically all definitions focusing on the components of involvement highlight family ownership as the pivotal criterion. However, no consensus is reached on a reasonable threshold of equity ownership. Whereas Anderson and Reeb (2003b) use a threshold of 5% fractional equity ownership, Gallo and Sveen (1991) require the family to own the majority of the stock, and Donckels and Fröhlich (1991) determine a threshold of 60% equity ownership for businesses to be classified as family businesses.[23] The problem with fixed thresholds of equity ownership is the artificial dichotomization of family versus nonfamily businesses with no further distinction within the two groups.

In response to this definition dilemma, Astrachan, Klein, and Smyrnios (2002) propose to use a continuous rather than a dichotomous scale in order to differentiate various levels of family influence. According to the so-called Power Subscale (PSC), a family can influence a business in a substantial way through its equity ownership stake and the proportion of family representatives who are members of the supervisory board and the management team. These

21 Proponents of the components-of-involvement approach assume that family involvement is sufficient to make a business a family business. Critics argue that family involvement is only a necessary condition and that family involvement must be directed towards behaviors that produce a certain distinctiveness of a family business. See Chrisman, Chua, and Sharma (2005) for a critical discussion.

22 See Chua, Chrisman, and Sharma (1999) and Handler (1989) for a detailed overview of alternative definitions of family businesses in the literature.

23 Jaskiewicz (2006) attributes the differences in ownership thresholds to country-specific, institutional, and cultural differences as well as to different types of family businesses in the research focus.

three channels of influence are viewed as additive and interchangeable. Family influence can then be measured along the PSC scale as follows (Klein, 2000):

$$PSC = \frac{Equity_{Family}}{Equity_{Total}} + \frac{Board_{Family}}{Board_{Total}} + \frac{Management_{Family}}{Management_{Total}}$$

According to Jaskiewicz (2006), the value of the PSC needs to be at least 0.5 in order for a business to classify as a family business.[24] This means that a company qualifies as a family business if a family controls at least 50% of the equity. The same is true if a family, for example, holds an equity stake of only 20% but fills at least three out of 10 seats on the board or management.[25] The level of family influence is the more distinctive the higher the PSC value is and reaches its maximum at a value of 3.0. In this case, the owning family controls 100% of the equity and fills all seats on the board and management with members of the family.

Following Klein (2000) and Jaskiewicz (2006), a family business can then be defined as an entity that is influenced by a family in a substantial way. This means that the family owns at least 50% of the equity; if the family owns less than half of the stock but still more than 20%, the lack of influence in ownership can be balanced through either influence on the board (percentage of seats on the supervisory board occupied by family members) or influence in the management (percentage of family members in the top management team). The main advantage of measuring family influence on a continuous rather than dichotomous scale is the resulting continuum of family business characteristics. Aside from identifying the extent of family influence, the approach also allows the manner of family influence on the business to be determined. Depending on whether this influence is derived from ownership, control, or management, it yields different types of family businesses: the family-owned business, the family-controlled business, and the family-managed business.

Family influence in a business is most prevalent in the time following the start-up phase of the business, that is, when the founder or the founding family is the main source of entrepreneurial drive and capital. As a result, family businesses are often associated with small or medium-sized companies. However, family ownership and management is also a widespread form of organization among well-established businesses at later stages of the

24 In a similar version, the concept is applied by Achleitner, Kaserer, Kauf, Günther, and Ampenberger (2009).

25 According to Jaskiewicz (2006), a family must hold at least 20% of the company's votingl rights as a necessary condition to the PSC approach.

corporate life cycle. Approximately nine out of 10 companies in Germany can be classified as family businesses (depending on the definition used). These family businesses provide 60% of all jobs, generate more than half of the GDP, and develop almost three quarter of all patents and are therefore commonly considered to be the core of the German economy (Schäfer, 2010). As of 2006, Hommel and Wölfer (2009) identify about 650 (private and public) family businesses in Germany and Austria with annual sales of more than €100m. The list is led by Volkswagen and BMW, which are both publicly listed companies but, at the same time, are dominated by their family owners. For example, the families Porsche and Piëch hold through their ownership of Porsche Automobilholding an indirect stake of 50.7% in Volkswagen and are also represented on the supervisory board (Volkswagen, 2014). At BMW, the Quandt/Klatten family owns a total stockholding of 46.7% and also participates in the supervisory board (BMW, 2014). According to a survey conducted by Institut für Familienunternehmen (2014), out of the 50 largest family businesses in Germany (as of 2013), 11 companies are publicly listed. Nine of these companies are also included in the *DAX*, a blue chip stock market index reflecting the 30 major German companies trading on the Frankfurt Stock Exchange.[26] In 2010, the Frankfurt Stock Exchange even designed two new stock indices to exclusively track family businesses, the *DAXplus Family* (including all family businesses trading in the prime standard) and the *DAXplus Family 30* (including the 30 largest and most liquid prime standard family businesses).[27]

2.3.2.3 Corporations

Intercorporate ownership emerges through the partial acquisition of shares by a (nonfinancial) company in another and is a common phenomenon in Germany. After World War II, a dense network of interlocking directorates and ownership ties between German companies evolved, which was generally referred to as "Deutschland AG". Managers at the center of the company network aimed to influence economic and political decisions far beyond the borders of their

---

26 Volkswagen, BMW, Continental, Fresenius, Henkel, HeidelbergCement, Fresenius Medical Care, Merck, Beiersdorf (sorted by annual sales as of 2013).

27 In order to qualify for inclusion in the DAXplus Family index, the founding family either has to own at least 25% of control rights or at least 5% of control rights if the family participates in the management or supervisory board (Deutsche Börse, 2010). Out of the 123 family businesses that were included in the DAXplus Family at index introduction, about 95% (117 companies) fulfilled both elements of the definition (required control of control rights and board membership). Only 23% of the index firms were characterized by family blockholdings of less than 25% (Achleitner, Kaserer, Kauf, & Volk, 2010). Alternative family indices are the *Hauck & Aufhäuser Familienindex Deutschland* and the *Credit Suisse Family Index*.

own companies. This long-standing, characteristic feature of German corporate governance has been attributed to companies' strategic interest in holding on to the comparative advantage of "coordinated capitalism". However, the density of the network has been eroded over the last 20 years. Vanishing capital ties imply a declining degree of strategic coordination among large German companies. This is mainly due to the increasing globalization and the rising importance of international corporations as well as changes in the German tax legislation and the introduction of the Securities Acquisition and Takeover Act (Wertpapiererwerbs- und Übernahmegesetz WpÜG) in 2002 (Beyer, 2002).

The German Monopoly Commission (*Monopolkommission*) provides a yearly analysis of intercorporate shareholdings among the 100 largest corporations in Germany and finds that the number of intercorporate shareholdings within this group has initially doubled from 73 in 1978 to 143 in 1996 and has declined since then to 58 cases in 2012 (Monopolkommission, 2014). The number of corporate owners has about halved from 31 in 1978 to 18 in 2012. The majority of these intercorporate shareholdings are due to commercial banks and insurance companies holding ownership shares in industrial companies and also in companies in their own industry. Focusing only on nonfinancial companies, the analysis identifies seven corporations holding stock in six other corporations in 2012. For example, Daimler holds 14.8% in EADS-Gruppe Deutschland, Siemens and Robert Bosch each own 50% in BSH Bosch und Siemens Hausgeräte, and Deutsche Lufthansa holds a 9.9% stake in Fraport.[28]

Intercorporate ownership ties are also quite common in France. Compared with Germany's starlike network, the French corporate network is more hierarchical and pyramidal (Comet & Pizarro, 2011). In contrast, the Anglo-American corporate governance system produces substantially lower levels of intercorporate ownership. This is due to U.S. antitrust laws being hostile to intercorporate ties.

2.3.2.4 Financial Investors

Financial investors – pension funds, insurance companies, and investment companies (mutual funds, investment trusts, hedge funds, private equity funds) – are major collectors of savings

[28] Robert Bosch and Siemens agreed that Robert Bosch would acquire Siemens' 50% stake in the joint venture BSH Bosch und Siemens Hausgeräte, which would then become a wholly owned subsidiary of the Bosch group. Completion of the transaction is expected in the first half of 2015 (Siemens, 2014).

and suppliers of funds to financial markets.[29] Most of their equity ownership in corporations is not held by the institutions themselves but rather in their role as financial intermediaries on behalf of the funds' beneficial owners. Due to the increasing institutionalization of pension benefits and the appeal of professional fund management, individuals who previously invested primarily through bank accounts or individual investment accounts now often channel their investments through financial institutions. This leads to a global trend of increasing ownership held by financial investors, especially in Continental Europe.

In Germany, the market value of total assets under institutional management as of 2012 amounts to 128% of the German GDP. This compares to 195% in the US and 222% in the UK (Çelik & Isaksson, 2014; Organisation for Economic Co-operation and Development, 2013). The huge difference is mainly due to the different pension system in Anglo-American countries.[30] Statistics further show that the value of assets in the stock market as a percentage of total institutional assets is significantly larger in the US and the UK than in Germany (Bank for International Settlements, 2007). Especially UK based insurance companies and pension funds are very much share capital minded and invest 32% of their resources in the stock market, whereas stock market investments by their counterparts in the US still account for 26% of their portfolio, as of 2005. In Germany, this ratio is significantly lower at 15%. This is mainly because German insurers invest only one fifth of their assets in equities and instead maintain substantial amounts of deposits and loans.

2.3.2.5 Commercial Banks

Germany traditionally has a strong bank-dominated financial system. Banks have played a pivotal role in the historical development of German corporations as they were the primary financiers of the German industrialization and the great wave of company foundings in the

---

[29] The relative importance of the different types of institutional investors varies across countries, partly reflecting the characteristics of retirement savings. In Germany, insurance companies are the largest category of institutional investors (in terms of assets under management), whereas in the UK, pensions funds and insurance companies likewise play a strong role, and in the US, investments funds are the dominant form of institutional savings (Organisation for Economic Co-operation and Development, 2013).

[30] Instead of paying pensions through repartition as, for example, in Germany, where the active population generates the pensions of the retired (i.e., no reserves are built up), Anglo-American countries have developed a capitalization system under which individuals save for their own pensions. These financial reserves are typically managed by financial institutions.

late 19th century. Germany's reconstruction after World War II was likewise financed by credit, again giving banks a central position in the German economy.[31]

The important role of banks as financial intermediaries is also enhanced by the German system of universal banking. In contrast to the Anglo-American banking system, which is relatively segmented, German banks offer a full spectrum of financial services to industrial companies, ranging from taking deposits and handling payment transfers to providing credit financing, dealing in securities, and underwriting public offerings. This *Hausbank* relation traditionally affects the financing practice of German corporations to a large degree: According to surveys by Deloitte (2012) and Kaserer, Fey, and Kuhn (2011), German midsize (*Mittelstand*) corporations make almost no use of capital markets and instead prefer bank loans as their dominant source of financing (following financing with own resources). As a result of the universal banking system and the strong reliance on credit financing, debt-to-equity ratios of German corporations tend to be much higher than in other countries: The debt-to-equity ratio for nonfinancial corporations in selected Euro area countries is, on average, 69% for the period 2000-11, whereas the ratio for German corporations exceeds the Euro average by approximately 20 percentage points (European Central Bank, 2012).[32]

The historically developed, tight relation between corporations and banks also results in a considerable bank ownership in German companies. According to monthly bank statistics provided by Deutsche Bundesbank (2014a), shareholdings of commercial banks in industrial companies have more than tripled in size from €9.2b in 1990 to €29.8b in September 2014. Out of 390 commercial banks in Germany, as of end-2012 (Deutsche Bundesbank, 2013), the "big four" (Deutsche Bank and Deutsche Postbank, Commerzbank, Hypovereinsbank/ Unicredit) hold about 90% of this volume. The concentration of bank ownership within the four largest institutions demonstrates the power of these banks but might also be the result of legal restraints: According to German banking law, commercial banks are not allowed to own an interest of more than 10% in a nonfinancial corporation if the share in the company's

[31] See, for example, Fohlin (2005) and Francke and Hudson (2012) on the historical evolution of Germany's system of close relations between commercial banks and industrial corporations.

[32] From the second quarter of 2008 onwards, the contribution of bank loan financing to overall debt financing of Euro area nonfinancial companies declined dramatically, assumingly due to restrictions in bank loan supply. Other sources of debt financing became more important. In particular, the issuance of debt securities by nonfinancial companies gained importance during the financial crisis (European Central Bank, 2012).

nominal capital, in terms of absolute value, exceeds 15% of the bank's liable equity. The aggregate amount of shareholdings in nonfinancial corporations must not exceed 60% of the bank's liable equity (§12 KWG). This limitation aims at reducing the risk of a contagion from distressed corporations to owning banks and thereby safeguards the solvency of the German banking industry.

In contrast to the German situation, bank ownership in the US is prohibited by law. The National Banking Act of 1864 specified activities constituting the core banking business, and although holding equity ownership in corporations was not included in this list of legal activities, courts exceptionally tolerated equity ownership if the shareholding had been acquired under a distressed loan and subsequently been sold in the near-term. In 1933, a comprehensive banking reform implemented under the Glass-Steagall Act addressed this issue and explicitly prohibited commercial banks from holding shares in nonfinancial companies in order to prevent banks from incurring liquidity problems and hence putting savers' deposits at risk. The Bank Holding Act of 1956 and the Gramm–Leach–Bliley Act of 1999 specified the regulation in more detail and continued to prohibit commercial banks from owning shares of nonfinancial corporations.[33]

2.3.2.6 Government

In Germany, government ownership is primarily the result of the transfer of the extensive state property of the former Third Reich to the succeeding Bundesrepublik (e.g., Viag, Veba, Salzgitter, Volkswagen, Saarbergwerke, Industrieverwaltungsgesellschaft) as well as the later formation of state-run institutions for the purpose of the reconstruction and development of the German economy (e.g., Kreditanstalt für Wiederaufbau). In the aftermath of World War II, it seemed desirable to direct the economy and control demand through government interventions and the provision of a fundamental infrastructure (aviation, railway traffic, telecommunication, and mailing, amongst others). The result was a so-called "mixed economy", an economic system in which both the private sector and the state played an important role. In the late 1970s, a more liberal understanding of the economy developed, and government ownership was put into question. The conservative-liberal government around Chancellor Helmut Kohl argued that the state should focus on its primary duties and responsibilities and consequently reduced the number of state owned shareholdings

[33] See Baums (1992b) for an illustration of the historic development of bank ownership in the US.

tremendously.[34] The privatization process continued further after the German reunification (the state ownership of the former German Democratic Republic has been privatized through the *Treuhandanstalt*). As of end-2012, the German government holds 111 direct shareholdings (66 of which are in corporations with operating businesses) and 591 "significant" indirect shareholdings (1991: 214 direct and 136 significant indirect shareholdings); the total number of direct and significant indirect shareholdings hence accounts to 702 (Bundesministerium der Finanzen, 2011; Bundesministerium der Finanzen, 2014b).[35] The three largest shareholdings are Deutsche Bahn (100% ownership equivalent to common stock in the amount of €2,150), Kreditanstalt für Wiederaufbau (47,19% ownership equivalent to a share in common stock in the amount of €1,769m), and Deutsche Telekom (15% ownership equivalent to a share in common stock in the amount of €1,655m). The current conservative Federal Minister of Finance Wolfgang Schäuble strives to continue the process of reducing government ownership (Bundesministerium der Finanzen, 2014a). However, the recent financial and economic crisis and its aftermath impedes these efforts as, for example, the initial public offering of Deutsche Bahn had to be cancelled due to weak market conditions, and, in addition, a so-called *Finanzmarktstabilisierungsfonds* had to be initiated in order to rescue banks from financial distress as a consequence of the global crisis.

Industrial countries worldwide witnessed a great degree of government ownership and regulation during the postwar years. By the 1970s, the often poor performance of government owned corporations and the increasing need to control government spending and debt initiated an international policy debate about the issue of government ownership itself, and by the 1990s, privatization had become a key aspect of economic reforms throughout the OECD area. Market liberalization, particularly in the EU, and technological changes that have rendered monopoly provision of certain goods and services obsolete (e.g., in the telecommunication sector) accelerated privatization initiatives worldwide. Over the last two decades, the OECD countries and increasingly also many non-OECD countries (especially in

---

34 See Eichel (2000) for a historic and political overview of the postwar privatization process in Germany.

35 Indirect government shareholdings are considered to be significant if the corporation's nominal capital exceeds €50,000, and the government ownership stake accounts at least for 25% of the company's capital.

Eastern Europe) have followed the example of Germany, France and the UK, which had been the pioneers of privatizing government owned corporations.[36]

2.4 Corporate Performance

Competition for customers, employees, capital, and further input factors makes performance essential to the survival and success of the firm. Corporate performance is therefore the ultimate dependent variable of interest in almost any area of management and corporate finance research. However, its measurement is one of the most challenging areas of inquiry.

2.4.1 Performance Dimensions

The narrowest definition of performance centers on organizational performance, which is assumed to reflect the fulfillment of the economic goals of a firm. This encompasses three specific areas of economically relevant firm outcomes: financial performance, stock market performance, and product market performance (Richard, Devinney, Yip, & Johnson, 2009).

In a broader sense, corporate performance is interpreted as a subset of the overall concept of organizational effectiveness (Venkatraman & Ramanujam, 1986). This wider performance dimension includes financial and operational performance but also emphasizes internal performance outcomes associated with more efficient or effective operations and other external measures that capture more than just economic considerations such as, for example, corporate social responsibility. The implementation of balanced scorecards in the 1990s has increased the attention given to the wider aspects of corporate effectiveness. However, balanced scorecards are individually tailored to a firm and can hardly be used to make objective comparisons between different companies. For the same reason, the use of the narrower concept of organizational performance generally dominates the use of the more general construct of organizational effectiveness in empirical research (Richard et al., 2009).

Performance can be measured either objectively (e.g., based on an established system such as internal accounting or systematic tracking by external agencies) or subjectively (e.g., based on perceptual assessments and evaluations by managers or external experts). Although objective and subjective measures are positively correlated (Wall et al., 2004), the latter might be affected

---

36 See Organisation for Economic Co-operation and Development (2003) for an overview of policies and practices of privatizing government owned corporations in the OECD countries.

by psychological or cognitive biases, which can lead to skewed and unrepresentative outcomes. The following elaborations therefore address the objective measures of performance and examine capital market and accounting performance measures. These measures target the financial, stock market, and product market outcomes that constitute performance.

2.4.2 Performance Measures

Given the multitude of performance concepts in the literature, the objective of the following discussion is not to give a comprehensive picture of all approaches but rather to focus on the performance measures common in the ownership literature. Table 2.3 summarizes the most frequently used performance measures.

2.4.2.1 Capital Market Performance

Capital market performance measures are based on stock market data of publicly traded companies. The greatest strengths of these measures are their ready availability and the almost instant adaption of stock prices to new publicly available information. Another advantage of capital market measures is that they are forward looking because stock prices (theoretically) reflect the discounted present value of expected future free cash flows. Stock prices also incorporate intangible assets more effectively than accounting data. Further, capital market performance measures are generally preferred over accounting measures in cross-country studies as they allow the comparison of performance measures regardless of national accounting conventions.[37]

Capital market performance measures can be divided into pure and hybrid measures. A common example for pure capital market performance measures is the share price return. This measure captures the gain (or loss) incurred by shareholders during a specific time period (usually one quarter or one year) and is defined as the change in stock price during the period expressed as a percentage of the value of the stock at the beginning of the period. Another (although less frequently used) measure purely based on stock market data is the share price

[37] A commonly cited example for the influence of accounting standards is the listing of Daimler Benz on the New York Stock Exchange in 1993. As a listing condition, Daimler was required to reconcile its earnings between German and US-GAAP: Under German accounting standards, the company reported a profit of DM 615mm. However, when reconciled to U.S. standards, this turned into a net loss of DM 1,839mm due to a removal of hidden reserves based income (Stice & Stice, 2014).

trend (excluding any cyclical components), which can be interpreted as an indicator of the quality of management and governance.

Only few ownership and performance studies are based on pure capital market performance measures. The greatest weakness of these measures is that they might not necessarily reflect the actual performance of the firm because capital market performance mainly depends on how much of the rent generated from the firm's activities is available for shareholders (in form of dividends or stock price increases). Furthermore, empirical evidence shows that stock prices do not always reflect an efficient appraisal of expected future cash flows as stock price movements can usually not fully be explained by economic rationalities (Roll, 1988). Instead, changes in stock price are, to a certain degree, also the result of market volatility (Shiller, 1981), momentum (Chan, Jegadeesh, & Lakonishok, 1996), or herding behavior among capital market participants (Graham, 1999). As a consequence, empirical ownership studies typically refer to hybrid forms of capital market performance measures, which use both stock market and accounting data.

A prominent hybrid measure of capital market performance is the market-to-book-value (MTB), which reflects the ratio of the company's market value to the book value of its assets. The calculation of MTB resembles the computation of the accounting performance measures ROA and ROE (see the following Section 2.4.2.2) and can be done twofold. Under the entity approach, the numerator refers to the market capitalization of the company's equity plus the market value (if applicable) of debt, and the denominator shows the book value of the company's total assets:

$$MTB\ (entity\ approach) = \frac{Market\ capitalization\ of\ equity + Market\ value\ of\ debt}{Book\ value\ of\ total\ assets}$$

Under the more frequently used equity approach, the numerator is limited to the market capitalization of the company's equity, and hence the denominator refers only to the book value of equity:

$$MTB\ (equity\ approach) = \frac{Market\ capitalization\ of\ equity}{Book\ value\ of\ shareholders'equity}$$

A ratio of greater than 1 implies that the market value of the company's equity is higher than its accounting value. However, unlike ROA and ROE, MTB does not provide any information on the ability of the company to generate earnings. Instead, MTB reflects investors' expectations of the management's ability to create future value from a given set of assets.

Another popular performance measure is Tobin's Q, which is defined as the ratio of the market value of a firm's assets to their replacement costs (Tobin, 1969):

$$Q = \frac{Market\ capitalization\ of\ equity + Market\ value\ of\ debt}{Estimated\ replacement\ cost\ of\ assets}$$

The measure is closely related to the entity approach of MTB. However, in contrast to MTB, which uses the book value of total assets as denominator, Tobin's Q applies the estimated replacement costs of the company's assets.[38] Consequently, instead of measuring the performance of the existing assets, Tobin's Q actually intends to measure the performance of a new investment assuming the possibility to reproduce the existing production capacity. A high value for Tobin's Q is usually a sign of valuable growth opportunities, that is, as long as Tobin's Q is greater than 1, it is profitable to invest in the reproduction of the production capacity.

One difficulty with the use of Tobin's Q is that assets are entered in the denominator not at the value shown in the firm's books but at what it would cost to replace them. However, the replacement values of a company's assets may be difficult to estimate (especially if assets are not traded on a market) largely because they are so specific to the firm. And even where replacement values are available, substantially more information is needed to construct this measure than the traditional MTB ratio (Damodaran, 2012). To cope with the problem of missing data on replacement costs of assets, the denominator of Tobin's Q is therefore frequently operationalized as the book value of equity and debt. Nonetheless, a further inapplicability of Tobin's Q relates to the nominator, which requires the market value of debt. As only a small portion of German companies' debt is traded, most of this debt lacks a market price. As a result, an approximation of Tobin's Q in the German context is commonly defined as the sum of the market value of equity and the book value of debt divided by the book value of total assets – which is similar to MTB:

$$Q(adapted) = \frac{Market\ capitalization\ of\ equity + Book\ value\ of\ debt}{Book\ value\ of\ total\ assets}$$

[38] In inflationary times, when the cost of replacing assets increases, Tobin's Q will generally be lower than the MTB. Conversely, if the cost of replacing assets declines much faster than the book value (e.g., as in the case of technology), Tobin's Q will generally be higher than the MTB (Damodaran, 2012).

The measure reflects the premium (or discount) at which the capital market values a firm's assets. A value of greater than one is generally interpreted as market optimism about the future profitability of a company. However, conclusions have to be drawn with care as the ratio works better for capital-intensive businesses than for companies with "soft" assets because accounting conservatism does not allow intangible assets to be recorded on the balance sheet. This produces inaccurately low book values and hence inflates the values of MTB or Tobin's Q. As a consequence, many ownership studies apply accounting measures as an additional means of corporate performance.

2.4.2.2 Accounting Performance

Accounting measures are widely used means of measuring corporate performance because they are readily available and rely on auditable sources. Furthermore, accounting measures do not require an exchange listing and hence are also applicable to performance studies examining privately held companies. Most important, accounting performance is directly under the firm's control and is not subject to psychological and behavioral influences (as opposed to capital market performance). In addition, there is evidence showing that accounting and economic returns are highly related (Danielson & Press, 2003).

A prominent performance measure based on accounting data is the return on assets (ROA). It is commonly calculated as the ratio of net income plus interest expenses after tax to average total assets:

$$ROA = \frac{Net\ income + Interest\ expense \times (1 - t)}{Average\ total\ assets}$$

The measure indicates how efficient a company is using its assets to generate earnings. The ROA can vary substantially across companies and is highly dependent on the industry. For example, companies operating in asset-intense industries (e.g., steel, automotive) typically display a lower ROA. Likewise, other companies may have assets that are "understated" due to high levels of intangibles and this produces higher ROAs.

Another popular accounting measure of performance is the return on equity (ROE). It is defined as the ratio of net income to average book value of shareholders' equity:[39]

$$ROE = \frac{Net\ income}{Average\ book\ value\ of\ shareholders'equity}$$

The measure indicates how efficient a company is using the resources provided by shareholders to generate earnings. According to the DuPont formula, ROE can be broken down in four components: profit margin, asset turnover, financial leverage and debt burden. The profit margin (net income divided by sales) examines the proportion of sales that finds its way into profit and is hence an indicator of profitability. The term asset turnover (sales divided by assets) shows how hard the firm's assets are being put to use and is thus an indicator of productivity, with a high ratio meaning that the firm is operating close to capacity. The product of the two terms is equal to ROA. Lastly, the financial leverage (assets divided by equity) shows the capital structure and relates the company's assets to the proportion that is financed with stockholders' equity, with a high ratio meaning that the firm uses more debt than equity. At the same time, the term debt burden (interest expenses after tax) becomes greater than zero. As a consequence of adding debt to the capital structure, ROE increases. Thus, ROE can be increased by improving the value drivers profitability and productivity (the product of which is ROA) or by altering the firm's capital structure (or simply by reducing the amount of shares outstanding).

One major difference between ROE and ROA is the consideration of debt. If a company carries no debt, shareholders' equity and total assets will be the same, which means that ROE and ROA will be equal. Adding debt to the capital structure would then lead to ROE becoming greater than ROA. In this regard, ROA is a better indicator of corporate performance when comparing companies with diverging capital structures. Another difference between ROE and ROA is the different perspective they take. In contrast to ROA, which aggregates the return to both shareholders and debtholders, ROE measures only the rate of return on shareholders'

39 As ROE measures the return on investment in equity, the numerator refers to net income, which mirrors cash flows that are available to equityholders after interest and taxes have been expensed. In contrast, ROA measures the return on investment in both equity and debt, and hence interest expenses are added back to the numerator in order to reflect cash flows that are available to all capital providers, both equity and debtholders.

equity. As a consequence, the choice between ROA and ROE also depends on the type of stakeholders for whom the performance measure is relevant.

A further accounting measure occasionally used in ownership and performance studies is sales or sales growth, which is the change in sales over the period, expressed as the difference between sales last period and those this period as a percentage of the sales last period. Sales (or alternatively, asset) growth quantifies the expansion of a corporation and is a key driver of long-term value. However, because the measure is focused on changes in size and not on changes in profitability, growth measures should always be coupled with profitability measures in order to obviate excessive and potentially value-destroying growth. Furthermore, the measure can be complicated to interpret when acquisitions and divestitures occur. A better performance measure is therefore the return on sales (ROS), which indicates how efficient a company is translating its sales into profit.

Less frequently used measures of accounting performance are variations of a firm's earnings such as earnings before interest and taxes (EBIT) or net income. Some of these profit measures (e.g., EBIT) have the advantage of being insensitive to changes in capital structure. However, they are not useful for performance comparisons across companies as they are not neutralized for differences in firm size.

Many ownership and performance studies apply accounting performance measures. However, a weakness of these measures is that they emphasize historic over future performance, whereas capital market performance measures are considered to be more forward looking. The use of accounting measures may also be limited by accounting choices. For example, accounting choices regarding the treatment of inventory or subsequent valuations of tangible and intangible assets allow companies to make use of these choices in such a way as to improve the appearance of financial statements. Window dressing thus leads to a distortion of accounting performance measures. Differences between IFRS, GAAP, and HGB standards lead to further complexities when comparing accounting performance measures between firms operating under differing accounting regimes. However, this is of no concern for the empirical analysis in this dissertation (which is based on a 2005-09 sample) because IFRS have been mandatory for all capital market oriented corporations within the EU since January 1, 2005.

Table 2.3: Common Measures of Performance

Performance measures	Comment
(a) Capital market performance	
Stock return	Change in stock price during the period expressed as a percentage of the value of the stock at the beginning of the period
Share price trend	Long-term share price trend, excluding any cyclical components
MTB	Ratio of the company's market value to the book value of its assets (entity vs. equity approach)
Tobin's Q	Ratio of the market value of a firm's assets to their replacement costs (according to the original definition). Alternatively, ratio of the market value of a firm's equity plus the book value of debt to the book value of its total assets (adapted definition)
(b) Accounting performance	
ROA	Ratio of net income plus interest expenses after tax to average total assets
ROE	Ratio of net income to average book value of shareholders' equity
Sales (asset) growth	Change in sales (assets) over the period, expressed as the difference between sales (assets) last period and those this period as a percentage of the sales (assets) last period
ROS	Ratio of net income plus interest expenses after tax to sales
Earnings before interest and taxes (EBIT)	Operating income, calculated as revenues minus costs of goods sold and administrative and selling costs
Net income	Bottom-line profit, defined as EBIT minus interest and taxes

3 Theoretical Framework

3.1 Introduction

The following chapter builds the theoretical framework around the research question of whether and how ownership structure affects performance.[40] The goal is to offer a rich theoretical analysis of the role of ownership in explaining variations in corporate performance. As the discussion is mainly grounded in the fundamental conflict between managers and owners when the former have the control, but the latter bear most of the wealth effects, Section 3.2 elaborates on agency theory, its consequences and the role of ownership structure as a mechanism to overcome shareholder-management conflicts. Building on agency effects as well as other, nonagency related arguments, Sections 3.3 and 3.4 concentrate on the concepts of ownership concentration and owner identity and provide theoretical explanations for the link between ownership and performance.

3.2 Theory Base

The foundation for research on corporate ownership structure is provided by the work of Berle and Means (1932) whose central premise is the recognition of problems resulting from the separation of ownership and control. Jensen and Meckling (1976) later expand these ideas through the introduction of agency theory, which will be briefly recapped below.

3.2.1 Early Approaches and Roots of Agency Theory

Until the early twentieth century, research on the theory of the firm models the firm as a *black box* operated so as to meet the marginal conditions with respect to cost and revenue, thereby maximizing profits.[41] Internal complexities of organizations are largely ignored. As a result, research based on the concept of marginal analysis has almost no implications for how firms are structured, or how they function internally. Thus, the black box view might be quite useful for addressing research questions regarding the effects of certain public policy measures, but it

40 See Learmount and Roberts (2006) for an elaboration of the notion *ownership of the firm* in the corporate governance literature and the meaning of *ownership* in philosophy, political theory, and law.

41 See Howey (1960) on the emergence of marginalism in economic theory.

does not seem appropriate to give useful insights to the development of a theory of the firm. In the following academic debate, many attempts have been made to overcome this limitation and to construct a theory of the firm that is adequate to explain the behavior of the disparate participants within the firm. The need for a revised theory of the firm was further spurred by the rising popularity of empirical studies on the separation of shareholders' formal ownership and managerial control (e.g., Berle & Means, 1932).

A new stream of research with important implications for a revised theory of the firm has been stimulated by the pioneering work of Coase (1937) who introduces the concept of transaction costs to explain the nature and limits of the firm. He further argues that the assignment of initial property rights is economically irrelevant if no transaction costs exist. With sufficient transaction costs however, initial property rights have a nontrivial effect because the specification of property rights determines how costs and rewards will be allocated among the participants in a firm. As the specification is generally effected through contracting, individual behavior in organizations, including the behavior of the managers, depends upon the nature of these contracts.

Managerial and behavioral theories of the firm developed independently of the transaction costs theory, even though the approaches are in fact highly complementary to each other as managerial and behavioral theories focus on the behavioral implications of the property rights specified in the contracts between the owners and the managers of the firm. Baumol (1959), Marris (1964) and Williamson (1964) suggest that managers, instead of maximizing corporate value or profit, seek to maximize their own utility. Ross (1973) builds on this argument and emphasizes the problem of uncertainty, which arises in all contractual arrangements when one party acts on behalf of or representative for the other party. By allowing transaction costs and informational asymmetries to cause incomplete contracts, managerial and behavioral theories hence abandon the assumption of a complete market. This leads to a methodological individualism, which does no longer consider corporations to be profit maximizing collectives but rather a "nexus for a set of contracting relations among individuals" (Jensen & Meckling, 1976, p. 310). The behavior of a corporation is then considered the equilibrium behavior of maximizing individuals with diverse and conflicting objectives. The economic focus on corporations is hence shifted to man-made institutions, incorporating the individual into economic theory. The agency theory in particular focuses attention on the nature of these contractual relations (Jensen & Meckling, 1976; Mitnick, 1975).

3.2.2 Agency Theory

The economic theory of agency provides the first formal technique for investigating contractual relations and is widely accepted in the strategic management literature as a link between ownership and corporate performance.

3.2.2.1 Origin of Agency Conflicts

An agency relation is based on a "contract under which one or more persons (the principal(s)) engage another person (the agent) to perform some service on their behalf, which involves delegating some decision making authority to the agent" (Jensen & Meckling, 1976, p. 308). The central assumption is that individuals are opportunistic, that is, they constantly aim to maximize their own interests.[42] Hence, there is no guarantee that the agent will always act in the best interest of the principal; there is rather a constant temptation for the agent to maximize his own utility, even at the expense of the principal. In case of incomplete information to the benefit of the agent, the principal cannot prevent those harming actions. An agency conflict thus arises when (a) utility functions of the principal and the agent conflict, and (b) information asymmetries exist.

3.2.2.2 The Shareholder-Management Conflict

The principal-agent conflict is a general contractual problem and exists in almost all cooperative efforts.[43] Economists however focus on two major conflicts: the shareholder-management conflict and the debtholder-management conflict. As this work concentrates on the relation of equity ownership and performance, only the first conflict is further considered. The shareholder-management conflict emerges from the separation of ownership and control in corporations with diffuse ownership structures and analyzes the relation between shareholders (i.e., principal(s)) and managers (i.e., agent(s)) of the firm. It assumes that a conflict of interests exists due to different utility functions of shareholders and managers:

---

[42] Criticism of agency theory has mainly been directed towards the assumption of purely opportunistic contract partners. Stevens and Thevaranjan (2005), among others, present a principal-agent model where the agent possesses some level of moral sensitivity, which causes him disutility if he provides less than the agreed-upon level of effort. In regard to the behavior of principals, it is argued that agency theory overlooks potential cheating by principals and glosses over issues of domination and authority. More recent research hence attempts to evaluate agency theory assumptions and their application to the firm from the perspective of philosophical anthropology (e.g., Fontrodona & Sison, 2006).

[43] See, for example, Mishra, Heide, and Cort (1998) for an examination of agency conflicts in relations between buyers and sellers.

Shareholders derive their utility from dividends and increases in the share price, whereas managers feature a much more complex utility function, which consists of pecuniary remuneration as well as of nonpecuniary aspects of their entrepreneurial activities such as prestige, career prospects, and other private benefits (Rappaport, 1986).

Agency conflicts manifest themselves in various situations (see Table 3.1). For example, a manager might forgo new profitable ventures simply because it requires too much trouble or effort to manage or to learn about new technologies (Jensen & Meckling, 1976). Avoidance of these personal costs represents a source of on-the-job utility, which the manager aims to maximize. The manager's low effort can result in the value of the firm being substantially lower than it otherwise could be. Furthermore, managers might have incentives to appropriate perquisites out of the firm's resources for their own consumption because they do not bear the full costs of these actions (Jensen & Meckling, 1976).[44] Examples for excessive perks range from an executive jet or a chauffeur-driven car to a large office and golf club memberships. This misuse of corporate assets misappropriates some of the firm's surplus and hence harms the value of the firm. A special form of misusing corporate assets refers to overinvestment, which occurs if managers pursue "pet projects" or execute other unprofitable investments in order to increase corporate size (Mann & Sicherman, 1991). For example, managers might perform large investments or undertake low-benefit or even value-destroying acquisitions in order to increase firm size because this empire building often has a positive effect on their prestige, compensation, and promotion. Furthermore, managers tend to have shorter time horizons to achieve returns on investment than shareholders (Narayanan, 1985). Compared with owners of a company, who are long-term oriented under the assumption of going concern, managers have a short-term focus as a result of fixed-term working contracts. Especially near retirement, senior managers might forgo profitable, long-term investments (e.g., investments in R&D) in favor of short-term gains (Dechow & Sloan, 1991). Finally, managers are more risk-averse than shareholders because more of their wealth is tied up in the ongoing business (Mann & Sicherman, 1991). Human capital invested in the firm typically represents a substantial portion of managers' wealth. Managers can hence decrease their own risk position by diversifying the firm's real asset portfolio. That is, managers reduce their

44 The early literature on managerial discretion focuses on the problem of managerial theft rather than that of shirking or empire building (see Shleifer & Vishny, 1997). This includes the expropriation of outputs and the sale of assets (managers can set up independent companies that they own personally and sell the output or even the assets of the main company to these firms at below-market prices).

personal risk, for example, by purchasing assets that are unrelated to the firm's primary line of business. This preference for asset diversification leads to suboptimal investment decisions, which are not in the interest of risk-neutral shareholders.

Table 3.1: Agency Conflicts in the Shareholder-Management Relation

Potential agency conflicts	Comment
Low effort	Managers tend to work less hard than shareholders expect them to.
Misuse of assets	Managers have incentives to consume excessive perks.
Overinvestment	Managers have incentives to realize even unprofitable investments.
Time preference	Managers tend to have shorter time horizons to achieve investment results than shareholders.
Risk preference	Managers prefer a diversified asset portfolio.

If the interests of managers and shareholders were perfectly aligned, managers would dilute all free cash flow to shareholders who would then be able to direct this cash to more efficient uses, and shareholder wealth would be maximized. However, in case of asymmetrical information to the benefit of managers (owing to their daily professional occupation with the company and the market), owners cannot prevent harming actions resulting from this misalignment of interests.

Information asymmetries between principals and agents generally occur in various forms (see Table 3.2). First, the principal might not be able to properly assess the agent's true quality before contract conclusion. This situation occurs, for example, if an applicant to a new job convinces the employer of his qualifications, thereby hiding any weaknesses. The uncertainty over the agent's hidden characteristics may thus lead to an adverse selection in the agent's engagement (Akerlof, 1970). Second, the agent might have the hidden intentions to opportunistically exploit the principal. This information asymmetry can cause adverse selection (before the contract conclusion) as well as a hold-up situation, where the principal recognizes the opportunistic behavior of the agent (after the contract conclusion) but cannot sanction him or prevent his harming actions due to his high dependency on the agent (Spremann, 1990). This situation occurs, for example, if a borrower increases the firm risk after the conclusion of the loan agreement (which involves fixed interest rates). Third, if after the contract conclusion the result of the agent's actions is also influenced by exogenous factors, the principal might observe these results but cannot draw conclusions on the direct efforts of the agent. The agent knows what actions he has taken, but they remain hidden to the principal (Caillaud & Hermalin, 2000). This situation occurs, for example, if sales growth cannot clearly be attributed to either successful marketing activities by the mandated salesman or to a general positive market environment. This creates a moral hazard conflict, which generally describes the risk of agents not putting forth their best efforts or shirking from their tasks once the contract has been concluded (Arnott & Stiglitz, 1988). Fourth, the principal observes both the result and the agent's efforts but might not have the knowledge to properly assess the outcome (Alparslan, 2005). This situation occurs, for example, if a customer has a car repair shop install a new coupler in his vehicle but does not have the know-how to assess the quality (and necessity) of the mechanic's work. Hidden information on the quality of the agent's work also leads to a moral hazard situation.

Table 3.2: Informational Asymmetries in Agency Relations

<table>
<tr><th></th><th>Hidden characteristics</th><th colspan="2">Hidden intentions</th><th>Hidden actions</th><th>Hidden information</th></tr>
<tr><td>Object of asymmetry</td><td>Characteristics of agent are unknown</td><td colspan="2">Intentions of agent are unknown or not avertable</td><td>Actions of agent are not observable (quantity uncertainty)</td><td>Actions of agents are not evaluable (quality uncertainty)</td></tr>
<tr><td>Time of appearance</td><td colspan="2">Before contract conclusion (ex ante)</td><td colspan="3">After contract conclusion (ex post)</td></tr>
<tr><td>Agency conflict</td><td colspan="2">Adverse selection</td><td>Hold-up</td><td colspan="2">Moral hazard</td></tr>
<tr><td>Conflict-solving mechanism</td><td colspan="2">Screening, self-selection, signaling, etc.</td><td>Mutual depen-dence etc.</td><td colspan="2">Monitoring, bonding, incentive alignment, etc.</td></tr>
</table>

3.2.2.3 Consequences From Shareholder-Management Conflicts

Adverse selection, hold-up situations, and moral hazard eventually hurt the welfare of both the principal and the agent because the principal anticipates the reduced utility and partially passes it on to the agent. Consequently, it should be in the interest of both parties to reduce these conflicts. However, it is generally impossible for the principal or the agent, at zero cost, to ensure that the agent will make optimal decisions from the principal's point of view. Most agency relations thus involve costly control mechanisms in order to prevent or mitigate agency conflicts. Nevertheless, in most cases there still remains some divergence between the agent's decisions and those decisions that would maximize the welfare of the principal. The difference between the first-best and second-best solution is called residual loss. The sum of these agency control costs and the residual loss constitutes agency costs inherent to any contractual relation between a principal and an agent (Jensen & Meckling, 1976).

In order to mitigate the risk of adverse selection, the principal might screen the agent, for example, by offering a set of compensation structures that allow for self-selection through the agent's choice (Rothschild & Stiglitz, 1976). At the same time, the agent might pursue credible actions to signal his qualification, for example, by documenting his educational track record (Spence, 1987). The agent's reputation also serves as a valuable instrument to reveal the agent's true character and intentions in previous contractual relations and thus might reduce the risk of adverse selection or a hold-up situation. However, as this dissertation deals with already existing contractual relations, adverse selection situations are not further considered.

In order to reduce agency conflicts resulting from hold-up situations and moral hazard (i.e., the lack of effort on the part of the agent), the principal might establish mutual dependencies by negotiating guarantees. He might also install appropriate incentives for the agent and incur monitoring costs designed to limit the dissenting behavior of the agent. Monitoring includes measures to control managers' behavior such as, for example, budget restrictions, operating rules, and reporting procedures as well as explicit monitoring activities through annual shareholders' meetings, one-on-one meetings with the management, participation in the supervisory board, or even legal action against management's policies (Chaganti & Damanpour, 1991). At the same time, the agent may be motivated to incur bonding costs (at the expense of his own utility) in the form of trust building actions to signal that he will not take actions that would harm the principal. In practice however, bonding is almost impossible to observe or quantify (Depken, Nguyen, & Sarkar, n.d.).[45]

3.2.2.4 Agency Control Mechanisms

Various internal and external mechanisms exist in corporate practice that either help align the interests of managers with those of shareholders or limit the agency costs that managers can produce (see Table 3.3). Particular attention has been paid to ownership structure as a key to more effective corporate governance. The main focus of this work is the empirical investigation of corporate ownership structures as a mechanism of corporate governance in Germany and the question of whether ownership concentration and owner identity do reduce agency costs. These potential effects of ownership structure are explained together with nonagency related effects in the following sections.

Apart from ownership structure, the firm's financing mix is also argued to influence the shareholder-management conflict. Several authors argue that high levels of debt and dividends reduce agency costs because fixed debt obligations limit the discretion of managers to misuse assets or invest in unprofitable ventures (e.g., Jensen, 1986). Debt also increases managers' exposure to market forces: In contrast to the situation in an all-equity financed company, where sloppy management may reduce shareholders' return but not threaten managers' utility, inferior performance of leveraged companies might lead rating agencies to downgrade the company, which in turn alerts shareholders to potential inefficiencies. Dividends also limit the cash available to managers, but they provide a weaker mechanism than debt payments because dividend payouts are not subject to the same legal obligation as debt service (Byrd, Parrino, & Pritsch, 1998). The company's financing mix hence is captured as control variable in the following empirical analysis.

Executive compensation is also suggested to be an important mechanism for aligning the interests of managers and shareholders (Jensen & Murphy, 1990). Effective compensation plans refer not only to the level of pay but also to the structure of the compensation package.

[45] In empirical research, bonding efforts can be proxied, for example, by the firm's advertising efforts and the firm's asset utilization rate (Depken, Nguyen, & Sarkar, n.d.). Increased advertising improves the firm's visibility and attracts attention from investors and regulators as potential monitors, which leads to lower agency costs. In contrast, agency costs will be higher for firms incurring a low sales-to-assets ratio as this might be the result of a lack of managerial effort (resulting in lower revenues) or the consumption of managerial perquisites (resulting in the firm purchasing unproductive assets).

Hence, three major components can serve to mitigate agency problems: fixed salary, bonuses linked to accounting-based performance measures, and stock options (Byrd et al., 1998).[46] In practice, information on managerial compensation packages has to be made publicly available since 2006 (§289 HGB and §315 HGB). However, publicly quoted companies are obliged to disclose only the total compensation of all board members. Although the German Corporate Governance Codex recommends a disclosure of compensation by name (DCGK §4.2.4), shareholders can vote against (especially family businesses prefer this confidentiality, for example Porsche AG). This control mechanism hence is not further examined.

Finally, the supervisory board acts as the ultimate internal control mechanism. The supervisory board is generally responsible for selecting, monitoring, and replacing the firm's management. By challenging managers' decisions, a strong board can limit the divergence of managers from shareholder wealth maximization.[47] But because board involvement is such a complex monitoring mechanism, it is difficult to objectively capture the intensity of involvement (Judge & Zeithaml, 1992). This aspect is also not further considered.

Moreover, there are also external mechanisms available such as the managerial labor market (Fama, 1980). Effective managers tend to have more future job opportunities (both within and outside the firm), and these prospects create incentives to limit excessive self-serving behavior at the expense of shareholders. Competition in product markets can also reduce managerial inefficiency if there is a common component to firms' costs, i.e. as one firm's costs fall, so do those of other firms. When costs fall, profit-maximizing firms expand, which in turn reduces product prices and gives self-serving managers less opportunity for discretionary behavior than if their firm's costs had fallen alone, and product prices had not changed (Hart, 1983). The market for corporate control (i.e., the threat of hostile takeovers) has been similarly argued to discipline managers because managerial slack that reduces shareholder value attracts opportunity investors and increases the likelihood that management will be dismissed following an acquisition (Manne, 1965). However, takeovers are an extremely expensive solution (Gedajlovic & Shapiro, 1998). The transaction costs of effecting a change in ownership are very high and therefore can deter such actions. Potential targets have also been

---

46 Granting managers stock options makes them owners of the company. This aspect of owner identity will be examined in the following sections.

47 The incentive to challenge managers is assumed to be greater if board members hold ownership stakes in the firm. This aspect of owner identity will be examined in the following sections.

limited by the frequent use of antitakeover devices. In addition, as takeovers tend to occur in waves, the use of the market for corporate control as a means of disciplining management may not be available at all time. Because of the serious limitations of the takeover market as the most important of the external constraints, it is commonly assumed that external constraints are in general less effective in disciplining managers than are internal instruments (Gedajlovic & Shapiro, 1998). External mechanisms are therefore not further considered.

Another argument for the focus on ownership concentration as the most relevant agency control mechanism is provided by its substitution effects for alternative control devices. For example, Nickell, Nicolitsas, and Dryden (1997) provide evidence to suggest that ownership concentration (and financial market pressure) can substitute for product market competition. In other words, the impact of competition on performance is lower when firms have a dominant external shareholder (or when they are under financial pressure). Rediker and Seth (1995) also investigate the interaction effects of agency control mechanisms and suggest that firms with high ownership concentration are not likely to be taken over. As a consequence, ownership concentration might be said to substitute for the threat of takeover as a governance device. The argument is empirically supported by Köke (2004) who analyzes a sample of 946 large German firms in the period 1987-94 and finds that high ownership concentration makes control changes less likely. This is consistent with the view that tight shareholder control acts as a substitute for disciplinary control changes.

Table 3.3: Agency Control Mechanisms in Existing Contracts

Mechanisms	Comment
(a) Internal control mechanisms	
Ownership structure	Ownership concentration and owner identity are major mechanisms to either help align the interests of managers with those of shareholders or limit the agency costs that managers can generate.
Capital structure	High levels of debt and dividends limit the discretion of managers to misuse assets or invest in unprofitable ventures, thereby reducing agency costs.
Executive compensation	Incentive compensation in the form of fixed salary, bonuses linked to accounting-based performance measures, and stock options serve to mitigate agency costs.
Supervisory board	A strong supervisory board limits the divergence of managers from shareholder wealth maximization by challenging managers' decisions.
(b) External control mechanisms	
Managerial labor market	Effective managers tend to have more future job opportunities and this creates incentives to limit self-serving behavior.
Product market	Managerial slack is lower under competition in the product market.
Market for corporate control	Managerial inefficiency that reduces shareholder value attracts investors and increases the likelihood that managers will be dismissed following an acquisition.

3.2.3 Summary

To conclude, agency theory demonstrates how agency conflicts arise as a result of imperfect contracting between shareholders and managers. Prerequisite is the assumption of different utility functions of shareholders and managers. In case of asymmetrical information to the benefit of managers, owners cannot prevent harming actions (low effort, misuse of assets, overinvestment, diverging time and risk preferences) resulting from this misalignment of interests. However, there exists a variety of mechanisms designed to mitigate these problems. Common to all agency control mechanisms is that they either align the incentives of managers and shareholders or limit the discretion of managers. Most control mechanisms are mutually compatible. Therefore, firms typically install several mechanisms at the same time (Byrd et al., 1998). These mechanisms form a complex, interrelated system, which shapes the corporate governance and agency costs in a firm. The focus of this work is to analyze ownership structure as the major control mechanism while controlling for the effects of capital structure as another important internal control mechanism.

3.3 The Concept of Ownership Concentration and Performance

Ownership concentration presents a source of power to limit the dissenting behavior of managers. The following discussion hence examines the arguments that have been offered in literature regarding the positive but also negative effects of ownership concentration on performance (and vice versa) and finally develops hypotheses for empirical testing.

3.3.1 Effects of Ownership Concentration on Performance

In the following presentation of arguments, potential agency effects of ownership concentration are discussed together with nonagency related effects. In order to assess implications for performance, the perspective of minority investors is taken, whose sole interest – assumingly – is to maximize the financial value of their investment in form of dividends and capital gains, which is reflected in the market value of the firm (Edwards & Weichenrieder, 2004; Putterman, 1993). In other words, ownership is primarily assessed in terms of its implications for firm value.

Monitoring argument

The monitoring argument is based on the assumption of agency conflicts between shareholders and managers (see Section 3.2.2) and predicts a positive effect of ownership concentration on corporate performance. Accordingly, the incentive to engage in monitoring activities will be low for shareholders who command only a small share in a firm because the costs of such efforts usually outweigh the individual benefits. Assuming that the product of monitoring is comparable to a public good with all shareholders enjoying gains on their own shares, small stockholders have an incentive to delay monitoring in the hope that any other shareholder will make the monitoring investment (Shleifer & Vishny, 1986). Dissatisfied shareholders owning small stakes rather sell out, favoring a "cheap exit" over an "expensive voice" (Bhidé, 1994, p. 132).

Because the benefits of monitoring increase with share size, and, at the same time, the incurred costs do not augment, the incentive to take action should increase with the investor's wealth commitment. A larger share size thus increases the cost efficiency of monitoring and, due to this higher incentive, enhances its usages, thereby avoiding the traditional free rider problem (Admati, Pfleiderer, & Zechner, 1994; Huddart, 1993). Moreover, a larger share size might even raise the shareholder's capability of control because blockholders are assumed to be better informed than average investors (Byrd et al., 1998). In addition, this deeper insight into the company also reduces the costs of explicit monitoring, which further increases cost efficiency. Thus, high ownership concentration leaves the shareholder not only highly incentivized to monitor the management but also capable of controlling them (and at lower costs). To conclude, large shareholders address the agency problem in that they have a general interest in profit maximization as well as enough control over the assets of the firm to have their interests respected. The monitoring argument hence suggests concentrating the stakes in a firm in the hands of only a few shareholders (Bushee, 1998; Shleifer & Vishny, 1997).

Overmonitoring argument

Another strand of literature, however, supports a negative effect of ownership concentration on performance. An argument closely linked to the monitoring argument is the overmonitoring argument. Burkart, Gromb, and Panunzi (1997) and Pagano and Roell (1998) argue that excessive monitoring by large shareholders reduces managerial discretion and constitutes a threat that reduces the level of noncontractible efforts by managers (e.g., searching for new investment projects). Reduced managerial effort and space for initiative eventually diminish firm performance.

Private-benefits-of-control argument

The private-benefits-of-control argument points to the potential costs of having large shareholders and predicts a negative performance effect (Barclay & Holderness, 1989; Zwiebel, 1995). The most obvious of these costs is that large shareholders tend to be undiversified and hence bear excessive risks (Demsetz and Lehn, 1985).[48] An even more fundamental problem is that large shareholders represent their own interests, which need not coincide with the interests of other investors in the firm (or other stakeholders).[49] In the process of using their control rights to maximize their own welfare, large shareholders can therefore redistribute

48 However, Shleifer and Vishny (1997) point out that the high levels of ownership concentration (e.g. in Germany) suggest that the lack of diversification is less of an issue for investors than is loss of control.

49 This variant of the classical principal-agent conflict is generally known as the principal-principal conflict.

wealth from others (Shleifer & Vishny, 1997). That is, they might use their position to exploit possibilities for beneficial actions that are likely to have a negative impact on performance (Johnson, Boone, Breach, & Friedman, 2000; Lemmon & Lins, 2003). Examples are insider trading, "sweetheart deals" with other companies they control, appointment of family members, targeted share repurchases, or withdrawal of corporate funds in form of excessive dividends. The power to influence company decisions and exploit private benefits of control increases with the concentration of ownership; minority shareholders usually cannot prevent those damages (apart from forming coalitions).

Cost-of-capital argument

An argument not linked to the agency theory is the cost-of-capital argument. It predicts a negative performance effect based on the liquidity reduction as a result of blockholdings. Accordingly, increased ownership concentration limits the number of shareholders who can participate in the trading of the firm's stock. This equals effectively a reduction of the stock's liquidity (Bolton & von Thadden, 1998). As a consequence, investors require higher returns on their equity investment in order to compensate them for the higher associated liquidity costs they bear (Amihud & Mendelson, 2000; Bhidé, 1994; Eleswarapu, 1997). This translates into higher cost of capital and hence a lower market value for any given level of expected cash flows generated by the company.

Natural selection argument

Another strand of literature predicts no effect of ownership concentration on performance. The argument relates to the Darwinian view of "natural selection" (Alchian, 1950; Friedman, 1953), which is based on the assumption that competition sorts out all inefficient organizations and structures, and hence all remaining organizational forms are equally efficient and consequently perform equally well. Demsetz (1983), Demsetz and Lehn (1985), Kole and Lehn (1997), and Cho (1998) later apply this argumentation to ownership structure, claiming that corporations with inefficient ownership structures will fail to survive in the long run. It is argued that alternative levels of ownership concentration influence a variety of costs and benefits occurring within the firm (e.g., monitoring, decision-making, transaction costs) that should be assessed with the same reasoning underlying any other production decision. This means that a decision by owners of a firm to alter the ownership structure from concentrated to diffuse (or vice versa) should be made in awareness of its consequences for loosening control. That is, the higher cost and reduced profit, which would be associated with this loss of control, should be offset by lower capital acquisition cost or other profit-enhancing aspects of diffuse ownership if shareholders choose to broaden ownership. The structure of ownership that emerges is hence an endogenous outcome of a competitive selection in which various cost advantages and disadvantages are balanced to arrive at an equilibrium with the optimal level of ownership depending on the particular company environment. As market forces generally push firms towards efficiency, firms are consequently forced to adopt value-maximizing ownership structures in order to ensure their survival.[50] Hence, ownership structures – whether diffuse or concentrated – that maximize shareholder wealth are those that emerge from the interplay of market forces. Accordingly, it can be argued that all existing ownership structures are equally efficient and hence perform equally. In order words, the natural selection argument states that existing ownership structures are equally efficient (depending on the particular company environment) because firms with inefficient ownership structures will fail to survive in the long run. Hence, no systematic generalized relation should exist between differences in ownership and variations in performance.[51]

However, a shortcoming of the natural selection argument is the definition of the time dimension "in the long run". It hence becomes difficult to differentiate an efficient firm from an inefficient firm that may just have not existed long enough to be already sorted out. Further, the assumption of a perfect selection mechanism appears unrealistic because structures are eliminated only if their inefficiencies are not outbalanced by the superiority of other organizational structures. As a result, only completely inefficient firms will be sorted out by the market.[52]

---

50 Market forces arise from the market for corporate control, which involves hostile takeovers or management buyouts but also the acquisition and sale of shares in ordinary exchange transactions.

51 Bahng (2002), Eckbo and Smith (1998) and Himmelberg, Hubburd, and Palia (1999) find no observable effect of ownership on performance in their empirical results, but, in contrast to the proponents of the natural selection argument who assume absence of any effects, they believe that positive and negative effects of ownership might offset each other (mutual neutralization argument). Nevertheless, this argument is not further considered in this dissertation as it appears questionable whether the various opposing effects are indeed equal in strength to outbalance each other.

52 This is typically the case in buyout transactions.

3.3.2 Reverse Effects of Performance on Ownership Concentration

Many studies support the effect of ownership concentration on performance, but there are also arguments for a reverse or bidirectional effect of performance on ownership concentration.

Information advantage argument

The information advantage argument assumes a positive effect of performance on ownership concentration. Due to their deeper insight into the company, large shareholders have incentives to capitalize on the information advantage and consequently increase their ownership stake when anticipating good financial performance. Analogously, they sell their shares when foreseeing a deterioration of financial performance. As a result, ownership in well-performing firms is expected to be more highly concentrated than in nonperforming ones Kole, 1996).

Natural selection argument

According to the natural selection argument, ownership concentration is determined by corporate performance in the sense that inefficient firms will fail to survive in the long run. As all remaining firms are expected to perform equally well, there is no pattern to derive a systematic effect from. Hence, the natural selection argument assumes no relation between performance and ownership concentration (see Section 3.3.1).

3.3.3 Summary and Hypotheses Development

Table 3.4 summarizes the hypothesized effects of ownership concentration on performance. On the one hand, the higher information base and influence of large shareholders is advantageous in reducing agency conflicts between shareholders and management. Monitoring is hence argued to result in improved firm performance. On the other hand, ownership concentration could also trigger managerial demotivation due to overmonitoring, which consequently would result in decreased firm performance. From certain ownership levels onwards, large shareholders might also use their power to treat themselves preferentially and consume private benefits of control at the expense of other shareholders and firm performance. Further, ownership concentration reduces market liquidity, which results in higher cost of capital and consequently a lower market value.

Consistent with the role of monitoring in reducing agency costs, performance is expected to improve with higher ownership concentration at first. However, as ownership gets beyond a certain point (which is impossible to determine ex ante), large owners get more likely to exploit private benefits of control. That is, the negative impact of ownership concentration due to private benefits of control but also due to overmonitoring and higher cost of capital is expected to be comparably strong at high levels of ownership concentration. Combining the two effects then leads to a curvilinear, bell-shaped relation between ownership concentration and performance. The following hypothesis is therefore proposed for empirical testing:

> *Hypothesis 1a: Corporate performance is a bell-shaped (first increasing, then decreasing) function of ownership concentration.*

At the same time, there might also exist reverse or bidirectional effects from firm performance on ownership concentration, which have to be taken into account in the empirical analyses. Accordingly, ownership in well-performing firms is expected to be more highly concentrated than in underperforming firms because large shareholders might capitalized on their better knowledge of the company and increase their ownership stake when assuming good performance and decrease it in case of unfavorable prospects. The following hypothesis is therefore formulated for empirical testing:

> *Hypothesis 1b: Ownership concentration increases with corporate performance.*

Table 3.4: Hypothesized Effects of Ownership Concentration and Performance

(a) Hypothesized effects of ownership concentration on performance

Performance effect	Rationale	Comment
Positive	Monitoring	Large owners are highly motivated and more capable of controlling the management, which decreases agency costs and eventually increases firm performance.
Negative	Overmonitoring	Excessive monitoring by large shareholders reduces managerial discretion and discourages managers from making extra efforts, which leads to a negative performance effect.
	Private benefits of control	Large shareholders exploit private benefits of control and expropriate corporate wealth, which negatively affects shareholder value.
	Cost of capital	Ownership concentration reduces stock liquidity thereby increasing cost of capital, which results in a lower market valuation.
Not observable	Natural selection	Market forces push firms toward value-maximizing ownership structures, and hence all existing structures are equally efficient and perform equally well.

(b) Hypothesized effects of performance on ownership concentration

Ownership concentration effect	Rationale	Comment
Positive	Information advantage	Large owners capitalize on their information advantage and consequently increase their ownership stake when anticipating good financial performance.
Not observable	Natural selection	Ownership concentration is determined by corporate performance in the sense that inefficient firms will fail to survive in the long run.

3.4 The Concept of Owner Identity and Performance

The previous elaborations on ownership concentration have demonstrated how large shareholders use their power to influence corporate performance (and vice versa). However, the commitment of owners and their willingness to engage in monitoring activities or alternatively to exploit private benefits may crucially depend on their identity. There is reason to assume that certain owner identities may present a higher degree of control or, alternatively, a higher level of rent extraction at any given level of shareholding. The following discussion therefore analyzes differences between various identities of owners and models their expected effect on corporate performance. Following, Thomsen and Pedersen (2000), the relative costs and benefits of ownership of each owner group are used as a benchmark for assessing its dominant objectives. The potentially reverse feedback from performance to ownership is also discussed in order to provide a complete picture of the relation. An empirical investigation is beyond the scope of this dissertation, though.

Finally, hypotheses on the effects of owner identity on performance are proposed for the sake of empirical testing, nonetheless knowing that the theoretical arguments on which they are based mainly relate to situations where ownership is dominated (or even fully held) by the respective owner identity. However, this is typically not the case for publicly listed companies, where the largest owner usually does not possess majority (or full) control. As a consequence, the actual performance effects are probably alleviated compared with theoretical expectations.

The accuracy of the hypotheses might be further limited by forced linearity of the relation between owner identity and performance. Although, it is likely that the effects of ownership in the hands of large shareholders are a nonlinear function of their stake sizes, empirical verification is technically hardly feasible given the large number of owner identity variables. This limitation is also inherent in many other studies focusing on owner identity effects.[53]

3.4.1 Individual Investor Ownership

There is very sparse literature on the relation between nonexecutive individual ownership and firm performance.[54] This is probably due to the fact that individual investors usually own only a small fraction of a company's shares and therefore have no significant influence on the firm's activities (Deutsche Bundesbank, 2014b). If individuals do possess a certain level of control, they are typically also involved in the firm's business through participation in the management or supervisory board in which case they would classify as insiders or family owners, respectively.

---

[53] Edwards and Nibler (2000), Lehman and Weigand (2000), Pedersen and Thomsen (2003), and Thomsen and Pedersen (2000) do not address this concern in their empirical analyses. Edwards and Weichenrieder (2004) test for the significance of quadratic terms in each largest shareholder types' control rights but find no evidence of nonlinearity.

[54] There is a rich literature on the performance of individual investors' self-managed stock portfolios (e.g., compared with market indices or professionally managed portfolios), though.

3.4.1.1 Effects of Individual Investor Ownership on Performance

The potential effects of individual ownership are discussed below.

Long-term commitment argument

Bøhren, Priestley, and Ødegaard (2006) provide evidence that the average duration of equity ownership is the longest among individuals (and industrial corporations) compared with other types of investors (with the exception of the government). This suggests that individual owners typically have little interest in speculation (Clark-Murphy & Soutar, 2004).[55] An explanation for this anomaly might be given by the personal relevance argument (as mentioned below). As a result of individual owners being patient and having less proclivity to pressure management to deliver short-term results, management is likely to adopt a long-term oriented investment focus, which will eventually increase company value (although short-term performance might be lower). Another aspect of individual owners' long-term commitment is that owners with a long holding period can be assumed to have particularly strong incentives to monitor. In addition, the long ownership duration gives individual owners time to learn about the firm and, as a consequence, should enable them to contribute as valuable monitors. The long-term commitment by individuals is therefore argued to be positively related to firm valuation.

Sleepy monitoring argument

Although the previous argument posits a positive effect of individual investors' long holding periods on their monitoring competence, individuals are generally considered to be less sophisticated investors.[56] According to De Bondt (1998), individual investors typically have no adequate understanding or are relatively incompetent of using company valuation techniques and hence can hardly assess the financial performance of firms (Pellens & Schmidt, 2014). In addition, they often lack adequate and relevant information (and acquisition thereof is costly) and are typically unfamiliar with the day-to-day-operations of the firm (Reeder, 1975). According to a survey by Shiller and Pound (1989), individual investors spend far less time on investment analysis than their institutional counterparts. The majority of individual investors do no analysis on their own prior to purchasing stock. As a consequence, individual owners

[55] For the case of Germany, supporting evidence is provided by a survey of 38,127 private investors of Deutsche Post DHL, according to which the majority of the respondents name long-term wealth accumulation and inflation protection as their primary investment objectives. Only 12% attach a high importance to short-term investment returns (Pellens & Schmidt, 2014).

[56] See Barber and Odean (2013) for an in-depth discussion of the behavior of individual investors.

are argued to have a serious disadvantage concerning their capability to engage in effective monitoring activities. This sleepy (passive) monitoring, however, might leave managers too much power to waste corporate resources on value-destroying activities.[57] Individual ownership is hence associated with a decreased financial performance.

Natural selection argument

Similar to the discussion on the performance effects of ownership concentration (see Section 3.3.1), it can be argued that market forces push firms towards efficiency and consequently to adapting the value-maximizing ownership structure considering costs and benefits of alternative owner types. The natural selection argument hence predicts no observable performance effects of private investor ownership.

3.4.1.2 Reverse Effects on Individual Investor Ownership

For the sake of completeness, potential reverse effects of performance on individual investor ownership are elaborated below. As there are hardly any studies dealing directly with the effects of corporate performance on individual ownership, literature on the behavior of individual investors is considered.

Reputation argument

As individuals are generally not considered to be sophisticated investors (as discussed above), perceptions of value often depend on coverage in the news or social media as well as tips from friends or financial advisors. In addition, many people are not capable of distinguishing good stocks from good companies (De Bondt, Werner F. M., 1998). Thus, firms that regularly appear in the news or have charismatic leaders who regularly appear in public are seen as good investment.[58] In contrast, companies that produce scandals and look bad in the public opinion

---

[57] Hansmann (1988) makes an important point insofar as for certain owners the costs of managerial opportunism may be worth bearing as alternative to having no ownership at all. This is because by virtue of having ownership, the owners in question are assured that there is no other group of owners to whom management is responsive: "It is one thing to deal with managers who are nominally your agents but serve you poorly; it is yet another to transact with managers who are actively serving owners with an interest clearly adverse to yours." (Hansmann, 1988, p. 276).

[58] For example, Apple benefited from its charismatic CEO Steve Jobs who created an extraordinary emotional tie between consumers and the company. As a consequence, Apple's shareholders were regularly blamed for being too emotional when they stuck to their shares even if the stock was commonly considered to be overpriced (Lazarus, 2013).

or operate in less reputable industries seem inherently unattractive investments.[59] Hence, the impact of the actual financial performance of a company on the level of individual ownership is expected to be low or even nonexistent. This conclusion is very closely linked to the personal relevance argument, which will be examined next.

Personal relevance argument

Aspara and Tikkanen (2010) analyze the concept of personal relevance and the potential effects of these perceptions on the individual's willingness to invest in certain companies as well as the tendency to be committed investors. They imply that individuals perceive certain companies as being personally relevant to them and hence identify with these companies in their roles of consumers or stakeholders.[60] This can lead individuals to give preferential treatment to a company, which may become manifest in an increased willingness to continue investing in or owning the company's stock, even beyond the willingness determined by the expected financial return-risk profile, and exhibit loyal and committed behavior towards the company. This loyalty and commitment may also lead individuals to require or being satisfied with lower expected financial returns from the company at a given risk level compared with institutional investors whose investment decisions and hence commitment is determined solely by the expected financial return-risk profile (Aspara, 2013).[61] As a consequence, the impact of performance on the level of individual ownership is expected to be low or even nonexistent.

Natural selection argument

The natural selection argument predicts no observable effects of performance on individual investor ownership (see Section 3.3.1).

---

59 For example, investors might refuse to place their money with tobacco companies, casino operators, or firearm manufacturers.

60 Personal relevance is motivated by the company or product brand being related to the individual's identity, self-image and personal values (Aspara, 2013). For example, if an individual has a preference for environmentally friendly products, he is likely to perceive companies committed to produce products causing less impact on the environment (e.g., electric vehicles) as being personally relevant.

61 For example, the stock of the German soccer club Borussia Dortmund has not performed well since its initial public offering in 2000 and distributed a mingy dividend of 6 cents per share only once. Nevertheless, the stock appears to be an attractive investment for many and is mainly owned by fans whose investment decisions are driven by their emotional ties instead of financial rationality ("Fußball-Aktien: Selten Erfolgs-geschichten", 2011; Gosenheimer, 2013).

3.4.1.3 Summary and Hypothesis Development

Table 3.5 summarizes the hypothesized effects of individual investor ownership on performance. Two contradicting arguments exist. According to the long-term commitment argument, individual investors are loyal owners who are believed to be beneficial for firm performance because they counter short-termism in the firm's investment decisions and have strong incentives to monitor. However, individual owners typically hold small ownership stakes due to their wealth constraints (see Section 2.3.2.1), and monitoring is therefore costly. At these very low levels of ownership, it appears hence more likely that the sleepy monitoring argument applies, which predicts a negative performance effect due to the incompetency of individual owners to effectively discipline the management. The effect on performance is even more negative if ownership is so dispersed that individual investors with an already small stake make up the largest owner. The following hypothesis is therefore formulated for empirical testing.

> *Hypothesis 2: Corporate performance decreases with ownership concentration in the hands of individuals.*

Table 3.5: Hypothesized Effects of Individual Investor Ownership and Performance

(a) Hypothesized effects of individual investor ownership on performance

Performance effect	Rationale	Comment
Positive	Long-term commitment	Individual investors are patient owners preferring sustainable long-term performance over short-term profits.
Negative	Sleepy monitoring	Individual investors are not capable of engaging in effective monitoring due to their lack of information, unfamiliarity with the business, and technical incompetence.
Not observable	Natural selection	Market forces push firms toward value-maximizing ownership structures, and hence all existing structures are equally efficient and perform equally well.

(b) Hypothesized effects of performance on individual investor ownership

Ownership effect	Rationale	Comment
Not observable	Reputation/ personal relevance	Individuals invest in companies if they perceive the company as being reputable or personally relevant to them and pay less or even no attention to the company's financial performance.
	Natural selection	Ownership concentration is determined by corporate performance in the sense that inefficient firms will fail to survive in the long run.

3.4.2 Insider Ownership

The effect of insider ownership on corporate performance has been intensively discussed since the evolution of the academic debate on agency conflicts. As a result, extensive research is found on the relation between managerial ownership and performance. In contrast, the shareholdings of board members have not captured the same research attention as that of managers because, from an agency theory perspective, board members should already represent the interests of shareholders. At the same time, however, board members have access to firm-specific information that may not be available to other shareholders and also possess some power to influence a company's decisions; board members could therefore also be treated as insiders (Kosnik, 1990). In the following discussion, the terms *insiders* and *managers* are used interchangeably and refer to both managers and board members (corporate executives).

3.4.2.1 Effects of Insider Ownership on Performance

The potential effects of insider ownership are discussed below.

Convergence-of-interest argument

As the main assumption of agency theory centers around the opportunistic behavior of managers, it can be argued that potentially harming actions might be constrained by higher managerial ownership because this increases the costs that mangers would have to bear themselves. As a consequence, the managerial utility function becomes more similar to that of shareholders, and managers are less likely to squander corporate wealth (Jensen & Meckling, 1976). Insider ownership hence serves to support the alignment between the interests of shareholders and insiders. This reduces potential agency conflicts and leads to a positive performance effect.

Entrenchment argument

Another strand of literature, however, supports a negative effect of managerial ownership on performance and points to offsetting costs of management ownership stakes (Fama, 1980; Fama & Jensen, 1983). Instead of reducing potential conflicts of interest through an alignment of interests, insider ownership is assumed to create a hold-up situation where shareholders recognize an opportunistic behavior of the manager but cannot sanction him or prevent his harming actions (see Section 3.2.2.2). In other words, the higher the level of managerial ownership, the easier it is for managers to entrench, that is, to protect themselves against disciplining actions and to reduce the probability of being replaced. By averting punishment or reducing the degree of sanction, insider ownership hence allows the management to extract larger perquisites from (other) shareholders at lower opportunity costs. As argued by Jensen and Ruback (1983), poor managers who resist being replaced might be the costliest manifestation of the agency problem. Consequently, a high level of managerial ownership is expected to lead to a performance loss.

Combined convergence-of-interest and entrenchment argument

Morck et al., (1988) merge the contradicting effects of the convergence-of-interest and entrenchment arguments to a combined, nonmonotonous effect: The performance effect resulting from the convergence-of-interest argument is expected to be positive and linear, whereas the performance effect from entrenchment is assumed to be a negative, nonlinear effect with a large gradient for medium levels of managerial ownership. The performance loss resulting from entrenchment is argued to be small at very low levels of managerial ownership but to increase with rising ownership stakes. At medium ownership levels, the negative performance effect is most distinct. Beyond medium ownership, the increasing performance loss is expected to level off as managers owning very high stakes might not be significantly more entrenched than those with medium stakes.

When combining the effects of the convergence-of-interest and entrenchment arguments, Morck et al. (1988) predict an *N-shape* (see Figure 3.1). At very low levels of ownership, the positive effect of the convergence of interest dominates the entrenchment because ownership stakes are yet too small to give managers any substantial control. The entrenchment effect then forces a negative effect at medium levels. At medium to high managerial ownership levels, the convergence-of-interest effect dominates again, turning the combined performance effect positive again (see Section 5.3.2.2 for a more detailed discussion of the empirical results).[62]

Figure 3.1: Combined Convergence-of-Interest and Entrenchment Effect

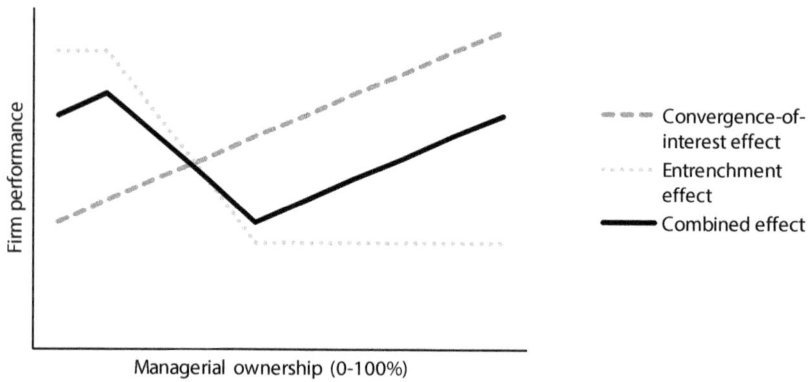

Note. Taken from Groß (2007).

62 In case of family firms, ownership by the founder or a member of the founding family may have effects on firm performance, which differ from those of insiders in general. For example, a founder may exert more control over the firm at any given level of ownership than other members of the management and may become entrenched at much lower levels of ownership than other managers (Morck et al., 1988).

Combined takeover premium and entrenchment argument

Underperforming firms are generally more likely to become the target of a hostile takeover after which the incumbent management is likely to be replaced (Kummer & Hoffmeister, 1978), but a high level of managerial ownership allows management to easily avert takeovers and hence retain control (Morck et al., 1988). As a consequence, raiders try to overcome managerial resistance by increasing the takeover premium. This is supported by Walkling and Long (1984) who find that the larger the financial gain for a target firm's managers, the less likely they are to resist a bid. A takeover premium typically leads to an increase of the target's share price and hence to a positive effect on capital market performance (takeover premium argument).

Stulz (1988) combines the hypothesized effects from the takeover premium and the entrenchment argument and predicts a bell-shaped relation between managerial ownership and performance (see Figure 3.2). At low levels of ownership, the positive performance effect from increasing takeover premia outweighs the entrenchment effect because managerial ownership stakes are yet too small to block takeover bids. Both effects balance at medium levels of ownership. With increasing managerial ownership however, managers control a sufficiently large fraction of ownership in order to entrench themselves and to oppose even value-maximizing takeover bids, thereby forcing a negative performance effect.

Figure 3.2: Combined Takeover Premium and Entrenchment Effect

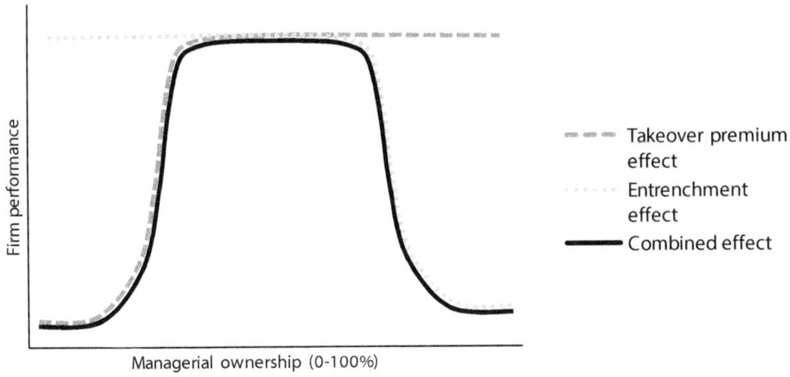

Note. Taken from Groß (2007).

Natural selection argument

The natural selection argument also applies to insider ownership and supports the absence of an observable effect of ownership on performance (see Section 3.3.1).

3.4.2.2 Reverse Effects on Insider Ownership

Apart from a variety of papers analyzing the effect of insider ownership on performance, few studies also deal with potential reverse or bidirectional effects of performance on insider ownership. For the sake of completeness, these effects are elaborated below.

Reward argument

The reward argument is closely linked to the convergence-of-interest argument, which assumes that stock ownership provides incentives for managers to take actions that maximize corporate performance (see Section 3.4.2.1). The reward argument, however, predicts a reverse causality in the ownership-performance relation and argues for firm performance as a determinant of managerial ownership (Kole, 1996). This is the case if firms grant their managers with equity ownership in order to reward them for good past corporate performance. As a consequence, improved financial performance leads to increased managerial ownership.

Compensation preference argument

According to Cho (1998), managers prefer equity compensation when they expect the firm to perform well and try to decrease the equity-based component of their remuneration when they anticipate an unfavorable firm performance. If their forecasts prove true (which is likely due to their insider knowledge), good performance correlates with high managerial ownership. However, Kaserer and Moldenhauer (2008) argue that Germany is different in this regard as stock-based compensation is less widespread than in Anglo-American economies, and insider ownership is often related to family control. The relation between insider ownership and performance in Germany is therefore expected to be less affected by reverse causality than in Anglo-American economies.

Along the lines of the compensation preference argument, it might also be argued that managers capitalize on their insider knowledge and increase their investment in the company when they expect the financial performance to improve and decrease their stockholdings when they anticipate the performance to deteriorate (Loderer & Martin, 1997). However, this argument is not expected to be relevant for the German market because insider trading is strongly prohibited in Germany (see Section 2.3.2.2).

Natural selection argument

Similar to the discussion on the effect of ownership concentration on performance (see Section 3.3.1), it can be argued that the ownership structure is determined by corporate performance in the sense that inefficient firms will fail to survive in the long run. As all remaining firms are expected to perform equally well, there is no pattern to derive a systematic effect from. Hence, the natural selection argument assumes no relation between performance and insider ownership.

3.4.2.3 Summary and Hypothesis Development

Table 3.6 summarizes the hypothesized effects of insider ownership on performance. Several contradicting arguments exist. According to the convergence-of-interest argument, managerial ownership aligns the utility functions of managers and shareholders and thereby increases corporate performance. At the same time, the entrenchment argument claims that managerial ownership reduces the power of controlling shareholders and thus enables managers to conduct wealth-destroying actions. The combination of the two arguments predicts an *N-shape* relation between managerial ownership and performance, with either the convergence-of-interest or the entrenchment effect dominating over the other, depending on the level of ownership.

As insider ownership plays an important role in Germany due to the large number of family controlled firms (see Section 2.3.2.2), the average level of insider (family) ownership is therefore supposed to be high. This is likely to lead to value-maximizing behavior by insider owners. As they personally bear the costs of potentially wealth-destroying actions, insiders are highly incentivized to make decisions that will maximize firm value. This positive performance effect is expected to dominate over any negative consequences from potential entrenchment (although the negative effects from entrenchment even outweigh any positive effects from increasing takeover premia). Consequently, the overall performance effect of insider ownership in the German market is expected to be positive. This leads to the following hypothesis for empirical testing:

> *Hypothesis 3: Corporate performance increases with ownership concentration in the hands of insiders.*

Table 3.6: Hypothesized Effects of Insider Ownership and Performance

(a) Hypothesized effects of insider ownership on performance

Performance effect	Rationale	Comment
Positive	Convergence of interest	Managerial ownership aligns the utility functions of managers and shareholders and hence reduces potential conflicts of interest.
Negative	Entrenchment	High managerial ownership reduces the power of shareholders to impose sanctions and thus allows managers to conduct harming actions at lower opportunity costs.
Depending on level of ownership: first positive, then negative, again positive	Combination of convergence of interest and entrenchment	At low levels of managerial ownership, the positive effects of the convergence of interest dominates any negative effects resulting from entrenchment, then the relation reverses at medium levels, and reverses again at high ownership levels.
Depending on level of ownership: first positive, then zero, lastly negative	Combination of takeover premium and entrenchment	At low levels of managerial ownership, raiders pay high takeover premia in order to overcome management's resistance to takeover bids and hence the share price rises. At high levels, negative performance effects from entrenchment dominate. The two effects balance at medium levels of managerial ownership.
Not observable	Natural selection	Market forces push firms toward value-maximizing ownership structures, and hence all existing structures are equally efficient and perform equally well.

(b) Hypothesized effects of performance on insider ownership

Ownership effect	Rationale	Comment
Positive	Reward	Well-performing firms reward their managers by granting them with equity ownership.
	Compensation preference	Managers prefer equity compensation when they expect their firm to perform well.
Not observable	Natural selection	Ownership concentration is determined by corporate performance in the sense that inefficient firms will fail to survive in the long run.

3.4.3 Intercorporate Ownership

Literature on intercorporate shareholdings is relatively sparse. Existing research on the determinants of intercorporate shareholdings so far has focused on the Japanese *keiretsu* system in which interfirm equity investments are an efficient way of disciplining members of closely interrelated business groups (e.g., Prowse, 1992) and on the prebid acquisition of target shares (*toehold purchase*) in the U.S. market for corporate control as a tool for influencing certain aspects of the bidding process (e.g., Mikkelson & Ruback, 1985). Although these aspects provide valuable insights into the role of intercorporate ownership, a toehold is a rare event in most firms' live, and the keiretsu system seems to be a unique Japanese phenomenon with no direct European parallel (Bøhren & Norli, 1997). Hence, not much is known about industrial companies as shareholders of other (European) companies.

3.4.3.1 Effects of Intercorporate Ownership on Performance

The potential effects of intercorporate ownership are discussed below.

Financial investment argument

The performance impact of intercorporate ownership strongly depends on the underlying motive. If corporations invest in other corporations simply because they have excess cash available to invest in return for dividends or capital gains, intercorporate investors basically do not differ from financial investors (see Section 3.4.4.1).[63] Intercorporate owners are therefore assumed to push firms in which they hold equity to increase performance. Although investing is not part of a nonfinancial corporation's core competencies, it is generally argued that corporations are more sophisticated than other types of investors (e.g., individual investors). Business insights and industry knowledge (depending on the industry in which the target company is active) also reduce the cost of acquiring information. Intercorporate ownership is therefore assumed to have a positive impact on performance.

Strategic investment argument

A second motive for intercorporate shareholdings is strategic investing, that is, the expansion of business opportunities (Allen & Philipps, 2000). The resulting business ties are mostly vertical, that is, between companies at different stages of the value chain. In this case, companies internalize their transactions with the provider of a critical input, which makes sense under conditions of high asset specificity and transaction frequency. Horizontal business relations intend to facilitate knowledge transfer and cost savings and typically aim at an

---

[63] Empirical research on the financial investment motive indicates that corporations typically purchase shares of other companies as part of a general cash-management program designed to lower the costs of holding an inventory of liquid assets. There is little evidence of entrenched managers diversifying firm-specific risk, "parking" free cash flow (when it should be paid out as dividends), or "grooming" white knights for future "lock-up" agreements (Bøhren & Norli, 1997; Eckbo, 1997).

ultimate integration of the two companies. Conglomerate ties mostly occur in form of corporate ventures, which strive for new add-on businesses.

In the light of strategic business ties, it is generally assumed that companies are more interested in maintaining a steady relation with business partners than in short-term gains (Thomsen & Pedersen, 2000).[64] Along these lines, intercorporate owners might be reluctant to exercise active monitoring due to potential conflict of interest pressures or strategic alignments of interest between the business partners (Kester, 1992). Generally, cooperation tends to reduce the beneficial effects on the firm value that could result from monitoring (Bhattacharya & Graham, 2009).[65] The advantages of strategic business ties therefore come at the cost of deficient monitoring. As a consequence, the overall effect of intercorporate ownership can be positive or negative, depending on the strength of the two contrary effects.

Natural selection argument

The natural selection argument also applies to intercorporate ownership and assumes the absence of a relation between ownership and performance (see Section 3.3.1).

3.4.3.2 Reverse Effects on Intercorporate Ownership

There are also potential reverse effects of performance on intercorporate ownership, which, for the sake of completeness, are elaborated below.

Vote-by-foot argument

If intercorporate investors do not differ from financial investors in their investment motive (see Section 3.4.4.2), then it can be assumed that they, similar to financial investors, elude the costs of monitoring and either agree with the management or vote by foot, that is, sell their stock in the case of policy disagreement (Brickley et al., 1988). As a consequence, overperforming corporations (in terms of accounting performance) attract a higher level of intercorporate investments than underperformers. This argument prevails especially at low levels of ownership where monitoring costs are relatively high.

---

64 In Germany, a number of special legal provisions apply in the case where the dominant owner in a corporation is another corporation. Most notably, §17 AktG enjoins dominant (corporate) owners from imposing unfavorable contracts on the corporation unless there is an adequate compensation.

65 The strategic investment argument is comparable to the self-dealing argument in the case of financial investor ownership, see Section 3.4.4.1.

Strategically driven investments argument

Intercorporate owners wishing to build equity positions in other corporations for strategic reasons might attach only little importance on the performance of the target company.[66] Performance is therefore assumed to have no (or little) effect on intercorporate shareholdings.

Natural selection argument

According to the natural selection argument, no systematic relation should exist between intercorporate ownership and performance (see Section 3.3.1).

3.4.3.3 Summary and Hypothesis Development

Table 3.7 summarizes the hypothesized effects of intercorporate ownership on performance. The predicted impact on performance strongly depends on the underlying motive for intercorporate shareholdings. First, corporations might invest in other companies in the course of a general cash-management program (financial investment argument). In this case, intercorporate investors basically act as financial investors pushing firms in which they hold equity to increase performance. Second, corporations might invest in other companies in order to expand business opportunities (strategic investment argument). Intercorporate ownership is then an important instrument to align incentives between firms to expand joint investment opportunities and to reduce the costs of generating business agreements and alliances. Tight business ties, however, might lead to a situation of conflict-of-interest pressures or strategic alignments of interest between the business partners where the possible gain of active monitoring faces an opportunity loss in the business relation, which might avert any monitoring incentives. The advantages of strategic business ties therefore come at the cost of deficient monitoring, with performance ultimately depending on the strength of the two contrary effects.

The expected overall performance effect of intercorporate ownership lastly depends on the assumed predominance of either the financial investment or the strategic investment

---

[66] For example, potential future threats to the business model due to the increasing environmental awareness in the market for automobiles prompted BMW in 2009 to enter a venture with SGL Carbon, Germany's leading manufacturer of carbon products (in 2009, SGL Carbon reported a net loss of €60m, reversing a gain of €190m in the previous year). Because of the strategic importance of the project, the automaker acquired a 16% stake in SGL. Susanne Klatten, a member of the Quandt family who controls BMW, independently bought 27% of SGL, thereby putting SGL Carbon effectively out of reach of rivals.

argument. For the German market, the analysis of intercorporate shareholdings among the 100 largest corporations (see Section 2.3.2.3) shows that most of these (German) corporations hold significant ownership stakes, typically ranging from 10% to 50% of their targets' equity. This could provide an indication of the predominance of the strategic investment argument. At the same time, the large size of these positions requires that corporations do indeed engage in monitoring their business partners' management simply because too much wealth is at risk. The evidence of corporations exhibiting an extraordinary long duration of equity ownership (see Section 3.4.1.1) further underpins this argumentation. As a consequence, a positive performance effect of intercorporate ownership is predicted. The following hypothesis is hence proposed for empirical testing:

> *Hypothesis 4: Corporate performance increases with ownership concentration in the hands of other nonfinancial corporations.*

Table 3.7: Hypothesized Effects of Intercorporate Ownership and Performance

(a) Hypothesized effects of intercorporate ownership on performance

Performance effect	Rationale	Comment
Positive	Financial investment	Corporations acquire ownership in other firms as financial investment and hence do not differ from financial investors pushing firms in which they hold equity to increase performance.
Positive or negative	Strategic investment	Corporations invest in other companies in order to benefit from strategic business opportunities. However, this might come at the cost of deficient monitoring incentives.
Not observable	Natural selection	Market forces push firms toward value-maximizing ownership structures, and hence all existing structures are equally efficient and perform equally well.

(b) Hypothesized effects of performance on intercorporate ownership

Ownership effect	Rationale	Comment
Positive	Vote by foot	Intercorporate owners investing for financial reasons either agree with management or vote by foot, that is, sell their stock, and are therefore attracted by well-performing corporations (in terms of accounting performance).
Not observable	Strategically driven investments	Intercorporate owners acquiring equity stakes in other corporations for strategic reasons attach less importance on the performance of the target company.
	Natural selection	Ownership concentration is determined by corporate performance in the sense that inefficient firms will fail to survive in the long run.

3.4.4 Financial Investor Ownership

Financial investors are major collectors of savings and suppliers of funds to financial markets. Their role has grown substantially in recent decades to such a degree that financial investors have emerged as the largest investor class in many countries. As a consequence, the relation between financial investor ownership and firm performance has been extensively studied in literature.

3.4.4.1 Effects of Financial Investor Ownership on Performance

The potential effects of financial investor ownership are discussed below.

Active monitoring argument

The central argument for a positive relation between financial investor ownership and performance is given by their role of active monitors. It is generally argued that due to their professional occupation with capital markets, industries and businesses, financial investors are better informed and more sophisticated than other types of investors.[67] Business insights and industry knowledge also reduce the cost of acquiring information. Thus, financial investors have the ability to monitor management more effectively and less costly compared with other types of investors.[68] As, for example, the performance of fund managers is typically measured in terms of financial success, they are also highly incentivized to take an active role in monitoring the management. This reasoning applies especially to private equity investors whose exit track record is dependent on the performance of their portfolio firms. Activist hedge funds also take an active role in realizing the value in their investments and are known to fight management. As alpha monitors, they wage proxy battles, liquidate assets and even force sales of companies in order to "unlock" shareholder value. In general, financial investors can therefore be seen as almost ideal monitors, thereby increasing corporate performance (Thomsen & Pedersen, 2000).

Myopic management behavior argument

An argument against a positive relation between financial investor ownership and corporate performance is that financial investors might prefer short-term returns and use their power to escalate the myopic investment behavior of the management (see Table 3.1). It is generally argued that managers tend to behave shortsighted if they have reason to assume that current earnings create a potential for misvaluation of the company's stock (Stein, 1989). This might occur if capital market participants either overreact to earnings declines related to long-term investments or underreact to cuts in strategically relevant R&D expenses that lead to a temporary increase in earnings. Managers especially fear a temporary stock misvaluation if it affects their stock-based compensation or endangers the prolongation of employment contracts. Further reasons such as the cost of equity in the case of near-term equity funding

---

[67] Corresponding to this argumentation, Hand (1990) uses institutional ownership (investment companies, banks, insurance companies, college endowments, money managers) as a proxy for sophisticated investors.

[68] Exceptions are exchange-traded funds, which deliberately do not monitor individual investee companies actively. As a consequence, they are regularly criticized for not taking advantage of their (enormous) power (e.g., Rottwilm 2015).

requirements or a possible takeover threat can also force managers to focus on the current stock price. Lastly, if managers expect the time horizon of influential investors to be rather shortsighted, they will adapt their investment behavior (thereby aggravating the time-preference problem) because a decline in earnings could otherwise trigger large stock sales causing the share price to fall. The sacrifice of long-term profits for short-term gains damages sustainable firm performance and therefore leads to a negative relation between financial investor ownership and long-term share price and future accounting returns (although, contemporary share price and current accounting performance are high).

In a survey of 400 CFOs by Graham, Harvey, and Rajgopal (2005), managers describe a trade-off between the short-term need to "deliver earnings" and the long-term objective of making value-maximizing investment decisions.[69] 78% of the interviewed CFOs admit to sacrifice long-term value to smooth earnings in order to avoid severe market reaction for underdelivering. There is empirical evidence that financial investors are indeed sensitive to earnings news. In an analysis of quarterly earnings announcements, Kim, Krinsky, and Lee (1997) find a positive relation between abnormal trading volume and the fraction of institutional ownership during the period immediately following an earnings announcement.[70] Literature states different possible reasons for the short-term focus of financial investors. First, due to fiduciary responsibilities arising from handling client capital, financial investors' performance and investment choices are continually monitored and rewarded based on their own (short-term) performance. Because fund sponsors use earnings of the portfolio firms (among others) as objective criterion to judge the prudence of an investment, financial investors may push harder than other types of investors on the firms they invest in to maintain high short-term earnings at the expense of long-term performance (Badrinath, Gay, & Kale, 1989). Financial investors can therefore be seen as key actors in creating the pressure for management's myopia. Second, the short-term focus of financial investors themselves might reduce insight and knowledge of the firm due to the only short-term occupation with the company.[71] In the presence of information gaps (especially in regard to R&D quality), financial

69 According to the survey, the two most important earnings benchmarks are quarterly earnings for the same quarter last year and the analyst consensus estimate.

70 Here, the term institutional ownership includes certain banks, insurance companies, investment advisors, investment companies, foundations, and large pension funds.

71 Alternatively, information gaps might also arise if financial investors hold too many firms with small stakes in their portfolio, which makes it not cost-efficient to monitor all firms.

investors might rely on current earnings as value proxy rather than trying to achieve a solid understanding of certain aspects of corporate strategy (Froot, Perold, & Stein, 1992). Short-term trading horizons can thus impact corporate investment horizons as financial investors may communicate their preference for short-term earnings directly to managers, thereby increasing the scope for underinvestment.[72]

As short trading horizons of financial investors seem to be a likely influence on myopic management behavior, institutional investors can be classified into three groups – *transient*, *dedicated* and *quasi-indexer* – in order to examine whether certain groups of institutional investors influence myopic management behavior more than others (Bushee, 1998; Porter, 1992).[73] Transient institutional investors are characterized by holding small ownership stakes in several firms and having a high portfolio turnover. They intend to maximize short-term gains and focus on value proxies such as current earnings. They are therefore expected to be most sensitive to fluctuations in earnings, thereby creating incentives for myopic management behavior. In contrast, dedicated institutional investors hold large positions in a few firms and trade infrequently.[74] Their large, long-term oriented holdings provide incentives to monitor managers and to rely on information other than current earnings to assess the company's performance, thereby attenuating the pressure for myopic management behavior. Lastly, the quasi-indexers use indexing or buy-and-hold strategies that are characterized by high diversification and low portfolio turnover. They are also committed to their portfolio firms but have greater flexibility than dedicated investors in terms of when and how much they can sell. It can be expected that the presence of quasi-indexers exacerbates incentives for myopic

72 In contrast to the common view of institutional investors as transient and myopic investors, Rajgopal and Venkatachalam (1997) provide evidence on the controversial role of institutions in corporate governance by investigating the relation between financial investor ownership and discretionary accounting behavior of managers. They find no indication of institutional investors encouraging myopic management behavior and instead argue that if institutions engage in active monitoring, managers will have reduced incentives to engage in earnings manipulation. This finding does not necessarily contravene the above mentioned argumentation of shortsighted institutional investors as the two views can be reconciled by the differentiation of institutional investor groups based on their investment behavior.

73 An example of a transient institutional investor is Numeric Investors L.P., a manager of international equity portfolios with very low ownership stakes in its portfolio companies and an above-average turnover of its portfolio holdings. An example of a dedicated institutional investor is Berkshire Hathaway, the insurance/holding company managed by Warren Buffett. An example for a quasi-indexer is the California Public Employees' Retirement System, which is characterized by a high ownership stability and small ownership stakes (Bushee, 2009).

74 Bøhren et al. (2006) provide evidence that the ownership duration generally grows as the fraction of shares held increases.

management behavior because their passive, fragmented ownership leads them to gather little information on the company and provides little incentive to monitor the management. The classification suggests that financial investors should not be considered to be a monolithic group of owners. Instead, there are different types of financial investors with differing utility functions, incentives and means of control; not all of them can be accused of escalating the myopic investment behavior of the management.

Self-dealing argument

An argument for a negative relation between financial investor ownership and performance results from business relations that investors might have with the company they own shares in (Pound, 1988). Due to conflict of interest pressures, financial institutions might then vote with management against their own interests. Hence, the utility function of institutional investors changes in view of other profitable business relations with the firm: The gain of active monitoring faces an opportunity loss in the business relation, which might avert the monitoring incentive of institutional investors. For example, an insurance company may hold an equity position in a company and, at the same time, act as its primary insurer. Voting against management may affect the firm's business relation with the incumbent management, whereas voting with the management results in no obvious penalty (Bhattacharya & Graham, 2009). It is also conceivable that institutional investors and management might find it mutually advantageous to strategically align their interests and cooperate, which eventually thwarts the beneficial effects on firm performance that could potentially result from financial investors' increased ability to monitor the management. Consequently, the presence of conflicts of interest and strategic alignment both predict a negative relation between financial investor ownership and firm performance. The argument, however, does not apply to financial investors such as, for example, pensions funds that have only an investment relation with firms they own equity in.

Based on the self-dealing argument, some authors, instead of classifying institutional investors according to their legal type of business (i.e., banks, financial investors) – as applied in this dissertation and, for example, by Baert and Vennet (2009) and Renneboog (2000) – categorize investors according to their potential business ties and differentiate between *pressure sensitive* and *pressure resistant* (or *pressure insensitive*) investors (Bhattacharya & Graham, 2009; Brickley et al., 1988). Investors classified as pressure sensitive are likely to maintain business relations with the firms in which they have an ownership share (e.g., banks, insurance companies), whereas investors classified as pressure resistant do not commonly have direct business relations with the companies in which they hold a position (e.g., investment and pension funds). It is argued that pressure resistant investors are more likely to actively control the actions of management and hence are the most capable of improving firm performance. Nevertheless, another strand of literature argues that this classification is mainly based on Anglo-American research and cannot be applied to studies in the Continental European context because institutional owners in Continental Europe typically have high levels of participation and therefore have a strong incentive to control the management (Ruiz-Mallorquí & Santana-Martín, 2011). Additionally, in contrast to the Anglo-American corporate landscape, dominant owners in Continental Europe are often represented at the supervisory board and therefore have the means to influence corporate decisions.

Natural selection argument

According to the natural selection argument, no systematic relation should exist between financial investor ownership and firm performance (see Section 3.3.1).

3.4.4.2 Reverse Effects on Financial Investor Ownership

For the sake of completeness, potential reverse effects of performance on financial investor ownership are elaborated below.

Vote-by-foot argument

It is argued that financial investors try to elude the costs of monitoring and, rather than taking an active role in the monitoring process, they tend to follow the so-called "Wall Street walk" according to which investors either agree with management or vote by foot, that is, sell their stocks in the case of policy disagreements (Admati & Pfleiderer, 2009; Brickley et al., 1988). As a result, underperforming firms have a low level of financial investor ownership. This argument applies in particular to quasi-indexers because their small shareholdings would cause disproportionally high monitoring costs and to transient investors because their short-term focus would make information gathering and monitoring costly and redundant as they would not benefit from the long-term performance increase through monitoring. Quasi-indexing and transient financial investors are therefore expected to avoid low-performing firms (Utete, 2008). In contrast, dedicated financial investors are less inclined to respond to temporary fluctuations in short-term performance and might be willing to take on these underperforming firms with a view to improving them.[75]

Information advantage argument

The information advantage argument regarding financial investor ownership resembles that of ownership concentration (see Section 3.3.2) and assumes a positive effect of performance on the level of financial investor ownership. Accordingly, financial investors are able to evaluate the firm's prospects more precisely than other types of investors due to their professional occupation with the company and the industry, in other words, the information advantage is not (necessarily) due to private information but rather due to financial investors' ability to better interpret publicly available information (Gibson, Safieddine, & Sonti, 2004). Financial investors thus increase their ownership stake when perceiving the firm as good investment and sell their shares when anticipating bad financial performance. The information advantage is especially pronounced with dedicated investors, whereas transient and quasi-indexing financial investors have assumingly less knowledge on their portfolio firms.

Natural selection argument

The natural selection argument assumes no relation between performance and institutional ownership (see Section 3.3.1).

3.4.4.3 Summary and Hypothesis Development

Table 3.8 summarizes the hypothesized effects of financial investor ownership on performance. Several contradicting arguments exist. According to the active monitoring argument, financial investors are assumed to be the most sophisticated and informed type of investor due to their professional occupation with capital markets, industries, and businesses.

---

[75] The proposition is supported by the increasing number of loan-to-own and mezzanine-to-own transactions in Europe during and after the latest financial crisis. That is, dedicated financial investors such as private equity (and hedge) funds identify target companies that are overleveraged and on the brink of bankruptcy but have a viable underlying business. Investors then acquire a debt position, or provide mezzanine with a view to swap for a potentially more valuable equity stake in the company following a financial restructuring (Andersson-Lindström & Weber, 2011). Loan-to-own can be illustrated by the example of the German roofing company Monier: In 2009, debt investors Apollo, Towerbrook Capital Partners and York Capital Management built up a 20% stake in Monier's senior debt in the secondary loan market and were able to successfully propose an alternative restructuring plan to that put forward by the incumbent equity sponsor. Post restructuring, the existing sponsor received no equity entitlement, and the three debt investors emerged as largest shareholders.

Financial investors have therefore the ability and incentives to monitor the incumbent management, and this will imply a greater pressure to maximize shareholder value. In contrast, the myopic management behavior argument assumes a difference between transient, dedicated and quasi-indexing investors based on their trading horizons, with the direction of the performance effect depending on the investor type.

The overall effect of financial investor ownership for the German market lastly depends on the dominant type of investors: Transient (and to a large degree also quasi-indexing) investors are assumed to have a negative effect on long-term performance due to their small, short-term investments, which induces management's myopia and provides less incentives to monitor. Dedicated owners, in contrast, have a long-term view on their typically large investments and are thus associated with a positive performance impact. According to Porter (1992), institutional investors in Germany typically hold larger and more long-term holdings than institutional investors in other economies and should therefore be characterized as dedicated owners. This argument is underpinned by the statistics revealing a high average ownership concentration in the German market and, at the same time, a significant importance of institutional investors as large shareholders (see Section 5.2.3). It is not clear, though, how the self-dealing argument influences the role of institutions as shareholders. The effect is likely to depend on the value of the business relation compared with the value of the equity investment; hence no general conclusions can be drawn. The following hypothesis is formulated for empirical testing:

> *Hypothesis 5: Corporate performance increases with ownership concentration in the hands of financial institutions.*

Table 3.8: Hypothesized Effects of Financial Investor Ownership and Performance

(a) Hypothesized effects of financial investor ownership on performance

Performance effect	Rationale	Comment
Positive	Active monitoring	Financial investors have the ability (and incentives) to monitor the management more effectively and less costly than other types of investors due to their business and industry knowledge, thereby contributing to corporate performance.
Depending on investor type: positive or negative	Myopic management behavior	Dedicated financial investors attenuate the pressure for myopic management behavior, whereas transient and quasi-indexing investors have a shortsighted time horizon and use their power to encourage myopic management behavior, which is associated with a negative impact on long-term performance.
Negative	Self-dealing	Financial investors might have business relations with the company, and actions against management may harm those relations.
Not observable	Natural selection	Market forces push firms toward value-maximizing ownership structures, and hence all existing structures are equally efficient and perform equally well.

(b) Hypothesized effects of performance on financial investor ownership

Ownership effect	Rationale	Comment
Depending on investor type: positive or negative	Vote by foot	Quasi-indexing and transient financial investors either agree with management or vote by foot, that is, sell their stock, whereas dedicated financial investors are willing to incur monitoring costs and invest in underperforming firms.
Positive	Information advantage	Dedicated financial investors capitalize on their information advantage and consequently increase their ownership stake when anticipating good financial performance.
Not observable	Natural selection	Ownership concentration is determined by corporate performance in the sense that inefficient firms will fail to survive in the long run.

3.4.5 Bank Ownership

German banks play a special role compared with other types of investors because they can combine debt- and equityholdings. As a consequence, quite a lot of research is found on the relation between bank ownership and firm performance. Literature focuses in particular on the advantages of the German bank-based financial system compared with the Anglo-American market-based system.

3.4.5.1 Effects of Bank Ownership on Performance

The potential effects of bank ownership are discussed below.

Asset management argument

As the internationalization of capital markets increased in the 1990s, a number of German banks voiced a desire to become global players in the same league as major American banks (Slager, 2004). In particular, the at that time "big three" (Deutsche Bank, Dresdner Bank, Commerzbank) became increasingly concerned with their yield on shareholdings. In redefining their strategies, these banks began to perceive shareholdings as part of their asset management (Beyer, 2002). The result of this process is an increased demand by (in particular large, internationally active) banks for pushing corporations in which they hold shares for profit maximization (Fiss & Zajac, 2004).[76]

Equity monitoring argument

The equity and debt monitoring arguments develop a perspective on bank ownership, which depends on the bank's role as creditor. According to the equity monitoring argument, the combination of debt and equity holdings gives banks additional power in disciplining corporate management. Barucci and Mattesini (2008) show that there is a complimentary between lending and equity holding, in other words, banks obtain valuable information (beyond disclosure requirements) from their lending relation from which they can benefit in their monitoring role as shareholder.[77] This risk-reducing effect might serve as explanation for the large bank ownership in Germany (considering the historically developed, strong role of banks as capital providers). Bank ownership should hence have a positive effect on firm value.

Debt monitoring argument

In contrast to the equity monitoring argument, the debt monitoring argument suggests that the combination of debt and equity also raises potential conflicts of interest, which might

---

76 The argument must be differentiated from speculative prop(rietary) trading, which occurs when banks trade stocks or other financial instruments on their own behalf with the goal to earn profits above that of market-making trading. Due to high losses during the financial crisis and tightened financial regulations such as the Volcker Rule in the US, basically all major banks have spun off their prop trading desks or have shut them down (Alich, 2009).

77 Vice versa, banks obtain inside information on the financial status of the firm through their role as shareholder and in turn might be more willing to advance credit lines, which eventually increases the firm's investable resources (with an expected positive effect on performance).

weaken the effectiveness of banks as monitors:[78] Shareholders have been argued to be less risk averse, especially when they hold a diversified portfolio of stock, whereas debtholders are inherently risk averse as they face the downside risk on their loan. Along these lines, it can be assumed that banks are interested in high reserves, whereas other types of shareholders are interested in high dividends. Another argument is that banks with an equity stake might bring pressure on the management to overcollateralize its loans (Baums, 1992a). As a result, equity ownership allows banks to influence financial and investment policies in order to protect the interests of the firm's existing creditors, and hence equity ownership might even become a substitute for loan covenants (Dittmann et al., 2010). Consequently, if banks are primarily interested in ensuring the service of their outstanding debt, they are less willing to challenge management decisions in the interests of shareholders (Brickley et al., 1988).[79] Bank ownership hence does not mitigate potential agency conflicts but rather enlarges and perpetuates these problems (Wenger & Kaserer, 1998) and is therefore associated with a negative effect on performance (provided that solvency remains ensured).

Natural selection argument

The natural selection argument also applies to bank ownership and predicts no observable performance effects of bank ownership (see Section 3.3.1).

3.4.5.2 Reverse Effects on Performance

There are also potential reverse effects of performance on bank ownership, which, for the sake of completeness, are elaborated below.

Distressed debt argument

The distressed debt argument states that banks have a high priority to safeguard their existing loans and wish to get actively involved in those companies where their (large) loans have a high probability to become distressed (*rescue operations*). In practice, equity ownership in

---

78 The debt monitoring argument is comparable to the broader argument of business relations in the context of financial investor ownership (see Section 3.4.4).

79 The case of Metallgesellschaft serves as an example of bringing the effectiveness of banks as corporate monitors into question: In 1993, the American affiliate of Metallgesellschaft, Germany's 14th largest industrial firm, experienced substantial losses on positions in energy futures and swaps, triggering an emergency recapitalization of the parent company. Deutsche Bank, as a major debtholder represented on the supervisory board, was regarded responsible for the debacle and scolded in the business press for insufficient and bad monitoring. See Edwards (1995) for a further discussion.

these companies is commonly realized through the increasingly popular instrument of debt-to-equity swaps under which companies undergoing a restructuring convert part of their outstanding debt into shares (Maier, 2009). As a result, banks are likely to hold shares in underperforming companies, which have a high likelihood to enter financial distress (and where recovery in case of financial distress would be difficult).

Natural selection argument

The natural selection argument makes a case for no observable relation between corporate performance and bank ownership (see Section 3.3.1).

3.4.5.3 Summary and Hypothesis Development

Table 3.9 summarizes the hypothesized effects of bank ownership on performance. Several contradicting arguments exist. On the one hand, a positive effect is predicted by the asset management argument, according to which banks perceive shareholdings as part of their asset management and therefore push these firms to adopt a profit maximizing orientation. The equity and debt monitoring arguments develop a perspective on bank ownership, which depends on the bank's role as creditor. Following the equity monitoring argument, banks obtain valuable information from their lending relation from which they can benefit in their monitoring role as shareholder. Bank ownership is therefore expected to positively influence performance. On the other hand, the debt monitoring argument suggests that the dual role of banks as providers of both debt and equity raises potential conflicts of interest, which might weaken the effectiveness of banks as monitors. If banks are primarily interested in ensuring the service of their outstanding debt, they are less willing to challenge management decisions in the interests of shareholders. Bank ownership is therefore associated with a negative effect on performance.

It is not clear whether the positive or negative effects of bank ownership dominate. It might even be argued that – as a result of combining debt and equity holdings – banks try to optimize across the entire range of relationships with a company (this would imply that conventional performance measures are not adequate instruments to capture the performance effect of bank shareholdings on firm performance). Sherman and Kaen (1997) weigh up the costs and benefits of bank ownership and come to the conclusion that banks typically hold larger loan positions than equity investments in portfolio companies. This is underpinned by statistics documenting the strong preference of German (Mittelstand) companies for bank debt (see Section 2.3.2.5). It appears therefore more realistic to assume that banks' voting power is used to ensure the service of their outstanding debt than to promote shareholders' interests (at least at low levels of equity ownership – which is reasonable to assume in the case of bank ownership). As a consequence, a negative performance effect (in terms of shareholder value) is expected. The leads to the following hypothesis for empirical testing:

> *Hypothesis 6: Corporate performance decreases with ownership concentration in the hands of commercial banks.*

Table 3.9: Hypothesized Effects of Bank Ownership and Performance

(a) Hypothesized effects of bank ownership on performance

Performance effect	Rationale	Comment
Positive	Asset management	Banks perceive shareholdings as asset management and push these firms to adopt a profit maximizing orientation.
	Equity monitoring	In their function as lenders, banks obtain valuable information from which they can benefit in their monitoring role as shareholder.
Negative	Debt monitoring	The combination of debt and equity holdings raises potential conflicts of interest, which weaken the effectiveness of banks as monitors (in the interest of other shareholders).
Not observable	Natural selection	Market forces push firms toward value-maximizing ownership structures, and hence all existing structures are equally efficient and perform equally well.

(b) Hypothesized effects of performance on bank ownership

Ownership effect	Rationale	Comment
Negative	Distressed debt	Banks have a high priority to safeguard their existing loans and wish to get actively involved in companies where their (large) loans have a high probability to default.
Not observable	Natural selection	Ownership concentration is determined by corporate performance in the sense that inefficient firms will fail to survive in the long run.

3.4.6 Government Ownership

The case of government ownership (versus private ownership) is an age-old topic in financial economics and occupies a vast literature (Shleifer, 1998). Economists in the 1930s and 1940s were quick to favor government ownership of firms as soon as market imperfections such as, for example, monopoly power were expected to occur (e.g., Lewis, 1949). In the 1960s and 1970s, however, failures of state ownership worldwide begun to accumulate, and advances in the theories of ownership and contracting have reopened the question of government versus private ownership (Friedman, 1962). Although there still remains some theoretical debate on the issue, most academic contributions today highlight the benefits of reducing the role of government as corporate owner.

3.4.6.1 Effects of Government Ownership on Performance

The potential effects of government ownership are discussed below.

Internalized regulation argument

The government might prefer to finance certain public policy goals through government ownership rather than through regulation in the private sector if a large amount of information would be required to regulate effectively. If an industry is changing rapidly or is highly technical in nature, ownership allows more flexible internal regulation of a firm and hence reduces regulatory monitoring and information costs. Shareholders may therefore appreciate government ownership as a less harmful alternative to other kinds of regulation (Eckel & Vermaelen, 1986). In addition, internal regulation may lead to more favorable policy treatment for the firm, and shareholders may also benefit from access to low-visibility subsidies via loan guarantees or below-market interest rates.

Government protection argument

The government may also acquire ownership (and grant additional subsidy) in order to prevent a firm from bankruptcy (Eckel & Vermaelen, 1986). If the subsidy benefits only bondholders or employees, there will be no positive effect on firm value. However, to the extent that shareholders were expecting to incur bankruptcy costs, they will also benefit, and stock prices will rise.

Political goals argument

Government ownership internalizes the relation between the public sector and corporations and functions as an institutional alternative to regulation. As a consequence, governments, unlike most other investors, generally invest for policy reasons rather than for the purpose of wealth creation (Templin, 2010). Their objectives are typically to maximize employment and wages, promote regional development by locating production in politically desirable rather than economically attractive districts, ensure national security, and provide low-price goods and services. These objectives generally aim at ensuring success in elections and a long tenure in power (Boubakri, Cosset, & Saffar, 2008). Political influence does not necessarily suggest that unsound financial decisions may result, but it is likely that political goals conflicts with profit maximization. According to Picot and Kaulmann (1989), low performance could be an indicator of the "price" that has to be paid for the specific goal priority. For example, politically-connected firms will be more reluctant to promote restructuring and initiate employee layoffs in order to decrease operating costs because such a decision would be politically costly. Government ownership is therefore associated with decreased performance (in terms of conventional performance measures).

Inefficient management argument

Picot and Kaulmann (1989) criticize the often insufficient quality of management in corporations with government ownership and argue that ties between public authorities and corporations might result in filling management positions according to political interests rather than performance related assessments of potential candidates. Politically-oriented managers, however, might have the wrong entrepreneurial skills, namely being better at dealing with politicians rather than effectively facing competitive market conditions (Barberis, Boycko, Shleifer, & Tsukanova, 1996). The primacy of political acceptability versus management skills also decreases the internal and external competition for management positions, which in turn might aggravate any potentially inefficient behavior of managers. In contrast to privately owned companies, which would have to face the threat of a takeover in the case of inefficient management, this threat does not exist for publicly owned companies as the privatization of such corporations depends not only on economic rationales but also on political factors. Hence, a low level of efficiency does not increase the probability of a takeover (and hence the probability of an exchange of the management). As a result, with an inefficient management installed, performance is expected to be lower in government owned companies than in corporations with other types of owners.

Undermonitoring argument

Alchian (1965/1996) theoretically predicts that publicly owned corporations are inherently less efficient than private firms. He argues that the key difference between public and private firms is the incentive and ability of owners to monitor. In the case of private firms, ownership is concentrated relative to the public sector, and ownership shares can be sold. As a result, private owners have the incentive to monitor management and to align managers' interests with their own. In the case of publicly owned corporations, ownership is diffused (assuming all citizens were owners), and shares of ownership have no price and cannot be sold. Thus, owners of public firms not only have little incentive to monitor management, and even if there would be such an incentive, they would free-ride on any monitoring efforts.

Along the same lines of argumentation, Picot and Kaulmann (1989) also predict that incentives for control of management behavior on the side of the owners are comparatively low in government owned corporations. This is because politicians acting as agents for the government are not directly affected by the performance of the companies in which the government is invested, whereas the wealth of private owners is directly dependent on the performance of their firms. This weak monitoring might leave managers too much power to waste corporate resources and pursue their own goals instead. A related problem is that without a market for ownership, information on the managerial performance of publicly owned corporations is insufficient and noncomparable. This combination of monitoring and information failure is noted by Lin, Cai, and Li (1998) who argue that although public and private systems of ownership may both suffer from collective-action problems in monitoring, the ability of markets to generate information gives private ownership a crucial advantage in the monitoring process compared with public owners. Kane (1999) makes a similar argument by noting that monitoring is particularly weak when ownership is diffuse and information is poor and that both situations arise in publicly owned corporations. In addition, it appears questionable whether politicians are actually capable to engage in effective monitoring activities due to, by nature, probably fewer business insights, less industry knowledge and less available time compared with professional investors.[80] These arguments suggests that problems of monitoring in the public sector will be serious relative to private monitoring and result in higher management discretion and worse public performance.

Natural selection argument

The natural selection argument also applies to government ownership and assumes the absence of any relations between ownership and performance (see Section 3.3.1).

3.4.6.2 Reverse Effects on Government Ownership

For the sake of completeness, potential reverse effects of performance on government ownership are elaborated below.

Policy driven investments argument

As government ownership pursues specific objectives that are different from those of private owners (see the government protection and political goals arguments discussed above), it can be assumed that performance plays only a minor role in the investment decision process.[81] Performance is therefore expected to have no effect on the level of government ownership.

Natural selection argument

The natural selection argument assumes the absence of any relation between performance and government ownership (see Section 3.3.1).

3.4.6.3 Summary and Hypothesis Development

Table 3.10 summarizes the hypothesized effects of government ownership on performance. A positive performance effect is to be expected as a result of internalized regulation as a less harmful alternative to external regulation. The government may also acquire ownership in

---

80 The example of Germany's much-delayed and expensive airport project Berlin-Brandenburg is insightful in this context: The airport's supervisory board, which is dominated by politicians from Berlin, Brandenburg, and the Federal Government rather than construction experts, is sharply criticized in the business press for doing a poor job of supervising and for failing to oversee fire-safety issues more rigorously while reportedly paying more attention to matters such as switching the floor tiles to a more stately limestone (Löhr & Schwenn, 2013).

81 Although there is the observation that the German government comes to the financial aid of companies (i.e., banks) facing severe financial difficulties as, for example, Commerzbank or Hypo Real Estate, this topic is beyond the scope of this dissertation because financial institutions are intentionally excluded from the analysis (see Section 5.2.1).

order to protect a firm from going bankrupt, which saves shareholders from incurring bankruptcy costs, thereby increasing market value. These arguments, however, appear to be relevant only for companies in regulated industries or for potentially distressed companies.

In contrast, the majority of companies with government ownership are expected to suffer from a negative performance effect as a result of political goals, inefficient management and weak monitoring by governments: The political goals argument states that government owners primarily pursue political goals (e.g., employment policy and structural policy) rather than wealth creation. This is likely to decrease financial performance. Along similar lines, the inefficient management argument assumes that managerial positions might be filled according to political interests rather than to personal performance records, which should lead to a low level of managerial efficiency and hence decreased financial performance. According to the undermonitoring argument, the potentially inefficient managerial behavior is aggravated due to government owners' comparatively little incentive as well as incompetency to effectively discipline the management. To conclude, government ownership is expected to lead to low performance (in terms of conventional performance measures). The following hypothesis is therefore formulated for empirical testing:

> *Hypothesis 7: Corporate performance decreases with ownership concentration in the hands of government authorities.*

Table 3.10: Hypothesized Effects of Government Ownership and Performance

(a) Hypothesized effects of government ownership on performance

Performance effect	Rationale	Comment
Positive	Internalized regulation	Shareholders appreciate government ownership as a less harmful alternative to external regulation.
	Government protection	Government ownership might protect a firm from going bankrupt, which saves shareholders from incurring bankruptcy costs, thereby increasing market value.
Negative	Political goals	Government ownership generally pursues political goals rather than wealth creation and hence has a negative effect on financial performance.
	Inefficient management	Managerial positions in government owned corporations might be filled according to political interests rather than to personal performance records, which could lead to a low level of managerial efficiency and hence decreased financial performance.
	Undermonitoring	Government agencies have little incentive and might not be capable to engage in effective monitoring activities.
Not observable	Natural selection	Market forces push firms toward value-maximizing ownership structures, and hence all existing structures are equally efficient and perform equally well.

(b) Hypothesized effects of performance on government ownership

Ownership effect	Rationale	Comment
Not observable	Policy driven investments	Governments generally invest for policy reasons rather than wealth creation upsides.
	Natural selection	Ownership concentration is determined by corporate performance in the sense that inefficient firms will fail to survive in the long run.

4 Related Literature

4.1 Introduction

As the variety of arguments brought forward shows, the relation between ownership and performance is complex. Theoretical arguments alone cannot unambiguously predict whether benefits of concentrated ownership outweigh its costs, or whether certain groups of owner identity have a more positive or more negative impact on company performance than others. Empirical research hence becomes important to examine which of the logically possible explanations is the most probable. The following chapter therefore presents the findings of major empirical studies. First, Section 4.2 addresses potentially moderating factors. Section 4.3 then reviews and evaluates the existing research on ownership structure and performance.

4.2 Moderating Factors

The empirical research on the effects of ownership on firm performance spans several decades and is still subject to controversy. The great variance in empirical evidence is in particular owing to three moderating effects (Hu & Izumida, 2008; Sáchez-Ballesta & García-Meca, 2007): the underlying corporate governance system, the applied measures of performance and ownership concentration, and the econometric techniques applied.

4.2.1 Corporate Governance System

There is some agreement in the literature to distinguish between two general systems of corporate governance: One is associated with the US and the UK, and the other is associated with Continental Europe and Japan.[82] The different characteristics of the two governance systems are summarized in Table 4.1. According to Hommel (1998), corporate governance follows a “carrot and stick”-approach. Internal control serves as the carrot and allows shareholders to closely interact with management and to create a tight relation between their own expectations and the management's incentive structure. In contrast, external control represents the stick, which controls management behavior through penalties provided by the

[82] See, for example, Grundfest (1990) and Short and Keasey (1999) for an in-depth cross-national comparison of corporate governance systems.

markets for corporate control and management labor. The key difference between the U.S. and the German governance system lies in the relative importance of these control mechanisms: In the US, control relies mainly on market sanctions to eliminate agency problems between owners and management, whereas in Germany, constraints on managerial behavior mainly appear to be internal and emanate from the various stakeholders in the firm.

Table 4.1: U.S. and German Corporate Governance Structures in Comparison

Control mechanisms	Corporate governance context	
	US	Germany
(a) Internal control mechanisms		
Ownership concentration	Low	High
Turnover of large equity blocks	High	Low
Owners	Pension and mutual funds	Banks, corporations
Investor orientation	Portfolio	Control
Financing	Equity	Debt
Long-term relation between banks and firms	Limited	Extensive
Value-based management incentive schemes	Important	Unimportant
Board structure	Single-tier	Two-tier
Board representation	Managers, outsiders	Owners, employees
Role of supervisory board/outside managers	Unimportant	Important
Decision-Making power of management	Significant	Large
(b) External control mechanisms		
Turnover on the market for management labor	High	Low
Regional segmentation of product markets	Low	Significant
Frequency of hostile takeovers	High	Low
Information available about publicly listed firms	Extensive	Limited
Shareholder protection	High	Low

Note. Adapted from Hommel (1998). The table is designed to indicate the salient comparative features of corporate governance structures across countries. It therefore highlights differences rather than absolute characteristics.

Gedajlovic and Shapiro (1998) argue that ownership concentration is only one (internal) dimension of corporate governance, and if one or more of the other (internal or external)

dimensions are actively present and force managers to maximize profits, then managerial discretion is limited even in the absence of a dominant shareholder, that is, ownership concentration becomes irrelevant and one should not find a relation between ownership structure and performance. Because Germany is characterized by a relative reliance on internal control mechanisms, which are, according to Gedajlovic and Shapiro (1998), generally assumed to be effective constraints, it can be concluded that in Germany, ownership concentration should play no relevant role to limit managerial discretion. However, the assumption of effective internal control mechanisms is challenged by Hommel (1998) who points to internal control deficiencies in German firms, and suggests that the control vacuum can only be filled with a market of corporate control as external control mechanism. Nevertheless, the market for corporate control faces serious limitations compared with other control instruments, which leads to the argument that market-based constraints are not powerful enough to fully constrain managers (see Section 3.2.2.4). As a consequence, ownership concentration is expected to be a relevant corporate governance mechanism in economies such as the US and the UK, which are characterized by a reliance on (comparably less effective) external constraints (Gedajlovic & Shapiro, 1998).

Ownership concentration is also assumed to be a relevant control mechanism if legal protection of shareholders as another external control mechanism is weak. For example, in corporate governance systems with comparably lower levels of legal protection of minority investors (as found in Continental Europe), investors are incentivized to increase their investment in order to have sufficient control over the firm to have their interests respected. Ownership concentration hence serves as a compensation for legal protection. Shleifer and Vishny (1997) thus propose that blockholder ownership has a more positive effect on firm value in countries with lower levels of investor protection because it is more necessary to counter managerial agency problems in these governance systems. In contrast, Thomsen, Pedersen, and Kvist (2006) refer to the existence of private benefits for controlling shareholders and argue that large shareholders have no incentives to give up control (and adopt a more dispersed ownership structure) because any benefits gained by selling more shares to the public must be shared with these investors. As a result, blockholder owners in Continental Europe will maintain ownership levels in excess of levels that maximize firm value. Hence, lower ownership concentration in Continental European firms could tend to increase firm value. This could be in particular the case for European firms with high levels of ownership concentration.

These arguments (although they come to different conclusions) suggest that the impact of ownership concentration is contingent upon the environmental context. Findings from studies based on Anglo-American samples may therefore not necessarily apply to Continental Europe (and vice versa). According to the specific economic environment, ownership structures (and types of shareholders) might imply different benefits and costs to firms, and the actual trade-off between these benefits and costs again is contingent upon the underlying governance context. That is, a specific corporate governance system may have an influence (which might also vary over time) on whether the ownership-performance relation is positive, negative, or insignificant. It is hence well worth to exercise caution in interpreting and generalizing results across national boundaries. Samples based on multicountry evidence have the advantage to cover the moderating effects of different underlying corporate governance systems.

4.2.2 Variable Measurement and Data Quality

Conflicting conclusions regarding the relation between ownership concentration and performance can also be partly attributed to different measures employed. With respect to measures of ownership concentration, most studies use the fraction of control rights owned by the largest shareholder, but there are also many variations to this (see Section 2.2.2 for a discussion on the differences between the various measures). With respect to measures of corporate performance, it turns out that Anglo-American studies mostly use Tobin's Q, whereas Continental European studies prefer MTB as performance measure due to differences in national accounting systems. Accounting performance measures such as ROA and ROE are also employed in many empirical studies either solely or as a complement of Tobin's Q. Venkatraman and Ramanujam (1986) suggest that these definitional differences play a major role in explaining the inconsistency of findings in empirical studies. In order to address this issue, the empirical analysis in this dissertation makes use of alternative measures of performance (see Section 5.2.2.2).

Another issue arises from data quality. Especially studies based on various data sources might suffer from definitional inconsistency. For example, Kole (1995) estimates separate regressions for the same sample from three different data sources and shows that the ownership coefficients are different and that their statistical significance varies. For this reason, ownership and performance data used for the empirical analysis in this work each originate from one single data source. A great amount of time is spent to ensure that the data are consistent and accurate.

4.2.3 Methodology

Different conclusions regarding the relation between ownership and performance are also owing to model specifications and estimation techniques applied. Most papers cited employ transversal analyses and use single equation ordinary least square (OLS) models. This methodology is in particular prevalent in (early) Anglo-American studies. Panel estimators for fixed- or random-effects models are commonly used for samples based on panel data. However, single-equation studies do not consider the possible endogeneity of ownership structure. In recent years, however, a growing number of studies have considered ownership concentration to be an endogenous variable. To a large degree, this has become possible due to the development of various econometric techniques that facilitate the endogenous treatment of variables (Hamilton & Nickerson, 2003). This is the case for simultaneous equation model techniques such as two-stage least squares (2SLS) using instrumental variables and generalized method of moments (GMM) estimation.[83] In order to address this issue, the empirical analysis in this dissertation applies several econometric techniques and contrasts the potentially different conclusions (see Section 5.4).

4.3 Review of Existing Studies

First, empirical studies on the relation between ownership concentration and performance are presented. Second, previous research on the relation between owner identity and performance is documented. As most of the existing empirical work is Anglo-American, special consideration is given to German and, more generally, to Continental European evidence.[84] A

83 GMM is an instrumental variable method, which applies to dynamic panel models where the lagged dependent variable also appears as explanatory variable.

84 The main criteria for inclusion in the literature review were frequency of citation and inclusion in highly cited review articles. Secondary criteria for inclusion were the use of statistical tests and sample size: Studies with extremely small sample sizes and studies that were based on anecdotal evidence were dropped. Event studies were also not considered in the review. Third, only studies based on samples from developed economies were included in the literature review because developing countries usually lack liquid and mature capital markets.

summary of the characteristics and main findings of the reviewed studies is provided in Table A.1.1 in the appendix.

4.3.1 Previous Research on Ownership Concentration and Performance

There are basically three strands of literature of relevance to the study of ownership concentration. One is a series of (mainly Anglo-American) studies of causes and effects of ownership concentration. These studies are mainly based on agency theory and view ownership structures as an efficient solution to risk allocation and incentive problems. They assume that ownership is exogenous, and causation runs only in one way (from ownership to performance). The second generation of ownership performance studies also considers the reverse direction of causation from performance to ownership and argues that, in equilibrium, ownership structure is endogenous. The third body of literature is concerned with international differences in corporate governance, and how these might be a substitute for ownership concentration as a mechanism to solve agency problems.

4.3.1.1 Studies Modeling a One-Way Causation

An early approach to the topic of ownership performance is made by **Hill and Snell (1988)** who address the issue of how corporate strategy and hence performance might be influenced by the corporate governance structure of firms in research-intensive industries. They argue that strategies pursued by shareholder controlled firms differ from those of manager controlled firms and theorize that managers favor diversification strategies, whereas shareholders prefer innovation strategies, which in turn are associated with greater profitability. The rationale for the predicted relations can be found in a consideration of risk/return aspects of the alternative strategies from the different perspectives of shareholders and managers. Most shareholders invest in a diversified portfolio of stocks in order to eliminate unsystematic risk. The riskiness of an individual stock hence does not matter to them as long as they can balance high risk stocks against low-risk stocks within their portfolio or are able to divest the stock if the performance of the firm starts to slip. In research-intensive industries, an emphasis on innovations is regarded as a high-risk strategy. Hence, although an innovation strategy may be attractive to portfolio investors, it is less favorable for managers who have to bear the consequences of failure and therefore rather prefer a low-risk imitator strategy. In regard to corporate diversification, it can be argued that diversification will not be preferred by shareholders as they usually hold a diversified portfolio. In contrast, managers favor extensive diversification as it increases the size if the firm and also provides an insurance against the failure of an innovation strategy. As a result of the different strategies preferred by shareholders and managers, the authors hypothesize that governance factors such as ownership concentration, management stockholdings, and outsider participation in the board will make it more likely that the firm places an emphasis on innovation and hence pursues strategies consistent with maximizing shareholder welfare. The study is based on a sample of 92 large firms in research-intensive industries in the US in 1980. In regard to ownership concentration, the results of OLS regressions show that concentration has a significant, positive impact on accounting profitability. However, the relation becomes insignificant once strategy is controlled for. This can be taken as evidence that the relation between ownership concentration and profitability is mediated by strategy, suggesting that shareholders influence firm performance indirectly through their impact upon strategy choice, which has a direct impact upon profitability.

Holderness and Sheehan (1988) analyze the role of majority shareholders and further address the issue of shareholder identity, assuming that the motivations and effects of large shareholdings may be different for individuals and corporations. Based on an U.S. sample of 114 public firms with a majority shareholder in 1978-84, they pair these majority owned firms with relatively widely held firms in the same industry and of the same size. They find that accounting rates of return and Tobin's Q are similar for majority owned and diffusely held firms as the differences lack statistical significance. In a further analysis, they conduct time series analyses by comparing the performance of firms when they have majority owners and when they don't. Rates of return are neither statistically lower nor higher during the majority-shareholder years. This suggests that majority shareholders have no pronounced effects on performance. They hence conclude that large block ownership is not motivated primarily as a means to expropriate or consume corporate wealth. Instead, attention should be paid to the effects of managerial large blockholdings as nine out of 10 majority shareholders in the sample firms are directly involved in firm management. That is, majority shareholders do not merely monitor management teams, they lead them. This suggests that benefits from managerial large blockholdings, rather than benefits from more effective monitoring alone, motivate large block ownership. Partitioning the sample by individual versus corporate majority shareholders reveals that the identity of large block shareholders appears to be important as individual majority-shareholder firms tend to underperform their comparison firms, whereas corporate-majority-shareholder firms do not. However, the differences are small and lack statistical significance.

Empirical research typically investigates the role of the largest shareholder or analyzes total blockholder ownership without considering its distribution, but **Konijn et al. (2001)** provide a different perspective on ownership concentration and examine the question whether a single large blockholder or a set of dispersed smaller blockholders is better for firm value. Literature makes different predictions on the effect of blockholder concentration on performance. On the one hand, there are arguments that highlight the advantages of dispersed blockholdings. For example, in the theories involving "exit" as the key governance mechanism, blockholder dispersion can be good for firm value even though splitting a block reduces the effectiveness of direct intervention ("voice"). Compared with a single large blockholder, dispersed blockholders internalize less of the market impact costs when collectively engaging in information-based trading. As a result, smaller dispersed blockholders have higher incentives to actually trade on information and therefore impound more information into prices. This disciplines managers ex ante to ensure that blockholders hold on to their stakes, thus increasing firm value. On the other hand, it can also be argued that blockholder dispersion has a negative effect on firm value. A second (or third) blockholder can be good for firm value if he monitors the first blockholder, but the incentive to monitor and the ability to impede any expropriation activities by the first blockholder require the other blockholder to be sufficiently large (or to form a coalition with other smaller blockholders). Too much dispersion hence can be bad for firm value. A fixed-effects regression of 3,722 firm-year observations for public U.S. firms in the period 1996-2001, shows that both the presence of any blockholders and their combined ownership share are negatively related to Tobin's Q. This suggests that there may be room for private benefits of control by blockholders, possibly at the expense of other stakeholders, thereby decreasing firm value. This supports Shleifer and Vishny (1997)'s view that the relevant agency problem to be addressed by corporate governance is the expropriation of small shareholders by controlling shareholders, rather the expropriation of (all) shareholders by managers. In a second model, they analyze the relation between blockholder dispersion and firm value by including a Herfindahl-Hirschman-Index to measure dispersion among the five top blockholders (more dispersion implies a lower value of the index). The coefficient is significant, positive, which means that a more dispersed blockholder base is negatively correlated with Tobin's Q. This results seems to support the arguments that focus on the contestability of the largest shareholder by other blockholders and state that dispersion limits the ability of smaller blockholders to effectively challenge the largest shareholder. However, the Herfindahl-Hirschman-Index reflects both the number of blockholdings and the symmetry between block sizes, and therefore might be a less clean measure of dispersion if block asymmetry is the crucial element. As an alternative, the number of blockholders and the Gini coefficient are used. The regression results show that the number of blocks is significantly negatively related, but there is no significant relation between firm value and block asymmetry measured by the Gini coefficient. It appears that dispersion operates largely through the number of blockholders rather than through block sizes. This casts doubt on the empirical relevance for arguments that push the contestability of the largest blockholder as the main mechanism for value creation under multiple blockholder structures.

A prominent study in the European market is the work of **Pedersen and Thomsen (1999)**. The paper examines the causes and effects of ownership concentration among the largest companies in 12 European countries (1990-93). As a reference point the paper takes the study on U.S. data by Demsetz and Lehn (1985) and examines whether their results hold in the European context. They find evidence that ownership concentration is negatively influenced by size (as a measure for risk) and positively by earnings volatility (as a measure for monitoring costs). But they also observe a nation effect, which is partly attributable to cross-country differences in institutions and regulation. As Demsetz and Lehn (1985), they find no significant relation between ownership concentration and performance. Estimates with a quadratic form of ownership concentration also produce insignificant results. The European evidence hence appears to be consistent with Demsetz and Lehn (1985)'s findings on U.S. firms. Ownership concentration might indeed be an endogenous variable with no effect on profitability.

In a subsequent study, **Thomsen and Pedersen (2000)** argue for performance as a bell-shaped function of ownership concentration as opposed to Demsetz and Lehn (1985)'s (and Pedersen and Thomsen (1999)'s) view of ownership as an endogenously determined variable with no effect on performance. They argue that the estimation of a quadratic relation is sufficiently flexible to catch both a general positive linear effect and a hypothetical entrenchment effect at high levels of ownership concentration. Running OLS regressions on MTB and ROA, they indeed find evidence of a bell-shaped effect with a maximum at 83%. As the bell graphically appears to be tilted, high ownership share of the largest owner is associated with increasing performance up to the point of majority control (51%). An increasing share has little effect beyond this point. For low ownership shares, the incentive effect is quantitatively important and statistically significant (the squared term is also statistically significant but quantitatively smaller). Furthermore, the authors note that the effect of ownership is qualitatively unchanged by including the identity of the largest owner as a categorical variable, which also turns out to be significant. The authors also address the possibility of a reverse direction of causality from performance to ownership structure in their OLS regression but assume that ownership structure is generally quite stable and does not adjust quickly to changing economic circumstances. The data show indeed a high structural stability, which makes it reasonable for them to regard ownership structure as an exogenous variable over the 5-year sample period. In order to examine the sensitivity of their results, the authors further test whether the observed changes in ownership concentration are correlated with performance in subsequent periods and find this to be the case. This approach provides some support for an effect of ownership structure on performance as predicted by theory, although it does not solve the issues of causality or simultaneity.

4.3.1.2 Studies Addressing Endogeneity of Ownership

Demsetz and Lehn (1985) are the first to address a certain level of endogeneity. Their research is related to an earlier paper by **Demsetz (1983)** where he argues that the structure of ownership varies systematically in ways that are consistent with value maximization, implying that ownership is an endogenous outcome balancing the costs (e.g., risk) and benefits (e.g., monitoring) of ownership. Hence, no systematic relation between ownership concentration and performance is to be expected (see Section 3.3.2). The study uses a 1980/81 sample of public firms in the US. They first estimate a model for ownership concentration and find that firm size, instability of profit rate (reflecting the control potential) and certain industries are empirically significant in explaining the variation in ownership structure. Then they use this predicted ownership variable to estimate a recursive regression model on firm performance including several other independent variables such as capital, advertising and R&D expenditures, size, and dummies for industry regulation. The explanatory power of the model is quite low, and no significant relation between ownership concentration and performance is found (the coefficients for the alternative measures of ownership concentration are even negative, although insignificant). The study is frequently cited in literature because Demsetz and Lehn (1985) are the first to conceptually and empirically provide support for the endogeneity of ownership concentration. However, their research design is criticized by Hill and Snell (1988) for not adjusting profit rates for industry differences. Another problem in Demsetz and Lehn (1985)'s analysis is that although they view ownership as endogenous and consequently use a recursive model to control for this endogeneity, only one way of causation is modeled because performance does not enter the ownership equation, and hence the possibility that ownership structure might be affected by firm performance is not examined. This issue is later revisited in a paper by **Demsetz and Villalonga (2001)** in a more explicit simultaneous equations setting where ownership structure is the dependent variable in one of the two equations, and firm performance is the dependent variable in the second equation. Their evidence supports the belief that (especially managerial) ownership is endogenously determined by performance but not the belief that ownership structure affects performance.

Another early study accounting for endogeneity of ownership to some degree is that of **Leech and Leahy (1991)**. The authors first apply OLS regressions on a sample of 470 publicly listed companies in the UK (1983) and analyze ownership structure both in terms of dichotomous control-type classifications and ownership concentration indices. The results for control types suggest that owner controlled firms (degree of control of largest shareholding exceeds 90% or alternatively 95%, or 99%) are more profitable and fast growing than manager owned firms (firms which are not classified as owner controlled): Profit margins rise by 1.89%, the rate of return on shareholders' capital by 4.54%, the rate of sales growth by 5.06% p.a., and the rate of growth of net assets by 10.59% p.a. Given a control type, ownership concentration implies a lower valuation ratio, profit margin, and growth rate of net assets. The authors explain, for example, the negative coefficient for the valuation ratio by means of a capital market discipline effect, which states that where ownership is concentrated, the market for shares is not well developed, and this is reflected in an adverse market valuation irrespective of the return on shareholders' capital. In a second step, the authors assume ownership structure as endogenous and analyze factors that are supposed to determine the variation on observed patterns of ownership among companies. As no simple relation between ownership concentration and control type was assumed, they do not expect to observe the same factors determining both concentration and control type.[85] For ownership concentration indices, their regression

[85] On the one hand, there is an evolution of control whereby increasing dispersion of ownership over time results in a transition from owner control to manager control. On the other hand, increasing dispersion does not necessarily lead to control loss in a minority-ownership controlled firm with growth financed by widening ownership.

analysis shows that concentration depends negatively on firm size and risk. Probit regression results for control type, however, are weak and depend on the classification used. They conclude that the control type is exogenous, whereas ownership concentration is endogenous, variations in the latter not necessarily having any implications for the former.

A multinational examination of the relation between ownership concentration and performance is provided by **Weiss and Hilger (2012)**. Using a sample of 1,079 firms from eight large economies, they find evidence of a curvilinear (first positive, then negative) effect of ownership concentration on Tobin's Q based on OLS regressions. However, when estimating 2SLS regressions in order to control for possible endogeneity, all ownership concentration variables turn insignificant. In a further analysis, they examine only firms with high ownership concentration (25% percentile) based on the assumption that there is a (negative) performance effect only at very high levels of ownership concentration, it should be more pronounced and easier to detect in this highly concentrated subsample than in the full sample. However, the results widely resemble those of the full sample. Using alternative performance measures does not affect the results. As a result, the analyses do not suggest a significant effect of either low or high levels of ownership concentration on performance when accounting for endogeneity by means of a 2SLS regression. The results are hence comparable to the findings of Demsetz and Villalonga (2001) that ownership concentration is endogenously determined.

For the case of Germany and the US, evidence on the role of the largest owner is provided by **Gugler and Weigand (2003)**. Based on a panel data set of 491 public U.S. corporations (1989-97) and 167 public German firms (1991-96), they estimate fixed-effects and fixed-effects instrumental variable regressions and find that when using instrumental variable techniques, managerial shareholdings have no statistically significant effect on performance, but the largest shareholder still affects performance. The point estimates of the coefficients of the largest owner yield that an increase in the stake of the largest shareholder increases performance (measured as ROA) until a stake of 28% (German sample firms) or 19% (U.S. sample firms) is reached, respectively. Performance deteriorates for further stake increases until 83% or 40%, respectively, before performance picks up again thereafter. This implies that the negative middle range in the cubic model is much wider for German firms (for ownership stakes of the largest owner from 28% to 83%) than for the U.S. sample firms (from 19% to 40%).

Edwards and Weichenrieder (2004) propose a method of distinguishing empirically between the beneficial and harmful effects of ownership concentration by obtaining separate measures of the control and cash flow rights of the largest shareholder. Based on a sample of 97 German nonfinancial firms in 1992, they run an OLS regression of performance on the size of voting and cash flow rights held by the largest (and second largest) owner.[86] The papers shows that greater holdings by the largest shareholder raise the value of the firms (greater monitoring of management and reduced incentives to exploit minority shareholders due to greater cash flow rights) but also lower the value of shares (greater private benefits of control due to greater control rights). The results show that, although the largest shareholders are able to gain private benefits of control at minority shareholders' expense, the net effect of equal increases in both the control and cash flow rights of the largest shareholder does not harm and, depending on the type of largest shareholder, may benefit minority shareholders.[87] In a further analysis, they estimate the effect of increased ownership by the largest shareholder on performance by estimating both the value of performance when the largest shareholder has all the control and cash flow rights in a firm and its value when these are zero. If it is assumed that there is no diversion of profits from minority shareholders in either of these two extreme cases, any difference in the estimated performance will reflect the effects of the change from no monitoring of management (when ownership is dispersed) to efficient monitoring (when the largest shareholder owns 100% of the control and cash flow rights).[88] The analysis shows that a change from completely dispersed ownership of a large company to ownership by a single shareholder can double the value of the company (depending on the type of shareholder).

86 The value of corporate equity is assumed to be determined by the minority shareholders in the corporations, whose only benefit from ownership of shares is the dividends they receive, and who are assumed to anticipate correctly the costs and benefits to them of owning shares in a company in which the largest owner may exert some control over its actions. The gross profits of a company are assumed to depend on the extent to which its management is subject to monitoring, which in turn depends separately on both the control and the cash flow rights of the largest shareholder.

87 The analysis finds that greater holdings by the second largest owners also tend to raise the value of shares, which may be due either to the effects of monitoring of management by the second largest shareholder or to the effects of monitoring the behavior of the largest shareholder and hence reducing the extraction of private benefits of control.

88 If ownership is completely dispersed, even the largest shareholder has not sufficient control rights to engage in diversion of profits from other shareholders, but there will also be no monitoring. If the largest shareholder owns all the control and cash flow rights, then no profits will be diverted because all profits accrue to the largest shareholder anyway, and the largest shareholder will have the correct incentives to engage in efficient monitoring because he internalizes all the benefits of doing so.

According to the authors, this provides evidence of the costs that shareholders in German corporations with dispersed share ownership suffer due to the lack of monitoring of management and might explain why so few large listed German corporations have completely dispersed ownership. In an alternative approach, the authors treat the ownership variables as endogenous and use instruments (size, age, risk) to estimate the regression model. However, a Hausman test of significance of the differences between the OLS and instrumental variable coefficient estimates finds that the instrumental variable model is inefficient, and hence there is no evidence that the results obtained are dependent on the inappropriate use of OLS as an estimation method.

In contrast to many previous studies that have documented (to some extent) a positive correlation between ownership concentration and firm performance, **Lehmann and Weigand (2000)** find that the presence of a single large shareholder does not necessarily enhance profitability. A fixed-effects regression of a sample of 361 mining and manufacturing firms (1991-96) finds ownership concentration to affect profitability (measured as ROA and ROE) significantly negatively at the 5% error level. The negative impact is a bit weaker for listed firms than for privately held firms, but the coefficient difference is not statistically significant. The authors also model a within-2SLS regression but find that there is no gain by endogenizing the ownership variable and instead prefer the fixed-effects model. These findings contradict both the hypothesis of the beneficial large shareholder as well as Demsetz and Lehn (1985)'s hypothesis of no ownership effect and instead support the view that large shareholders inflict costs on the firm (e.g., rent extraction, too much monitoring, or infighting).

4.3.1.3 Multicountry Studies

In the early 1990s, an institutional view on ownership structures emerged, which conjectures the traditional economic view according to which companies will tend to adopt optimal structures because this will promote their efficiency and competitiveness. Roe (1993) argues that if the economic model is universal, similar ownership structures should exist across countries: "There is a best way to make steel, and presumably there is a best way to organize large steel firms." (Roe, 1993, p. 28). However, comparative analyses provide evidence of fundamental differences between market economies such as the US and Germany or Japan. According to the institutionalists, the differences suggest that differing histories, cultures and paths of economic development better explain the differing structures than economic theory alone. For example, U.S. banks are prevented by legislation from holding shares in industrial companies, whereas German banks are not so constrained, which leads to path dependency of bank ownership in Germany. The institutional view hence regards ownership structures as highly dependent on national regulation. The question then arises whether ownership is primarily determined by economic theory, or whether there is a choice of models.

Pedersen and Thomsen (1997) criticize the nation effect as formulated by Roe (1993) as an all-encompassing argument for differences between economies. According to their view, the highly liquid structure of the American stock market can also be explained by the size of the largest U.S. firms, which made it necessary to diversify ownership and eventually created the large American stock market (compared with other nations). They present a quantitative analysis of ownership structures among the hundred largest, nonfinancial companies in each of twelve European countries in the year 1990 and expect the frequency of different ownership modes to depend on the existence of institutions complementary to these modes - after controlling for differences in company size and industry. Their study indeed reveals differences between nations giving the impression of a strong nation effect. For example, dispersed ownership is common in the UK, foreign ownership is predominant in Belgium and Spain, and government ownership is common in France and Italy but rare in the rest of Europe. They explain these differences in ownership structure by historical and geographical differences that have shaped the economic development of these nations (historical waves of nationalization and privatization, industrialization, industry structure, etc.). Remarkably, the different patterns of ownership structures between the twelve European nations are still existent after controlling for firm size and industry. To further explore the nature of the nation effect, the authors then analyze the extent to which institutional differences can explain national ownership patterns. Results from a multinominal logistic regression show that stock market size, banking concentration, frequency of dual class shares, and openness of the economy can explain two thirds of the nation effect. The study hence presents support for Roe (1993)'s argumentation and complements his work on a more qualitative basis. However, there is still uncertainty about the nature of the nation effect due to the limited number of nations covered in the analysis, and it may also be likely that other factors such as, for example, geographical location, tax systems and cultural differences also influence national ownership structures.

Early cross-country studies on ownership concentration are primarily concerned with international differences in corporate governance at the country level and tend to emphasize qualitative (cultural, political, and historical) determinants of ownership structure, whereas more recent studies have emerged as a synthesis between the systems literature and agency theory. This line of research emphasizes that corporate governance structures may be a substitute for ownership concentration as a mechanism to solve agency problems. **Gedajlovic and Shapiro (1998)** contribute to this view and examine the relation between ownership concentration and performance in Canada, France, Germany, the UK, and the US. The purpose of their study is to determine whether the relation between ownership concentration and performance varies across countries in ways that are related to national differences in corporate governance. They assume that a positive relation between ownership concentration and firm performance exists only if internal and/or external constraints do not exist or operate imperfectly. When other agency control mechanisms are installed, managerial discretion will be limited even in the absence of a dominant shareholder. Based on the different characteristics of the corporate governance systems (see the discussion in Section 4.2.1), they expect a positive relation between ownership concentration and performance in the UK and US and no relation in Germany, France, and Canada. Results from OLS regressions on 1,030 medium to large public companies in these five countries for the period 1986-91 indicate that important and statistically significant differences do in fact exist across the countries studied.[89] For the U.S. subsample, the coefficient of ownership concentration is significant, negative, whereas the coefficient for the squared measure is significant, positive, that is, ownership concentration effects are positive but are only present in firms with high levels of ownership concentration. Unlike for the U.S. sample, no significant effects are found for the U.K. subsample, which is surprising but might imply that the internal constraints facing U.K. managers are more effective at resolving agency problems than assumed. For the German subsample, similar effects as for the US are found. Ownership concentration therefore does not appear redundant in terms of limiting agency conflicts. This finding may indicate that the

[89] Seifert, Gonenc, and Wright (2005) examine the effects of ownership on performance using a sample of firms from four countries and, like Gedajlovic and Shapiro (1998), find no universal relation (across the four countries) between the ownership variables and performance. As there are nevertheless significant relations found within the various nations, one could conclude that ownership structure matters indeed, but it matters because of specific local laws or the effects of other governance mechanisms in the specific country. Alternatively, the authors suggest that, because there is no consistent relation across countries, the ownership effect is minimal. This line of reasoning would then be consistent with Demsetz and Lehn (1985).

German corporate governance system has more in common with the U.S. system than is commonly assumed. In particular, it may suggest that the role of German banks as a means of internal constraint may commonly be exaggerated. For the French and Canadian subsample, no significant effects are found, as expected.

Thomsen et al. (2006)'s work concentrates on Continental Europe and finds a different shape of the ownership concentration and performance relation. They apply random-effects models and Granger causality tests to a sample of 876 of the largest EU and U.S. firms for the 1988-98 period and find no significant association between blockholder ownership and prior or subsequent firm performance in either the US or the UK. However, in Continental Europe they identify a negative association between ownership and both market valuation and accounting profitability. Further analysis reveals that the negative performance effect is significant only for companies with initial levels of blockholder ownership of at least 10%. It hence appears that the system effect is attributable to (or at least covaries with) a high level of ownership concentration. This is in line with La Porta, Lopez-de-Silanes, Shleifer, and Vishny (2000) who point to private benefits as a cause of low market valuation and high levels of blockholder ownership in countries with low levels of investor protection. Given the high level of ownership concentration in Continental Europe, further increases tend to lower firm value, or the market tends to respond to decreases in ownership concentration through stock price appreciation. Lower levels of investor protection in Continental Europe imply larger private benefits of control than in the US and the UK. When blockholder control is relaxed, the market may therefore respond positively. The private benefits might also explain why large owners have not already adjusted their shareholdings to maximize firm value.

In an analogous manner, **Kirchmaier and Grant (2005)** also argue that blockholder ownership in Germany has tended to exceed the level that maximizes firm value. They use a sample of 473 of the sum of the largest 110 nonfinancial companies in each of the five largest European economies in the period 1992-2002 and group them into three ownership categories: legal control (where the largest shareholder or alternatively the three largest shareholders control more than 50% of the control rights), de-facto control (where the largest shareholder or alternatively the three largest shareholders exceed the national mandatory bid threshold, which in Germany is at 30% of the votes), and widely held firms (where no shareholder or alternatively the three largest shareholders own a percentage of control rights above the mandatory bid threshold). As performance variable, they use the average quarterly share price returns and employ a filter technique to isolate the long-term share price trend from cyclical effects. They then examine the performance differences for the various ownership categories. Results for the German subsample show that the best performing companies are widely held, companies under de-facto control are the next best performing group and legal control – which is the dominant form of ownership of the German sample firms – performs worst. The differences are statistically significant (when analyzing the three largest shareholders) between the widely held group and both the de-facto and legal control group (for Spain and France, results are similar, and no conclusions can be drawn for Italy and the UK). The authors attribute the fact that the dominant form of ownership in Germany is the worst performing ownership category to the existence of private control benefits due to the low minority investor protection; That is, large shareholders maintain ownership levels in excess of the level that maximizes firm value because they also value the private benefits of control. This indicates that existing German ownership structures are inefficient.

4.3.1.4 Summary

The empirical research on the effects of ownership structure on firm performance spans several decades but has failed to reach any conclusions as to whether ownership concentration does significantly affect performance. Most of the early studies model a one-way causation running from ownership concentration to performance. However, cross-sectional regressions of performance on ownership concentration may be misleading as well as statistically incorrect because the results are contaminated by the potential effect of performance on ownership concentration. With the second generation of ownership studies, clear progress has been made in the empirical literature. The first reflects the need to consider the endogenous nature of ownership structure. The second, a consequence of the previous one, refers to the use of techniques enabling researchers to tackle endogeneity and address an assessment of analysis over time. Studies taking endogeneity into account tend to find weaker evidence of a relation between ownership concentration and performance. But despite the wealth of research, the question remains whether large owners contribute to the solution of agency problems, or whether they exacerbate them. Since the 1990s, a third body of literature has emerged that is concerned with international differences in corporate governance. These authors propose that institutional differences at the country level account for a considerable portion of the differences in ownership concentration.

4.3.2 Previous Research on Owner Identity

Most studies on ownership concentration are concerned simply with examining the percentage of shares owned by single parties and make no attempt to identify the party controlling a particular block of shares. However, it is quite likely that there are differences in motives and behavior arising from differences in goals and objectives of owner groups. Ignoring this may fail to provide valuable insights into the relation between ownership and firm performance. There is hence a clear need for explicit consideration to be given to the identity of shareholder parties, both internal and external to the firm.

4.3.2.1 Individual Investor Ownership and Performance

The effect of nonexecutive individual ownership has attracted limited attention in literature. To the best of knowledge, no empirical research exists that focuses solely on the relation between individual ownership and performance.

An approach is made by **Mínguez-Vera and Martín-Ugedo (2007)** who analyze the influence of ownership structure on firm value using sample of 95 public Spanish firms for the 1998-2000 period. First, they examine the influence of major shareholders, with special attention to nonlinear and piecewise relations, but the within-group panel data estimation finds no significant effect of large blockholdings on firm value. In a second step, they investigate the type of main shareholder and distinguish between institutional and individual or family investors (no executive function is required). Their evidence shows that the presence of an individual or family investor as the major shareholder has a favorable influence on Tobin's Q. The authors assume that it is harder for individuals to diversify their portfolios (compared with institutional investors), which might make them more interested in management's oversight. Finally, a possible two-way relation (endogeneity) between ownership concentration and firm value is considered. Results from 2SLS panel data regressions reveal a positive effect for ownership by major shareholders on firm value, although the opposite relation is not significant. This result is contrary to the insignificant relation obtained by simple panel data regression and is also opposed to Demsetz and Villalonga (2001)'s conclusion that the value of the firm has a negative influence on ownership concentration, whereas it does not affect Tobin's Q. The authors hence conclude that the results for Spanish firms might be a consequence of a real incentive to oversee managers, given that the market for corporate control is not as established as in the US.

4.3.2.2 Insider Ownership and Performance

Within the field of owner identity, insider ownership is the most popular topic and has been extensively studied. As a result, plenty of research contributions exist. The most frequently cited work is the paper by **Morck et al. (1988)** who look at the relation between managerial ownership and performance in a 1980 sample of 371 public firms in the US. To test the theoretically derived convergence-of-interest and entrenchment arguments, they estimate piecewise linear regressions allowing for slopes to change at two turning points, 5% and 25%, and find that in some ranges of ownership (below 5% and over 25%, however with the coefficient for the latter not being significant), Tobin's Q is positively related to managerial ownership, but in others, a negative relation is found.[90] The findings suggest that the convergence-of-interest effect is more important at both low levels and high levels of insider ownership, but the entrenchment effect is dominant at the medium levels of ownership. The results are fairly robust to alternative specifications (with different breakpoints) but are not robust, however, to the use of accounting profit as an alternative performance measure. All in all, Morck et al. (1988)'s characterization of the influence of managerial ownership on performance has gained broad acceptance among researchers in financial economics, and a number of related papers provide supporting evidence of a nonmonotonic ownership-performance relation with varying turning points.

Consistently, **Chen, Hexter, and Hu (1993)** find a similar relation to that reported by Morck et al. (1988). Using a sample of 500 large, listed U.S. firms in 1976, 1980 and 1984, they try linear, quadratic and cubic specifications and find that corporate performance rises when management ownership is between 0% and 5-7% and falls as ownership increases to 10-12% (beyond this range results are not stable). Like Morck et al. (1988), they contribute this slope of the relation to managerial incentives (at very low levels of insider ownership) and managerial entrenchment (beyond that range).

[90] Morck, Shleifer, and Vishny (1988) arrived at turning points of 5% and 25% as a result of examining a variety of piecewise regressions. The specification including two turning points at 5% and 25% provided the "best" regression models as it had the lowest sum of squared errors. The theoretical justification for these particular numbers is not very strong. However, they note that the choice of 5% is supported by the fact that this is the mandatory disclosure level of ownership by the SEC. The choice of a 25% turning point is motivated by the assumption that 20-30% is a managerial ownership level beyond which a hostile bid for the firm could not succeed.

McConnell and Servaes (1990) examine the relation between insider ownership and Tobin's Q for a large sample of 1,173 public firms in 1976 and for another large sample of 1,093 public firms in 1986. For both samples, they find a significant, squared relation between performance and the fraction of shares owned by insiders as Tobin's Q increases until insider ownership reaches approximately 40-50% and then slightly decreases. Their results are robust to the inclusion of the same control variables used by Morck et al. (1988) and to the use of ROA as an alternative performance measure. After adjusting their sample to make it more comparable to the sample used by Morck et al. (1988), they attempt to replicate Morck et al. (1988)'s piecewise linear regression but find only a significant, positive relation for insider ownership between 0% and 5%. No significant relation is identified beyond 5% insider ownership. In addition to insider ownership, the authors also examine the effect of institutional ownership and find a positive effect on performance. An interesting finding is that no performance effect is found when analyzing blockholder ownership in general. This implies that most blockholders take a passive attitude toward management. Only when block ownership is combined with ownership by insiders, the coefficients are significant.

Another paper in support of Morck et al. (1988)'s findings of a nonmonotonic relation between ownership and performance is the work by **Hermalin and Weisbach (1991)**. Their study of 134 listed U.S. firms for the years 1971, 1974, 1977, 1980 and 1983 replicates Morck et al. (1988)'s work but uses a panel data set instead of a cross-section, which allows them to control for possible simultaneity between ownership and performance. Using pooled OLS, they find that Tobin's Q rises with managerial ownership up to a stake of 1%, decreases in the range of 1-5% (but statistically not significant) and becomes positive again in the range of 5-20% (but statistically not significant) and turns negative for ownership levels exceeding 20%.[91] Next, they reestimate the equations treating managerial ownership as endogenous (with the lagged values of ownership as their instruments). As a result, the sign on the ownership variables remain the same, but the sizes of the coefficients become larger. When using EBIT as an alternative measure of performance, the relation is similar. The authors argue that the positive performance effect at low ownership levels results from increasingly aligned interests

[91] Hermalin and Weisbach (1991) use slightly different breakpoints than Morck et al. (1988) because they have data on very low levels of managerial ownership that Morck et al. (1988) do not. Hence, lower breakpoints are chosen in order to make use of their data. However, they note that results using Morck et al. (1988)'s inflection points are similar, though less pronounced.

of managers and shareholders. Beyond 1%, performance declines with ownership because the increasing insulation from disciplinary devices such as the takeover market more than offsets the increased alignment of interests. These results, which were obtained using an instrumental variable technique controlling for endogeneity, hence confirm the findings of Morck et al. (1988) and McConnell and Servaes (1990) and suggest that the results of this prior research were not driven by its assumption of exogenous shareholdings.

Nevertheless, **Kole (1996)** casts doubt on the persistence of a nonmonotonic relation between managerial ownership and performance and reconsiders Morck et al. (1988)'s causal interpretation. The author argues that if the accumulation of equity by mangers occurs randomly across firms, then evidence of a relation between ownership and performance reveals the direct incentive effects of managerial stockholdings. However, if firms differ systematically in ways that also affect the cumulation of stockholdings by managers (e.g., through the firms' compensation policy), then the characterization of the relation between performance and ownership as indicative of incentives is too narrow. This reversal of interpretation from ownership determining performance to performance driving ownership is examined empirically by introducing previous firm performance (measured by average sales growth over the previous four years and by current year's market-adjusted abnormal return) into Morck et al. (1988)'s model. Using the same data sample as Morck et al. (1988), the author finds that the nonmonotonic relation is dampened once past performance is added, which suggests that the ownership-performance relation incorporates both rewards and incentives. Further *pseudo-causality* tests (by varying the point in time at which firm performance is measured) present new evidence that supports a rewards interpretation of the ownership-performance relation: Rather than firm performance being determined by the level of managerial ownership of equity, firm performance is a determinant of managerial ownership.

Cho (1998) further explores the possibility that (insider) ownership and performance are endogenously determined. Using a data set of 326 public manufacturing firms in 1991, he first replicates Morck et al. (1988)'s study and finds a similar nonmonotonic relation between Tobin's Q and management shareholdings.[92] Then, he estimates a simultaneous equation regression instead of OLS and finds that corporate value affects insider ownership positively.

[92] Following Morck et al. (1988), Cho (1998) assumes two changes in the slope and uses a grid search technique to identify the two breakpoints at 7% and 38% at managerial ownership.

This suggests that managers in firms with superior performance or with better investment opportunities hold a larger fraction of their firm's shares (presumably as the outcome of an accordant compensation contracting process). In contrast, the estimations do not show any evidence that insider ownership affects corporate performance, a finding, which contrasts with the OLS regression results, thereby reversing the interpretation of the relation between ownership structure and corporate value. Thus, this finding raises again important questions regarding the implicit assumption that ownership structure is exogenously determined and suggests that studies not accounting for endogeneity may be misspecified.

In the context of acquisitions of 867 publicly traded firms in the US during the 1978-88 period, **Loderer and Martin (1997)** also examine the empirical evidence on whether managerial stock ownership fosters better firm performance. Tobin's Q, sales, standard deviation and variance of the firm's stock returns are used to explain insider holdings. The simultaneous equations yield no evidence of larger managerial ownership boosting performance maybe because management is already effectively disciplined by competition in product and labor markets. In contrast, performance appears to affect how much stock executives want to hold in their firm. However, different from Kole (1996) and Cho (1998), the authors find evidence that performance is indeed a negative predictor of insider ownership. Higher performance hence induces smaller holdings. One possible interpretation is that Tobin's Q ratios measure growth opportunities already capitalized in the stock price. There is therefore little reason to hold stock of firms with high Tobin's Q ratios. In fact, as a large fraction of managers' human capital might already be tied to their firms' fortunes, high Tobin Q ratios could induce them to liquidate at least part of their stockholdings. It is also possible that underperforming firms try to redress the situation by increasing management's stakes – on what appears to be the now debatable assumption that higher managerial ownership stakes improve performance.

Holderness, Kroszner, and Sheehan (1999) replicate for 1935 (1,236 public firms in the US) and 1995 (3,759 public firms in the US) central aspects of Morck et al. (1988)'s study. They confirm a positive relation between firm performance and managerial ownership in the 0-5% range of managerial shareholdings but, unlike Morck et al. (1988), they do not find a statistically significant relation beyond 5% managerial shareholdings. They also confirm the endogeneity of managerial ownership.

Himmelberg, Hubburd, and Palia (1999) extend the research by proposing an equilibrium interpretation of the observed differences in ownership structure across firms. Rather than interpreting low ownership levels as evidence of a suboptimal compensation design, they argue that the compensation contracts observed in the data are endogenously determined by the contracting environment, which differs across firms in both observable and unobservable ways. In particular, low levels of managerial ownership might well be the optimal incentive arrangement for a firm if the severity of agency conflicts between managers and shareholders happens to be low for that firm. Himmelberg et al. (1999) extend the Demsetz and Lehn (1985) study by adding new variables to explain the variation in ownership structure. The results show that a large fraction of the cross-sectional variation in managerial ownership is explained by unobserved firm heterogeneity. They then investigate the degree to which this heterogeneity makes managerial ownership an endogenous variable in models of firm performance by using a fixed-effects panel data model and instrumental variables to control for unobserved (time-invariant) firm effects. Their performance measure is Tobin's Q although they claim that similar results are produced if ROA is used as performance measure. They fit linear and quadratic regressions and find that changes in management holdings have no significant impact on performance. However, when they control for endogeneity of ownership by using instrumental variables, they find a quadratic form of the effect of ownership on performance, but this evidence is tentative because of the weakness of their instruments. Himmelberg et al. (1999)'s interpretation of the findings differ, for example, from Kole (1996) who also argues that managerial ownership is endogenous but interprets this as a consequence of causality operating into the opposite direction (from performance to ownership). Himmelberg et al. (1999), in contrast, emphasize the importance of unobserved heterogeneity in the contracting environment across firms, which causes endogeneity as opposed to reverse causality.

Short and Keasey (1999) extend the so far primarily U.S. based literature by examining a U.K. based sample. Their analysis of key differences between the U.S. and U.K. governance systems suggests that management should become entrenched at higher levels of ownership in the UK. Some of the reasons for this suggestions are that U.K. managers do not have the same freedom as their U.S. counterparts to mount takeover defenses, and institutional investors in the UK are more able to coordinate their monitoring activities. Based on a sample of 225 listed U.K. firms over the period 1988-92, they estimate a cubic model of managerial ownership and confirm the general findings of a nonlinear relation between managerial ownership and performance as suggested by Morck et al. (1988). That is, management moves from alignment to entrenchment to alignment as their ownership stakes in the firm increase. Calculations carried out on the ownership coefficients reveal that, when using ROE as performance measure, the turning points on the cubic function of managers' ownership are 16% (a maximum point) and 42% (a minimum point). Thus, performance is positively related to managers' ownership in the 0-16% range, negatively related in the 16-42% range and positively related when managers' ownership exceeds 42%. The results are robust to the alternative use of MTB as performance measure, which indicates turning points at 13% and 42%. The analysis hence confirms that U.K. managers become indeed entrenched at higher levels of ownership (13%/16-42%) than their U.S. counterparts (5-25%). A limitation of this study is, however, that the authors do not examine the potentially misspecifying impact of endogeneity on their results.

Most studies are limited to the use of one or two turning points in the ownership function, but **Davies, Hillier, and McColgan (2005)** contribute to literature by suggesting to add further turning points at higher ownership levels. They argue that at high levels of managerial ownership when external market discipline becomes ineffective, entrenchment behavior will resurge. With equity holdings around 50%, managers will have implicit control of their company but still do not have objectives completely aligned to external shareholders. Only at very high levels of managerial ownership are incentives aligned to that of other shareholders. Their data set consists of 802 industrial, publicly quoted firms in the UK in the year 1995. Using OLS regressions, they specify a quintic function, which leads to two local maximum points at 7% and 51% and two minimum points at 26% and 76%. More specifically, performance increases for managerial ownership levels of 0-7%, decreases for levels of 7-26%, turns positive again in the 26-51% range, decreases in the 51-76% range and increases for ownership levels beyond 76%. All ownership coefficients in the quintic model are statistically significant. To analyze the effects of endogeneity, they carry out a simultaneous equation analysis and find that Tobin's Q is found to be significantly and positively related to the level of managerial ownership. The finding that although managerial ownership is determined by performance, performance itself is determined in part by managerial ownership is at odds with Cho (1998) and Himmelberg et al. (1999) but consistent with the work by Morck et al. (1988).

Evidence in the case of Spain is provided by **de Miguel, Pindado, and de la Torre (2004)**. They construct a data panel of 135 nonfinancial, listed companies for the period ranging from 1990-99. First, the authors examine the relation between ownership concentration and performance (measured as the market value of shares). To control for unobservable heterogeneity and to avoid potential endogeneity of ownership, they estimate the GMM by applying an instrumental variable estimator (with all available lags of all the right-hand side variables in the model being used as instruments). The results suggest that performance increases with ownership concentration up to a level of 87% (presumably as a result of the monitoring effect) and decreases for ownership concentration beyond this breakpoint (presumably as a consequence of the expropriation effect). In a second model, the authors investigate an insider ownership model and estimate a curvilinear model. They find indeed a cubic specification with the effect being positive up to an insider ownership value of 35%, then turning negative within the range of 35% and 70% and positive again beyond a value of 70% (the results for the last ownership range are consistent with Davies et al. (2005)'s finding of a positive performance effect of insider ownership values beyond 76%). They authors interpret this evidence as support of both the hypothesized convergence-of-interest and the entrenchment effect. They further conclude that Spanish insiders get entrenched at higher ownership levels than their U.S. and U.K. counterparts and refer, for example, to Morck et al. (1988) who show that U.S. managers get entrenched when ownership ranges from 5% to 25%. As possible explanation for this discrepancy, the authors point to differences in corporate governance (see Section 4.2.1).

Turning the focus particularly to Germany, **Kaserer and Moldenhauer (2008)** argue that studies from Anglo-American countries seem to be significantly affected by endogeneity as in these countries insider ownership seems to be mainly driven by management's compensation contracts. In contrast, insider ownership in Germany is often related to family control, stock-based compensation is less widespread, and the market for corporate control is less developed. Based on a pooled data set of 648 firm observations for the years 1998 and 2003, evidence is found to support a significant and positive relation between firm performance (measured by the stock price performance over 60 months, MTB, and ROA) and insider ownership. The relation seems to be robust even if a 2SLS approach is applied in order to account for potential endogeneity. They also search for curvilinear and piecewise-linear relations but find no support for nonlinear specifications. Furthermore, the results hold for a subsample of firms with no stock-based compensation program. Overall, the results hence indicate that insider ownership might be an important variable explaining the long-term value creation in the corporate sector.

Contrary evidence, however, is found by **Groß (2007)** who conducts a study of 521 nonfinancial German firms in the years 2000 and 2003. Empirical results from simultaneous equations show that insider and institutional ownership both have a negative effect on firm performance (measured as Tobin's Q). General ownership concentration has a negative performance effect until an ownership level of 39% and has a positive effect from there on (which is even increasing for a share size above 80%). The reverse effect of performance on ownership concentration is not significant, but high performance levels (Tobin's Q greater than 0.7) have a negative effect on insider and institutional shareholdings.[93] The author concludes that because managerial ownership has a negative effect on performance, managerial stock remunerations appear counterproductive. In contrast, higher general ownership concentration grants a better corporate governance. Following the implications of the results, shareholders have to fear more agency conflicts with management or with institutional investors and less value losses through blockholders. Finally, the author combines the different ownership aspects into a four-equations system and also examines the effect of ownership concentration and institutional shareholdings on insider ownership. Ownership concentration has a positive effect on insider ownership, whereas institutional ownership has a negative effect. The positive effect of ownership concentration could be caused by the controlling shareholder preferring stock-based compensation of the management given the false assumption of a positive interest alignment. If the substitution effect of monitoring mechanisms is used as explanation, the shareholders must even have an additional false explanation, that of a negative effect of ownership concentration on performance. Also for institutional ownership, the substitution effect of monitoring mechanisms is based on false expectations. In order to explain the negative effect of institutional ownership on insider shareholdings, institutional owners have to impact performance in a positive way. Then, a high institutional shareholding would reduce the demand for managerial ownership as agency mechanism. Another explanation for the negative relation between institutional and insider ownership is that institutional investors know about the negative entrenchment effect of managerial ownership and thus have an aversion to managerial ownership (and consequently do not promote stock-based remuneration).

---

93 Potential explanations for the negative effect of performance on institutional shareholdings are the realization of a gain, diversification considerations, and a planned sale as exit channel. The negative effect on managerial ownership is also contradicting the assumptions. Its negative impact could originate from a perceived decreased utility of managerial ownership as agency mechanism if the firm is already performing well (Groß, 2007).

Special Case: Family Ownership and Performance

The question of whether family ownership leads to superior firm performance has evoked a large number of empirical investigations. A frequently cited paper is the work by **McConaughy, Walker, Henderson, and Mishra (1998)**. Based on a sample of 219 public firms in the US for the period 1986-88, they show that founding-family controlled firms (defined as firms whose CEOs are either the founder or a member of the founder's family) have a higher MTB and are more efficient (in terms of sales growth, which can be viewed as a proxy for better management and also lower agency costs) than firms matched with respect to industry, size and managerial ownership. They find value and efficiency unrelated to the managerial level but instead related to who the owner-managers are. That is, what is significant is whether the owner-managers are founders (or related to the company founders) because founders run their firms more efficiently than managers without founding-family ties. The authors provide an agency explanation for this result: Family ties apparently align management and firm interests better than managerial ownership does in the absence of such ties and consequently produce superior results.

Another prominent study is the work by **Anderson and Reeb (2003a)** who also investigate the effect of family ownership and family CEO status. For their investigation, they use a sample of 403 public, nonfinancial and nonutility firms in the US from 1992 through 1999. They create a binary indicator variable, which equals one when founding families hold shares in the firm and/or when founding-family members are present on the board. Using fixed-effects models, the authors find that family firms exhibit better accounting and market performance than nonfamily firms (e.g., Tobin's Q in family firms is 10% higher than in nonfamily firms). An estimation of a squared ownership function indicates a bell-shaped function with a maximum point at 31% of ownership. Accordingly, firm performance is increasing until families own about one third of the firm's equity. Beyond this level, performance begins to decline but is still better than in nonfamily firms. The results do not change when 2SLS regressions are estimated in order to account for potential endogeneity. Further testing suggests that the greater performance in family firms, relative to nonfamily firms, stems from those firms in which a family member serves as the CEO. This is presumably because family members possess unique, value-adding skills and view themselves as the stewards of the firm. Consistently,

Villalonga and Amit (2006) offer further evidence of the “family premium” being mainly due to founder CEOs.[94]

In terms of European evidence, **Jaskiewicz (2006)** collects data for 785 quoted firms in Germany, France and Spain for the year 2003.[95] Having determined each firm's PSC, he classifies firms with a PSC value of at least 0.5 and a family ownership of 20% as family firms (see Section 2.3.2.2). OLS regression results indicate a linear positive effect of family influence on accounting performance for German and French corporations (for Spain no significant performance effect is found). Regressions using dummy variables for different PSC brackets find that the positive performance effect is the strongest for companies with a medium level of family influence. A further investigation reveals that not only the absolute level of family influence, but also the channel through which family influence is exercised has important effects on performance. In contrast to family representation on the supervisory board, which is not associated with performance, the representation of family owners in the management team is clearly related to performance and follows a bell-shaped function. That is, with increasing family representation in the management team, performance increases (due to increased monitoring), but as soon as family members fill more seats in the management team than they should be entitled to according to their capital share, performance decreases (due to private benefits of control, overmonitoring, or below-average qualification of family managers).

Turning the focus particularly to Germany, **Andres (2008)** contributes to literature by explicitly separating the family effect from general blockholder effects. Firms are classified as family firms either if the founder or family members hold more than 25% of the shares, or if the founding family owns less than 25% of the control rights but is represented on the

---

94 In an additional analysis, Villalonga and Amit (2004) summarize nine frequently used definitions of family firms, ranging from a least restrictive (“One or more family members are officers, directors, or blockholders.”) to a very restrictive definition (“The family is the largest shareholder, has at least 20% of the votes, one family officer and one family director, and is in 2nd or later generation.”). Regression coefficients of the different family firm dummies indicate that the value effect of family firms ranges widely depending on how family firms are defined. Their most remarkable finding, however, is that when family firms are run by descendants, the premium turns into a discount. Thus, in contrast to Anderson and Reeb (2003a) who argue that both founder and descendant CEOs are associated with improved firm performance, Villalonga and Amit (2004) find that firm value is destroyed when descendants serve as CEOs.

95 See Maury (2006) for further evidence from Western Europe. Consistent with previous literature, he finds that family ownership is associated with higher profitability and higher valuations compared with nonfamily firms. However, the value benefits tend to disappear in countries with below-average shareholder protection (such as Germany).

supervisory board or in the management team. Based on a data set of 275 public firms from 1998 through 2004, the paper shows that family firms are not more profitable than widely held firms. The analysis further reveals that firm performance is highest for family firms in which the founder is still active as CEO. Moreover, it appears that family firms also outperform other types of blockholders with stakes of at least 25%. In random-effects regressions of performance on different blockholder types (government, financials, corporations, individuals without links to the company, families, management), family blockholder ownership is the only variable showing significant and positive coefficients. The effect on ROA is between 3.1% and 4.5% per year (depending on the model). The results are robust to alternative econometric specifications and seem to be robust to endogeneity concerns. Evidently, families seem to add value to a company in a way that distinguishes them from all other types of blockholders. However, the performance of family firms is only better in firms in which the founding family is still active either on the supervisory board or in management. These results point out that families are only able to induce positive performance effects if they have a deeper relation with their business and act as stewards of the firm. If families are just large shareholders without active involvement, the performance of their companies is not distinguishable from other firms. It thus appears that not only are the blockholder position and the monitoring incentives it entails relevant but the identity of owners as well.

Edwards and Weichenrieder (2004) enrich the literature by comparing the effect of several ownership groups (individuals/families, corporations, banks, public sector bodies, foreign firms) for a sample of German firms (see Section 4.3.1.2 for a review of the study in the context of general ownership concentration). OLS regression results demonstrate that higher control rights of the largest shareholder significantly lower the market value of equity, with the effect being more negative if this shareholder is a bank or a corporation than if it is a family (the effects of public and foreign ownership are also negative but statistically insignificant). This suggests that such large shareholders are in a particular good position to divert profits from minority shareholders, perhaps by exploiting business relations between themselves and the firm in which they hold the largest stake. However, more control rights of the largest owner significantly raise the market value of equity (for all types except for public sector bodies), with the effect being significant, positive if this shareholder is a family, a corporation, or a foreign firm. This is consistent with greater cash flows rights increasing this shareholder's incentives to engage in monitoring, thus reducing profit diversion. As a result, the authors conclude that the effect of owner identity on performance depends on the extent to which the controlling shareholder's control rights exceed his cash flow rights. Especially for family and foreign large owners, the net effect of equal increases in the control and cash flow rights on performance statistically significant and positive. In a further analysis, the authors find that the estimated proportional changes in performance when control and cash flow rights owned by the largest shareholder jointly increase from zero to 100, is large and significant if the largest shareholder is a family or a foreign firm. This suggests that a change from completely dispersed ownership to full ownership by a single shareholder of these types has substantial effects on the extent of monitoring of management. The implied estimate of the value of efficient monitoring of management by these types of shareholders relative to no monitoring of management is very high.

4.3.2.3 Intercorporate Ownership and Performance

Not much is known about industrial firms as owners of other industrial firms. Empirical evidence on large diversified U.S. firms suggests that diversification might hurt performance (e.g., Lang & Stulz, 1994).[96] However, this strand of research deals with the performance of companies generating sales in many segments and is not necessarily applicable to the case of firms holding publicly traded shares in other companies and the question of how performance of the target companies is affected by the diversification and hence subsequent shareholdings by other corporations. Although, to the best of knowledge, no studies exist that focus mainly on intercorporate ownership and firm performance, empirical insights are still generated as a corollary of studies dealing with several ownership groups including corporate owners. The results of these studies are interspersed in the relevant sections covering the main focus of the respective studies.

4.3.2.4 Financial Investor Ownership and Performance

In recent years, there has been an increased focus in empirical literature on the role of institutional investors in monitoring, disciplining and influencing corporate managers. A body of research has emerged that examines institutional shareholders' monitoring function

96 Lang and Stulz (1994) find that firms that become diversified appear to perform poorly before becoming more diversified. The authors reason that diversifying firms may seek growth through diversification because they have exhausted growth opportunities in their existing activities.

concerning the discretion used by corporate managers in reporting profits.[97] For example, **Chung et al. (2002)** analyze earnings management through discretionary accounting accruals based on an U.S. sample of 12,478 firm-year observations for the 9-year period 1988-96. Their results show that when investment institutions collectively own a large percentage of a company's equity, managers are deterred from (fully) pursuing opportunistic earnings management through discretionary accrual choices. This is probably because of direct pressures from investment institutions as well as from indirect pressures, which arise when managers believe that it is futile to engage in opportunistic earnings management because the institutions can "see through" accounting manipulations and price securities properly. In this regard, the evidence seems to be consistent with institutional investors monitoring and constraining the self-serving behavior of managers. The results are corroborated by a later study by **Hadani, Goranova, and Khan (2011)**, among others.

Along the same lines, **Katz (2009)** examines a sample of 147 private firms in the US going public between 1980 and 2005. Results indicate that firms that are backed by private equity sponsors have higher earnings quality than those without private equity sponsorship, engage less in earnings management and report more conservatively both before and after an initial public offering. Moreover, private equity backed firms that are majority owned by private equity sponsors exhibit superior long-term stock price performance after they go public. For example, the mean of the 1-year abnormal returns is 19.1% for firms majority owned and -9.3% for firms minority owned by private equity sponsors. The author attributes these results to professional ownership and tighter monitoring exhibited by private equity investors. In addition, the study finds that abnormal returns and industry adjusted ROA are significantly larger for firms owned by larger private equity sponsors with greater capital under management and providing a higher level of monitoring and support due to these repeated players' concern for their reputation. Along the same lines (but with different conclusions), **Dharwadkar, Goranova, Brandes, and Khan (2008)** suggest that portfolio characteristics affected owners' motivation and capacity to monitor and find that the beneficial effect of monitoring by large institutional owners are offset by their portfolio characteristics, that is, increases in the size of portfolio holdings, number of blockholdings, portfolio turnover, and even the importance of a particular holding reduce the monitoring effectiveness.

---

[97] Earnings management potentially exacerbates informational asymmetries between shareholders and management and misleads market participants regarding the firm's financial situation.

In contrast to the majority of studies crediting institutional investors with superior monitoring, **Renneboog (2000)** finds no evidence of a monitoring role by institutional investors based on a sample of 186 Belgium firms publicly listed during the period 1989-94. The paper addresses the question of how corporate control is exerted in nonperforming public companies and studies whether the board's composition is instrumental for adequate monitoring proxied by enforced management turnover. Results indicate that the presence of large share blocks held by institutional investors are not related to board restructuring. In contrast, management replacement is influenced by large corporate owners and family owners. The paper also investigates whether the ownership structure plays a performance-induced disciplining role, but a surprising finding is that none of the owner groups seems to be involved with disciplining management when performance is poor. The author attributes the lack of institutional investor involvement to potential conflicts of interests (which does not concern other groups of owners) and questions the corporate control role of large shareholders in general.

Apart from to the monitoring aspect of institutional ownership, another body of empirical research focuses on institutional investors' alleged pressure for myopic management behavior. A prominent paper in this context is the work of **Bushee (1998)** who addresses the question of whether institutional investors create or reduce incentives for corporate managers to reduce investment in R&D to meet short-term earnings goals. Based on a sample of 13,944 firm-year observations between 1983 and 1994 in the US, the author tests whether institutional ownership affected R&D spending for firms that could reverse a decline in earnings with a reduction in R&D. The results indicate that managers are less likely to cut R&D to reverse an earnings decline when institutional ownership is high, implying that institutions are sophisticated investors who indeed serve a monitoring role in reducing pressures for myopic behavior and ensuring that managers choose R&D levels to maximize long-term value rather than to meet short-term earnings goals. However, the analysis also indicates that a large proportion of ownership by institutions that have high portfolio turnover and engage in momentum trading significantly increase the probability that managers reduce R&D to reverse an earnings decline. The results hence support the widely argued view that short-term oriented behavior of institutions creates pressures for managers to sacrifice R&D expenditures for the sake of higher current earnings – but only for firms with high levels of institutional owners exhibiting transient ownership characteristics (i.e., high portfolio turnover, diversification, and momentum trading) and not for institutional investors as a whole.

Wahal and McConnell (2000) reach a different conclusion when analyzing expenditures for property, plant and equipment (PP&E) and R&D for about 2,500 U.S. firms from 1988 to 1994. They find no evidence of institutional investors causing managers to behave myopically – regardless of the institutions' investment style. In contrast, they are able to document a positive relation between industry-adjusted expenditures for PP&E and R&D and the fraction of shares owned by institutional investors. The authors suggest viewing institutions as a buffer between impatient individual shareholders and managers, which allows managers to focus on projects with long-term payoffs. A basis for such a view is that institutional investors may have an information advantage relative to individual shareholders. As a consequence, institutional owners might be more likely to withstand the temptation to judge managers on the basis of short-term reported earnings than do individuals.

Kochhar and David (1996) use a data set of 135 manufacturing firms in the US with institutional shareholders in 1989. Applying an outcome-based measure of innovation, their results indicate that institutions do not foster short-term orientation on the part of firm managers. When differentiating between pressure sensitive and pressure resistant institutions, they find the coefficient on pressure resistant institutions to be significant, positive (no conclusion can be reached on pressure sensitive institutional owners). The results hence suggest that institutions resistant to managerial influence are associated with greater innovations in firms, whereas institutional owner that are susceptible to that influence, do not exhibit such an association.

Yet another body of research addresses the self-dealing argument and suggests that the incentive to monitor varies within the institutional investor community depending on potential business relations between institutional investors and the firms they own equity in. Also based on the differentiation between pressure sensitive and pressure resistant institutions, **Brickley et al. (1988)** analyze a sample of 201 U.S. firms that proposed management-initiated antitakeover amendments in 1984. They find evidence that firms with greater holdings by pressure resistant institutions are more likely to oppose management's recommendations (especially when the proposal reduces shareholder wealth), whereas firms with greater holdings by pressure sensitive shareholders have more proxy votes casted in favor of management's recommendations. They conclude that the management of some institutions might face conflicts of interest between their fiduciary responsibilities to their beneficiaries and other objectives such as value maximization for the owners of the institution.

Bhattacharya and Graham (2009) also refer to the distinction between pressure sensitive and pressure resistant shareholders and are among the first to investigate the potential endogeneity between firm performance and institutional equity ownership. Their dataset includes 98 public firms in Finland with institutional ownership in 2004. Results from 3SLS point at a considerable two-way feedback between performance and institutional ownership. The analysis notes feedback from the voting power associated with ownership stakes, which affects performance and also finds feedback from performance, measured as Tobin's Q, which determines owners' equity stake holding. In addition, the study documents a negative relation between institutional ownership concentration and performance, which suggests that, on average, a more equal distribution of voting power among the three largest institutional owners enhances firm performance by 0.1% (the effect is stronger for pressure resistant than for pressure sensitive institutions). At the same time, the results also indicate that firm performance increases the possibility of a more equal distribution of voting power by institutions. On average, this effect ranges from 0.8% to 2.7% (the effect is larger for firms controlled by pressure sensitive institutions).

Thomsen and Pedersen (2000) enrich the literature by comparing the effect of several owner groups (institutions, banks, corporates, families/individuals, government) in a study of 435 of the largest European companies over the period 1990-95 (see Section 4.3.1.1 for a review of the study in the context of general ownership concentration). The authors hypothesize that owner types have different objectives with implications for corporate strategy and performance. OLS regression results find that companies tend to have higher MTBs if their largest owner is a bank than if it is an institutional investor. In contrast, corporate, family and government ownership has a significant, negative influence on MTB compared with institutional investors. An interpretation of these results may be that these owners tend to place more emphasis on nonprofit goals than do financial investors. The effects on ROA are qualitatively the same as on MTB. A positive effect of bank ownership and negative effects of family and government identity relative to institutional investors are found. However, sales growth is higher in firms whose largest owner is another company or a family. The discrepancy between profitability and sales growth seems to be consistent with the interpretation that for a given ownership share, financial investors induce companies to increase shareholder value, whereas corporate and family owners are more concerned with growth and survival. In a further analysis of interaction effects, the authors find that ownership concentration also depends on owner identity. As expected, a high ownership share is associated with a higher MTB value for institutional investors than for other ownership types. The reason may be that more decision-making power allocated to the market-oriented institutional investors induces companies to adopt shareholder value maximizing strategies.

Lehmann and Weigand (2000) also examine the effect of different owner types (financial institutions including banks, industrial corporations, individuals/families, foreign owners) for a sample of German firms (see Section 4.3.1.2 for a review of the study in the context of general ownership concentration). The authors argue that the willingness of owners to engage in monitoring may crucially depend on who they are. In other words, the location of control rights (i.e., the identity of owners) can be a more important determinant of the degree of control exerted by owners than ownership concentration. The authors use firms with another firm as largest shareholder as base group and document a positive but statistically insignificant effect of ownership concentration on ROA. The coefficient differences on ownership concentration resulting from within-regressions are significant, negative for firms owned by individuals/families, different large owners or firms that experienced a change in owners during the observation period. In contrast, a significant, positive impact of ownership concentration on profitability is found for firms with financial institutions as largest shareholders. According to the authors, this latter result is consistent with the view that financial institutions/banks are better (more efficient) monitors so that agency costs are lower.

Comparable evidence is provided by **Pedersen and Thomsen (2003)** who compare the effect of several owner groups (individuals/families, financial institutions, corporations, government) in a study of 214 of the largest European companies over the period 1992-95. Results from 3SLS find a positive two-way feedback between general ownership concentration and performance (measured as MTB). The authors then estimate the regression model separately by the identity of the owners in order to test for differences between owner categories. They find that financial ownership has a large positive effect on firm value as financial owners apparently use their owner power to increase shareholder value (financial ownership is, in turn, positively affected by firm value). The same effects are found for intercorporate ownership. In contrast, ownership in the hands of individuals or families has no effect on firm value (individual ownership increases with firm value, though). The authors presume that although agency considerations point to the value of a convergence of interest in the case of insider ownership, risk aversion, entrenchment and capital rationing may reduce the competitiveness of closely held family businesses. Finally, government ownership is found to lower firm value (while low firm value is found to increase the level of government ownership). This might indicate inferior performance, but government ownership follows a different logic compared with private ownership because governments might not necessarily aim for shareholder value creation.

4.3.2.5 Bank Ownership and Performance

Cable (1985) was the earliest researcher analyzing the relation between bank ownership and corporate performance in Germany. He studies a 1970 sample of 48 large nonfinancial firms and finds that bank ownership enhances performance, which he attributes to market power effects and efficiency gains. However, he relies on a small sample and uses a debatable performance measure, as he divides the income of equityholders by total assets (i.e., the numerator of ROE is divided by the denominator of ROA).

Gorton and Schmid (2000) empirically investigate the influence of German banks on the performance of German firms for two large and two small samples of publicly listed and private firms in 1986 and 1975 and provided support for Cable's study. They find that bank control rights from equity ownership significantly improve firm performance beyond what nonbank blockholders could achieve. An increase of the bank's control rights from equity ownership by one percentage point changes the MTB by 0.23% in the small sample and by 0.41% in the large sample. The power of the banks cannot be due to the fact that they are blockholders because banks are included in the Herfindahl-Hirschman-Index. Hence, banks appear to be special in positively affecting corporate performance. They conclude that banks have a financial incentive to improve the performance of firms and find no evidence that banks extract private value to the detriment of firm performance.

Edwards and Nibler (2000) investigate a cross-section of 156 of the largest nonfinancial German firms in 1992 and find a positive relation between firm performance and the largest shareholder being one of the three big banks (the coefficient is similar in size to that of individuals/families without a majority of control rights as largest shareholder). The estimated coefficient for other banks being the largest shareholder is positive but not significantly different from zero. Performance is not affected by an increase in either the largest or the second largest shareholder's control rights if this shareholder is a nonbank firm. They reason that firms whose largest shareholders are nonbank firms could be part of a pyramidal ownership structure, which enables owners to separate their control from cash flow rights, thereby extracting private benefits of control.

Agarwal and Elston (2001) reach a less benign conclusion regarding the role of banks in German corporate governance than previous studies. Their sample consists of 100 large firms for the period 1970-86. The study finds no evidence to support the hypothesis that bank ownership influences profitability or growth of the firm. Thus, the benefits of increased access to capital and monitoring of firms by banks do not seem to be realized in either higher profitability or stronger growth. In addition, the interest payment to debt ratio is significantly higher for bank-influenced firms, which supports the assumption that German universal banks might engage in rent-seeking activities and provides evidence of a conflicting interest between creditors and shareholders (for example, by redistributing the rents away from shareholders towards themselves in the form of higher interest payments or by influencing firms to undertake less risky projects). The results are corroborated by a later study by **Chirinko and Elston (2006)**.

Dittmann et al. (2010) analyze the role of bankers on the boards of German nonfinancial companies for the period 1994-2005 and find that bankers on the board of firms where their banks hold significant equity stakes cause a decline in the valuations of these firms. Furthermore, they find little evidence that bankers simply represent their interests as shareholders and monitor management (just as any other blockholder might do). They hypothesize that if banks are concerned about their equity investments, bankers should seek representation on the boards of underperforming firms as these companies seem to indicate a stronger need for intervention by their owners. However, the analysis shows that banks are represented on those boards where firm valuation is in fact higher and use their board seats to promote their own business as lenders and M&A advisors.

For the case of Spain, **Ruiz-Mallorquí and Santana-Martín (2011)** use a sample of 111 nonfinancial firms over the period 1996-2009 and analyze the impact of dominant owners' control rights on firm value. They distinguish between dominant shareholders that are banks and those that are investment funds and find that when a bank is the dominant shareholder, the control rights of that owner are negatively related to firm value. They reason that dominant bank owners are likely to extract private benefits due to the fact that banks can maintain business relations with the firms in which they hold positions. An increase in the voting power in the hands of the second and third largest shareholders is associated with an increase in firm value, which suggests that the presence of other large shareholders tends to decrease expropriation by a dominant bank shareholder.

Outside of Europe, Japan is well comparable to Germany (and Continental Europe, in general) in such a way that Japanese banks can establish debt and equity positions in the same firms (in contrast, U.S. regulations force the separation of stockholders from lenders). Using a 1986 sample of 373 Japanese firms, **Morck et al. (2000)** find that higher ownership by main banks (a firm's largest creditor) is associated with lower firm valuation. The estimation implies that a 1% increase in main bank ownership corresponds to a drop in Tobin's Q of 0.21. Firm valuation is the lowest, when bank ownership is at 5%. At higher levels of bank ownership, however, this relation is mitigated and, in some specification, even reversed. The authors argue that this relation reflects both costs and benefits of equity holdings by banks: At modest levels of ownership, bank ownership might be large enough to endow banks with substantial power but not large enough to align bank interests with those of shareholders. In addition, the authors investigate the possibility of endogeneity of bank ownership and sort firms based on their change in Tobin's Q over certain time intervals and examine the changes in bank ownership of the firms with the largest declines in valuation (alternatively, they control for endogeneity by using bank ownership data that are lagged by ten years). They are, however, unable to find evidence that Japanese banks increased their ownership positions in firms as a response to poor firm performance. This result is corroborated by a later study by **Kang, Shivdasani, and Yamada (2000)** in the context of takeover bids.

4.3.2.6 Government Ownership and Performance

The empirical literature on government ownership and performance emerged after Alchian (1965/1996) theoretically predicted that publicly owned corporations would be inherently less efficient than private firms (see Section 3.4.6.1). Early work compared public and private corporations within the same industry and focused on utilities and infrastructure in industrialized economies. Subsequent research also looked into more competitive industries and developing nations. The wave of privatizations in developed economies during the 1970s finally opened a new way of empirical analysis as same-firm performance before and after privatization could be compared. Shirley and Walsh (2000) review existing literature in the period from 1970 to 2001 and find that out of the 52 studied included in their review, 32 studies conclude that the performance of private as well as privatized firms is significantly superior to that of publicly owned firms.[98] 15 studies either find that there is no significant relation between ownership and performance, or that the relation is ambiguous. Only five studies find a superior performance of public firms.

Although inconsistent with the theoretical predictions, **Meyer (1975)**'s work is among few studies that provide early evidence of a superior performance of publicly owned corporations. During the 1970s, the anxiety over petroleum shortages raised the question of ownership by the public sector, and a central issue of the academic debate was whether the type of owner influenced the adaption of new innovations and other costs of providing services. As it appeared difficult to identify particular innovations, Meyer (1975) implied a relation between technology sets and costs functions and studied the cost functions of 30 randomly sampled public and private utilities. He finds significantly lower costs for public firms (assuming operating costs as an indicator of the degree to which new technologies or organization methods are adopted) and attributes the difference in cost structures to public firms purchasing inputs at lower prices and employing technologies with lower operating cost, which have not been adopted in the private sector. The findings are consistent with the results by **Pescatrice and Trapani (1980)** who extend the analysis by controlling for technology differences among the sample firms. A cost differential of 24-33% is estimated, which indicates that publicly owned utilities perform better than their privately owned counterpart. They interpret this cost differential as a result of the effective regulation of private firms (and public firms minimizing cost). According to a similar study by **Färe, Grosskopf, and Logan (1985)**, the major source of inefficiency in privately owned firms is due to the lack of allocative (price) efficiency.

In contrast to the previously cited studies, **Atkinson and Halvorsen (1986)** find no difference in the performance of privately owned and publicly owned utilities in the US.[99] Assuming that cost efficiency of firms will be less the weaker is the relation between managers' utility and firm profits, they model utility maximizing behavior of managers as cost minimization subject

[98] Another highly cited review article is the study by Megginson and Netter (2001). Their review also supports the proposition that privately owned firms are more efficient and more profitable than otherwise comparable government owned firms.

[99] Atkinson and Halvorsen (1986) criticize Färe, Grosskopf, and Logan (1985), who use the same data sample but find a different result for using a nonparametric approach that does not provide information on possible differences in the relative use of inputs.

to shadow rather than market prices of inputs. The estimation results indicate that the two types of firms are equally cost inefficient (holding output constant, inefficiency increases the average quantities demanded of capital and labor and decreases the average quantity demanded of fuel).

Many studies on government ownership pertain to sectors where firms are highly regulated and have geographic monopolies (e.g., electricity, water supply, garbage collection) and therefore do not directly compete with each other. However, these findings must be interpreted with care and cannot be used to make inferences about the effect of ownership type on performance in competitive environments. A work that incorporates this aspect by using a different research setting is the research of **Kole and Mulherin (1997)** who study a sample of U.S. corporations in which the government holds a large block of equity during and following World War II. Concurrent with the entry of the US into the war, the government seizes enemy owned assets, including stakes of between 35% and 100% in American subsidiaries of German corporations.[100] The government retains ownership in these vested companies for periods ranging from one to 23 years and, as a sizable shareholder, elects the management, which sets corporate policy. This setting allows studying the effects of an ownership change on firm performance, ceteris paribus. The authors identify five vested companies for which they are able to develop industry controls but find no performance differences after vesting and the 5-year period following the sale by the government. For the three firms with publicly traded equity, the change in equity value is also not significantly different than that of the control group. They conclude that government owned firms benefit from monitoring mechanisms that are comparable to their counterpart in the private sector. However, the generalizability of the results is limited as the firms in the sample are subject to interim administratorship by the government rather than full-fledged government ownership.

One widely cited research in favor of private ownership is the study by **Megginson et al. (1994)**. The work compares the pre- and postprivatization financial and operating performance of 61 companies from 18 countries and 32 industries that experienced full or partial privatization through public share offerings during the period 1961-90. The results

[100] For example, the German pharmaceutical company Schering had its U.S. assets been seized in 1941 and placed under government administratorship. In 1952, the company was released, and its assets were sold to the private sector (later merged with Plough Inc. and recently acquired by Merck & Co. Inc.).

document that, after being privatized, firms increase sales, become more profitable (the mean increase in ROA after government divestiture is 2.5%), increase their capital investment spending and improve their operating efficiency. The results hold when comparing firms operating in competitive versus noncompetitive (regulated) industries and when comparing industrialized and developing country privatizations. The authors are not able to document the causes of these performance improvements after privatization but feel that the most likely explanation is that (even partial) private ownership allows the internalization of the benefits of performance improvements. The study by **D'Souza and Megginson (1999)** use the same sample selection criteria as in Megginson et al. (1994) but focuses on the period from 1990 through 1996 and also documents significant increases in profitability after privatization (in fact, the significance levels of the profitability variables are much greater than in the previous study conducted by Megginson et al. (1994).

Boardman and Vining (1992) look explicitly on competition and ownership and consider the theoretical claim that competition in product markets (i.e., no market failures in the product markets) can be a more important determinant of allocative efficiency than whether a firm is publicly owned or privately owned. This can be due either to inefficient monitoring by owners in privately held firms or to efficient political monitoring in publicly owned firms. However, using Canadian data from the year 1986, the authors find no support for a primacy of competition versus ownership and instead demonstrate the importance of ownership for both technical and allocative efficiency. They do not rule out that competition might improve performance in some cases but conclude that ownership matters indeed: Although privately owned firms also engage in rent-seeking activities where possible, they will try to maximize realizable rents by keeping down production costs. As a consequence, private ownership might be preferable from an efficiency perspective.

Along the same lines, **Picot and Kaulmann (1989)** examine a sample of Fortune's *The foreign 500* for the years 1975-84, covering six Western industrial nations. The study is confined to corporations that act in unregulated markets and that are exposed to competition. Companies from the public service sector are therefore excluded from the sample. Evidence yields that government owned corporations are throughout less profitable (and less productive) than privately owned corporations. The authors conclude that the disadvantages in performance of government owned companies are mainly caused by the differences in the property rights structure: In government owned corporations, the right to coordinate resources is mainly in the hands of the managers, whereas the right to appropriate profits is in the hands of the governments. Therefore, an attenuation of property rights can be concluded. Incentives for control by the owners are much weaker than in privately held corporations because politicians acting as agents for the government are not directly affected by the appropriation of profits (or losses), whereas the wealth of private owners is directly affected by the performance of their firms. This indicates that government ownership potentially leaves management too much freedom to waste corporate resources compared with private ownership.

More recent literature on the relation between government ownership and performance mainly focuses on economies such as China, the world's largest state sector currently under transition.[101] For example, **Beirne, Liu, and Sun (2013)** examine firm ownership transformation in China and also compare the performance impacts of different methods taken to restructure the ownership of state firms, such as full versus partial privatization. Based on a sample of 1,184 companies during the period 1997-2003, they find that partial privatization, that is, the mix of government and private ownership, emerges as the best performing type of ownership model in terms of improved labor productivity after the reform. Because the association with the government implies political support and business connections, which might be necessary to vitalize performance, partially privatized firms can gain the best synergy of both state support and private business strength. The experience of the Chinese reform hence shows that the political context and system are important influencing factors on ownership preference for a firm.

4.3.2.7 Summary

Overall, there is clear evidence that simply examining ownership in terms of the percentage of shares owned by the largest party of shareholders does not provide a full account of the story. The major conclusion to arise from the literature review on owner identity groups is that it is not appropriate to treat all owners as a homogenous group with a singular interest on

[101] In the course of an economic reform process started in the 1990s, China established two stock exchanges (Shanghai and Shenzhen) but is still reluctant to fully commit itself to privatization and argues that partial privatization could produce efficiency gains while maintaining control. Under the mantra of "grasp the large, release the small", the Chinese government still maintains high levels of ownership in large or "strategically" important companies (i.e., in the finance, energy, and telecommunications sector). However, the success of this strategy is heavily dependent on the willingness of investors to buy into the formula "private money, government control". Given increasing local government debt problems, thin profitability and overcapacity, a further wave of privatization seems to be inevitable ("Privatisation in China", 2011; Wildau, 2014).

maximizing shareholder value. In contrast, some types of shareholders may be entirely passive investors, whereas others are more active and engage in monitoring. Various motivations and abilities of different types of shareholders may hence result in their distinctive effectiveness to influence major corporate decisions and value. As a consequence, there is a clear need to incorporate the identity of owner groups into the empirical investigation of the effect of ownership structure on performance.

5 Research Design

5.1 Introduction

This chapter develops the research design for the subsequent empirical analyses. Section 5.2 describes the used data, and Section 5.3 outlines the model. Finally, Section 5.4 introduces the econometric approach to be applied to the data.

5.2 Data

The research design is grounded on the description of the applied sample selection process and variables used. This is followed by descriptive statistics.

5.2.1 Sample Selection and Data Sources

The data sample used for the empirical analyses is based on companies included in the *composite DAX* (*CDAX*). The index comprises all companies listed in the *general standard* and *prime standard* segments at the Frankfurt Stock Exchange and reflects the performance of the overall German equity market.[102] The sampling period spans the 5-year period from 2005-09 and covers all major phases of an economic cycle, including a phase of expansion (2005), boom (2006-07), contraction (2008), and recession (2009).[103] The sample consists of all companies included in the index at year-end.

The initial sample pool includes 745 firms. First, 18 companies issuing only preferred stock (Vorzugsaktien) but no common stock (Stammaktien) are excluded from the sample. Preferred stock typically has a priority over common stock in the payment of dividends but carries no control rights. This class of shares can thus not be considered in an ownership-performance

[102] The general standard is subject to minimum statutory requirements for EU-regulated markets. The prime standard requires companies to meet further international transparency requirements. Admission to the prime standard is also a prerequisite for inclusion in the selection indices *DAX*, *MDAX*, *TecDAX*, and *SDAX*.

[103] Voß and Müller (2011) classify the period 2004/2005–09 as the seventh economic cycle since 1945. An economic cycle is commonly defined by identifying changes in the GDP compared with the previous year and is typically characterized by a phase of expansion (2005: +0.7%), a phase of booming economic growth (2006: +3.7%, 2007: +3.3%), a phase of contraction (2008: +1.1%), and finally a phase of recession (2009: -5.1%). Most recent statistics on the German GDP are provided by Statistisches Bundesamt Deutschland (2012). See Schirwitz (2007) for an in-depth discussion of identifying economic cycles in Germany.

analysis. Second, following, for example, Edwards and Weichenrieder (2004), McConnell and Servaes (1990), and Pedersen and Thomsen (1999), 152 financial firms are also excluded from the sample. As a result of legal requirements, these companies have a different capital structure and different income measuring rules. Their inclusion in the sample would therefore lead to a lack of comparability concerning accounting based performance variables. 12 firms operating in the public utilities sector are also excluded due to peculiarities in their operational and regulatory conditions (Barontini & Caprio 2006; Marchica, 2008; Mura, 2007; Villalonga & Amit, 2006). Third, three companies changed their business model significantly during the sample period and continued operations as financial firms. These companies are dropped from the analysis in the respective years only. Fourth, two companies are also dropped from the analysis as they can be identified as shells. Fifth, one company is not included in the analysis because its headquarter is outside of Germany. Finally, 68 firms are not considered because of missing or incomplete ownership and/or performance data.[104] The final sample encompasses 489 companies (*I*) or 2,118 firm-year observations (*N*). Table 5.1 summarizes the sample selection process.

Table 5.1: Sample Selection Process

Sample selection	Number of companies (*I*)	Number of observations (*N*)
All firms included in the CDAX at year-end 2005-09	745	3,121
less: Firms issuing only preferred stock	18	77
less: Financial firms (SIC codes 6xxx)	152	615
less: Public utility firms (SIC codes 49xx)	12	57
less: Firms transforming to financial firms	3	7
less: Firms operating as shells	2	7
less: Firms headquartered outside of Germany	1	1
less: Firms with missing ownership and/or performance data	68	239
Final sample	489	2,118

[104] Data unavailability is almost always due to missing or incomplete performance data and concerns mostly firms having filed for bankruptcy or being liquidated.

The structure and pattern of the sample, by number of annual observations per company, is given in Table 5.2 and Table 5.3.

Table 5.2: Structure of the Sample

Number of annual observations per company	Number of companies (*I*)	Number of observations (*N*)
5	332	1,660
4	60	240
3	45	135
2	31	62
1	21	21
Total	489	2,118

The data set is constructed as a short panel, consisting of repeated observations on many companies over few time periods ("small T, large N"), which is the standard case for panel data analyses.[105] The panel is unbalanced, with some firms having more observations than others: 332 companies remain in the sample for the entire period, whereas 70 companies enter, and 94 companies leave the sample during the 5-year period. The missing time periods in the panel structure have several reasons and do not necessarily result from self-selection of the sample firms: Corporations mainly enter the CDAX through initially going public or through changing market segments. Main causes for dropping out of the CDAX are squeeze-outs, M&A, insolvency proceedings, or changes of market segments.

105 In contrast, a long panel consists of a small cross-section of companies observed for many time periods.

Table 5.3: Pattern of the Sample

Pattern	Number of companies (*I*)	Percentage of companies
2005 - 2006 - 2007 - 2008 - 2009	332	67.9%
2005 - 2006 - 2007 - 2008	35	7.2%
2007 - 2008 - 2009	26	5.3%
2006 - 2007 - 2008 - 2009	25	5.1%
2005 - 2006	18	3.7%
2005	17	3.5%
2005 - 2006 - 2007	17	3.5%
2008 - 2009	9	1.8%
2006 - 2007	4	0.8%
Other patterns	6	1.2%
Total	489	100.0%

Table 5.4 gives an overview of the sample distribution across industries based on the first two digits of the standard industry classification (SIC) codes.[106] The companies in the sample belong to eight broad industries. Noteworthy is the high proportion of industry sectors such a heavy manufacturing (35.2%), services (31.9%) and light manufacturing (18.4%).

[106] The Standard Industrial Classification (SIC) is a widely used system for classifying industries by a hierarchical four-digit code: The first digit of a firm's SIC code designates the major industrial sector, and the subsequent digits refer to more detailed industry levels. The detailed code list is available from the U.S. Securities and Exchange Commission (n.d.). SIC codes are designed to describe a company's type of business according to the company's (manufacturing) processes rather than its actual products. In case of conglomerates, more than one code may apply, yet a main code is assigned based on sales statistics. See Klein (1998) for a further discussion on SIC codes.

Table 5.4: Sample Distribution by SIC Code

SIC (first two digits)[a]	Industry sector	Explanation	Number of companies (*I*)	Percentage of companies
01	Agriculture and forestry	Agricultural production-crops	2	0.4%
15, 16, 17	Mining and construction	General building contractors and operative builders, heavy construction contractors, construction special trade contractors	7	1.4%
20, 22, 23, 24, 25, 26, 27, 28, 29	Light manufacturing	Food, tobacco, textile mill, apparel, lumber and wood, furniture, paper, printing and publishing, chemicals, petroleum	90	18.4%
30, 32, 33, 34, 35, 36, 37, 38, 39	Heavy manufacturing	Rubber, stone, clay and glass, primary metal, fabricated metal, industrial and commercial machinery and computer equipment, electronic and electric equipment, transportation equipment, measuring, analyzing and controlling instruments, other manufacturing	172	35.2%
42, 44, 45, 47, 48	Transportation and communications	Motor freight transportation and warehousing, water transportation, transportation by air, transportation services, communications	28	5.7%
50, 51, 52, 53, 54, 57, 59	Wholesale and retail trade	Wholesale trade with (non-)durable goods, retail trade with building materials, merchandise stores, food stores, home furniture, other retail	34	7.0%
70, 72, 73, 75, 78, 79	Services I	Hotels, personal services, business services, automotive repair, motion pictures, amusement and recreation services	139	28.4%
80, 87,89	Services II	Health services, engineering, accounting, research and management services, other services	17	3.5%
Total			489	100.0%

[a]Financial firms (SIC codes 6xxx) and public utility firms (SIC codes 49xx) are excluded from the analysis.

Figure 5.1 provides an overview of the sample distribution by annual revenues. A small percentage (2.6%) of the observations reports revenues of less than €1m (small firms). 29.5% of the observations have revenues between €1m and €50m (medium-sized firms). Given that the sample consists of publicly listed companies, it is not surprising that two thirds of the observations make revenues of more than €50m (large companies), with a considerably large fraction of observations (19.5%) exceeding even €1b (super large firms).

Figure 5.1: Sample Distribution by Annual Revenues

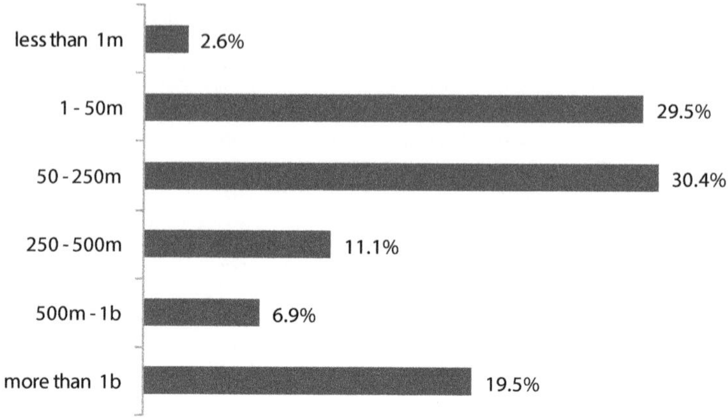

Note. N = 2,111 (for seven sample observations, revenues are missing). Annual revenues are in €.

Information about ownership structure is manually collected from *Hoppenstedt's* yearly publication *Aktienführer* and complemented by researching historical annual reports and contacting the company's department for investor relations.[107] Only shareholdings of 5% or more of a company's equity are included in the analysis.[108] Capital market and accounting data as well as further company statistics come from the database *Standard & Poor's Capital IQ*.

5.2.2 Variables Used

The use of ownership and performance variables is based on the theoretical discussion on in Chapter 2. The selection of control variables is dictated by literature and data availability.

---

[107] Companies gain knowledge of their shareholder structure through the issuance of registered shares (instead of bearer shares) and periodic surveys conducted by external research centers and depository banks. A further source of shareholder identification is the mandatory registration of share transactions crossing certain thresholds (3%, 5%, 10%, 15%, 20%, 25%, 30%, 50%, 75%) of equity ownership with the BaFin in accordance with WpHG §21.

[108] According to Deutsche Börse (2014), shareholdings of less than 5% of a company's equity are considered to be free float and are commonly reported only on an aggregated basis. Consequently, shareholdings of less than 5%, even when reported in *Hoppenstedt* or corporate press releases, are excluded for reasons of data consistency. This rule is applied in many German studies, for example Andres (2008), Kaserer and Moldenhauer (2008), Lehmann and Weigand (2000) and is also a common international threshold; see, for example, Anderson and Reeb (2003a) and Maury (2006).

5.2.2.1 Ownership Variables

Ownership variables compromise measures of ownership concentration and measures of owner identity. As the ownership variables are not simply downloaded from an existing database but manually collected within the scope of this work and cross-checked for consistency, the probability of data error is minimal. Therefore, no data processing is applied to avoid a reduction of information.

Ownership Concentration Variables

As the measure of ownership concentration should reproduce the existence and power of a controlling shareholder, the fraction of shares held by the largest shareholder are captured in the variable *OWN1*.[109] The ownership concentration measure is extended to further shareholders by using the aggregated shares of the two and three largest owners, *OWN12* and *OWN123*, respectively. Furthermore, in order to consider the case of more than one large owner, the shareholding of the largest owners divided by the shareholding of the second largest is considered in the variable *OWN1/OWN2*. A further concentration measure is *BLOCK*, which captures the fraction of shares held in blocks of 5% or more. Finally, the Herfindahl-Hirschman-Index is used to measure the symmetry of the share size over all shareholders. The variable *HHI* is calculated as the sum of the squared percentages of ownership shares, $HHI = \sum_{i=1}^{N} P_i^2$, where P_i is the percentage of shares held by shareholder i. All ownership measures used in the analysis refer to directly held control rights.

Owner Identity Variables

Measures of owner identity are derived by classifying shareholders into six main categories and aggregating the share sizes (in %) held by one identity group. Accordingly, no difference is assumed in the utility function and the behavior of shareholders with different share sizes (Groß, 2007). In addition, binary variables for the identity of a specific shareholder (e.g., the largest shareholder) are created. The following owner identities are included in the analysis:

- Individual investors: Individual shareholders with no executive involvement in the company are subsumed under the group of private investors (*PRIVATE*).

[109] Furthermore, a logistic transformation is applied, as suggested by Demsetz and Lehn (1985), in order to obtain a symmetrical distribution of the ownership concentration variable. Regression results are very close to those of the untransformed variable (see Footnote 157).

- Insiders: Members of the management (*MGMT*) and supervisory board (*BOARD*) as well as their family members (based on their last names) are classified as insiders (*INSIDER*).[110]
- Corporations: Owners are categorized as corporate when they are another public or private nonfinancial company (*CORP*), either domestic (*DCORP*) or foreign (*FCORP*).
- Financial institutions: This ownership category covers shareholdings by insurers and investment companies as well as holding companies (*FINAN*) and further distinguishes between domestic (*DFINAN*) and foreign (*FFINAN*) institutions.[111]
- Banks: This group of investors includes commercial banks and depository banks exercising proxy votes (*BANK*).
- Government: Ownership in the hands of a national government, local authorities, or government agencies is also included in the analysis (*GOV*).

Corporations can also hold own stock (treasury shares), but because the following analysis aims to analyze the relation between ownership and corporate performance, treasury stock is not considered to be a relevant ownership and is therefore excluded from the analysis. Employee ownership is also dropped from the analysis for reasons of consistency because this type of shareholding is typically reported only on an aggregated basis but in fact consists of single equity stakes below the 5%-threshold. Finally, in very few cases where it is not possible to precisely classify shareholdings into one of the main ownership categories, ownership is also not included in the analysis.

5.2.2.2 Performance Variables

Performance and control variables are inspected for outliers.[112] Extreme values are then cross-checked for consistency by comparing them with data from earlier or later observations on the same company and by researching the company's annual reports. The probability of measurement or transcription errors is therefore minimal. Based on the assumption that the outliers are not false but genuine and important, variables are then winsorized only at the 1st

---

[110] According to WpHG §15a, stock transactions by family members of mangers or members of the supervisory board have to be treated alike as directors' dealings.

[111] If private investors (e.g., Susanne Klatten) are invested via an investment trust (in this case, Skion GmbH), their ownership share is classified as institutional rather than as private because it appears reasonable to assume that their motivation and behavior is comparable with that of an investment company.

[112] See Williams (2015) for a guidance on how to detect outliers using Stata.

and 99th percentiles in order to minimize the impact of extreme values and, at the same time, avoid a reduction of information.[113] This approach is also applied, for example, by Baert and Vennet (2009) as well as Douma, George, and Kabir (2006). The alternative of labeling them as missing values is problematic and a deletion of the observations could significantly reduce the sample size. This results in a loss of potentially valuable information and could force a truncation error. Thus, the concept of winsorizing is preferred over excluding (trimming) affected values. Following Williams (2015), regression models are fitted both with and without extreme values, but coefficient estimates barely change (results not displayed).

Capital market performance

The empirical analysis in this dissertation focuses on capital market performance as the primary measure of corporate performance. The emphasis on capital market performance arises from the power that the stock market possesses over publicly listed companies in pushing firms to adopt value-increasing strategies: First of all, a high market value decreases the likelihood of a hostile takeover and hence ensures the survival of the firm (and thereby protects the management from being replaced). Firms can even use their own stock as a cheap currency to make acquisitions of other companies. Finally, a high market value is useful to raise fresh money (by issuing new stock or convertible debt) in order to finance new projects and expand operations.

As a measure of capital market performance, an adapted version of Tobin's *Q* is used, which is calculated as the sum of the market value of equity and the book value of debt at fiscal year-end divided by the book value of total assets.

Accounting performance

As a robustness check, the empirical analyses refer to accounting performance measures such as ROA and ROE, where *ROA* is calculated as earnings before interest and taxes (EBIT) at fiscal year-end divided by the average value of total assets during the respective fiscal year, and *ROE* is computed as earnings from continuous operations at fiscal year-end divided by the average value of equity during the respective fiscal year.

---

[113] Alternatively, boundaries for winsorizing can be defined, for example, as the 5th and 95th percentiles (as applied, e.g., by Maury & Pajuste, 2005). Another procedure is the use of the interquartile range (as applied, e.g., by Gross, 2007). The majority of ownership and performance studies, however, do not report any data processing procedures.

5.2.2.3 Control Variables

A suggested by Demsetz and Villalonga (2001) and also Weiss and Hilger (2012), R&D expenditures, capital expenditures and the debt ratio are included in the regression in order to control for investments in intangible assets, differences in methods of depreciation and the leverage of a firm. On the one hand, these variables control for variances across firms in terms of performance; on the other hand, they reduce differences in the performance measures caused by accounting artifacts. In addition, sales growth is also frequently identified as being likely to have an impact on performance and is therefore also included as control variables (e.g., Driffield, Mahambare, & Pal, 2007; Groß, 2007).[114]

Financial leverage

Financial leverage (*DEBT*) commonly refers to the ratio of total debt to total assets (e.g., Driffield et al., 2007; Gugler & Weigand, 2003). Although there is an abundance of research aiming to explain the relation between financial leverage and performance, literature remains unclear as to whether debt has a positive or negative effect on performance. From a tax perspective, debt has a positive effect on accounting performance because the German tax system treats debt favorably and allows tax deductibility up to a certain degree.[115] This saves corporate income tax payments (compared with equity financing), thereby increasing net income and hence profitability. The effect of debt financing on the market value (that is, the present value of expected future free cash flows discounted at the firm's weighted average cost of capital), however, is ambiguous because, despite the increased proportion of the firm's cash flows that could be passed on to investors in form of higher returns, it is not clearly predictable how debt financing impacts the costs of financing.[116]

From a product market perspective, debt can be used to increase production to gain a strategic advantage over industry rivals, thereby boosting sales growth (and hence profitability). According to Campello (2006), leverage above the industry average can be associated with

[114] See Welch (2003) for a summary of control variables used by previous studies in modeling the relation between ownership structure and corporate performance.

[115] Under the interest ceiling rules (*Zinsschranke*), interest deductibility is generally possible for net interest expenses (interest expense less interest income) of up to 30% of EBITDA.

[116] In regard to cost of financing, there is no universally valid prediction whether debt financing decreases a firm's weighted average cost of capital (due to the favorable tax treatment of debt), increases it (due to the increasing pretax cost of debt as well as higher demanded rates of return for equity investments resulting from an increased probability of financial distress and bankruptcy), or leaves it unchanged.

market share gains obtained at the expense of average-leveraged industry rivals. However, after a certain threshold, more debt leads to sales underperformance. Especially when market demand for a firm's product heads south, excessive debt can become a major obstacle. Opler and Titman (1994) and González (2013) find that highly leveraged firms lose substantial market share to their more conservatively financed competitors in industry downturns (due to increasing indirect costs of financial distress). In other words, high leverage can lead to above-average declining sales during industry downturns and also cuts down on the firm's earnings (due to fixed interest expense obligations) but, at the same time, can enhance sales growth, especially during industry upturns. Leverage thus magnifies the effects of business risk (that is, the instability of operating profits and operating returns on assets). As a result, it is not possible to generalize the expected effect of leverage on corporate performance.

From an agency perspective, the effect of financial leverage on performance is inconclusive. On the one hand, debt financing disciplines managers and raises their pressure to perform, that is, to reduce wasteful spending and to increase their efforts because debt reduces the free cash flow at the disposal of managers (Jensen, 1986; Stulz, 1990). Indeed, debt implies fixed interest payments, which must be met by managers under the threat of bankruptcy (which could result in managers' replacement) if these obligations are not satisfied. Debt thereby induces (additional) monitoring by lenders. Consequently, financial leverage should have a positive impact on corporate performance (both, profitability and market value). On the other hand, financial leverage provides incentives to shareholders to invest in riskier projects than those preferred by debtholders due to the asymmetry of investment returns and losses (Jensen & Meckling, 1976). However, conflicting interests between shareholders and debtholders can also force managers to forgo risky projects such as investments in R&D (La Rocca & La Rocca, 2007; Myers, 1977). This argument is especially relevant for firms in the growth stage.[117] Furthermore, a high level of debt may limit the firm's ability to raise fresh capital, which again might force a firm to pass up valuable investment opportunities. This suggests that higher financial leverage is correlated with lower (long-term) profitability and market value.

---

[117] See Damodaran (n.d.) for an analysis of the relative relevance of advantages and disadvantages of financial leverage across a firm's life cycle.

Investment activities

Following Cho (1998) and Demsetz and Lehn (1985), two proxies for investment activities are included: capital expenditures (*CAPX*), which constitute investments in fixed assets (such as property, plant, or equipment) and are defined as the ratio of capital expenditures to total assets, and investments in R&D (*RDX*), which are measured as the ratio of R&D expenditures to total assets.

The effect of capital expenditures on profitability is expected to be moderately negative. As capital expenditures are assumed to generate benefits over multiple periods, IAS 16 *Property, Plant, Equipment* requires them to be capitalized and written off as depreciation over their useful life. As the expenses are spread over multiple years, the capitalization treatment of capex lowers net income but only to a moderate degree. In contrast, the effect of R&D expenditures on profitability depends on the distinction between expenditures occurring in the research and in the development phase: IAS 38 *Intangible Assets* requires development costs to be activated on the balance sheet as intangible asset if certain criteria are met, whereas research costs must be expensed in the year they occur. The treatment of research costs as expense thus has the effect of immediately lowering net income. As a consequence, the relation between R&D expenditures and (short-term) profitability is expected to be highly negative for firms incurring relatively high research costs, whereas the relation should be moderately negative for firms having relatively high development costs classifying for capitalization.

The effect of investment activities on firm valuation is ambiguous (Woolridge & Snow, 1990): On the one hand, it seems reasonable to assume that the relation is positive because the capital market should reward managers for undertaking investments. This is due to potential improvements in production or the exploration of valuable growth opportunities that will boost the company's sales and increase profitability (and consequently with a positive effect on valuation). By the same token, it might also be plausible to predict no stock market reaction because the capital market does expect managers to undertake periodic investments in order to maintain their firm's competitiveness. On the other hand, it might also be possible to assume a negative relation between investment activities and firm valuation for firms owned by institutional investors who, in pursuit of superior quarterly performance, might disdain long-term investments because they reduce short-term earnings. However, this arguments seems to be more relevant for the U.S. market than for Germany.

Growth

The growth of sales (*GRO*) is included to control for the influence of growth on performance. The variable is naturally expected to have a positive impact on profitability as growth increases net income, all else equal.[118] In contrast, the effect on firm valuation should be moderate because share prices already reflect expectations of growth prospects.

Other control variables

In order to control for industry-specific effects such as industry maturity or intensity of competition, which might affect the level of profitability, or cyclical variations in capital market based performances having an industry-specific component, industry dummies are defined based on the first two digits of the standard industrial classification (SIC) code.[119] Further, time dummies are included for each year of the sample period.

5.2.2.4 Summary

The variables used and their definitions are summarized in Table 5.5.

---

[118] Some authors argue that the inclusion of growth in a regression on profitability would lead to a simultaneous equation bias due to the two-way nature of the relation between profitability and growth (e.g., Radice, 1971). This is because, on the one hand, sales growth is a natural driver of profitability, but, on the other hand, profit also provides the funds for growth and facilitates the borrowing of external capital for expansion. Moreover, agency theory predicts a bias towards using profits for the purpose of growth because managers, acting in self-interest, would not care as much for paying dividends as they would for pursuing growth (Marris & Mueller, 1980). However, the facilitating effect of internal funds and the problem of information asymmetries tend to be more pronounced for smaller firms than for the larger ones. As a consequence, the following empirical analysis, which is based on a sample of large, publicly listed firms, is not expected to suffer from simultaneity between growth and profitability. Furthermore, the simultaneity argument does not apply for the relation between growth and firm valuation.

[119] See, for example, Anderson and Reeb (2003a) and Andres (2008).

Table 5.5: Definition of Variables Used

Variable name	Definition
(a) Ownership concentration variables	
OWN1	Control rights held by the largest shareholder (in %)
OWN12 (OWN123)	Aggregated control rights of the two (three) largest shareholders (in %)
OWN1/OWN2	Ratio of the control rights held by the largest shareholder and the second largest shareholder
BLOCK	Fraction of control rights held in blocks of 5% or more
HHI	Herfindahl-Hirschman-Index: sum of the squared percentages of control rights
(b) Owner identity variables	
PRIVATE	Aggregated control rights in the hands of private investors with no executive involvement in the company
INSIDER	Aggregated control rights in the hands of insiders: members of the management (MGMT) and supervisory board (BOARD) as well as their families
CORP	Aggregated control rights in the hands of nonfinancial companies: domestic (DCORP) and foreign (FCOPR)
FINAN	Aggregated control rights in the hands of financial institutions: domestic (DFINAN) and foreign (FFINAN)
BANK	Aggregated control rights in the hands of commercial banks
GOV	Aggregated control rights in the hands of national government, local authorities, or government agencies
PRIVATE (dummy)	Binary variable, which takes the value of 1 if the largest owner is a private investor with no executive function and 0 otherwise
INSIDER (dummy)	Binary variable, which takes the value of 1 if the largest owner is an insider and 0 otherwise. Also: MGMT (dummy), BOARD (dummy)
CORP (dummy)	Binary variable, which takes the value of 1 if the largest owner is a nonfinancial company and 0 otherwise. Also: DCORP (dummy), FCORP (dummy)
FINAN (dummy)	Binary variable, which takes the value of 1 if the largest owner is a financial institution and 0 otherwise. Also: DFINAN (dummy), FFINAN (dummy)
BANK (dummy)	Binary variable, which takes the value of 1 if the largest owner is a commercial bank and 0 otherwise
GOV (dummy)	Binary variable, which takes the value of 1 if the largest owner is a national government, local authority or government agency and 0 otherwise

(continued)

Table 5.5: Definition of Variables Used (continued)

Variable name	Definition
(c) Corporate performance variables	
Q	Sum of the market value of equity and the book value of debt divided by the book value of total assets (adapted version of Tobin's Q)
ROA	EBIT divided by the average value of total assets
ROE	Earnings from continuous operations divided by the average value of equity
(d) Control variables	
DEBT	Total debt divided by total assets
CAPX	Capital expenditures (investments in fixed assets) divided by total assets
RDX	Investments in R&D divided by total assets
GRO	Sales growth, year to year

5.2.3 Descriptive Statistics

Table 5.6 shows the correlations of the variables used in the estimations. As expected, high and statistically significant correlations are found among the alternative measures of ownership concentration as well as among the alternative measures of accounting performance. These correlations, however, do not cause any problems for the statistical regressions. The control rights of intercorporate owners have a medium and statistically significant correlation to almost all measures of ownership concentration. This indicates that intercorporate owners are often among the largest shareholders. The relatively small magnitude of the correlations between the other variables, albeit in many cases statistically significant, does not suggest any severe multicollinearity issues.

Multicollinearity refers to a situation in which two or more independent variables are highly (although not perfectly) correlated (Greene, 2012). This impacts estimation efficiency severely (Mela & Kopalle, 2002): Small changes in the data may produce wide swings in the parameter estimates, coefficients may have very high standard errors and low significance levels even though they are jointly significant, and the R-squared for the regression is quite high, and coefficients may have the "wrong" sign or implausible magnitudes. A common means to identify multicollinearity is tolerance, which measures the degree to which each independent variable is explained by a set of other independent variables. Tolerance is calculated as $T_{ij} = 1 - R_{ij}^2$, where R_{ij}^2 is the adjusted auxiliary R^2, that is, the adjusted R^2 of the regression of the independent variables on each other. The higher the tolerance, the smaller is the degree of multicollinearity and hence the bias of the variables. An alternative measure of multicollinearity is the variance inflation factor (VIF), which is calculated simply as the inverse of the tolerance value, or $VIF = 1/(1 - R_{ij}^2)$. The VIF translates the tolerance value, which directly expresses the degree of multicollinearity, into an impact on the estimation process because the square root of the VIF ($\sqrt{VIF}$) reflects the degree to which the standard error has been increased due to multicollinearity. As the standard error is increased, it makes the confidence intervals around the estimated coefficients larger, thus making it harder to demonstrate that the coefficient is significantly different from zero. VIF's in excess of 10 (and tolerances of less than 0.10) are generally considered to be problematic (Wooldridge, 2009). For the variables used in the following analysis, high VIF's are found for the alternative ownership concentration measures and for the alternative measures of firm performance, which is logical and has no effects on the models (results not displayed). VIF's for all other independent variables are not critical. The absence of multicollinearity is hence confirmed.[120]

[120] In addition, the statistical software package Stata, which has been used for the empirical analyses, checks for multicollinearity and automatically excludes the relevant variable(s). However, this was not the case in regard to the reported analyses.

Table 5.6: Correlation Matrix of Variables

	(1)	(2)	(3)	(4)	(5)	(6)	(7)
(1) OWN1	1.000						
(2) OWN12	**0.951*****	1.000					
(3) OWN123	**0.907*****	**0.985*****	1.000				
(4) OWN1/OWN2	**0.766*****	**0.594*****	**0.526*****	1.000			
(5) BLOCK	**0.930**	**0.930**	**0.971**	0.443	1.000		
(6) HHI	**0.966*****	**0.914*****	**0.873*****	**0.789*****	**0.802*****	1.000	
(7) PRIVATE	-0.020	0.032	0.060***	-0.129***	0.091***	-0.040**	1.000
(8) INSIDER	0.022	0.075***	0.097***	-0.081***	0.123***	-0.384**	-0.047**
(9) CORP	0.498***	0.482***	0.465***	0.391***	0.435***	**0.527*****	-0.106***
(10) FINAN	0.322***	0.368***	0.392***	0.170***	0.414***	0.316***	-0.156***
(11) BANK	-0.022	0.020	0.053**	-0.054**	0.081***	-0.015	-0.014
(12) GOV	-0.046**	-0.027	-0.024	-0.048**	-0.015	-0.046*	-0.025
(13) Q	0.035	0.029	0.023	0.038*	0.017	0.048**	-0.022
(14) ROA	0.086***	0.077***	0.064***	0.064***	0.045**	0.080***	-0.053*
(15) ROE	0.048**	0.029	0.015	0.051**	-0.003	0.044**	-0.057**
(16) DEBT	-0.009	0.013	0.028	-0.047**	0.034	-0.016	0.037*
(17) CAPX	-0.008	0.010	0.011	-0.045**	0.008	-0.021	-0.067***
(18) RDX	-0.140***	-0.156***	-0.149***	-0.064***	-0.128***	-0.129***	-0.024
(19) GRO	-0.067***	-0.065***	-0.062**	-0.396	-0.063**	-0.060**	-0.059**

(continued)

Table 5.6: Correlation Matrix of Variables (continued)

	(8)	(9)	(10)	(11)	(12)	(13)	(14)
(8) INSIDER	1.000						
(9) CORP	-0.235***	1.000					
(10) FINAN	-0.312***	-0.328***	1.000				
(11) BANK	-0.067***	-0.065***	-0.012	1.000			
(12) GOV	-0.043**	-0.028	-0.036	0.096***	1.000		
(13) Q	0.059***	0.022	-0.029	-0.036	-0.021	1.000	
(14) ROA	0.086***	0.058***	-0.050**	-0.016	0.014	0.016	1.000
(15) ROE	0.059***	0.027	-0.048**	-0.012	0.016	0.013	**0.699***
(16) DEBT	0.005	-0.007	0.005	0.064***	0.063***	-0.100***	-0.116***
(17) CAPX	-0.045***	0.003	-0.006	-0.007	0.091***	0.008	0.166***
(18) RDX	0.023	-0.096***	-0.025	-0.050**	-0.031	0.252***	-0.252***
(19) GRO	0.046*	-0.030	-0.033	-0.037	-0.145	0.175***	0.179***

(continued)

Table 5.6: Correlation Matrix of Variables (continued)

	(15)	(16)	(17)	(18)	(19)
(15) ROE	1.000				
(16) DEBT	-0.204***	1.000			
(17) CAPX	0.124***	0.120***	1.000		
(18) RDX	-0.121***	-0.217***	-0.054**	1.000	
(19) GRO	0.136***	-0.074***	-0.094***	-0.019	1.000

Note. Values over 0.5 are shown in bold. Asterisks denote statistical significance of the reported variables at the 0.01 (***), 0.05 (**) and 0.1 (*) level. The definition of variables can be found in Table 5.5.

Table 5.7 provides descriptive statistics of the variables used in the estimation. The ownership variables are bounded to the range of 0.010 and one. A minimum of 0.010 is due to the introduction of phantom investors with a stake of 1% for firms with no significant shareholders.[121] Average shareholder concentration measured by the stake of the largest owner is around 0.383 with a standard deviation of 0.264. This provides evidence of a very high ownership concentration and is in line with findings from previous studies for the German

[121] Lehmann and Weigand (2000) suggest assuming hypothetical shareholdings of 1% for firms with no significant shareholders.

market (see the discussion relating to Figure 5.2). Regarding the various owner types, the statistics show average share sizes of about 0.035 (standard deviation: 0.105) held by individual investors, 0.104 (0.189) by insiders, 0.002 (0.019) by the government, 0.131 (0.264) by corporations, 0.011 (0.054) by banks and 0.246 (0.272) held by financial institutions. These results are roughly in line with findings from previous studies for the German market (see the discussion relating to Figure 5.3).

The average Tobin's Q of 1.180 suggests a general overvaluation of the German stock market during the sample period.[122] At the same time, the standard deviation is very high (0.979), which reflects the particular characteristics of the sampling period covering all major phases of an economic cycle. The high level of Tobin's Q found in the sample compares with results from other studies.[123] For example, Achleitner, Kaserer, Kauf, Günther, and Ampenberger (2009) analyze 700 German companies for the 1998-2008 period and obtain an average Tobin's Q of 1.7 for family businesses and 1.5 for nonfamily businesses. For an earlier period (1999-2004), Chua, Eun, and Lai (2007) find in a cross-country study of nonfinancial companies in 49 countries a Tobin's Q ratio of 1.27 for German companies, which is close to their sample average of 1.30. Dittmann et al. (2010) reports an average Tobin's Q of 1.54 for a sample of 167 DAX 100 firms in the period 1994-2005 (with the highest value of 1.64 in 1998 and the lowest value of 1.26 in 2002).

ROA averages at 2.041% and has a high standard deviation of 8.974, which reflects both the varying macroeconomic conditions during the sample period and a great variance in operative performance among the sample firms. Kaserer and Moldenhauer (2008) obtain a similar result in their examination of 220 nonfinancial public German firms and find an average ROA of 2.747% (5.449%) in 2003 (1998). The above mentioned study of Achleitner et al. (2009) computes an average ROA of -1.9% for family businesses and 3.3% for nonfamily businesses. A surprising finding is that the average ROE of the sample firms is negative with -1.623%, and has a very high standard deviation of 40.947, which reflects large difference among the sample firms. For an earlier time period (2000 and 2003), Groß (2007) also finds a negative ROE of

[122] However, the high value of Tobin's could also be indicative of a systematic underreporting of assets due to accounting conservatism (see Section 2.4.2.1).

[123] However, a comparison of empirical studies is hampered by the use of differing computation methods of Tobin's Q.

-0.127% in her study of German public firms. Achleitner et al. (2009) obtain a slightly positive ROA of 0.4% for family businesses and even 11.3% for nonfamily businesses.

Table 5.7: Descriptive Statistics of Variables

Variable	Observations	Mean	Standard deviation	Minimum	Maximum
OWN1	2,118	0.383	0.264	0.010	0.996
OWN12	2,118	0.472	0.263	0.020	1.000
OWN123	2,118	0.513	0.262	0.030	1.000
OWN1/OWN2	2,118	19.770	29.912	1.000	99.550
BLOCK	2,118	0.529	0.264	0.000	0.996
HHI	2,118	0.241	0.245	0.010	0.996
PRIVATE	2,118	0.035	0.105	0.000	0.802
INSIDER	2,118	0.104	0.189	0.000	0.966
CORP	2,118	0.131	0.264	0.000	0.996
FINAN	2,118	0.246	0.272	0.000	0.987
BANK	2,118	0.011	0.054	0.000	0.982
GOV	2,118	0.002	0.019	0.000	0.382
Q	2,033	1.180	0.979	0.201	6.340
ROA	2,081	2.041	8.974	-37.703	22.673
ROE	1,997	-1.623	40.947	-225.653	69.318
DEBT	2,072	0.191	0.189	0.000	0.883
CAPX	2,118	0.040	0.040	0.000	0.204
RDX	2,118	0.030	0.058	0.000	0.308
GRO	1,625	7.069	31.412	-73.934	155.193

Note. The definition of variables can be found in Table 5.5.

Figure 5.2 shows the aggregated size of shareholdings of the *g*-th largest owner and reveals a high ownership concentration for the sample firms. With an average stake of 38.3%, the largest shareholder alone is able to exercise a blocking minority.[124] On average, the largest shareholder can therefore be considered to be a dominant owner who effectively controls the firm. This gives justification for the use of the percentage share of the largest owner as a main ownership

[124] In fact, the average stake of the largest owner must be assumed to be even larger because the calculation includes 70 observations with no significant shareholders for which phantom investors holding a stake of 1% have been introduced (see Footnote 121).

concentration variable. The second and third largest owners hold comparatively smaller shareholdings of 8.9% and 4.1%, respectively. On an aggregated basis, the three largest owners together hold 51.3% of the shares in a firm, which grants them the majority of votes at shareholders' meetings. The aggregated size of shareholdings of the largest three owners is therefore also considered a major ownership concentration measure. Stockholdings of any further shareholders are negligibly small, though.

The high ownership concentration found in the sample compares well to results of other ownership performance studies for the Continental European market. For example, Groß (2007) reports an average size of 44.4% for the largest shareholder in a sample of 521 German public companies in 2000 and 2003. Edwards and Weichenrieder (2004) find a mean stake of 47.3% for the largest shareholder in 1992 sample of 97 German public firms. Richter and Weiss (2013) obtain an average aggregated share size of 48.44% for the largest five shareholders in a subsample of 100 German public companies in 2007. For the Spanish market, Mínguez-Vera and Martín-Ugedo (2007) obtain a mean of 29.4% for the stake of the main shareholder and 56.1% for the shares of the five major shareholders in a sample of 95 public companies for the 1998-2000 period. Alonso-Bonis and de Andrés-Alonso (2007) find an average size of 43.33% for the fraction of shares owned by the largest shareholder in a Spanish sample of 101 public companies for the 1991-97 period. For a sample of 217 Norwegian public companies for the 1989-97 period, Bøhren and Ødegaard (2006) determine an average shareholding of 29.0% for the largest owner, 55.9% for the largest five owners and 67.5% for the largest ten owners.

Figure 5.2: Aggregated Size of Shareholdings of the *g*-th Largest Owner(s)

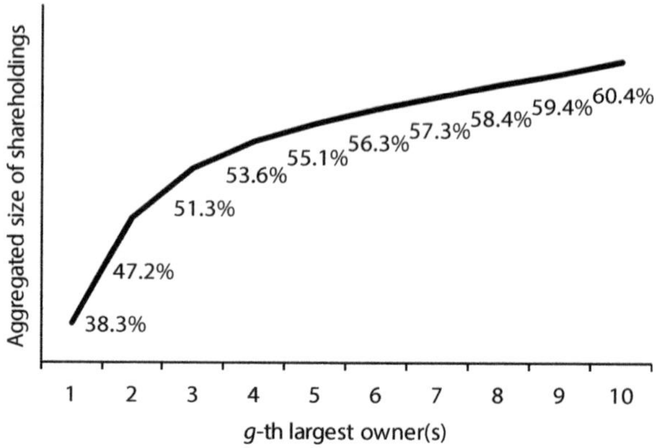

Note. *N* = 2,118. The calculation includes phantom investors with a stake of 1% for firms with no largest and no second largest shareholder.

A comparison of firms exhibiting a very low ownership concentration (lowest 25%) to firms with a particularly high ownership concentration (highest 25%) finds that the former operate mainly in heavy manufacturing and transportation. This is not surprising as these industries require high capital resources and hence a broad investor base. Firms with a high ownership concentration are comparably more active in light manufacturing and wholesale/retail trade. In the remaining industries, both types of firms are about equally distributed.

Table 5.9 presents difference-in-means tests using low and high ownership concentration as the discriminating variable. The first subsample includes firms with an ownership concentration of up to 16.6%, and the second subsample consists of firms with an ownership concentration of more than 55.4%. The t-tests find that the Tobin's Q does not differ much between the two groups. However, the group with high ownership concentration reports a significantly higher ROA than the group with low ownership concentration (3.067 versus 0.977). However, these results have to be interpreted with care as the same firms might be included in both groups if their ownership concentration changes from low to high (or vice versa) during the sample period. The explanatory power of t-tests is therefore limited in the case of panel data.

Table 5.8: Difference-In-Means Tests: Ownership Concentration

Performance and control variables	Full sample	Low ownership concentration (25%-quantile)	High ownership concentration (1 - 75%-quantile)	t-statistics
		OWN1 < 16.6%	*OWN1* > 55.4%	
Q	1.180	1.233	1.242	-0.127
ROA	2.041	0.977	3.067	-3.734***
ROE	-1.623	-1.916	1.652	-1.491
DEBT	0.191	0.177	0.180	-0.258
CAPX	0.040	0.039	0.038	0.333
RDX	0.030	0.045	0.019	7.259***
GRO	7.069	8.685	5.126	1.576
Maximal *N* (*I*)[a]	2,118 (489)	528 (154)	530 (183)	

Note. Ownership concentration is measured as the size of shares owned by the largest shareholder (*OWN1*). Asterisks denote statistical significance of the reported variables at the 0.01 (***), 0.05 (**) and 0.1 (*) level. The definition of variables can be found in Table 5.5.
[a]The actual number of observations (firms) depends on data availability and hence differs for each t-test.

Table 5.9 analyzes the change in ownership concentration over time. Differences-in-means tests with ownership concentration in different years as discriminating variable provide evidence that ownership is not changing significantly over 1-year periods. However, this is not surprising as large blocks of shares usually cannot be sold in a short-term. Second, management often tries to prevent block trades as they are very likely to cause severe stock price effects, which might potentially harm other shareholders. Lastly, in case a large blockholder might nevertheless be able to quickly sell his investment, this change in ownership is captured in the t-test analysis only if the buyer acquires only part of the stock offering (or collects additional stocks in the company) so that the concentration of ownership for the respective firm changes. The results hence have to be interpreted with care. In contrast to the stable ownership concentration in the short-term, ownership concentration does significantly change over the period of two to three years. For example, between 2006 and 2009, average ownership concentration increases from 35.5% to 39.6%. Comparable evidence is provided by Maury and Pajuste (2005). Gugler and Weigand (2003) and Thomsen and Pedersen (2000) conclude from the stickiness of ownership concentration (in the short-term) that it might make it more likely that ownership is exogenous to performance.

Table 5.9: Differences-In-Means Tests: Change in Ownership Concentration Over Time

Year *x* vs. year *y*	Entire sample period	Year *x*: ownership concentration	Year *y*: ownership concentration	t-statistics
2005 vs. 2006	0.383	0.371	0.372	-0.094
2006 vs. 2007	0.383	0.368	0.373	-0.254
2007 vs. 2008	0.383	0.368	0.392	0.012
2008 vs. 2009	0.383	0.376	0.395	-0.973
2005 vs. 2007	0.383	0.365	0.375	-0.592
2006 vs. 2008	0.383	0.362	0.391	-1.547
2007 vs. 2009	0.383	0.360	0.396	-1.943*
2005 vs. 2008	0.383	0.364	0.396	-1.707*
2006 vs. 2009	0.383	0.355	0.396	-2.112**
2005 vs. 2009	0.383	0.365	0.400	-1.723*
Maximal *N* (*I*)[a]	2,118 (489)	842 (421)	842 (421)	

Note. Ownership concentration is measured as the size of shares owned by the largest shareholder (*OWN1*). The subsamples contain only companies that are included in the full sample for (at least) both of the two years in consideration. Asterisks denote statistical significance of the reported variables at the 0.01 (***), 0.05 (**) and 0.1 (*) level. The definition of variables can be found in Table 5.5.

[a]The actual number of observations (firms) depends on data availability and hence differs for each t-test.

After having examined the concentration of ownership, the emphasis is now placed on the identity of owners. Figure 5.3 presents the average size of the aggregated shareholdings of the various owner types. Accordingly, the group of financial investors dominates, on average, 24.6% of a company's stock. Other large shareholder groups are corporations holding an average stake of 13.1% and insiders with an average stake of 10.4%. Individual investors (3.5%), commercial banks (1.1%) and government entities (0.2%) appear to play only a minor role. In contrast to the statistics on ownership concentration, the facts about owner identity are hardly comparable to other performance studies due to differing classifications of owner groups. Kaserer and Moldenhauer (2008), however, apply a roughly comparable owner classification and find similar results for the average ownership structure for a sample of 290 CDAX nonfinancial firms in 2003. Accordingly, companies' equity is dominated, on average, by insiders (29.0%), corporations (19.4%) and financial institutions (8.7%). In contrast, the stockholdings are much smaller for commercial banks (2.9%), government entities (1.2%), and individual investors (0.8%). Free float is, on average, 36.0%, treasury shares account for 0.7%, and others hold a remaining 1.2% of a company's shares.

Figure 5.3: Average Shareholder Structure

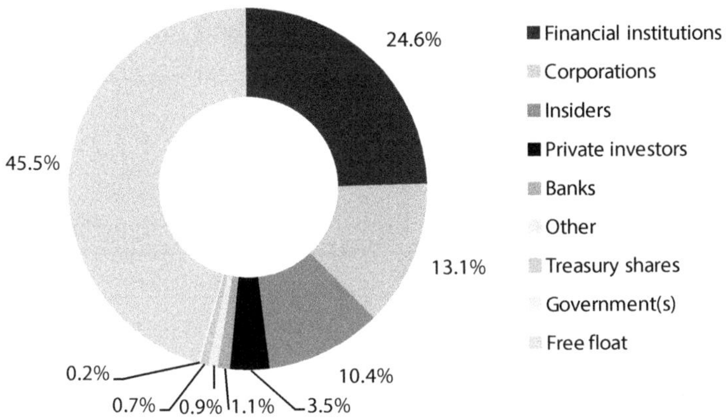

Note. N = 2,118.

Table 5.10 shows the frequency by which each owner type is found among the firm's five largest owners over the sample period.[125] Rank one is assigned to the largest owner, rank two is the second largest, and so on. Accordingly, financial institutions are the largest owners in 48.2% of the observations. An interesting finding is that institutions are dominant across all owner ranks. Considering that the size of stakes continuously decreases with the owner rank (see Figure 5.2 on this aspect), institutional investors – as a group – are present across the entire range of stake sizes. This evidence can be interpreted as an indication for the activity of different types of financial investors such as transient and quasi-indexing institutional investors, which are characterized by small ownership stakes, and dedicated institutions, which prefer larger stakes (see Section 3.4.4). Nonfinancial corporations are the largest owners in 21.6% of the observations and the second (third) largest owners in only 12.5% (7.3%) of the cases. Their preference for being the largest owner supports the notion that corporations invest for strategic reasons (which implies active control and monitoring) rather than for financial considerations (see Section 3.4.3). Another important group of large investors are insiders.

[125] In 92.6% of the observations, between one and five owners (with a stake of 5% or more) are identified. In 4.1% of the cases, more than five large stakeholders are present, and in 3.3% of the observations, ownership is so dispersed that no large shareholder exists.

They are the largest owners in 21.3% of the observations and the second (third) largest owners in 20.4% (20.7%) of the cases. This suggests that insiders are active across the entire range of stake sizes and have no preference for certain stake sizes (again considering that the size of stakes continuously decreases with the owner rank). As expected, private investors, banks and government entities are relatively uncommon as largest owners.

Table 5.10: Frequency Distribution Across Owner Types to be Among the Company's Five Largest Owners

Owner types	Owner rank				
	1	2	3	4	5
Private investors	6.4%	9.5%	14.9%	14.0%	7.0%
Insiders	21.3%	20.4%	20.7%	20.3%	19.1%
Corporations	21.6%	12.5%	7.3%	6.3%	5.5%
Financial institutions	48.2%	53.6%	53.0%	55.9%	61.8%
Banks	1.9%	3.6%	4.1%	3.4%	6.5%
Government(s)	0.6%	0.4%	0.0%	0.2%	0.0%
Total	100.0%	100.0%	100.0%	100.0%	100.0%

Table 5.11 examines the relevance of owner types according to the size of shareholdings.[126] As expected from the previous statistic on owner ranks, financial investors are found to be the dominant type of shareholder across all stake sizes, and corporations play a major role among the (super-) majority owners. In contrast, insiders hold both small and medium to large stake sizes but are hardly represented among the supermajority owners. Private investors settle for comparably smaller ownership stakes, which is probably due to their limited financial resources compared with other owner types.[127] As expected, banks and government entities are mostly represented among smaller owners and play no significant role compared with other types of investors.

[126] The sample includes 5,034 shareholdings of more than 5%. These are held by financial institutions (52.2%), insiders (20.6%), corporations (14.4%), private investors (9.5%), banks (3%), and the government (0.4%).

[127] If individual investors owned a higher stake, they would probably wish to take a seat in the company's advisory board – in which case they would classify as insiders.

Table 5.11: Relevance of Owner Types According to Size of Shareholdings

Owner types	Size of shareholdings					Average fraction held
	5.0 - 14.9%	15.0 - 24.9%	25.0 - 49.9%	50.0 - 74.9%	>75.0%	
Private investors	11.3%	9.9%	7.1%	5.6%	2.5%	15.8%
Insiders	19.6%	21.1%	28.1%	25.1%	2.8%	21.1%
Corporations	7.8%	15.5%	16.7%	30.3%	45.6%	38.4%
Financial institutions	57.2%	49.7%	44.7%	38.7%	48.4%	19.8%
Banks	3.7%	3.5%	2.7%	0.2%	0.7%	14.6%
Government(s)	0.4%	0.3%	0.7%	0.0%	0.0%	16.9%
Total	100.0%	100.0%	100.0%	100.0%	100.0%	

Table 5.11 also provides supplemental information on the average fraction of shareholdings across owners' investment universe. Accordingly, if corporations invest in other firms, their shareholdings average at 38.4%. Again, this high share provides an indication of the predominance of strategic over financial investment motives. In comparison, the average stakes of other owner types are much smaller: Insiders and financial institutions hold, on average, only 21.1% and 19.8%, respectively. Government entities, private investors and bank opt for even smaller stakes.

5.3 Model

This section specifies the model structure of the ownership-performance relation and elaborates on several modeling aspects, which need to be considered in order to minimize the potential specification error and the subsequent bias of results.

5.3.1 Model Structure

To analyze the relation between ownership and performance, the latter is regressed against ownership structure (ownership concentration and owner identity). The equation can be expressed as follows:

$$\boxed{Performance} = f\{\boxed{Ownership}, \boxed{Controls}\}$$

Performance ↑	Ownership ↑	Controls ↑
Q, ROA, ROE	*Concentration*: *OWN1(2,3), OWN1/OWN2, BLOCK, HHI* *Identity*: *PRIVATE, INSIDER, CORP, FINAN, BANK, GOV*	*DEBT, RDX, CAPX, GRO*

where performance is alternatively measured as *Q*, *ROA*, or *ROE*. Ownership concentration considers six alternative variables (*OWN1*, *OWN12*, *OWN123*, *OWN1/OWN2*, *BLOCK*, *HHI*). Owner identities include *PRIVATE*, *INSIDER*, *CORP*, *FINAN*, *BANK*, and *GOV*. The model also includes a set of common control variables, namely *DEBT*, *CAPX*, *RDX* and *GRO* as well as industry and year dummies (the definition of variables can be found in Table 5.5).

5.3.2 Modeling Aspects in the Ownership-Performance Relation

Crucial model aspects are, most important, the endogeneity of ownership structure but also the question of linearity of effects as well as the timing of effects.

5.3.2.1 Endogeneity of Ownership Structure

There are three situations in which endogeneity is present: (a) errors-in-variables, (b) omitted variables, and (c) simultaneous causality (Bascle, 2008).[128] The first source of endogeneity, the errors-in-variables problem, arises when the true value of a regressor is unobserved due to a measurement error. An example is given by Berger and Hann (2003) who investigate the effect of new reporting standards on firms' industry classification system. Before 1997, managers had a relative freedom to inaccurately report in which their firm was active. After 1997, new SIC standards require that more disaggregated information is provided in order to give a more accurate and less subjective representation of a firm's scope. A study on the relation between business diversification and performance based on pre-1997 SIC data can thus be confronted with an endogeneity problem arising from measurement error.

The second source of endogeneity is the issue of omitted variables. This problem arises if a variable, which affects the dependent variable and is correlated with one or more independent variables, is omitted from the regression.[129] This occurs if data are unavailable or if the variable is unobservable, which both leads to a misspecification of the model. The omitted information is referred to as unobserved heterogeneity.[130] Not controlling for unquantifiable firm characteristics may yield biased results, as shown, for example, by Moulton (1986), because the effect of the omitted variable is captured in the error term, which makes the error term being correlated with some of the independent variables. As a result, the exogeneity condition (error

---

[128] An alternative, although less frequently discussed, source of endogeneity arises from the possibility that current values of the explanatory variable are a function of past values of the dependent variable (Wintoki, Linck, & Netter, 2012). Accordingly, it can be argued that current observations of the ownership structure may not be completely independent of past firm performance. For example, the reward argument (see Section 3.4.2.2) assumes that firms grant their managers with equity ownership in order to reward them for good corporate performance in the past. It is hence likely that the effect of performance on ownership is lagging. Neglecting this source of (dynamic) endogeneity can have consequences for inference. This is especially true because the difficulty in identifying exogenous instruments (see Section 5.4.3) in many cases means that analyses are often based on panel data and fixed effects estimates. Fixed effects estimation can potentially thwart the bias arising from unobservable heterogeneity, but this comes at the expense of a strong exogeneity assumption – which is questioned assuming a dynamic nature of the ownership-performance relation. To deal with the issue of dynamics, Wintoki et al. (2012) suggest to further extent the analysis through the use of dynamic panel estimators such as the GMM.

[129] If the omitted variable is uncorrelated with the independent variables, the error term does not correlate with the independent variables, and hence no inference problem exists.

[130] The term heterogeneity refers to variation across individual units of observation. Unobserved heterogeneity describes variation that cannot be observed because of its relation to unobservable and hence omitted variables.

term with zero mean conditional on the independent variables) is violated, and the endogeneity problem arises. An example for unobservable variables is provided by Pindado and Requejo (2012) who construct a model to explain a firm's investment activities dependent on the firm's cash flows, Tobin's Q and previous year's investment rate. The model does not include any information on the propensity of the management to undertake investment projects because this information cannot be observed by researchers. However, it is reasonable to assume that there are managers who are more prone to undertake investments than others. The example hence demonstrates the difficulty to enter the (unobservable) behavior of individuals into a model. Another example for individual heterogeneity affecting both firm value and ownership structure is provided by Himmelberg et al. (1999) who examine whether certain firm characteristics affecting performance make insider ownership endogenous. Their results show that both value and insider ownership are explained by common characteristics (common cause), some of which are unobservable and that the omission of these characteristics may lead to biased conclusions regarding the influence of insider ownership on performance because of the relation between the former and the omitted variables, which in turn leads to a correlation between the error term and the ownership variable.

The third source of endogeneity is simultaneous causality and occurs if the causality runs in both directions, from the independent variable to the dependent variable and from the dependent variable to the independent variable. When there is simultaneous causality, the dependent variable and the error term are correlated, and OLS estimation picks up both forward and backward effects, thereby producing biased and inconsistent coefficients. A classic illustration of the simultaneity problem points at the hypothetical question of whether an increase in the size of a city's police force would lower the average murder rate (Wooldridge, 2009). However, the police force size cannot be assumed as being exogenously determined because a city's spending on law enforcement (and hence the number of police officers) is at least partly determined by its expected murder rate. As a consequence, a simultaneity bias would arise if OLS was used to estimate this relation. The problem of simultaneity is potentially inherent in many corporate finance and management studies and also affects the ownership-performance relation. Although a large body of literature suggests that certain ownership structures drive performance, this research is plagued with simultaneity issues, and it cannot be ascertained whether the causation is actually reversed, that is, whether performance drives ownership. The existence of hypotheses of effects in both directions (see

Sections 3.3 and 3.4) provides support for the simultaneity assumption. Hence, it appears inevitable to incorporate endogeneity in the econometric model.

Pindado and de la Torre (2004) examine the ownership-performance relation and address the question about the main source of endogeneity in this specific context. They focus on testing whether the endogeneity of ownership is a consequence of the individual heterogeneity that affects both firm performance and ownership, or a result of the simultaneity that exists between the two variables. Based on a panel data set of 135 public nonfinancial firms in Spain for the period 1990-99, the authors estimate a fixed-effects model and regress insider ownership and the level of ownership concentration against market capitalization. As controls, they include variables that might influence both value and ownership structure (and may thus be potential sources of endogeneity): intangible assets, market share, size, and leverage. They argue that the omission of these variables would make ownership an endogenous variable because a correlation between the error term and the ownership variable might exist. The inclusion of intangible assets and market share follows Himmelberg et al. (1999)'s argumentation. In regard to size, it is assumed that firm size is negatively related to ownership concentration because the larger the firm is (and hence the larger its capital resources are), the more difficult it is to own a certain fraction of the firm's equity because more owners have to commit more of their wealth (Demsetz & Lehn, 1985). Debt is also argued to have a negative effect on ownership concentration because large shareholders have to bear a higher risk of a given stake in a leveraged firm. However, risk aversion implies that they will purchase additional shares only at lower, risk-compensating prices. Increased costs of capital hence discourage shareholders of larger firms from attempting to maintain highly concentrated ownership levels.

If, as suggested by Himmelberg et al. (1999), the endogeneity is due to model misspecification, a certain correlation between ownership and the individual effect should exist, which is affected by the inclusion or omission of the common determinants. In other words, if the omission of one of the proposed control variables in the model leads to a higher correlation between ownership variables and the individual effect, it must be considered to be a source of endogeneity. However, if the endogeneity stems from an alternative source, the simultaneity or inverse causality between ownership and value, ownership variables are expected to correlate with the random disturbance once the individual effect has been controlled for.

Pindado and de la Torre (2004) first compute the correlation coefficients between ownership variables and the individual effect. They then omit one by one the control variables when estimating regression models and afterwards compare the resulting correlations with the corresponding one obtained from the estimation of the models containing all controls. Second, the correlation coefficients between ownership variables and the random disturbance are computed. All in all, their analysis of the correlation coefficients between ownership variables and the error term casts doubt as to whether the included control variables, which are sources of unobserved heterogeneity, are actually sources of endogeneity of the insider ownership and ownership concentration variables. In regard to simultaneity, the results provide evidence that insider ownership as well as ownership concentration are indeed endogenous and that this endogeneity is not caused by unobserved heterogeneity but by its simultaneity with value. Pindado and de la Torre (2004) hence suggest controlling for endogeneity by using instrumental variables techniques.[131]

5.3.2.2 Linearity of Ownership Effects

There is no consensus about the assumed shape of the ownership-performance relation in the literature. Although most studies suppose a linear effect, a large number of studies actually provide evidence of a nonlinear relation (see Table A.1.1).

A frequently modeled shape of the relation between (managerial) ownership concentration and performance is given by Morck et al. (1988). They use a piecewise regression with two turning points of 5% and 25%, thereby dividing the function into three parts. For the first range from 0% to 5%, they find a significant, positive relation between ownership and performance, whereas evidence on the second part of the function from 5% to 25% indicates a significant, negative relation. For the last range of the function ending at 100%, they find a positive but insignificant effect. The empirical result is hence a two parted function with a maximum at 5%. Many studies have copied this approach and find a significant, positive relation of ownership and performance in the first range from 0% to 5% (e.g., Holderness et al., 1999). Others adjust the range size. For example, Chen et al. (1993) identify a range from 0% to 5-7% for which they provide evidence of a positive effect. Many studies also confirm the negative relation for the second part of the function. Chen et al. (1993) again alter the second

[131] The application of simultaneous equation models or instrumental variable regressions is a standard textbook approach to tackle endogeneity (e.g., Greene, 2012; Wooldridge, 2009).

turning point to 10-12% and also find a negative relation for their definition of the second piece of the function. However, for the last range of the function ending at 100%, none of these studies finds significant evidence of an effect. Other studies such as McConnell and Servaes (1990) divide the ownership levels into two regions and produce a bell-shaped relation between managerial ownership and performance peaking at 40-50%. In contrast, Hermalin and Weisbach (1991) divide the managerial ownership levels into four regions: less than 1%, 1-5%, 5-20% and greater than 20%. They find that at levels greater than 20%, performance significantly decreases with ownership.[132] Davies et al. (2005) use even five ownership ranges from 0-7%, 7-26%, 26-51%, 51-76% and 76-100% and find similar results for the first three regions as Morck et al. (1988). Beyond an ownership level of 51%, they document a first decreasing and then increasing performance effect of increasing managerial ownership. Figure 5.4 illustrates the discussed effect shapes.

Figure 5.4: Effect Shapes of the (Insider-) Ownership-Performance Relation in Selected Empirical Studies

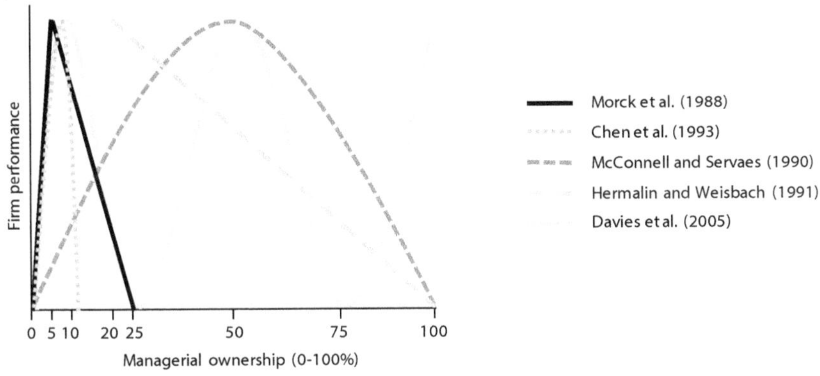

Note. Only statistically significant parts of the respective functions are shown.

The different inflection points are a result of differences in the data samples (size of firms, institutional differences), the choice and measurement of the variables used (and whether or not the endogeneity of ownership is taken into account), and the treatment of outliers Chen et al. (1993). A further explanation for the differences is the estimation method used. The

[132] They also find that at levels of ownership of less than 1% performance significantly increases with ownership.

problem with studies applying a squared or cubic model is that they force the function to follow a pre-determined either quadratic or cubic shape. Linear-piecewise regressions, in contrast, are more flexible and can proxy more complex functions. But the disadvantage is that coefficients on the ownership variable are allowed to change only at pre-determined levels of ownership. However, there is no theoretical guidance for the choice of turning points on the piecewise regression.

Based on this discussion, the following empirical analyses test simple linear models but also consider more complex functions in order to control for potential nonlinearities in the relation between ownership and performance.

5.3.2.3 Timing of Effects

Most studies of the effect of ownership and performance focus on assessing the effect of current ownership on current performance.[133] However, it is possible that current ownership affects performance in the next period, that is, performance can be expected to adjust with delay to changes in ownership structure. The process of adjustment to changes in the explanatory variables may hence depend on the passage of time, which indicates the use of lagged versions of these factors as regressors (Wintoki, Linck, & Netter, 2012). Consequently, in order to protect against a potential timing error, the empirical analyses in this work will also include models using lagged ownership structures.

5.4 Econometric Approach

The analysis of panel data captures variation across units (similar to regressions on cross-section data) but also variation over time. Panel data methods are therefore more complicated than cross-section data and require the use of much richer models and estimations methods. Characteristics, advantages and challenges of panel data as well as the various models and estimators applied in the empirical analysis are outlined below.

5.4.1 Advantages and Limitations of Panel Data Sets

Observations in the data set involve two dimensions: a cross-sectional dimension (indicated by the superscript i) and a time series dimension (indicated by the superscript t). By blending the

[133] This practice is due to static data samples in many ownership and performance studies.

interindividual differences and intraindividual dynamics, panel data have several advantages over cross-sectional or time series data:[134] A major advantage of panel data is that they often have large numbers of observations and hence are rich in content. This leads to an increased precision in estimation (Hsiao, Mountain, & Illman, 1995). Panel data usually contain more degrees of freedom and more sample variability than cross-sectional data, which may be viewed as a panel with $T = 1$, or time series data, which is a panel with $N = 1$, hence improving the efficiency of econometric estimates.

A second attraction of panel data is the greater capacity for constructing and testing more complicated behavioral models than purely cross-section or time series data. For example, the effectiveness of social programs is better studied and modeled with panels (Hsiao, 2007): Evaluating the effectiveness of certain program using a cross-sectional sample typically suffers from the fact that those receiving treatment are different from those without. In other words, one does not simultaneously observe what happens to an individual when he receives treatment, or when he does not.

Another important advantage is the possibility to control for the impact of missing or unobserved and hence omitted variables (Baltagi, 2005). In contrast to time series and cross-section studies, which do not control for the individuality of firms and therefore run the risk of obtaining biased results, panel data suggest that firms are heterogeneous. If these unobserved individual-specific effects are assumed to be time-invariant, panel data methods offer several ways to obtain consistent estimates, which will be discussed in the subsequent sections.

A further attraction of panel data includes the possibility to reveal dynamics that are difficult to detect with cross-sectional data (Dougherty, 2011). Although this advantage is shared by repeated cross-section data (from which pseudo-panel data can be constructed), panel data with repeated observations on the same unit typically allow more of the variation in the micro data to be used in constructing parameter estimates.

---

[134] Econometric analyses are traditionally based on cross-section (sample of a number of observational units all drawn at the same point in time) or time series data structures (set of observations drawn of the same observational unit at a number of points in time). However, the increasing availability of databases and the plummeting costs of computation and software distribution during the last decades have led to the emergence of time series cross sections (panel data structures) that consist of the same cross-sectional units observed at several points in time.

Lastly, the availability of panel data may simplify statistical inference (Hsiao, 2007): For example, measurement errors usually lead to underidentification of an econometric model. However, the availability of multiple observations for a given unit may allow researchers to make different transformations to induce different and deducible changes in the estimators and hence to identify an otherwise unidentified model.

The frequently cited limitations of panel data such as data collection problems, distortions of measurement errors and selectivity problems apply mainly to panel surveys and are of minor relevance for the following empirical analyses as the data are retrieved from well established data bases and are cross-checked for consistency. The only concern might be the short time series dimension of short panels covering only a limited time span for each unit. This means that asymptotic arguments rely crucially on the number of individuals tending to infinity (Baltagi, 2005). However, this argument is less relevant for the following empirical analysis as the sample period spans a 5-year period covering all major phases of an economic cycle and therefore would hardly benefit from a further extension of the time series dimension.

5.4.2 Fundamental Panel Methods

Basic panel estimation methods include the pooled OLS estimator as well as the fixed-effects and random-effects estimators. The methods differ mainly in their treatment of unobserved heterogeneity and their capability of capturing the panel aspect of the data structure. The methods are briefly introduced in the following subsections.[135]

5.4.2.1 Pooled OLS Estimation

Pooled sample estimators, or population-averaged estimators, ignore the panel structure of the data and simply regress a dependent variable on an intercept and the regressors using both between (cross-section) and within (time series) variation in the data.

A pooled OLS estimator assumes a model of the following form:

$$y_{it} = \alpha + \boldsymbol{x}'_{it}\boldsymbol{\beta} + (\alpha_i - \alpha + \varepsilon_{it}) \qquad (1)$$

where i indexes observational units and t indexes time, y_{it} denotes the dependent variable, and $\boldsymbol{x}'_{it}$ is a vector of independent variables. Any time-specific effects are assumed to be fixed

[135] This section draws from Baltagi (2005), Cameron and Trivedi (2005), Cameron and Trivedi (2010), Dougherty (2011), Giesselmann and Windzio (2012), Greene (2012), Hsiao (2007), and Wooldridge (2009).

and already included as time dummies in the regressors. The model explicitly includes a common intercept α, and the firm-specific (time-invariant) effects $\alpha_i - \alpha$ are centered on zero.

The OLS estimation is the best linear unbiased estimator, and no other estimator will produce better coefficients if the least squares assumptions hold (Gauss-Markov Theorem). The key assumptions needed for OLS to produce consistent estimates of the parameters are: (a) The error term has a mean of zero conditional on the independent variables (zero conditional mean, i.e., strict exogeneity), (b) disturbances are uncorrelated with each other (no autocorrelation) and have a constant variance (homoskedasticity), and (c) there are no linear relations among the independent variables (no perfect collinearity).[136]

However, OLS estimation is inconsistent in case of unobserved heterogeneity. As discussed in the previous Section 5.3.2.1, individual heterogeneity represents a firm-specific performance effect, which remains constant over time but is unobservable. As OLS ignores time-invariant firm-fixed effects (unquantifiable firm characteristics or, in other words, unobserved firm heterogeneity) entirely, the regression may yield biased results because the effect is captured in the error term, which makes the error term being correlated with some of the independent variables. As a result, an endogeneity problem arises, as the correlation between a regressor and the fixed effects in the error term violates the most important OLS estimation assumption, the exogeneity condition, specifying that the error term has an expected value of zero given any regressor, that is, $E(u_{it}|\boldsymbol{x}_{it}) = 0$.

It is not possible to estimate a model that contains a firm-specific effect as an independent variable because there would be as many variables that capture the individual effect as the number of companies included in the sample. A solution to the problem of unobserved heterogeneity is therefore either (a) to manipulate (transform) the model in such a way that the fixed effects are removed and estimate the coefficients based on the transformed model (within-transformation, and to some degree also random-effects transformation), or (b) endogenous variables are instrumented with variables that are assumed to be uncorrelated with the fixed effects (2SLS estimation). These approaches are discussed below.

---

[136] See von Auer (2007) for a comprehensive examination and interpretation of all assumptions needed to make the OLS technique applicable.

5.4.2.2 Fixed- and Random-Effects Estimation

A way to tackle unobserved heterogeneity is to apply fixed or random effects models. The crucial distinction between the two approaches is whether the fixed effects are permitted to be correlated with the regressors (fixed-effects model) or not (random-effects model).

Fixed-effects model

A fixed-effects (FE) model has the following form:

$$y_{it} = \alpha_i + \boldsymbol{x}'_{it}\boldsymbol{\beta} + \varepsilon_{it} \qquad (2)$$

where the error is $u_{it} = \alpha_i + \varepsilon_{it}$. The regressors are permitted to be correlated with the time-invariant component of the error (α_i), but it is assumed that the regressors are uncorrelated with the idiosyncratic error (ε_{it}).

Again, it is not possible to jointly estimate $\alpha_1 \ldots \alpha_N$ and $\boldsymbol{\beta}$ because for a short panel, asymptotic theory relies on $N \to \infty$, and so does the number of fixed effects to estimate (incidental-parameters problem). It is therefore essential to control for the nuisance α_i before estimating the parameter $\boldsymbol{\beta}$.

A solution to the incidental-parameters problem is the within-groups estimator, which transforms the equation in such a way that the fixed effects α_i are eliminated.[137] For this, the mean values of the variables for each individual i are calculated:

$$\bar{y}_i = \bar{\boldsymbol{x}}'_i\boldsymbol{\beta} + \bar{\varepsilon}_i$$

Next, the original observations are expressed as deviations from these individual means.[138] This is known as the within-groups estimation because it is explaining the variations around

[137] Another way to estimate the parameters of a fixed-effects model is the least-squares dummy-variable (LSDV) estimation. This method brings the unobserved effect explicitly into the model and defines a set of dummy variables A_i, where A_i is equal to one in the case of an observation relating to individual i and zero otherwise. The unobserved effect is then being treated as the coefficient of the individual-specific dummy variable, the $\alpha_i A_i$ term representing a fixed effect on the dependent variable y_i for individual i. Having respecified the model in this way, it can be fitted using OLS. However, the LSDV method is not suitable for short panels where T is fixed and $N \to \infty$, given the need for a large number of dummy variables. Furthermore, it can be shown mathematically that the LSDV method is identical to the within-groups method (the only difference is in the number of degrees of freedom).

[138] Firms for which only a single time period is observable play no role in a fixed-effects model because the time-demeaning for such observations yields all zeros, which are not used in the estimation.

the mean of the dependent variable in terms of the variations around the means of the explanatory variables for the group of observations relating to a given individual:[139]

$$y_{it} - \bar{y}_i = (\boldsymbol{x}_{it} - \bar{\boldsymbol{x}}_i)'\boldsymbol{\beta} + (\varepsilon_{it} - \bar{\varepsilon}_i)$$

As the mean of the time-invariant α_i is itself α_i, theses individual effects are removed from the transformed equations. OLS is then used to estimate these transformed equations. Because α_i has been eliminated, OLS leads to consistent estimates of $\boldsymbol{\beta}$ even if α_i is correlated with $\boldsymbol{x}_{it}$, as is the case in the fixed-effects model. The fixed-effects estimator hence eliminates the inconsistency produced by OLS estimates. This result is a great advantage of panel data. Consistent estimation is possible even with endogenous regressors, provided that they are correlated only with the time-invariant component of the error α_i and not with the time-varying component of the error ε_{it}. A disadvantage of the within-estimator, however, is that any regressors that remain constant for each individual will drop out of the model. The estimator is also limited in the presence of time-varying regressors that vary only little over time.[140]

Random-effects model

A random-effects (RE) model also has the following form:

$$y_{it} = \alpha_i + \boldsymbol{x}'_{it}\boldsymbol{\beta} + \varepsilon_{it} \tag{2}$$

It is assumed that the individual-specific effects are purely random, implying that α_i is distributed independently of the regressors (whereas in the fixed-effects model, α_i is permitted to be correlated with the regressors). That is, $Cov(\boldsymbol{x}_{it}|\alpha_i) = 0$. In other words, the distinction between fixed and random effects is whether the unobserved individual effect embodies elements that are correlated with the regressors in the model, not whether these effects are stochastic or not.

---

139 Because the within-estimator provides a consistent estimate of the fixed-effects model, it is often called the fixed-effects estimator, though the first-difference estimator also provides consistent estimates in the fixed-effects model (Cameron & Trivedi, 2010).

140 An alternative estimator for fixed-effects models is the first-difference (FD) estimator. In contrast to the within-estimator, which applies a mean-difference transformation, the first-difference estimator first-differences by subtracting previous from current observations. The first-difference transformation also removes the fixed effect, but a weakness is that the first sample year is missing. In addition, it is less eligible for unbalanced panels because sample gaps are magnified. If, for example, y_{it} is missing, then both Δy_{it} and $\Delta y_{i,t+1}$ are missing in the transformed data. As a consequence, the within-estimator is preferred over the first-difference estimator for the empirical analyses in the course of this dissertation.

Under these random-effects assumption, the parameter $\boldsymbol{\beta}$ can be consistently estimated in a pooled OLS procedure. But because α_i is in the composite error in each time period, the u_{it} are serially correlated across time:

$$Cor(u_{it}, u_{is}) = \sigma_\alpha^2/(\sigma_\alpha^2 + \sigma_\varepsilon^2) \text{ for all } s \neq t \tag{3}$$

where $\sigma_\alpha^2 = Var(\alpha_i)$, and $\sigma_\varepsilon^2 = Var(\varepsilon_{it})$. This serial correlation in the error term can be substantial, and, because the usual pooled OLS standard errors ignore this correlation, they will be incorrect. A solution to the serial-correlation problem is the use of generalized least-squares (GLS). Define

$$\lambda = 1 - \sqrt{\sigma_\varepsilon^2/(\sigma_\varepsilon^2 + T\sigma_\alpha^2)} \tag{4}$$

which is between zero and one.[141] $\hat{\lambda}$ is a consistent estimator of λ. The transformed equation then turns out to be

$$(y_{it} - \hat{\lambda}\bar{y}_i) = \alpha(1 - \hat{\lambda}) + (\boldsymbol{x}_{it} - \hat{\lambda}\bar{\boldsymbol{x}}_i)'\boldsymbol{\beta} + \{(1 - \hat{\lambda})\alpha_i + (\varepsilon_{it} - \hat{\lambda}\bar{\varepsilon}_i)\} \tag{5}$$

where the overbar again denotes the time averages. The equation hence involves quasi-demeaned data on each variable. Compared with the within-estimator, which subtracts the time averages from the corresponding variable, the random-effects estimator subtracts a fraction of that time average, where the fraction depends on σ_ε^2, σ_α^2 and the number of time periods T. The GLS estimator is simply the pooled OLS estimator of Equation 5. Hence, the random-effects estimator is the feasible GLS estimator of $\boldsymbol{\beta}$.

The random-effects estimator is consistent if the random-effects model is appropriate. It is inconsistent if the fixed-effects model is appropriate because the correlation between $\boldsymbol{x}_{it}$ and α_i implies correlation between the regressors and the error.

Advantages of the random-effects estimator are that it yields estimates of all coefficients, and thus marginal effects, even those of time-invariant regressors, and that $E(y_{it}|\boldsymbol{x}_{it})$ can be

141 If $\hat{\lambda}$ is close to zero, the random-effects estimates will be close to the pooled OLS estimates. This is the case when the unobserved effect, α_i, is relatively unimportant (because it has small variance relative to σ_ε^2). It is more common for σ_α^2 to be large relative to σ_ε^2, in which case $\hat{\lambda}$ will be closer to one. As T gets large, $\hat{\lambda}$ tends to one, and this makes the random-effects and within-estimates very similar.

estimated. The big disadvantage is that these estimates are inconsistent if the fixed-effects model is appropriate.[142]

5.4.2.3 Choice of the Appropriate Estimation Method

Although the OLS estimator is easy to use and has a benchmark character in the empirical literature, it is hardly relevant for the analysis of panel data. This is because consistency of the pooled OLS estimator requires that $E(u_{it}|\boldsymbol{x}_{it}) = 0$ in the model $y_{it} = \alpha + \boldsymbol{x}'_{it}\boldsymbol{\beta} + u_{\text{it}}$. If this assumption fails so that $\boldsymbol{x}'_{it}$ is endogenous, individual-effects models such as the fixed- and random-effects model can provide alternative ways to obtain consistent results. The pooled OLS estimator is hence used only as a reference model in the course of this dissertation.

Consistency in the fixed-effects model $y_{it} = \alpha_i + \boldsymbol{x}'_{it}\boldsymbol{\beta} + \varepsilon_{it}$ requires the weaker assumption that $E(\varepsilon_{it}|\alpha_i, \boldsymbol{x}_{it}) = 0$. Essentially, the error has two components: the time-invariant component α_i correlated with the regressors that can be eliminated through differencing and a time-varying component ε_{it} that is uncorrelated with the regressors.

The random-effects model adds an additional assumption and requires that α_i is distributed independently of $\boldsymbol{x}'_{it}$. This is a much stronger assumption because it implies that $E(\varepsilon_{it}|\alpha_i, \boldsymbol{x}_{it}) = E(\varepsilon_{it}|\boldsymbol{x}_{it}) = 0$, as assumed by the pooled OLS model.

For the analysis of an individual-effects model, the fundamental question is therefore whether the firm-specific effects are fixed (i.e., correlated with the regressors) or random (i.e., not correlated with the regressors). If the effects are fixed, then the pooled OLS and the random-effects estimators are inconsistent.[143] Instead, the within-estimator needs to be used. If effects are random, both the random-effects and the fixed-effects (as well as the OLS) estimators are consistent. However, the fixed-effects estimator is less desirable because using only within-

---

[142] An alternative estimator for random-effects models is the between-estimator. The between-estimator uses only between-variation (i.e., cross-sectional variation) in the data and is analogue of a cross-section regression, which is the special case $T = 1$, that is, the data is collapsed with one (time-averaged) observation per individual. In practice, the between-estimator is rarely used because the pooled estimator and the random-effects estimator are more efficient (Cameron & Trivedi, 2010). Moreover, taking away the within-variation of the data would leave out valuable information from panel data sets.

[143] The inconsistency of the random-effects estimator in the fixed-effects model follows from the fact that as $T \to \infty$, the individual fixed effects α_i are not estimated but are viewed as realizations of random variables with zero mean. The violation of the assumption $E(u) = 0$ for the regression model leads to inconsistency.

variation leads to less efficient estimation and inability to estimate coefficients of time-invariant regressors. The models and appropriate estimators are summarized in Table 5.12.

Table 5.12: Models and Appropriate Estimators

Estimator of β	Assumed model		
	Pooled	Random effects	Fixed effects
Pooled OLS	Consistent	Consistent	Inconsistent
Within	Consistent	Consistent	Consistent
Random effects	Consistent	Consistent	Inconsistent

Note. Adapted from Cameron and Trivedi (2005). Shaded columns visualize the consistent estimators.

When choosing between models, three statistical tests are commonly applied:[144] the Chow F-test for poolability, the Lagrange Multiplier test for the presence of random effects, and the Hausman test for fixed effects. The test procedures are discussed in detail in Section 6.1.1.1.

Apart from statistical specification tests for choosing the most appropriate model, it appears even more important that methodological decisions can be logically reasoned (Giesselmann & Windzio, 2012; Halaby, 2004; Verbeek, 2004). Accordingly, the empirical estimation method has to match the research question and variable characteristics. This means that for longitudinal research questions, which by definition are interested in the effects of time-variant variables, a methodology should be chosen that models longitudinal data and uses only intrasubject variability in order to construct coefficients. This is commonly the case for fixed-effects models. In contrast, for transversal research questions, which by definition are not interested in the effects of time-variant variables, a methodology should be chosen that refers to differences in levels and uses intersubject variability in order to estimate coefficients. Fixed-effects models are not appropriate as they eliminate these level differences and cancel out any

[144] Another view on the question of which estimator to use is proposed by Petersen (2009). He argues that it is more fruitful to think of the estimators as reporting on different aspects of the data. No estimator is then necessarily better, they just answer different questions. The OLS estimator reports roughly what one would get with cross-sectional data. The within-estimator provides evidence of whether effects hold within firms across time, whereas the random-effects estimators can be thought of as a weighted average of the between- and within-estimator and reports whether effects hold both across firms and within firms across time. Consequently, the different estimators are just different ways of describing the data, each yielding relevant insights in its own rights.

time-constant variables. Instead, random effects models (or pooled OLS) should be applied. A further motive for a longitudinal research design is the intention to control for unobserved heterogeneity (time-invariant firm-specific characteristics). If it can be theoretically ruled out that there are no omitted variables or, if existent, that they are uncorrelated with the explanatory variables, random-effects models produce unbiased estimates of the coefficients, use all the data available (because between-variation is not thrown out) and produce the smallest standard errors. However, this is not only a very restrictive assumption, but is also inconsistent with the actual motive for using panel data: The advantage of panel data over cross-sectional data to control for unobserved heterogeneity is not being capitalized on. If, in contrast, omitted variables do exist, and if these can be assumed to correlate with the variables in the model through time-invariant effects, fixed-effects models are preferred because they provide a means for controlling for omitted-variable bias. To summarize, fixed-effects models are an appropriate estimation method for analyzing panel data with a longitudinal research question and time-variant variables – as it is the case for the empirical work in this dissertation. The further empirical analysis therefore emphasizes the interpretation of results from fixed-effects models (within-estimation).

5.4.3 Advanced Panel Methods

Advanced panel methods focus on instrumental variable estimation, without and with fixed effects. Although both estimation approaches tackle simultaneous causality, they differ in their treatment of unobserved heterogeneity and their capability of capturing the panel aspect of the data structure. The methods are briefly introduced below.

5.4.3.1 Pooled 2SLS Estimation

Although the unobserved heterogeneity can be removed through the transformation of the equations, the model still suffers from potential endogeneity as a result of regressors being determined simultaneously with the dependent variable. A solution to address this endogeneity problem is the use of an instrumental variables (IV) method.[145]

The instrumental variable estimator provides a consistent estimator under the strong assumption that valid instruments $\boldsymbol{z}$ exist that have the property that changes in $\boldsymbol{z}$ are

[145] This section draws from Baum (2006), Baum, Schaffer, and Stillman (2003), Cameron and Trivedi (2010), Greene (2012), Wooldridge (2002), and Wooldridge (2009).

associated with changes in $\boldsymbol{x}$ but do not lead to changes in y (except indirectly via $\boldsymbol{x}$). That is, instruments $\boldsymbol{z}$ have to be found that satisfy the following conditions:

- The instruments must be correlated with the variable x that needs to be explained, that is, $cov(z, x) \neq 0$ (relevance condition), and at the same time
- the instruments must be uncorrelated with the error term u, that is, $E(u|z) = 0$ (validity or exogeneity condition).[146]

The idea is first to regress the variable to be instrumented on the instruments to obtain the fitted values, which can then be used in the second-stage regression on the equation of interest. The model to be fitted is called a structural equation, and assumes the following form:

$$y_{1it} = \boldsymbol{y}'_{2it}\boldsymbol{\beta}_1 + \boldsymbol{x}'_{1it}\boldsymbol{\beta}_2 + u_{it}; \quad i = 1, \dots, N \tag{6}$$

where the dependent variable y_{1i} depends on m endogenous regressors, denoted by $\boldsymbol{y}_{2it}$, and K_1 exogenous regressors, denoted by $\boldsymbol{x}_{1it}$. The regression errors u_{it} are assumed to be uncorrelated with $\boldsymbol{x}_{1it}$ but are correlated with $\boldsymbol{y}_{2it}$:

$$\begin{array}{l} \boldsymbol{y}'_{2it} \rightarrow y_{1it} \\ \uparrow \;\; \nearrow \\ u_{it} \end{array}$$

This correlation leads to the OLS estimator being inconsistent for $\boldsymbol{\beta}$. To obtain a consistent estimator, the existence of at least m instrumental variables $\boldsymbol{x}_2$ for $\boldsymbol{y}_2$ that satisfy the assumption that $E(u_{it}|\boldsymbol{x}_{2it}) = 0$ are required:

$$\begin{array}{l} \boldsymbol{x}'_{2it} \rightarrow \boldsymbol{y}'_{2it} \rightarrow y_{1it} \\ \qquad\quad \uparrow \;\; \nearrow \\ \qquad\quad u_{it} \end{array}$$

The instruments $\boldsymbol{x}_2$ need to be correlated with $\boldsymbol{y}_2$ so that they provide some information on the variables being instrumented. One way to motivate this is to assume that each component y_{2j} of $\boldsymbol{y}_2$ satisfies the first-stage equation (reduced-form model):

$$y_{2jit} = \boldsymbol{x}'_{1it}\boldsymbol{\pi}_{1j} + \boldsymbol{x}'_{2it}\boldsymbol{\pi}_{2j} + v_{jit}; \; j = 1, \dots, m \tag{7}$$

[146] Whereas the relevance condition can be easily tested, the validity condition cannot be tested because the condition involves the unobservable residual. Therefore, this condition has to be taken on faith.

The first-stage equations have only exogenous variables on the right-hand side. The exogenous regressors $\boldsymbol{x}_1$ in Equation 7 can be used as instruments for themselves. The challenge is to come up with at least one additional instrument $\boldsymbol{x}_2$. This can be difficult because $\boldsymbol{x}_2$ needs to be a variable than can be legitimately excluded from the structural Equation Model 6 for y_1.

Equation 6 can be more simply written as

$$y_{it} = \boldsymbol{x}'_{it}\boldsymbol{\beta} + u_{it} \tag{8}$$

where the regressor vector $\boldsymbol{x}'_{it} = [\boldsymbol{y}'_{2it}\ \boldsymbol{x}'_{1it}]$ combines endogenous and exogenous variables, and the dependent variable is denoted by y rather than y_1. The instrument vector can be similarly obtained as $\boldsymbol{z}'_{it} = [\boldsymbol{x}'_{1it}\ \boldsymbol{x}'_{2it}]$ where $\boldsymbol{x}_1$ serves as the ideal instrument for itself and $\boldsymbol{x}_2$ is the instrument for $\boldsymbol{y}_2$.

If there are more instruments available than regressors (overidentified model), the most efficient estimator is the two-stage least-squares estimator (2SLS).[147] The term 2SLS arises because the estimator can be computed in two steps: First, the first-stage regression given in Equation 7 is estimated by OLS, and second, the structural regression given in Equation 6 is estimated by OLS with endogenous regressors replaced by predictions from the first step.

Finally, the question arises of how to identify suitable instruments. Reiss and Wolak (2007) discuss the difficulty of finding an instrumental variable and cynically suggest that the best instrumental variable could be constructed by simply adding a computer-generated independent identically distributed random error to the explanatory variable. The new variable would then satisfy the criteria to be a valid instrument because it is uncorrelated with the error term and yet correlated with the original variable (by construction). Maddala (1977, p. 154) also points to the challenge of finding and justifying appropriate instruments and asks "Where do you get such a variable?".

Larcker and Rusticus (2010), among others, proposes to find instruments outside the model in order to solve the identification problem. Accordingly, the ideal instrument is the result of a "natural experiment" in which an event changes the endogenous variable but leaves the other aspects of the economic system unaffected. In the accounting and corporate finance literature,

---

[147] The econometric literature proposes several types of instrumental variables methods with the most commonly used being 2SLS (two-stage least squares), LIML (limited information maximum likelihood), JIVE (Jackknife IV), 3SLS (three-stage least squares), and GMM (generalized method of moments).

changes in regulation are occasionally used as a quasi experimental treatment. However, one concern about such studies is that it is difficult to disentangle the effect of the specific legislation from all other developments occurring around the same time. Further, if the legislation allows exemptions for certain firms, the causal inferences might even be strengthened. It is therefore generally difficult to identify outside instruments that are uncorrelated with the error term and, at the same time, contain sufficient information on the independent variables that need to be instrumented. This applies especially to the ownership-performance relation where the basic problem is that for many variables that plausibly determine the optimal level of ownership, it is also possible to argue that the same variables might plausibly affect corporate performance.

Nevertheless, previous research on the ownership-performance relation suggests that firm size and risk might be used as instruments.[148] It is possible to construct arguments under which either size or risk could be correlated with firm performance, though. For example, if high values of Tobin's Q are assumed to reflect future growth opportunities, such firms might generally be smaller (or larger) and might also have more volatile stock prices due to the greater uncertainty about future growth prospects. However, Himmelberg et al. (1999) counter that these arguments seem weaker than the arguments against other potential instruments. They further claim that it is generally argued in studies of fixed investment that deviations of Tobin's Q from its equilibrium value are explained by the costs of adjusting the capital stock and that these adjustment costs are proportional to the investment rate. Therefore, the inclusion of R&D intensity and the investment rate (as well as the advertising intensity) should control for future growth opportunities. This argument eliminates the a priori case for including the size and volatility variables in the performance equation and thus provides an

[148] Richter and Weiss (2013) analyze determinants of ownership concentration and provide empirical support for the relative importance of country-level factors. Applying hierarchical linear models to a sample of 900 firms in nine countries, they find that firm-level factors account for a large part (about 74%) of the total variance in ownership concentration, but only 6% of the firm-level variance can be attributed to commonly emphasized firm characteristics such as firm size and firm-specific risk. The explanatory power of industry-level factors is also quite low as they can explain only 2% of the variance in ownership concentration. In contrast, the relative importance of country-level factors such as legal origin and shareholder protection is the highest as they account for 24% of the total variance in ownership concentration (accordingly, ownership concentration is found to be intermediate in civil law countries (especially in Germany) and the lowest in countries with a common law tradition, and shareholder protection has a similar (although weaker and negative) effect on ownership concentration).

argument for omitting these variables from the performance equation and using them as instruments for ownership instead (validity condition).

Following Himmelberg et al. (1999)'s argumentation, firm size is included as one instrument for ownership in the following empirical analysis. Size is likely to be relevant because it is expected to be negatively correlated with ownership (relevance condition).[149] The larger the firm the greater the value of a given fraction of ownership and therefore the greater the costs, all else equal, of a controlling holding. Personal wealth constraints may then prevent owners from increasing their share of equity ownership commensurate with the increase in firm size (Demsetz & Lehn, 1985).[150] Moreover, acquiring a significant share in a large firm likely leads to suboptimal portfolio diversification. Investors may then incur the resulting costs either in form of decreased portfolio performance or in form of transaction costs associated with redressing optimal performance.

As another instrument for ownership, risk is included in the analysis. An obvious effect of risk on ownership concentration is the increase of the nondiversification cost of large shares (relevance condition). According to Demsetz and Lehn (1985)'s argumentation, an attempt to preserve concentrated ownership in the light of the firm's larger capital resource needs requires a small group of owners to commit more wealth to a single company. Risk aversion, however, implies that they will purchase additional shares only at a lower, risk-compensating price. This increased cost of capital discourages owners of large firms from attempting to maintain highly concentrated ownership. Consequently, a negative relation is implied for risk and ownership concentration. At the same time, it can also be argued that uncertainty has an increasing effect on ownership concentration (Demsetz & Lehn, 1985). One of the main advantages of a higher ownership concentration is the greater incentive for large blockholders to monitor. High uncertainty, and hence high risk, leads to more volatile businesses, and the more volatile a business is due to frequent decisions and unforeseen developments, the greater the need to monitor managerial performance. This effect favors a higher ownership concentration for firms with a relatively high risk due to the increase in monitoring incentives. According to Demsetz and Lehn (1985), the positive effect of risk on monitoring incentives is

[149] The negative relation is empirically supported, for example, by Demsetz and Lehn (1985) and Pedersen and Thomsen (1999).

[150] Although investors may use debt to acquire a given share of equity, this involves transaction costs and interest payments.

particularly prevalent at low risk levels but decreases with increasing risk. In contrast, the negative effect of risk on portfolio diversification is relatively small at low levels of ownership concentration but gains relevance with increasing risk. Consequently, at low risk levels, the monitoring incentives outweigh diversification considerations, whereas at high risk levels, the opposite effect holds. Taking the two opposing effects into account, Demsetz and Lehn (1985) hence argue that uncertainty or risk has an inverse *U-shaped* effect on ownership concentration.[151] The squared risk is therefore also added to the set of instrumental variables.

Having reasoned that size and risk are both valid and relevant instruments, diagnostics for weak instruments are performed on the candidates.[152] Size is expressed as annual sales and total assets.[153] Risk is measured as beta, which reflects the covariance of a firm's stock price with the national market portfolio.[154] This sensitivity is calculated by the slope of a regression of the weekly or monthly stock market prices on the DAX over a 1-, 3- or 5-year period.

Table 5.13 shows the correlation between the endogenous variable ownership concentration and instrument candidates. Accordingly, the correlation between annual sales (*REV*) and total assets (*TA*) with ownership concentration ranges from -0.106 to -0.150 (with all correlations being significant at the 0.01 level), depending on the measure of ownership concentration. As the two measures annual sales and total assets correlate about equally high with ownership concentration, and total assets is the common choice in literature, the latter is used in the empirical analysis as instrument. In regard to risk, the correlation between the various risk measures and ownership concentration ranges from -0.197 to -0.403 (with all correlations being significant at the 0.01 level), depending on the measure of ownership concentration. As

[151] The bell-shaped relation is empirically supported, for example, by Demsetz and Lehn (1985) and Richter and Weiss (2013).

[152] Leech and Leahy (1991), for example, argue for firm age as another instrument because the passage of time might reduce ownership concentration as large shareholdings by founders and their families become fragmented (e.g., through the need to attract new shareholders in order increase the capital basis), leading to an eventual loss of control. Therefore, a negative effect of age on ownership concentration can be expected. However, they are not able to provide empirical support for their argument. The empirical analysis in the course of this dissertation also finds no indication for age being a strong instrument due to a very low correlation with the endogenous regressor.

[153] Alternatively, size can be measured as market value of the firm's equity (see, for example, Demsetz & Lehn, 1985 and Richter & Weiss, 2013).

[154] Alternatively, financial risk can be measured by the standard deviation of the rate of return (see, for example, Demsetz & Lehn, 1985 and Leech & Leahy, 1991). However, the standard deviation of the rate of return reflects total risk (including idiosyncratic, diversifiable risk), whereas beta measures systematic, nondiversifiable risk. Only the latter is relevant for (portfolio) investors.

RISK2, the weekly beta on a 3-year basis, provides the highest correlation with ownership concentration, it is the preferred risk measure.

The instruments do not show a particularly high correlation with the endogenous regressor, which might lead to efficiency loss using instrumental variables compared with OLS (due to the inability of the instruments to properly explain the variation in the instrumented variable). But the correlations are not so low as to immediately flag a problem of weak instruments.

Table 5.13: Correlation Matrix of External Candidates for Instruments

		(1)	(2)	(3)	(4)	(5)	(6)	(7)
(1)	OWN1	1.000						
(2)	OWN123	**0.907*****	1.000					
(3)	HHI	**0.966*****	**0.873*****	1.000				
(4)	REV	-0.121***	-0.150***	-0.106***	1.000			
(5)	TA	-0.122***	-0.144***	-0.108***	**0.940*****	1.000		
(6)	RISK1	-0.294***	-0.340***	-0.301***	0.208***	0.181***	1.000	
(7)	RISK2	-0.346***	-0.403***	-0.349***	0.236***	0.212***	**0.751*****	1.000
(8)	RISK3	-0.197***	-0.209***	-0.198***	0.055**	0.042*	0.435***	0.331***
(9)	RISK4	-0.261***	-0.281***	-0.263***	0.057***	0.046**	0.380***	**0.503*****
(10)	RISK5	-0.244***	-0.288***	-0.241***	0.030	0.024	0.315***	0.415***

(continued)

Table 5.13: Correlation Matrix of External Candidates for Instruments (continued)

		(8)	(9)	(10)
(8)	RISK3	1.000		
(9)	RISK4	**0.594*****	1.000	
(10)	RISK5	0.430***	**0.672*****	1.000

Note. Shaded cells visualize the relevant parts of the matrix. Values over 0.5 are shown in bold. Asterisks denote statistical significance of the reported variables at the 0.01 (***), 0.05 (**) and 0.1 (*) level. *REV* refers to annual sales (revenues), and *TA* refers to total assets. *RISK1* and *RISK2* are the weekly beta on a 1- and 3-year basis, respectively, and *RISK3*, *RISK4* and *RISK5* reflect the monthly beta on a 1-, 3- and 5-year basis, respectively. The definition of the remaining variables can be found in Table 5.5.

The estimation then consists of two regressions. The first-stage regression determines the level of ownership concentration and looks as follows:

$$Ownership\ concentration = g\begin{Bmatrix} firm\ performance, firm\ size, \\ firm\ risk, firm\ risk^2 \end{Bmatrix} \quad (9)$$

The model relies on the previous discussion on instruments available for ownership concentration and has in similar versions also been used by Leech and Leahy (1991), Mínguez-Vera and Martín-Ugedo (2007) and Weiss and Hilger (2012). The model also includes firm performance as it can be argued that firm performance is likely to influence ownership structure as ownership is to influence performance. This relation is the reason that renders OLS estimations useless for determining the effect of ownership concentration on performance.

Having determined the ownership concentration with the help of the first-stage regression, the second-stage regression includes the ownership measure as well as various control variables and uses firm performance as the dependent variable. The equation relies on an adapted version of a model initially developed by Demsetz & Villalonga (2001) and has in similar versions also been used by Seifert et al. (2005) and Weiss and Hilger (2012). Estimating the second-stage regression will give information on the relevance of ownership concentration on firm performance. The second-stage regression looks as follows:

$$Performance = f\begin{Bmatrix} ownership\ concentration, \\ debt, capex, rdex, grow \end{Bmatrix} \quad (10)$$

The final, combined model is in the form of:

$$Performance = f\begin{Bmatrix} g\begin{pmatrix} performance, firm\ size, \\ firm\ risk, firm\ risk^2 \end{pmatrix}, \\ debt, capex, rdex, grow \end{Bmatrix} \quad (11)$$

5.4.3.2 Within-2SLS Estimation

The within-estimator removes unobserved heterogeneity through the transformation of equations but does not address potential endogeneity as a result of regressors being determined simultaneously with the dependent variable, and the instrumental variables method tackles reverse causality but does not approach unobserved heterogeneity. A solution to this dilemma is provided by the panel 2SLS estimation.[155]

The panel 2SLS estimation is again based on the individual-effects model, which has two errors components, α_i and ε_{it}:

$$y_{it} = \alpha_i + \boldsymbol{x}'_{it}\boldsymbol{\beta} + \varepsilon_{it} \tag{2}$$

The within-estimator provides consistent estimates of the coefficients of the time-varying regressors under a limited form of endogeneity of the regressors as $\boldsymbol{x}_{it}$ may be correlated with the fixed effects α_i but not with ε_{it} (see Section 5.4.2.2). The panel 2SLS estimation now considers a richer type of endogeneity, with $\boldsymbol{x}_{it}$ being correlated with ε_{it}. Then the within-estimator becomes inconsistent, and instruments $\boldsymbol{z}_{it}$ are required that are correlated with $\boldsymbol{x}_{it}$ but are uncorrelated with ε_{it}, that is, $E(\varepsilon_{it}|\alpha_i, \boldsymbol{z}_{i1}, \dots, \boldsymbol{z}_{it}, \dots, \boldsymbol{z}_{iT}) = 0$ so that instruments and errors are uncorrelated in all periods.

The panel 2SLS procedure is first to suitably transform the individual-effects model to control for α_i and, second, to apply 2SLS to the transformed model. The procedure is basically the application of 2SLS to the within-estimation: The within-2SLS estimator performs a within-2SLS regression of $y_{it} - \bar{y}_i$ on an intercept and $\boldsymbol{x}_{it} - \bar{\boldsymbol{x}}_i$ with the instruments $\boldsymbol{z}_{it} - \bar{\boldsymbol{z}}_i$.

The instrument identification strategy is the same as used with pooled data (see Section 5.4.3.1): Exogenous regressors are instrumented by themselves, whereas for endogenous variables, additional variables are obtained that do not directly determine y_{it} but are correlated with the variable being instrumented.

Common postestimation test procedures are the Hansen's J-statistic of overidentifying restrictions to examine the validity of the instruments, the test of under- and weak identification to prove the relevance of the instruments, and finally the test for regressor endogeneity. The procedures are discussed in detail in Section 6.1.2.1.

5.4.4 Summary

To summarize, the panel methods mainly differ in their treatment of unobserved heterogeneity, simultaneous causality and their capability of capturing the panel aspect of the

155 This section draws from Baltagi (2005), Cameron and Trivedi (2010), and Semykina and Wooldridge (2010).

data structure (see Table 5.14): The pooled OLS estimator assumes that all explanatory variables are uncorrelated with unobserved heterogeneity and are also strictly exogenous. The within-estimator tackles the problem of unobserved heterogeneity as it allows for correlation between the explanatory variables and the fixed effects. However, within-estimation does not address potential endogeneity as a result of regressors being determined simultaneously with the dependent variable.

A solution to this problem is to use instrumental variable techniques. The pooled 2SLS tackles simultaneous causality but does not remove unobserved heterogeneity. The within-2SLS allows ownership to be correlated with the idiosyncratic errors and, at the same time, addresses simultaneity through the use of instruments.

Both, the within-estimator and the within-2SLS estimator take the longitudinal structure of the panel data into account and hence are able to capture dynamic effects that are not visible in cross-sections. For this reason, the within-estimator and the within-2SLS appear to be superior to the pooled estimators. The following empirical analyses therefore focuse on results from these two estimation methods and refer to pooled models only when necessary (results are displayed in Appendix A.2-A.4, though).

Table 5.14: Comparison of Panel Methods

Estimation method	Issues in panel data analysis addressed by various estimation methods		
	Longitudinal data structure	Unobserved heterogeneity	Simultaneous causality
Pooled OLS	✗	✗	✗
Within	✓	✓	✗
Pooled 2SLS	✗	✗	✓
Within-2SLS	✓	✓	✓

Note. Shaded rows visualize the preferred estimation methods.

6 Empirical Analyses

The following chapter empirically addresses the research question of whether and how ownership structure affects performance.[156] Two aspects of ownership are examined: First, Section 6.1 deals with the effect of ownership concentration. Second, Section 6.2 examines the impact of owner identity. Finally, Section 6.3 conflates the two effects to a combined model in order to capture the effect of ownership concentration as a function of the identity of owners. The analyses include an adequate testing of the hypotheses developed in Chapter 3 and take reference to major findings and approaches reviewed in Chapter 4. Special attention is being paid to the differences of various econometric approaches, as discussed in Chapter 5, and their consequences for the empirical results and the interpretation of findings. Section 6.4 closes the chapter with a summary and discussion of results.

6.1 Ownership Concentration Effects

In the following section, the performance effect of ownership concentration, that is, the existence and strength of controlling shareholders, is assessed. The analyses consist of a base case as well as econometric variations of this.

6.1.1 Base Case

The base case analyzes linear effects of ownership concentration on performance, assuming a model with fixed effects.

6.1.1.1 Linear Within-Regression Results

Table 6.1 presents the within-regression results for ownership concentration models, using cluster-robust standard errors. Models 1.1-1.6 use Tobin's Q as the dependent variable and apply six alternative measures of ownership concentration. The results find the coefficient of the control rights held by the largest owner to be 0.396 (Model 1.1).[157] This indicates that, for a

[156] The analyses are performed using the statistical software package Stata version 12.1.

[157] When a logistic transformation of the *OWN1* variable is used (see Footnote 109), the coefficient is positive as well (0.135, significant at the 0.05 level). As results are very close to those of the untransformed variable but interpretation is not as straightforward, the raw data is preferred for further analyses (see also Chaganti & Damanpour, 1991; Mínguez-Vera & Martín-Ugedo, 2007).

given firm, an increase of the control rights held by the largest shareholder by 100 basis points results, on average, in an increase of firm performance measured by Tobin's Q by 0.396 basis points.[158] Figure 6.1 illustrates the relation graphically. The coefficients for the shareholdings by the two largest and the three largest shareholders are also significant, positive. The size of the coefficients is in descending order, which supports the assumption that the largest shareholder has the greatest influence on performance (which is also reflected in the fact that the average size of the largest shareholder is by far larger than the shareholding of the second largest shareholder in the sample). The ratio of the control rights held by the largest shareholder and the second largest shareholder also has a significant, positive coefficient, which is however diminutive in size. Both the fraction of shares held in blocks and the Herfindahl-Hirschman-Index have a positive coefficient, but only the latter is also significant.

Among the control variables, only growth has a significant, positive, albeit very small effect on performance. The small size of the coefficient is not surprising because the market value already reflects growth prospects and hence does not respond much if anticipated growth is realized (see Section 5.2.2.3).

In regard to the explanatory power of the models, R-squared for the within-variation averages at around 16% (15.8% in the controls-only model), where the R-squared based on the within-estimation can be interpreted as the amount of time variation in the y_{it} that is explained by the time variation in the explanatory variables. In other words, the R-squared (within) describes the goodness of fit for the observations that have been adjusted for their individual means. The R-squared (between) describes the goodness of fit for the N different individual means. The low value of around 3% is unsatisfactory but not surprising because R-squared (between) is not optimized by the within-estimator (for a between regression, this R-squared attains a maximum). Finally, the R-squared (overall) of about 6% corresponds to the usual R-squared of an OLS regression. Thus, the within-estimator is fitted to a pooled regression. As the R-squared (overall) is not very close to the R-squared (within), it can be assumed that individual heterogeneity is high, which indicates that a pooled regression might not be applicable, and hence the within-regression is preferred (for the sake of completeness, the results of a pooled OLS regression are displayed in Appendix A.2, though).

[158] The alternatively applicable first difference estimator confirms the results from the fixed-effects estimations and finds that an increase in the control rights held by the largest shareholder by 100 basis points from one year to the next leads to an average performance increase by 0.431 basis points (results not displayed).

Sigma u (α), the standard deviation of the individual effect α_i, is about 0.9; Sigma e, the standard deviation of the idiosyncratic error ε_{it}, is about 0.5, depending on the model.[159] As sigma u is roughly twice the value of sigma e, the individual-specific component of the error appears to be much more important than the idiosyncratic error. Rho represents the interclass correlation of the error, or, in other words, rho is the fraction of the variance in the error due to the individual-specific effects. For the within-models, the rho estimates of around 0.8 are quite high.

Figure 6.1: Linear Within-Regression Result for Ownership Concentration Model 1.1 – Graphic Presentation of Results

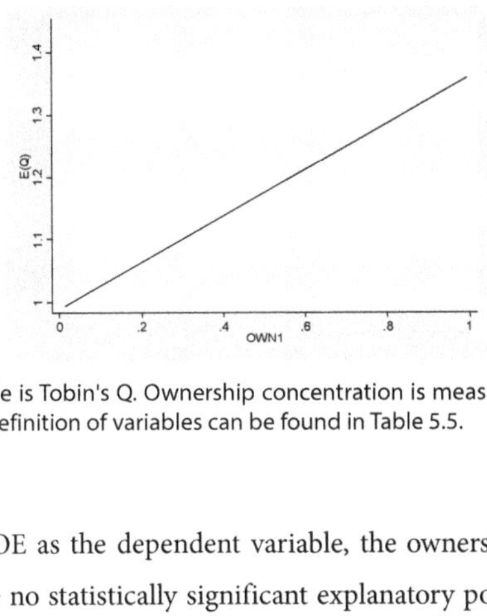

Note. The dependent variable is Tobin's Q. Ownership concentration is measured as the control rights of the largest owner (*OWN1*). The definition of variables can be found in Table 5.5.

When using ROA or ROE as the dependent variable, the ownership concentration variables increase in size but have no statistically significant explanatory power (results not displayed). The insignificance of effects might be explained by the circumstance that the regression models analyze the effect of current ownership on current performance. In contrast to capital market performance measures such as Tobin's Q, which respond promptly to relevant changes in ownership structure, accounting performance adopts slowly. Effects are hence expected only in future periods. Among the control variables, sales growth again has a significant, positive effect on firm performance. High levels of debt turn out to have a significant, negative impact, which seems to support the theoretically argued underinvestment in projects with a positive net present value resulting from fixed interest payment obligations. R&D expenditures, as

[159] The combined error in the individual-effects model $\alpha_i + \varepsilon_{it}$ is referred to as $u_i + e_{it}$ in Stata.

expected, have a significant, strongly negative coefficient. The R-squared (within) decreases to around 13% (ROA) and 12% (ROE), respectively.

It is worth mentioning that it is not possible to consider industry dummies in a fixed-effects model directly because these variables lack time series variation and thus are perfectly correlated with the firm-fixed effects, which are being removed from the transformed equation when applying a mean-difference transformation (see Section 5.4.2.2). Demeaning the firm performance variable with respect to the industry or the general market (i.e., industry- or market-adjusting), although widely used in empirical finance research, is not applicable for panel data because this approach may lead to severe biases as empirically demonstrated by Gormley and Matsa (2014a). This is because any estimation that transforms the dependent variable but not the independent variables will yield inconsistent estimates by failing to account for correlations across independent variables within these groups. In practice, such within-group correlations are commonplace. This can be illustrated using the example of a firm-level capital structure estimation where leverage is regressed against ROA, bankruptcy risk and MTB: Because firms in the same industry are subject to common demand and technology shocks, their ROA and bankruptcy risk exhibit positive within-industry correlation. Within-industry correlation in leverage, the dependent variable, results as well. However, by industry-adjusting only leverage but not the regressors, the industry-adjusting approach to remove the underlying industry-level heterogeneity is inconsistent. As a consequence, the estimation then suffers from an omitted-variable problem. In contrast, within-estimators are consistent because they are equivalent to demeaning both the dependent and independent variables so as to remove the unobserved heterogeneity. Rather than industry-adjusting a dependent variable, Gormley and Matsa (2014a) therefore suggest to estimate a model with industry-fixed effects. Following this argumentation as well as the work by Gugler and Weigand (2003) who present results for both firm-fixed- and industry-fixed-effects specifications, alternative models with industry-fixed effects (instead of firm-fixed effects) are computed (results not displayed), but the fundamental regression findings do not change:[160] For example, the coefficient of the control rights held by the largest owner is 0.457 (significant at the 0.05 level).

---

[160] Combining both firm- and industry-fixed effects is hardly practical due to high computational capacity requirements (see also Gormley & Matsa, 2014b).

Table 6.1: Within-Regression Results for Ownership Concentration Models

Dependent variable: Q	Controls only	Model 1.1	Model 1.2	Model 1.3	Model 1.4	Model 1.5	Model 1.6
OWN1		0.396*** (0.150)					
OWN12			0.377** (0.173)				
OWN123				0.310* (0.187)			
OWN1/OWN2					0.002** (0.001)		
BLOCK						0.232 (0.178)	
HHI							0.421*** (0.136)
DEBT	0.331 (0.325)	0.375 (0.329)	0.361 (0.335)	0.346 (0.338)	0.347 (0.324)	0.344 (0.355)	0.367 (0.330)
CAPX	0.739 (0.629)	0.782 (0.627)	0.750 (0.620)	0.746 (0.621)	0.848 (0.633)	0.759 (0.623)	0.774 (0.625)
RDX	0.923 (0.853)	0.805 (0.855)	0.800 (0.856)	0.831 (0.857)	0.898 (0.853)	0.849 (0.858)	0.849 (0.854)
GRO	0.002* (0.001)	0.002* (0.001)	0.002* (0.001)	0.002* (0.001)	0.002* (0.001)	0.002* (0.001)	0.002* (0.001)
Constant	1.129*** (0.075)	0.981*** (0.095)	0.958*** (0.113)	0.979*** (0.080)	1.074*** (0.080)	1.013*** (0.123)	1.032*** (0.082)
R^2-within	0.158	0.165	0.165	0.162	0.163	0.161	0.166
R^2-between	0.043	0.034	0.032	0.035	0.045	0.037	0.041
R^2-overall	0.064	0.059	0.058	0.060	0.067	0.062	0.065
Sigma u (α)	0.888	0.888	0.889	0.888	0.885	0.888	0.885
Sigma e	0.452	0.450	0.451	0.451	0.451	0.452	0.450
Rho	0.794	0.795	0.796	0.795	0.794	0.794	0.794

Note. The analysis is based on 1,560 firm-year observations (452 firms). Asterisks denote statistical significance of the reported variables at the 0.01 (***), 0.05 (**) and 0.1 (*) level. Cluster-robust standard errors are in parentheses. All estimations include time dummies (estimated coefficients are not reported). The definition of variables can be found in Table 5.5.

In order to compare these results to alternative model specifications, random-effects estimations are also performed – although it has been theoretically argued that fixed-effects models are preferred over random-effects models for analyzing panel data with a longitudinal research question and time-variant variables, as it is the case for this empirical work (see Section 5.4.2.3). The random-effects estimations confirm the results from the fixed-effects models and find a statistically significant coefficient of 0.396 basis points for the control rights held by the largest shareholder.[161] Results are presented in Appendix A.3. In order to provide supporting evidence of the appropriateness of the fixed-effects model as preferred estimation, several specification tests are applied. The results are presented in Table 6.2.

First, the F-test for poolability developed by Chow (1960) tests for the presence of individual effects and can be used to choose between the pooled model and the fixed-effects model. The null hypothesis is that there are no individual effects, that is $\alpha_i = 0$. In this case, no panel models need to be specified as all individuals are sufficiently homogenous, and therefore the same coefficients apply across all individuals. If the null hypothesis is rejected, the fixed-effects model is preferred. Otherwise the pooled model is appropriate. As a test result, a p-value of 0.000 is obtained, which leads to a strong rejection of the null hypothesis, and hence the fixed-effects model is preferred over the pooled OLS model. The F-test thereby confirms the theoretically reasoned preference.

Second, the Lagrange Multiplier (LM) test developed by Breusch and Pagan (1980) tests for the presence of random effects and can be used to choose between the pooled model and the random-effects model. The null hypothesis is that individual-specific error variance components are zero, that is, $\sigma_u^2 = 0$ or equivalently $Cor(\varepsilon_{it}, \varepsilon_{is}) = 0$ for $t \neq s$. In this case, no significant difference across individuals would exist (i.e., no panel effect). If the null hypothesis is rejected, the random-effects model is preferred. Otherwise, the pooled model is appropriate. As a test result, a p-value of 0.000 is obtained, which leads to a strong rejection of the null hypothesis, and therefore the random-effects model is preferred over the pooled OLS model. Hence, both the F-test and the LM test reject the pooled OLS model. Instead, individual-effects models such as the fixed- and random-effects model are preferred.

---

161 The alternatively applicable between-estimator confirms the results from the random-effects estimations and finds that the average performance is 0.486 basis points higher for firms where the control rights of the largest shareholder are, on average, 100 basis points higher.

Third, as the key consideration in choosing between a random- and a fixed-effects approach is whether α_i and $\boldsymbol{x}'_{it}$ are correlated, Hausman (1978) proposed a test for fixed effects based on the difference between the estimable coefficients of time-varying regressors in a random- and a fixed-effects model.[162] Under the null hypothesis that individual effects are random, both estimators should be similar because both are consistent. Accordingly, as the fixed-effects approach is consistent when α_i and $\boldsymbol{x}'_{it}$ are correlated but the random-effects approach is inconsistent, a statistically significant difference is interpreted as evidence against the null hypothesis. The test of fixed effects (0.396) against random effects (0.365) yields $t = 0.031 \ / \ 0.081 = 0.382$ for the coefficient of the control rights held by the largest shareholder.[163] The difference is comparably higher for the control variables, and the overall statistic therefore has a p-value of 0.000. This leads to a strong rejection of the null hypothesis, and hence the fixed-effects model is preferred over the random-effects model. In a fixed-effects model, the random-effects estimator cannot be used because only the within-estimator is consistent. As a consequence, the within-estimator is preferred for the analyses.

[162] The standard approach of using cluster-robust standard errors implicitly presumes that estimators are not efficient. Then the Hausman test is incorrect. The statistical significance is therefore tested in the appropriate auxiliary regression by using standard errors (if, however, cluster-robust standard errors for the random effects differ substantially from default standard errors, α_i and ε_{it} are not i.i.d., and hence the random-effects estimator is not efficient. In this case, a robust version of the Hausman test would be needed). When running the Hausman test, it is specified that both covariance matrices are based on the (same) estimated disturbance variance from the efficient estimator. Lastly, the Hausman test is based only on time-varying regressors (and hence industry effects are excluded from the equations).

[163] The coefficient from the random-effects estimation used as input for the Hausman test differs slightly from the one previously reported in the results section (0.365 vs. 0.396). This is because the Hausman test requires the absence of time-invariant variables, such as the SIC. In contrast, this requirement does not affect the coefficient derived from the fixed-effects estimation as this method cancels out time-invariant variables anyway.

Table 6.2: Results from Model Specification Tests (OLS vs. FE vs. RE) – Ownership Concentration

Models	Specification test	Test statistic	Interpretation
OLS vs. FE	F-Test $H_0: \alpha_i = 0$	F(9, 451) = 28.990 Prob > F = 0.000	⇒ H_0 is rejected: FE preferred over OLS
OLS vs. RE	LM test $H_0: \sigma_u^2 = 0$	Chibar2(1) = 820.920 Prob > chibar2 = 0.000	⇒ H_0 is rejected: RE preferred over OLS
FE vs. RE	Hausman test H_0: Difference in coefficients is not systematic.	Chi2(9) = 45.390 Prob > chi2 = 0.000	⇒ H_0 is rejected: FE preferred over RE

Note. Tests are based on models using Tobin's Q as dependent variable and the control rights held by the largest shareholder (*OWN1*) as ownership concentration variable. Results are robust to the use of alternative measures of performance and ownership concentration.

6.1.1.2 Summary

To summarize, the results from linear within-regressions (the base case) provide evidence of a positive relation between ownership concentration and firm valuation, taking into account the panel structure of the data set and eliminating any fixed effects: According to the within-estimator, an increase of control rights held by the largest shareholder by 100 basis points results, on average, in an increase of firm performance measured by Tobin's Q by 0.396 basis points. The effect shape is robust to the use of alternative ownership concentration measures. The use of ROA or ROE as alternative dependent variables produces comparable results but these lack statistical significance, which might, however, be explained by the slow adoption of accounting performance to changes in ownership concentration. Finally, model specification tests corroborate the presence of individual effects and consequently confirm the preference of panel methods over a pooled OLS estimation. Further, it is both theoretically argued and econometrically proven that these firm-specific effects do indeed correlate with the variables in the model, which eventually justifies the appropriateness of the within-estimator.

6.1.2 Variations of the Base Case

After having examined the (linear) relation between ownership concentration and performance based on a model with fixed effects, the possibility of alternative specifications is now investigated.

6.1.2.1 Instrumental Variable Regression Results

So far, the analysis avoided to address the problem of reverse causality. A commonly proposed solution to the problem of simultaneous causality is to find instrumental variables for endogenous independent variables. An instrumental variable estimation is then applied to a model with fixed effects.

Table 6.3 presents the within-2SLS regression results for ownership concentration models, using cluster-robust standard errors.[164] Models 4.1-4.3 use Tobin's Q as a measure of performance and apply three alternative measures of ownership concentration. Accounting performance (measured as ROA), firm size (measured as total assets), firm risk (measured as the weekly beta on a 3-year basis) and its squared measure are employed as instruments (see Section 5.4.3 for an in-depth discussion of the instrument identification strategy). Results of the first-stage regressions to determine ownership concentration show that the coefficients of the instruments carry the expected signs (with risk being significant at the 0.01 level). Then, the second-stage regression is performed to determine firm performance. Compared with the within-estimations, the coefficients of the ownership concentration measures are smaller. For example, the control rights held by the largest owner have an estimated beta coefficient of 0.141, whereas this is 0.396 in the within-regression. More important, however, only the Herfindahl-Hirschman-Index is significant at the 0.01 level, whereas the control rights held by the largest and the three largest owner(s) do not carry a significant coefficient. Hence, the estimations do not definitely provide evidence of an effect of ownership on performance.

Among the control variables, only growth carries a significant, positive coefficient. In regard to the fit of the models, the alternative specifications do not differ as all three have an equally high root mean square error of about 0.449.[165]

When using ROA or ROE as the dependent variable, ownership concentration has still no explanatory power (results not displayed).[166] The absence of effects might, again, be explained

---

[164] The panel 2SLS estimators are obtained by using the Stata module *xtivreg2* written by Schaffer (2005).

[165] The R-squared has no statistical meaning in the context of panel 2SLS regressions (Sribney, Wiggins, & Drukker, 1999). Some authors report the root mean square error (root MSE) instead. The root MSE is the square root of the variance of the residuals and can be interpreted as the standard deviation of the unexplained variance. It indicates the absolute fit of the model to the data (with lower values of the root MSE implying a better fit).

by the circumstance that the regression models analyze the effect of current ownership on current performance. Among the control variables, sales growth, again, has a significant, positive effect on firm performance. High levels of debt turn out to have a significant, negative impact, which seems to provide evidence of the theoretically argued underinvestment in projects with a positive net present value resulting from fixed interest payment obligations. R&D expenditures, as expected, have a significant, strongly negative coefficient.

[166] In the models with ROA or ROE as the dependent variable in the second-stage regression, Tobin's Q (instead of ROA) is included in the instrument set in the first-stage regression.

Table 6.3: Within-2SLS Regression Results for Ownership Concentration Models

	Model 4.1		Model 4.2		Model 4.3	
	First stage	Second stage	First stage	Second stage	First stage	Second stage
Dependent variable:	OWN1	Q	OWN123	Q	HHI	Q
Exogenous variables:						
DEBT	-0.107**	0.391	-0.057	0.387	-0.083**	0.373
	(0.047)	(0.337)	(0.063)	(0.324)	(0.041)	(0.324)
CAPX	-0.147	0.670	-0.065	0.659	-0.122	0.656
	(0.136)	(0.624)	(0.148)	(0.629)	(0.136)	(0.629)
RDX	0.302*	0.845	0.283*	0.839	0.183	0.880
	(0.158)	(0.862)	(0.163)	(0.859)	(0.138)	(0.857)
GRO	-0.001	0.002**	-0.001	0.002**	-0.001**	0.002**
	(0.001)	(0.001)	(0.001)	(0.001)	(0.001)	(0.001)
Instruments:						
ROA	0.001		0.001		0.001	
	(0.001)		(0.001)		(0.001)	
TA	-0.001		-0.001		-0.001	
	(0.001)		(0.001)		(0.001)	
RISK2	-0.117***		-0.108***		-0.115**	
	(0.042)		(0.041)		(0.046)	
RISK2 (SQ)	0.034		0.023		0.027	
	(0.026)		(0.030)		(0.028)	
Instrumented variable:						
OWN1		0.141				
		(0.824)				
OWN123				0.189		
				(0.790)		
HHI						0.002***
						(0.823)
Root MSE	0.105	0.449	0.105	0.449	0.101	0.450

Note. The analysis is based on 1,509 firm-year observations (418 firms). Asterisks denote statistical significance of the reported variables at the 0.01 (***), 0.05 (**) and 0.1 (*) level. Cluster-robust standard errors are in parentheses. All estimations include time dummies (estimated coefficients are not reported). The definition of variables can be found in Table 5.5.

To summarize, the within-2SLS analyses do not definitely suggest a significant effect of ownership on performance when accounting for endogeneity. However, the reason might be that the instruments are weak. As a consequence, formal diagnostics on weak instruments need to be performed.

First, a Hansen's J-statistic of overidentifying restrictions is performed. A crucial assumption on the validity of an instrumental variable estimation is that the chosen instruments are valid, that is, that they are uncorrelated with the error term, and that the excluded instruments are correctly excluded from the estimated equation (validity condition). This assumption can be tested using Hansen (1982)'s J-statistic of overidentifying restrictions, which is calculated as $N \times R^2$ from a regression of the instrumental variable equation's residuals on the full set of instruments (both the included exogenous variables and those instruments that do not appear in the equation). The J-statistic is distributed χ^2 with degrees of freedom equal to the degree of overidentification $j - k$ (with j being the number of instruments and k being the number of regressors) under the null hypothesis that all instruments are orthogonal to the error. A high p-value on the Hansen test can be interpreted as a proof of validity of the instrumental variable results. A p-value of less than 0.05, and hence a rejection of the null hypothesis, casts doubt on the validity of the instruments and implies that the instruments do not satisfy the required orthogonality conditions, either because they are not truly exogenous, or because they are being incorrectly excluded from the regression.[167] As a result of the test, the Hansen J-statistic is statistically highly insignificant, which indicates that the instruments are valid. Results are displayed in Table 6.4.

[167] The main problem with Hansen's J-statistic is that it is weakened by the use of a large number of instruments. By definition, if the number of instruments is greater than the number of observations, it will deliver a p-value of 1, which is meaningless. Moreover, Bowsher (2002) argues that even keeping the instrument count below N does not always safeguard the Hansen test and demonstrates that in situations with too many instruments for a given value of N, it is possible to produce inflated J-statistics with implausibly high p-values. Roodman (2009) therefore suggests to view p-values above 0.25 with concern and to limit the number of instruments.

Table 6.4: Test of Overidentifying Restrictions

Test of overidentifying restrictions H_0: Instruments are valid			
Hansen's J-statistic	Chi-sq(3)	= 5.947	
	p-value	= 0.114	⇒ H_0 is accepted: instruments are valid

Note. The test is based on models using Tobin's Q as dependent variable and the control rights held by the largest shareholder (*OWN1*) as ownership concentration variable. Results are robust to the use of alternative measures of performance and ownership concentration.

Second, good instruments should not only be valid but also relevant. A common postestimation test procedure is hence to perform tests of under- and weak identification. Results are displayed in Table 6.5. The first part of the table reports the test statistic for Kleibergen and Paap (2006)'s test of underidentification. The test examines whether the equation is identified, that is, whether the excluded instruments are relevant, meaning correlated with the endogenous regressor. The null hypothesis of the test is that the matrix of reduced form coefficients has a rank of $k - 1$, that is, that the equation is underidentified. The statistic is distributed χ^2 with degrees of freedom $= j - k + 1$. A p-value of less than 0.05 on the Kleibergen test statistic, and hence a rejection of the null hypothesis, can be interpreted as a proof for the equation being properly identified. As a result of the test, a p-value of 0.004 is obtained, which indicates that the null can be rejected, proving that the model is identified. In other words, the instruments do provide enough information to properly identify the model. However, this result should be treated with caution because weak-instruments problems – that is, instruments being correlated with the endogenous regressor but only weakly – may still be present. Much attention in the econometric literature has been devoted to this topic. What is surprising is that, as Bound, Jaeger, and Baker (1995) have shown, the weak-instruments problem can arise even when correlations between the regressor and the instruments are highly significant. Hence, rejecting the null of underidentification based on the test of overidentifying restrictions and conventional significance levels is not sufficient.

Much attention in the econometrics literature has been devoted to the problem of weak instruments. When searching for plausible instruments for a potentially endogenous regressor, it is, due to the difficulty to identify good instruments, common to find that the candidates are only weakly correlated with the endogenous variable in question. However, using such variables as instruments is likely to produce estimates with standard errors that are larger than those on OLS estimates. Furthermore, if the potential instruments are only weakly correlated with an endogenous explanatory variable, then even a weak correlation between the instruments and the error in the original equation will lead to a larger inconsistency in the instrumental variable estimate of β than in the OLS estimate. Another issue is that the 2SLS produces large estimation biases – albeit in the same direction as OLS estimates (which are biased due to endogeneity). Bound et al. (1995) point to the consequences of the weak-instruments problem for empirical work and conclude that using instruments, which jointly explain little of the variation in the endogenous variable, can do more harm than good: "The cure can be worse than the disease." (Bound, Jaeger, & Baker, 1993, p. 1).

The second part of the table therefore implements the two formal tests for weak instruments proposed by Stock and Yogo (2005). Both test are built on Cragg and Donald (1993)'s F-statistic for joint significance in the first-stage regression but use different critical values based on different criteria. The first test addresses the concern that the estimation bias of the 2SLS estimator resulting from the use of weak instruments can be large, sometimes even exceeding the bias of OLS. To apply the test, the largest acceptable bias of the 2SLS estimator relative to OLS is chosen. Stock and Yogo (2005) compiled critical values that vary with the chosen relative bias toleration (as well as with the number of endogenous regressors and the number of exclusion restrictions). If the F-statistic exceeds the critical value of the test, the null hypothesis of weak instruments is rejected. As a test result, a critical value of 10.270 is obtained for a 10% relative bias tolerance (which is a commonly used threshold). As the F-value of 7.688 does not exceed the critical value of the test, the hypothesis of weak instruments cannot be rejected. This means that the estimator is weakly identified in the sense that it is subject to bias that is unacceptably large. Only if an estimation bias of 20% relative to OLS was accepted, the F-value would exceed the critical value of 6.71, and the hypothesis of a weakly identified equation could be rejected.

The second test for weak instruments addresses the concern that weak instruments can lead to size distortion of Wald tests on the parameters. The Wald test is a statistical significance of the endogenous regressor in the structural equation model [$\boldsymbol{\beta}_1 = 0$ in Equation 6] at a 5% level. Under weak identification, the Wald test rejects too often. The test statistic is based on the rejection rate r (e.g., 10%) that is acceptable if the true rejection rate should be the standard 5%. Weak instruments are defined as instruments that will lead to a rejection rate of r when the true rejection rate is 5%. To apply this test, a tolerance for the size distortion of the Wald test is chosen. The test statistics provide the critical value that varies with the chosen relative bias toleration and with the number of endogenous regressors and the number of exclusion restrictions. If the F-statistic exceeds the critical value of the test, the null hypothesis of weak instruments is rejected.[168] As a result of the test, a critical value of 24.580 is obtained if a distortion of a 5% Wald test based on the 2SLS estimator is tolerated, so that the true size can be at most 10%. As the F-value of 7.688 does not exceed the critical value of the test, the hypothesis of weak instruments cannot be rejected.

To conclude, the chosen instruments appear to be valid but only to some degree relevant. The potential weakness of the instruments does not only make the estimates likely to be imprecise but might also bias the results. Conclusions from the within-2SLS estimator hence have to be drawn with care.

---

[168] Baum, Schaffer, and Stillman (2007) recommend using the Kleibergen-Paap rk Wald statistic, as the robust analog of the Cragg-Donald statistic, to test for weak identification in the presence of clustering. Nonetheless, with a value of 3.764, the conclusions from the test do not change.

Table 6.5: Weak Instruments Diagnostics

Underidentification test H_0: Equation is underidentified			
Kleibergen-Paap statistic	Chi-sq(4)	= 15.484	
	p-value	= 0.004	⇒ H_0 is rejected: Instruments are relevant
Weak identification test H_0: Instruments are weak			
Cragg-Donald F-statistic	= 7.688		
		Stock-Yogo weak identification test critical values for Number of endogenous regressors: 1 Number of excluded instruments: 4	
2SLS relative bias	5 %	16.850	⇒ H_0 is accepted: Instruments are weak (instruments are strong if a 20% relative bias tolerance is accepted)
	10%	10.270	
	20%	6.710	
	30%	5.340	
2SLS size of nominal 5% Wald test	10%	24.580	⇒ H_0 is accepted: Instruments are weak
	15%	13.960	
	20%	10.260	
	30%	8.310	

Note. The test is based on models using Tobin's Q as dependent variable and the control rights held by the largest shareholder (*OWN1*) as ownership concentration variable. Results are robust to the use of alternative measures of performance and ownership concentration.

So far, external constructs (performance, firm size, firm risk and its squared measure) have been used as instruments. An alternative is the use of internal instruments. Examples for internal instruments commonly used in the corporate finance literature are industry averages and lagged endogenous variables.[169] An example for the use of industry averages as instruments is provided by Lev and Sougiannis (1998) who apply the average level of R&D expenditures of the other firms within an industry as an instrument for a given firm's R&D expenditures. The industry R&D level is obviously unaffected by firm idiosyncratic shocks,

[169] An alternative approach – although less frequently used – is the construction of ranked instrumental variables. Accordingly, after the endogenous variables have been ordered by size, the number of rank rather than the actual value is used as instrument. The rank is correlated with the original value but, because it is a rank, should not be correlated with the error term. The approach of using ranked endogenous variables as instruments is criticized, for example, by Larcker and Rusticus (2010) because, by construction, both the exogenous and the endogenous parts determine the rank. Hence the instruments obtained this way will have the same problems as the underlying endogenous variable.

thereby limiting its correlation with the original regression residual, and, at the same time, the correlation between a firm's R&D expenditures (the original variable) and the industry average (the instrument) is generally high. In this case, the industry average appears to be a successful instrument.[170] However, in the case of ownership and performance, this method does not appear reasonable as the correlation between the a firm's ownership structure and the industry average is not consistent across all industries (see Section 5.2.3). As a consequence, the construction of lagged endogenous variables as instruments seems to be a more promising approach in this particular field of research.

The use of ownership variables from a period other than the current period as instruments has the attraction of being highly correlated with the variable being instrumented. Table 6.6 shows the correlation between the endogenous variables and their values lagged by one, two, or three years, respectively. As expected, the instrument candidates show a statistically highly significant and strongly positive correlation with the endogenous variables (which can be explained by the stickiness of ownership concentration over time). The lagged variables are therefore likely to be relevant instruments (relevance condition). Theoretically, the lagged variables might also be valid instruments because they are not contemporaneously correlated with the error term, assuming the error term is not autocorrelated (validity condition).

[170] Larcker and Rusticus (2010) doubt that using industry aggregates as instrumental variable would generally resolve direction of causality or correct for omitted variable. This is because industry aggregates combine both the exogenous and the endogenous parts of the original variable. This approach will only work when the exogenous part of the original variable varies across industry, whereas the endogenous part varies only within industry. However, it appears more likely that both parts of the original variable vary across industry.

Table 6.6: Correlation Matrix of Internal Candidates for Instruments

		(1)	(2)	(3)	(4)	(5)	(6)	(7)
(1)	OWN1	1.000						
(2)	OWN123	**0.907*** **	1.000					
(3)	HHI	**0.966*** **	**0.873*** **	1.000				
(4)	OWN1_l1	**0.882*** **	**0.809*** **	**0.845*** **	1.000			
(5)	OWN1_l2	**0.790*** **	**0.733*** **	**0.747*** **	**0.884*** **	1.000		
(6)	OWN1_l3	**0.693*** **	**0.647*** **	**0.644*** **	**0.793*** **	**0.887*** **	1.000	
(7)	OWN123_l1	**0.805*** **	**0.879*** **	**0.766*** **	**0.904*** **	**0.815*** **	**0.744*** **	1.000
(8)	OWN123_l2	**0.728*** **	**0.792*** **	**0.685*** **	**0.811*** **	**0.903*** **	**0.814*** **	**0.891*** **
(9)	OWN123_l3	**0.642*** **	**0.703*** **	**0.595*** **	**0.741*** **	**0.817*** **	**0.899*** **	**0.809*** **
(10)	HHI_l1	**0.856*** **	**0.779*** **	**0.876*** **	**0.965*** **	**0.846*** **	**0.757*** **	**0.871*** **
(11)	HHI_l2	**0.766*** **	**0.704*** **	**0.773*** **	**0.855*** **	**0.964*** **	**0.853*** **	**0.782*** **
(12)	HHI_l3	**0.671*** **	**0.622*** **	**0.666*** **	**0.769*** **	**0.860*** **	**0.964*** **	**0.714*** **

(continued)

Table 6.6: Correlation Matrix of Internal Candidates for Instruments (continued)

		(8)	(9)	(10)	(11)	(12)
(8)	OWN123_l2	1.000				
(9)	OWN123_l3	**0.907*** **	1.000			
(10)	HHI_l1	**0.966*** **	**0.873*** **	1.000		
(11)	HHI_l2	**0.882*** **	**0.809*** **	**0.845*** **	1.000	
(12)	HHI_l3	**0.790*** **	**0.733*** **	**0.747*** **	**0.884*** **	1.000

Note. Shaded cells visualize the relevant parts of the matrix. Values over 0.5 are shown in bold. Asterisks denote statistical significance of the reported variables at the 0.01 (***), 0.05 (**) and 0.1 (*) level. Annexes *l1*, *l2* and *l3* to the ownership concentration variables refer to the value of the variables lagged by one, two and three years, respectively. The definition of the remaining variables can be found in Table 5.5.

Following the analyses of, for example, Gugler and Weigand (2003), Hermalin and Weisbach (1991), and Maury and Pajuste (2005), the previously presented within-2SLS models are reestimated, using the lagged values of ownership concentration as instruments. In the first step, ownership concentration is lagged by one year and used as instrument in the within-2SLS regression of performance measured as Tobin's Q against ownership concentration measured as the size of control rights held by the largest owner (plus a set of control variables). The first lag is chosen because its correlation with the current value of the variable is the highest compared with more distant lags, and therefore it seems to be the most credible instrument.

Using the second lag in addition is not reasonable because the main effect is already captured in the shorter lag structure.[171] This assumption is confirmed by testing for redundant instruments. An instrument is redundant if the asymptotic efficiency of the estimation is not improved by using it. The test statistic is a likelihood-ratio test based on the correlation between the regressors and the instruments with and without the instrument being tested. Under the null hypothesis, the specified instrument is redundant. With a p-value of 0.091 and 0.796 for the 1- and 2-year lag, respectively, the test statistic indicates a higher redundancy of the 2-year lag. Consequently, the analysis includes only the 1-year lag of ownership concentration. The underidentification test (Kleibergen-Paap statistic) and the weak identification test (Cragg-Donald F-statistic) indicate no weak-instruments problems.[172] Estimation results provide no evidence of a statistically significant effect of ownership concentration on performance (results not displayed).[173] The results are robust to the use of alternative measures of ownership concentration. When using ROA as the dependent variable, results do not change.

In the second step, the 1-year lagged ownership concentration variable is used in addition to the previously externally identified instruments (performance, firm size, firm risk and its squared measure). Test statistics prove that the instruments are both relevant and valid. This is an advantage over the previously used instrument set, which appeared to be valid but only to some degree relevant. Weakness of the instruments is no longer a problem. But again, estimation results provide no evidence of a statistically significant effect of ownership concentration on performance (results not displayed). The results are robust to the use of alternative measures of ownership concentration. When using ROA as the dependent variable, results do not change.

---

[171] In addition, the longer the lags used, the smaller the sample size because observations for which lagged values are unavailable are dropped from the estimation.

[172] The test of overidentifying restrictions (Hansen's J-statistic) is impossible to perform in an exactly identified model (one endogenous regressor and one instrument) because residuals and right-hand side variables are uncorrelated by construction. Instead, instrument validity relies on persuasive arguments, economic theory and norms established in previous empirical studies.

[173] Similarly, replacing the endogenous ownership structure with its lagged values in a within-estimation also produces no statistically significant coefficients for ownership concentration (results not displayed). This is not surprising as the absence of a relation between past values of ownership structure and current capital market performance can be explained by the nearly instant adoption of stock prices to new, relevant information.

Although lagged values seem to be natural candidates for instruments, this approach is not very often applied in practice. The reason for this is that although the lagged values can be argued to fulfill the validity condition by being uncorrelated with the error term, they also have to have the property that changes in the instrument variable are associated with changes in the endogenous variable but do not lead to changes in the dependent variable, except indirectly via the instrumented variable (see Section 5.4.3). In other words, the instruments need to be variables that can be legitimately excluded from the original equation of interest. However, in the case of ownership and performance, it cannot be argued that the lagged value of ownership would be without any direct effect on current performance. Hence, using lagged variables as instruments does not enable one to escape the endogeneity problem. The estimates might still be distorted by simultaneity bias, and hypothesis testing is invalid (Reed, 2013).

Finally, an important postestimation procedure is the test of regressor endogeneity. Under the null hypothesis that the specified endogenous regressors can actually be treated as exogenous, the test statistic is distributed as χ^2 with degrees of freedom equal to the number of regressors tested for endogeneity. The endogeneity test is defined as the difference of two Hansen statistics: one for the equation with the smaller set of instruments where the suspect regressor is treated as endogenous and one for the equation with the larger set of instruments where the suspect regressor is treated as exogenous. Under the null hypothesis both the smaller set of instruments and the additional, suspect instruments are valid. As a result of the test based on the originally used instrumental variables (performance, firm size, firm risk and its squared measure), a high p-value of 0.845 is obtained, which indicates that the hypothesis of exogeneity of the ownership concentration variable cannot be rejected. This finding is robust to the alternation of the applied instrumental variables, as previously discussed. Results are displayed in Table 6.7.

To conclude, the test of regressor endogeneity does not provide any evidence to support the reciprocal dependence of ownership and performance. This means, that, contrary to the theoretical arguments developed in Section 3.3.2, no reverse effects of performance on ownership concentration can be empirically detected. As a consequence, ownership concentration has to be treated exogenously. This implies that the within-2SLS estimator is still consistent but can be much less efficient than the within-estimator. The results without instrumenting for ownership concentration are therefore be more accurate. Furthermore, it is worth mentioning that the findings are in accordance with results from model specification tests for 2SLS models without fixed effects, which also could not reject the null hypothesis of regressor exogeneity (see Appendix A.4).

Table 6.7: Endogeneity Test

Test of regressor endogeneity H_0: Regressor is exogenous			
Endogeneity test statistic	Regressor tested: *OWN1*		
	Chi-sq(1)	= 0.038	
	p-value	= 0.845	⇒ H_0 is accepted: Regressor is exogenous

Note. The test is based on models using Tobin's Q as dependent variable and the control rights held by the largest shareholder (*OWN1*) as ownership concentration variable. The instrument set includes performance, firm size, firm risk and its squared measure. Results are robust to the use of alternative measures of performance and ownership concentration as well as to the alternation of the instrument set.

6.1.2.2 Nonlinear and Piecewise-Linear Regression Results

To test for nonlinear and piecewise-linear ownership effects, two model specifications are applied. The first series of models tests for a nonlinear relation between ownership and performance and includes the square and the cube of the ownership concentration variables. The second series of models tests for a piecewise-linear relation between ownership and performance and replaces the variable *OWN1* by subvariables for certain levels of ownership concentration.

Nonlinear ownership effects

Table 6.8 presents the within-regression results for ownership concentration models assuming squared and cubic effects on performance. Models 6.1-6.6 use Tobin's Q as the dependent variable and apply six alternative measures of ownership concentration. Models 6.3 reveals a negative but statistically insignificant coefficient of the size of shares owned by the three largest owners and a positive coefficient of its squared (SQ) term (0.871, significant at the 0.05 level). This suggests that performance increases if the three largest owners hold more than 35.6% of a company's shares. For ownership concentration below this breakpoint, the effect on performance is negative but this part of the function lacks statistical explanatory power. Figure 6.2 displays the identified relation graphically. Overall, this effect shape provides some support for the positive performance effect identified in the linear base case (see Section 6.1.1).

Nonetheless, the effect is not robust to the alternation of ownership concentration measures. No evidence of a cubic (CB) relation between ownership concentration and performance is found. Finally, with an R-squared (within) of around 17%, the explanatory power of the models does not increase much compared with the linear models.

Figure 6.2: Nonlinear Within-Regression Result for Ownership Concentration Model 6.3 – Graphic Presentation of Results

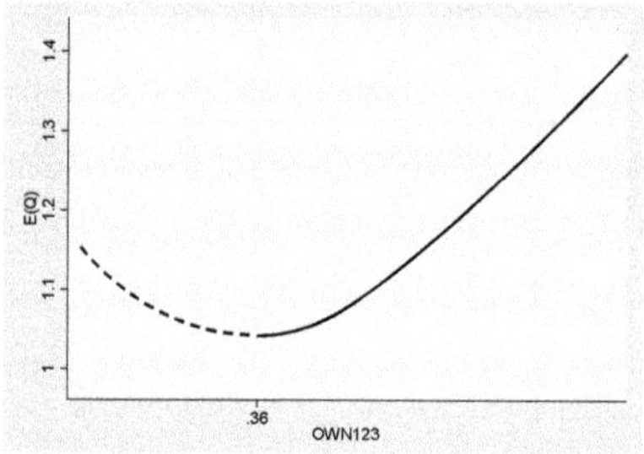

Note. The dashed line marks the statistically insignificant part of the function. The dependent variable is Tobin's Q. Ownership concentration is measured as the control rights of the three largest owners (*OWN123*). The definition of variables can be found in Table 5.5.

When using ROA as the dependent variable, there is no evidence of a squared relation between ownership concentration and performance, however, the results indicate a cubic (*N-shaped*) relation when using the shares held by the three largest owners as a measure of ownership concentration (results not displayed): The effect of ownership is first positive (25.715, significant at the 0.05 level), turns negative (-52.620, significant at the 0.1 level) and is positive (32.785, but not significant) at high levels of ownership (results not displayed). This suggests that accounting performance increases if the three largest owners hold more than 35.6% of a company's shares, decreases until their ownership reaches a level of 71.9% and increases again thereafter (with the last part of the function lacking statistical significance). With an R-squared (within) of around 13%, the explanatory power of the models does not increase much compared with the linear models. The use of ROE as the dependent variable does not produce any statistically significant coefficients.

Table 6.8: Within-Regression Results for Ownership Concentration Models, Quadratic and Cubic Relations Assumed

Dependent variable: Q	Model 6.1	Model 6.2	Model 6.3	Model 6.4	Model 6.5	Model 6.6
OWN1	0.038 (0.639)	-0.076 (1.041)				
OWN1 (SQ)	0.368 (0.559)	0.672 (2.514)				
OWN1 (CB)		-0.216 (1.812)				
OWN123			-0.621 (0.515)	-1.492 (0.916)		
OWN123 (SQ)			0.871** (0.416)	3.066 (2.460)		
OWN123(CB)				-1.484 (1.744)		
HHI					0.378 (0.669)	-0.529 (1.393)
HHI (SQ)					0.052 (0.718)	2.696 (3.418)
HHI (CB)						-1.984 (2.433)
DEBT	0.372 (0.328)	0.372 (0.329)	0.344 (0.332)	0.324 (0.332)	0.367 (0.329)	0.373 (0.324)
CAPX	0.781 (0.629)	0.775 (0.629)	0.695 (0.624)	0.689 (0.624)	0.776 (0.621)	0.749 (0.626)
RDX	0.848 (0.861)	0.850 (0.862)	0.898 (0.860)	0.899 (0.860)	0.853 (0.855)	0.906 (0.870)
GRO	0.002* (0.001)	0.002* (0.001)	0.002* (0.001)	0.002* (0.001)	0.002* (0.001)	0.002* (0.001)
Constant	1.038*** (0.156)	1.047*** (0.170)	1.169*** (0.176)	1.246*** (0.159)	1.036*** (0.113)	1.091*** (0.144)
R^2-within	0.166	0.166	0.166	0.167	0.166	0.167
R^2-between	0.042	0.042	0.041	0.038	0.042	0.046
R^2-overall	0.065	0.065	0.065	0.063	0.066	0.069
Sigma u (α)	0.885	0.885	0.886	0.887	0.885	0.884
Sigma e	0.450	0.451	0.450	0.450	0.450	0.450
Rho	0.794	0.794	0.794	0.795	0.794	0.794

Note. The analysis is based on1,560 firm-year observations (452 firms). Asterisks denote statistical significance of the reported variables at the 0.01 (***), 0.05 (**) and 0.1 (*) level. Cluster-robust standard errors are in parentheses. All estimations include time dummies (estimated coefficients are not reported). The definition of variables can be found in Table 5.5.

Piecewise-linear ownership effects

Following Mínguez-Vera and Martín-Ugedo (2007), the division points are first set at 10% and 25%: The first variable, *OWN1*(0-10%) includes concentration variables up to 10%, such that if the level of concentration (measured by *OWN1*) is below this threshold, the *OWN1*(0-10%) variable is equal to *OWN1* and if higher takes the value 10%. The second variable *OWN1*(10-25%) is set to zero if *OWN1* is below 10%, equals the value of *OWN1* minus 10% if *OWN1* is between 10% and 25%, and is 25% if *OWN1* is greater than or equal to 25%. The third variable *OWN1*(25-100%) is zero if *OWN1* is lower than 25% and equals *OWN1* minus 25% otherwise. To summarize:

$$OWN1(0-10\%) = \begin{cases} OWN1 & if\ OWN1 < 0.1 \\ 0.1 & otherwise \end{cases}$$

$$OWN1(10-25\%) = \begin{cases} 0 & if\ OWN1 < 0.1 \\ OWN1 - 0.1 & if\ 0.1 \leq OWN1 < 0.25 \\ 0.25 & otherwise \end{cases}$$

$$OWN1(25-100\%) = \begin{cases} 0 & if\ OWN1 < 0.25 \\ OWN1 - 0.25 & otherwise \end{cases}$$

In a second model, the division points are set to 25% and 50%, reflecting important thresholds for minority and majority control in the German corporate governance context. The procedure is analogous to the previous described model.

For model 3, again following Mínguez-Vera and Martín-Ugedo (2007), only one break point is used, which is set at 50% of the size of shareholdings of the largest owner. *OWN1*(0-50%) takes the value of *OWN1* if it is less than 50% and 50% otherwise. *OWN1*(50-100%) takes the value of zero if *OWN1* is less than 50% and the value of *OWN1* minus 50% otherwise. To summarize:

$$OWN1(0-50\%) = \begin{cases} OWN1 & if\ OWN1 < 0.5 \\ 0.5 & otherwise \end{cases}$$

$$OWN1(50-100\%) = \begin{cases} 0 & if\ OWN1 < 0.5 \\ OWN1 - 0.5 & otherwise \end{cases}$$

The fourth model establishes an ownership share of 75% as the break point, in reference to Gedajlovic and Shapiro (1998) and Mínguez-Vera and Martín-Ugedo (2007). The procedure is analogous to the previous described model.

Table 6.9 presents the within-regression results for ownership concentration models assuming a piecewise-linear effect on performance. Models 7.1-7.4 use Tobin's Q as the dependent variable and apply alternative breakpoints to *OWN1*. Separate line segments are then fitted to each interval. Model 7.1 finds a positive effect of ownership concentration on performance at levels of ownership above 25% (0.353, significant at the 0.05 level). Model 7.3 also finds a positive effect of ownership on performance if the share of the largest shareholder exceeds 50% (0.582, significant at the 0.1 level). This indicates a positive performance effect at high levels of ownership concentration. R-squared (within) is at around 17%.

These findings support the results obtained from the squared models, which also revealed a significant performance effect at high levels of ownership concentration. At low concentration levels, however, evidence is less conclusive. There are indications of a potentially negative impact on performance if ownership concentration is low, although the effect is statistically not significant. This concern is reinforced by the findings from the squared models, which also documented a negative but, again, statistically insignificant relation at low levels of ownership concentration.

Figure 6.3: Nonlinear Within-Regression Result for Ownership Concentration Models 7.1 and 7.3 – Graphic Presentation of Results

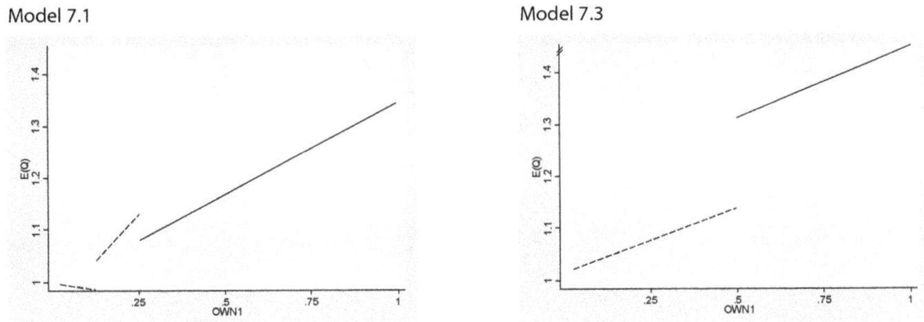

Note. Model 7.1 includes two division points of the function specified at 10% and 25% of the size of the control rights of the largest owner. Model 7.3 captures one division point at 50% (with the y-axis being discontinued, the actual slope of the function is steeper than illustrated). Dashed lines mark statistically insignificant parts of the functions. The dependent variable is Tobin's Q. Ownership concentration is measured as the control rights of the largest owner (*OWN1*). The definition of variables can be found in Table 5.5.

When using ROA as the dependent variable, the picture changes (results not displayed). A positive effect of ownership concentration is found if the share of the largest owner is below 10% (31.692, significant at the 0.05 level). At ownership levels exceeding 75%, a negative performance effect is identified (-16.671, significant at the 0.1 level). The explanatory power of the models is about 13%. These findings conflict with the results from the estimations based on Tobin's Q as performance measure and are also not consistent with the results from the cubic model indicating a first positive, then negative, and again positive accounting performance effect of the shareholdings by the three largest owners. The use of ROE as the dependent variable does not produce any statistically significant results. The findings from the models based on Tobin's Q are thus not robust to alternations of the performance variable.

To conclude, results from nonlinear and piecewise-linear regression models generally support the overall positive effect of ownership concentration on firm value, particularly at high levels of ownership concentration. At the same time, however, they yield a first indication that the relation might not be consistent across all ranges of ownership concentration. However, conclusions have to be drawn with care as nonlinear regressions suffer from serious limitations. That is, by specifying squared or cubic models, certain underlying relations are assumed a priori, and this eventually limits the flexibility for fitting the data. The piecewise-linear approach overcomes this problem (however, it might also be argued that the quadratic specification is advantageous over the piecewise-linear specification in that the turning point is endogenous instead of being specified in advance). Nonetheless, a major drawback of the piecewise-linear models is that the continuity of first derivatives is not carried at sampled points, which limits the accuracy of interpolations.

Table 6.9: Within-Regression Results for Ownership Concentration Models, Piecewise-Linear Relations Assumed

Dependent variable: Q	Model 7.1	Model 7.2	Model 7.3	Model 7.4
OWN1(0-10%)	-0.214 (1.135)			
OWN1(10-25%)	0.516 (0.497)			
OWN1(25-100%)	0.353** (0.141)			
OWN1(0-25%)		0.316 (0.665)		
OWN1(25-50%)		0.221 (0.275)		
OWN1(50-100%)		0.439 (0.346)	0.582** (0.261)	
OWN1(0-50%)			0.230 (0.376)	
OWN1(0-75%)				0.357 (0.235)
OWN1(75-100%)				0.679 (0.815)
DEBT	0.377 (0.333)	0.377 (0.330)	0.373 (0.328)	0.373 (0.329)
CAPX	0.771 (0.628)	0.781 (0.628)	0.788 (0.626)	0.792 (0.623)
RDX	0.772 (0.865)	0.809 (0.864)	0.850 (0.864)	0.811 (0.885)
GRO	0.002* (0.001)	0.002* (0.001)	0.002* (0.001)	0.002* (0.001)
Constant	1.001*** (0.151)	0.994*** (0.173)	1.020*** (0.137)	0.991*** (0.110)
R^2-within	0.167	0.167	0.166	0.166
R^2-between	0.026	0.035	0.041	0.037
R^2-overall	0.053	0.061	0.065	0.062
Sigma u (α)	0.891	0.887	0.885	0.887
Sigma e	0.450	0.450	0.450	0.451
Rho	0.796	0.795	0.794	0.795

Note. The analysis is based on 1,560 firm-year observations (452 firms). Asterisks denote statistical significance of the reported variables at the 0.01 (***), 0.05 (**) and 0.1 (*) level. Cluster-robust standard errors are in parentheses. All estimations include time dummies (estimated coefficients are not reported). The definition of variables can be found in Table 5.5.

6.1.2.3 Restricted Cubic Spline Regression Results

Cubic splines (also referred to as natural splines) are generally defined as piecewise-polynominal line segments whose function values and first and second derivatives agree at the boundaries where they join. The boundaries of these segments are called knots, and the fitted curve is continuous and smooth at the knot boundaries (Smith, 1979).[174] To avoid instability of the fitted curve at the extremes of the covariate, a common strategy is to constrain (restrict) the curve to be a straight line before the first knot or after the last knot (Orsini & Greenland, 2011). Cubic spline functions offer a convenient way to model nonlinear relations when the underlying mechanisms are not known. For these purposes, cubic splines provide great flexibility for fitting data and can assume virtually any shape, hence being very much less likely to be biased than are quadratics or other polynominals, or linear piecewise regressions.[175]

The restricted cubic spline function of a scalar variable x (in this case, ownership concentration) can be expressed as (Durrleman & Simon, 1989):

$$S(x) = \beta_{00} + \beta_{01}x + \sum_{i=1}^{K-2} \beta_{i3} \begin{Bmatrix} (x - t_i)_+^3 - (x - t_{K-1})_+^3 \times \frac{(t_K - t_i)}{(t_K - t_{K-1})} \\ +(x - t_K)_+^3 \times \frac{(t_{K-1} - t_i)}{(t_K - t_{K-1})} \end{Bmatrix} \; ; i = 1, \dots, K \quad (12)$$

where K is the number of knots, and $t_1 < t_2 < \cdots < t_K$ are the positions of the knots in the range of x. The plus-function $(x - K)_+$ is defined as $x - K$ if $x \geq K$ and zero otherwise.

In order to model a restricted cubic spline regression, $K - 2$ spline variables are introduced. A spline variable (x_i) can be written as:

$$x_i = (x - t_i)_+^3 - (x - t_{K-1})_+^3 \times \frac{(t_K - t_i)}{(t_K - t_{K-1})} + (x - t_K)_+^3 \times \frac{(t_{K-1} - t_i)}{(t_K - t_{K-1})} \; ; i = 1, \dots, K - 2 \quad (13)$$

These variables are activated as x increases in the following way: For $i = 1, \dots, K - 2$, if $x < t_i$, then $x_i = 0$; for $t_i < x < t_{K-1}$, then $x_i = (x - t_i)^3$; for $t_{K-1} < x < t_K$, then x_i has two cubic terms, whereas for $x > t_K$ it has three terms, which add to zero. Instead of the linear predictor βx, the linear predictor $\sum_{i=0}^{K-2} \beta_i x_i$ where $x_0 = x$, is used. This requires the estimation of $K - 1$ regression coefficients.

---

174 The term *spline* comes from a tool – long thin strips of wood, called spline – that has historically been used by engineering draftsmen to draw in a smooth curve between specified points.

175 The difference between fitting data to a quadratic or cubic polynominal equation and using the cubic spline method is that a polynominal fits one equation to all the data, whereas a cubic spline uses a different cubic equation for each adjacent pair of data points.

A crucial issue in spline regression is the choice of the location and number of knots. A standard approach is to place knots at evenly spaced intervals in the data (Keele, 2008). This procedure avoids arbitrary choices and ensures that there is enough data with each region of x to get a smooth fit. Harrell (2001) recommends to place three knots at the 10%, 50%, 90% percentiles, four knots at the 5%, 35% 65%, 95% percentiles, five knots at the 5%, 27.5%, 50%, 72.5%, 95% percentiles and so on. Even more important than the location of knots is the number of knots because the number of knots chosen affects the amount of smoothing applied to the data by controlling the piecewise fits. Increasing the number of knots increases the number of piecewise functions fit to the data allowing for greater flexibility. However, a too large number of knots results in a spline model that interpolates between the data points because more knots shrink the amount of data used for each piecewise function. Thus, if the number of knots is too small, the spline estimate will overly smooth with little variability, whereas a too large number of knots increases variability in the fit and may result in overfitting. A commonly applied approach to determine the appropriate number of knots is based on Akaike (1973/1998)'s information criterion (AIC). The AIC is expressed as the negative likelihood penalized by the number of parameters in the model. The idea then is to select the model that minimizes the AIC relative to a series of models specified for the given data (in itself, the absolute value of AIC has no meaning). Specifically, AIC aims to find the best approximating model to the unknown true data-generating process.

Table 6.10 shows the AIC values according to increasing numbers of knots of cubic splines from five (minimum number of knots commonly used for large data sets) to seven (maximum number of knots). The most satisfactory choices are the models with five and six knots, respectively.[176] Plotting the models shows that the overall shape of the fitting does not change substantially when increasing the number of knots from five to six (graphics not displayed). However, the model with six knots has a knot placed at 26% of ownership rights held by the largest owner, which is an interesting knot location from a theoretical perspective because 25% marks the threshold for minority power. Hence, the model with six knots is preferred.

[176] In general, the model with the minimum AIC is to be preferred. In this analysis, this is the model with six knots (AIC = 1,411.704). But according to Burnham and Anderson (2002)'s rules of thumb, there is also substantial level of empirical support for models whose AIC value is at most two points higher than the minimum AIC value. Here, this is the case for the model with five knots (AIC = 1,412.481).

Table 6.10: AIC Values for Various Restricted Cubic Spline Models for Ownership Concentration Models

Number of knots	Percentiles of regressor (%)[a]	Values of regressor (%)	AIC[b]
5	5, 27.5, 50, 72.5, 95	5.3, 17.6, 31.0, 53.1, 89.3	1,412.481
6	5, 23, 41, 59, 77, 95	5.3, 15.1, 26.2, 42.0, 58.0, 89.3	1,411.704
7	2.5, 18.3, 34.2, 50, 65.8, 81.7, 97.5	1.0, 11.8, 22.1, 31.0, 50.0, 65.2, 95.0	1,417.891

[a]Knot locations are expressed in fixed percentiles of the regressor (in this case, ownership concentration measured as *OWN1*), as suggested by Harrell (2001). [b]Values of AIC are calculated using Tobin's Q as dependent variable.

Table 6.11 presents the within-regression results for ownership concentration-performance models using restricted cubic splines.[177] A disadvantage of cubic splines is that the numeric results for the individual spline variables are uninterpretable (Durrleman & Simon, 1989; Vittinghoff, Glidden, Shiboski, & McCulloch, 2012). A standard solution to this problem is to pretend that these parameters do not exist, which is why the regression is commonly referred to as *nonparametric regression* (Newson, 2012). The resulting fit can be interpreted only graphically. Figure 6.4 therefore displays the regression results graphically. The graphs on the left-hand side display the adjusted predictions of corporate performance against the spline variable and the graphs on the right-hand side show the marginal effect of the spline variable, that is, the change in predicted performance for a unit change in ownership concentration (this is the first derivative of the corresponding curve shown on the left-hand side).

Model 8.1 uses Tobin's Q as the dependent variable and measures ownership concentration as the size of shares held by the largest owner. The latter is divided into five equally spaced spline variables with six knots at 5.3%, 15.1%, 26.2%, 42.0%, 58.0%, and 89.3% of the control rights held of the largest owner. This means that, for example, spline one contains observations with ownership shares between 5.3% and 15.1%. The graphic presentation of the results indicate a positive relation between ownership concentration and performance in spline two (15.1% ≤ *OWN1* ≤ 26.2%) and spline four (42.0% ≤ *OWN1* ≤ 58.0%). In spline five (58.0% ≤ *OWN1* ≤ 89.3%), the positive effect is still existent but levels off (marginal effect is slightly decreasing). This means that dominant shareholders owning between 15.1% and 26.2% and beyond 58% are beneficial for performance (measured as Tobin's Q). In contrast to the largely positive

177 Regressions using restricted cubic splines are performed by using the Stata module *postrcspline* written by Buis (2008).

effect shape, a negative association between ownership concentration and performance is identified in spline one (5.3% ≤ *OWN1* ≤ 15.1%) and spline three (26.2% ≤ *OWN1* ≤ 42.0%), although the marginal effect is positive. To summarize, corporate performance increases with ownership concentration in splines two and four. At the same time, corporate performance decreases with ownership concentration in splines one and three.[178]

Model 8.2 measures ownership concentration as the size of shares held by the three largest owners.[179] The corresponding graphs basically show the identical curve as the previous model but are shifted to the right (which appears logical considering the additional, although small, influence of the second and third largest owners). Accordingly, the relation between ownership concentration and performance is negative in splines one and two (7.6% ≤ *OWN123* ≤ 44.4%) with a local minimum at 41.0% (a minimum in model 8.1 is located at 13.9%). The relation then turns positive for ownership concentration values in splines three and four (44.4% ≤ *OWN123* ≤ 73.2% with a local maximum at 62.0% (a maximum in model 8.1 is located at 29.2%). In spline five (73.2% ≤ *OWN123* ≤ 93.6%), the function experiences a further local minimum at 76.0% of ownership concentration (a minimum in model 8.1 is located at 44.1%). From then on, corporate performance increases even with positive marginal effect. The alternative measurement of ownership concentration such as the size of shares held by the two largest owners essentially produces the same curve shape (results not displayed).

Model 8.3 measures ownership concentration as the value of the Herfindahl-Hirschman-Index.[180] By squaring the percentages of ownership shares, large blocks are weighted larger so that a higher Herfindahl-Hirschman-Index value (with a minimum of 0.01 and a maximum of 1.00) can be interpreted as a rising inequality of shares (which is equivalent to an increasing ownership concentration). Compared with the previous two models, the graphs yield consistent results as the relation between ownership concentration and performance is

[178] Replacing current ownership concentration with its lagged values produces no statistically significant spline variables according to the Wald tests 1 and 2 (results not displayed), meaning that the employed ownership concentration variables are not relevant to the model. This is in line with the findings from linear within-regressions (see Footnote 173) and is not surprising as the absence of a relation between past values of ownership structure and current capital market performance can be explained by the nearly instant adoption of stock prices to new and relevant information.

[179] The AIC criterion yields an optimal number of six knots located at 7.6%, 29.0%, 44.4%, 57.4%, 73.2%, and 93.6% of the control rights held of the three largest owners.

[180] The AIC criterion yields an optimal number of six knots located at values of HHI of 0.01, 0.05, 0.10, 0.21, 0.36, and 0.80.

negative at low levels of ownership concentration (local minimum at *HHI* = 0.05), turns positive (local maximum at *HHI* = 0.13), is negative (local minimum at *HHI* = 0.25), positive again at high levels of ownership concentration (local maximum at *HHI* = 0.67) and finally levels off with a marginal effect of close to zero.

A common diagnostic is the Wald statistic (Wald test 1), which tests for the overall significance of the spline terms in the model under the null hypothesis that all coefficients are zero, that is, $\beta_1 = \beta_2 = \cdots = \beta_{k-1} = 0$. For model 8.1, the small p-value of 0.007 clearly leads to a rejection of the null hypothesis, as desired. This confirms the overall importance of ownership concentration for predicting performance. The same conclusion can be reached for models 8.2 and 8.3 with p-values of 0.019 and 0.001, respectively.[181]

An additional version of the Wald statistic (Wald test 2) tests for the significance of all nonlinear spline terms in the model (Orsini & Greenland, 2011). One characteristic of restricted cubic splines in the default Stata setup is that the first of the $k-1$ spline variables is just the untransformed predictor, so that all nonlinearity is captured by the other $k-2$ variables. Hence, an F-test of the latter can be conducted in order to test the null hypothesis that the coefficients of the nonlinear terms are zero, that is, $\beta_2 = \beta_3 = \cdots = \beta_{k-1} = 0$. This is basically a test for departure from linearity. For model 8.1, the null cannot firmly be rejected as the p-value of 0.164 indicates linearity beyond the first knot. As a consequence, the linear model is preferred over the cubic spline model. However, models 8.2 and 8.3 yield p-values of 0.051 and 0.100, respectively, and hence provide support for the superiority of the nonlinear models. As model 8.2 basically displays the same curve shape as model 8.1, it seems justifiable to also accept the nonlinearity of model 8.1 despite the high p-value in the Wald test 2.

When using ROA as the dependent variable, the Wald test 1 produces high p-values of 0.15, 0.14 and 0.28, respectively, (depending on the measure of ownership concentration used). This means that the null hypothesis that the coefficients of all regressor are zero cannot be rejected. This casts doubt on the overall significance of the spline variables. In addition, the Wald test 2 yields high p-values of 0.16, 0.11 and 0.36, respectively (depending on the measure of ownership concentration used), which indicates that the cubic model is not optimal. The same holds if ROE is used as the dependent variable.

---

[181] Replacing current ownership concentration with its lagged values again produces no statistically significant spline variables according to the Wald tests 1 and 2 (results not displayed).

To conclude, the results from within-regressions using restricted cubic splines confirm the generally positive relation between ownership concentration and performance identified in the previous analyses and, at the same time, confirm the concerns of a negative relation at low concentration levels. A drawback of the use of restricted cubic splines is that it does not allow addressing potential endogeneity as a result of regressors being determined simultaneously with the dependent variable. The same problem potentially occurs with linear within-regressions – although this is of no relevance for the empirical analyses in the course of this dissertation because the test of regressor endogeneity is not able to prove that ownership concentration is indeed an endogenous variable (see Section 6.1.1.1).[182]

[182] Stata does not support the estimation of restricted cubic splines using within-2SLS regressions.

Figure 6.4: Within-Regression Results for Ownership Concentration Models, Using Restricted Cubic Splines – Graphic Presentation of Results

Model 8.1 - Dependent variable is Q, ownership concentration variable is *OWN1*

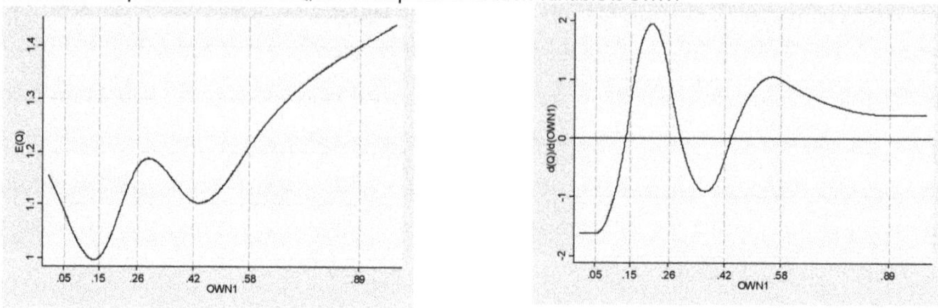

Model 8.2 - Dependent variable is Q, ownership concentration variable is *OWN123*

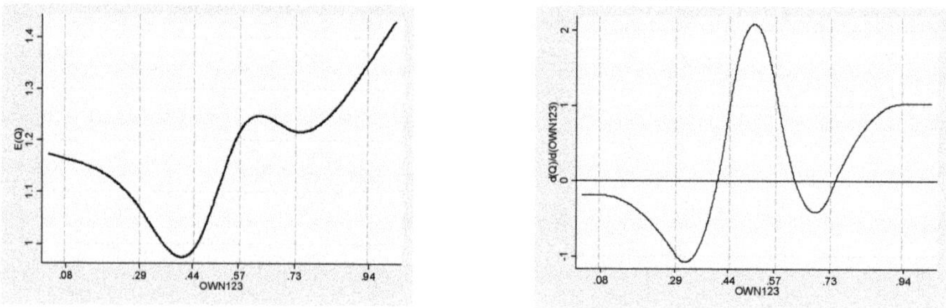

Model 8.3 - Dependent variable is Q, ownership concentration variable is *HHI*

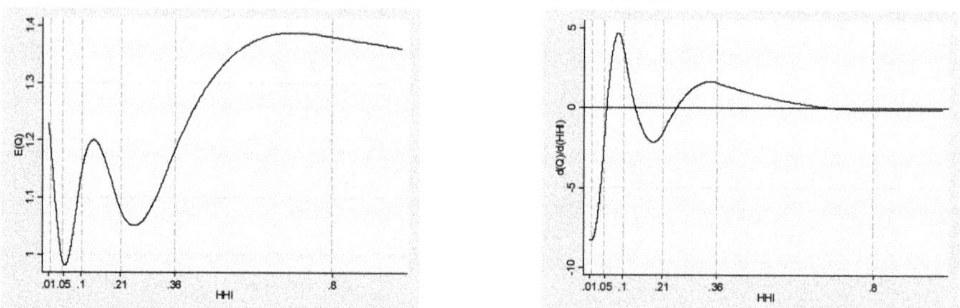

Note. The figures display the effect of ownership concentration (alternatively measured as *OWN1*, *OWN123* and *HHI*) on performance (measured as Tobin's Q) after using restricted cubic splines in a within-regression. The graphs on the left-hand side display the adjusted predictions of corporate performance against the spline variable, and the graphs on the right-hand side show the marginal effect of the spline variable (this is the first derivative of the corresponding curve shown on the left-hand side). All predicted and marginal effects are estimated at the means of the remaining covariates. The dashed, vertical lines indicate the position of the knots (with the number of the knots depending on the best model fit). The definition of variables can be found in Table 5.5.

Table 6.11: Within-Regression Results for Ownership Con-centration Models, Using Restricted Cubic Splines

Dependent variable: Q	Model 8.1	Model 8.2	Model 8.3
spline 1	-1.620*	-0.184	-8.301**
	(0.984)	(0.499)	(3.638)
spline 2	53.501*	-4.216	1,024.745**
	(29.912)	(4.810)	(433.803)
spline 3	-141.255*	36.215	-1.973.984**
	(80.315)	(25.784)	(939.178)
spline 4	130.632*	-90.016	1,121.212**
	(78.952)	(58.441)	(484.309)
spline 5	-60.775	89.515	-210.405**
	(46.607)	(64.596)	(103.727)
DEBT	0.362	0.311	0.348
	(0.335)	(0.330)	(0.325)
CAPX	0.773	0.599	0.748
	(0.625)	(0.619)	(0.616)
RDX	0.885	0.839	0.930
	(0.865)	(0.863)	(0.868)
GRO	0.002*	0.002*	0.002*
	(0.001)	(0.001)	(0.001)
Constant	1.145***	1.165***	1.285***
	(0.150)	(0.153)	(0.165)
R^2-within	0.170	0.171	0.174
Wald test 1	3.250***	2.730**	4.880***
Wald test 2	1.640	2.290**	1.900*

Note. The analysis is based on 1,560 firm-year observations (452 firms). Asterisks denote statistical significance of the reported variables at the 0.01 (***), 0.05 (**) and 0.1 (*) level. Cluster-robust standard errors are in parentheses. All estimations include time dummies (estimated coefficients are not reported). Model 8.1 uses the shares held by the largest owner (*OWN1*) as spline variable, model 8.2 uses the shares held by the three largest owners (*OWN123,*) and model 8.3 employs the Herfindahl-Hirschman-Index (*HHI*). Wald test 1 is a test of joint significance of all spline terms, whereas Wald test 2 is a test of joint significance of all nonlinear spline terms in the model. The definition of variables can be found in Table 5.5. A limitation of cubic splines is that the numeric results for the individual spline variables are uninterpretable. Instead, the resulting fit can be interpreted only graphically.

6.1.2.4 Summary

Several variations of the base case model have been examined. First, instrumental variable regressions are performed. To summarize, results provide evidence of a small but positive effect of ownership concentration on performance measured as Tobin's Q only if using the Herfindahl-Hirschman-Index as concentration measure. Alternative measures of ownership concentration yield positive but statistically insignificant coefficients. This is also the case when altering the measure of performance. Compared with the base case model, the within-2SLS estimator takes into account the problem of reverse causality by replacing the ownership concentration variables with the instruments performance, firm size, firm risk and its squared measure. Formal diagnostics confirm both the validity (i.e., the instruments are uncorrelated with the error term) and relevance (i.e., the instruments are correlated with the variable that needs to be explained) of the instruments. However, tests for weak instruments indicate that the instruments are weak (i.e., the instruments are only weakly correlated with the variable that needs to be explained). This can lead to an estimation bias and a size distortion of Wald tests on the parameters. In an alternative model approach, lagged values of ownership concentration variables are used as instruments, and test diagnostics indicate no weak-instruments problem. Again, estimations provide no evidence of a statistically significant effect of ownership concentration on performance. This finding is robust to the use of alternative measures of ownership concentration and to the performance definition. Results do not change when conflating lagged values of ownership concentration with the originally used instrument set. However, although these findings indicate an absence of effects of ownership concentration on performance, conclusions have to be drawn with care. This is because there is no econometric proof of endogeneity of ownership concentration. Ownership concentration should therefore be treated as exogenous. This implies that the within-2SLS estimator is still consistent but can be much less efficient than the base case within-estimator (documenting a positive relation between ownership concentration and performance), which is hence to be preferred over the within-2SLS estimator.

A second variation of the base case model is the examination of nonlinear and piecewise-linear ownership effects. To summarize, results from the within-regressions including squared measures of ownership concentration provide evidence of a positive relation between ownership concentration (measured as the control rights held by the three largest owners) and performance (measured as Tobin's Q) beyond 35.6%. There are indications of a negative performance effect at low levels of ownership concentration, although the effect shape is statistically insignificant and not robust to the use of alternative measures of ownership concentration or performance. The positive relation at high levels of ownership concentration is supported by results from piecewise-linear ownership concentration models, which provide evidence of a positive relation between ownership concentration and performance if the largest owner holds – depending on the applied division points – more than 25% or more than 50% of the company's shares. At low concentration levels, however, evidence is still less conclusive. The piecewise-linear regression models find, again, indications of a potentially negative impact on performance if ownership concentration is low, although the effect is statistically insignificant and not robust to the alternation of performance measures.

Third, a further variation of the base case model is the use of restricted cubic splines. Compared with the piecewise-linear model specifications, cubic spline functions provide more flexibility to model nonlinear relations when the underlying mechanisms are not known because they can assume virtually any shape. To summarize, results from the within-regressions using restricted cubic splines confirm the generally positive relation between ownership concentration and performance measured as Tobin's Q but find that the relation is nonlinear with a negative effect at low levels of ownership concentration, a bell-shaped effect at medium levels of ownership concentration, and a positive effect at high levels of ownership concentration. More specifically, performance is positively related to ownership concentration in the hands of the largest owner for ownership levels between 13.9% and 29.2% and beyond 44.1%. At the same time, performance is negatively related to ownership concentration in the hands of the largest owner for ownership levels below 13.9% and between 29.2% and 44.1%. The effect shape is robust to the alternation of ownership concentration measures. For example, when using the size of shares held by the three largest owners, the general effect shape does not change except for a shift to the right, which is a logical consequence of the increased number of shareholders considered in the ownership concentration measure. Performance is then positively related to ownership concentration for ownership levels between 41.0% and 62.0% and beyond 76.0%. At the same time, performance is negatively related to ownership concentration for ownership levels below 41.0% and between 62.0% and 76.0%.

The results from the within-regressions using restricted cubic splines are supported by the previous findings from models using squared ownership concentration terms according to which performance increases if the three largest owners hold more than 35.6% of a company's shares; this is close to the turning point of 41.0% identified in the restricted cubic spline regression model. The results also receive support from the previous findings from models estimating a piecewise-linear relation according to which the relation between ownership concentration (measured as the size of shares held by the largest owner) and performance is significant, positive for ownership levels beyond 25% or 50%, respectively, depending on the chosen division points of the piecewise-linear regressions; this is close to the turning points of 29.2% and 44.1%, respectively, beyond which the ownership concentration effect turns positive in the restricted cubic spline regression. Finally, the within-regressions using restricted cubic splines affirm the concerns raised in the squared and piecewise-linear regression models of a potentially negative performance effect at low levels of ownership concentration and provide indeed confirmatory evidence.

6.2 Owner Identity Effects

The previous section has examined the effect of ownership concentration on corporate performance. However, this mirrors only one dimension of ownership structure and does not provide a full account of the story. The other dimension is the identity of owners, which will be assessed in the following analyses.

6.2.1 Identity of General Shareholder Base

In order to capture the identity of the general shareholder base, six owner identity variables are applied, reflecting the aggregated sum of shares held by all shareholders classified as individual investors, insiders, corporations, financial investors, commercial banks, or government agencies. A central assumption is that there are no differences in the utility function and the behavior of shareholders with the same identity (see Section 2.3).

Table 6.12 presents the within-regression results for owner identity models, using cluster-robust standard errors. Models 9.1-9.3 use Tobin's Q as the dependent variable. According to the results from model 9.1, the coefficient of the control rights held by corporations is 0.315, (significant at the 0.1 level) and the coefficient of the control rights held by financial institutions is 0.408 (significant at the 0.05 level). This indicates that, for a given firm, an increase of the control rights held by corporations or financial institutions by 100 basis points results, on average, in an increase of firm performance, measured by Tobin's Q, by 0.315 or 0.408 basis points, respectively. The coefficient of the control rights held by individual investors is also positive but statistically insignificant. Insiders, banks and government agencies exhibit a negative but statistically insignificant influence on performance.

Among the control variables, only growth has a statistically significant and positive, albeit very small effect on performance. In regard to the explanatory power of the models, R-squared for the within-variation is 17.3% (15.8% in the controls-only model). Again, it is not possible to consider industry variables in a fixed-effects model (see Section 6.1.1.1). However, the omission of industry dummies does not affect the validity of the results because the computation of alternative models with industry-fixed effects (instead of firm-fixed effects) does not change the fundamental regression findings (results not displayed): The coefficient of corporate shareholdings is still positive (0.486, significant at the 0.05 level) and that of financial investors' shareholdings is positive as well (0.237) but not statistically significant.

When using ROA as the dependent variable (results not displayed), the coefficients of the control rights in the hands of corporations and financial institutions are still positive but insignificant. A surprising finding is that the coefficient of insider ownership turns positive and (9.268, significant at the 0.1 level). This means that although insider ownership is not appreciated by the capital market as being value-enhancing, it apparently has a large, positive effect on accounting performance. Among the control variables, sales growth has, again, a significant, positive effect on firm performance. High levels of debt turn out to have a significant, negative impact. R&D expenditures have a significant, negative coefficient. The R-squared (within) decreases to around 12%. When using ROE as the dependent variable, coefficients of all ownership variables are insignificant.

Model 9.2 focuses on the significant, positive effects identified for the aggregated control rights in the hands of corporations and financial investors and further differentiates between domestic and foreign owners. In the case of corporations, both domestic (*DCOPR*) and foreign (*FCORP*) corporations have a positive performance impact but only the effect of foreign corporations is statistically significant (0.505, significant at the 0.05 level). The reverse is true for financial institutions where, again, both domestic (*DFINAN*) and foreign (*FFINAN*) institutions are positively associated with performance but only the effect of domestic institutions is statistically significant (0.494, significant at the 0.05 level).

Model 9.3 investigates the negative but insignificant effects identified for the aggregated control rights in the hands of insiders and further differentiates between members of the management and members of the supervisory board. An interesting finding is that the negative relation between insider ownership and performance is driven by the negative performance effect of ownership in the hands of managers (-1.009, significant at the 0.1 level).[183] In contrast, the coefficient of ownership in the hands of supervisory board members is positive but statistically insignificant. It is surprising to find that the opposite conclusion can be reached when using ROA as the dependent variable (results not displayed): The previously discussed positive relation between insider ownership and accounting performance appears to be driven by the positive effect of ownership in the hands of managers (17.136, significant at the 0.05 level), and the coefficient of ownership in the hands of supervisory board members is also positive but statistically insignificant. This contradicting evidence indicates that insider ownership has a positive effect on accounting performance, whereas capital market participants doubt the value-enhancing potential of management ownership and consider these firms less attractive, which eventually results in a lower market valuation compared with firms with a lower level of managerial ownership.

A limitation of these models is the assumption of linearity. However, adding squared owner identity terms reduces the R-squared to a low value of 8.2%, which means that the goodness of fit is much smaller than that for the linear model.[184] In addition, conclusions have to be drawn with care as the within-estimator does not address the problem of reverse causality. As a consequence, it cannot be concluded in which direction causality runs. This limitation cannot be econometrically overcome due to the very large number of instruments that would be required in a simultaneous equations setting.

---

[183] When adding a squared term of management holdings to the model, the negative effect of management ownership appears to turn positive after a certain breakpoint; however, both effects are statistically insignificant. The linear model is hence preferred.

[184] The estimation of restricted cubic splines (as in the case of ownership concentration models) is technically not feasible with more than one independent variable.

Table 6.12: Within-Regression Results for Owner Identity Models

Dependent variable: Q	Controls only	Model 9.1	Model 9.2	Model 9.3
PRIVATE		0.040 (0.312)	0.070 (0.311)	0.119 (0.265)
INSIDER		-0.373 (0.370)	-0.346 (0.368)	
MGMT				-1.009* (0.561)
BOARD				0.213 (0.368)
CORP		0.315* (0.185)		0.316* (0.178)
DCORP			0.166 (0.248)	
FCORP			0.505** (0.211)	
FINAN		0.408** (0.185)		0.425** (0.170)
DFINAN			0.494** (0.226)	
FFINAN			0.234 (0.170)	
BANK		-0.391 (0.401)	-0.315 (0.394)	-0.382 (0.403)
GOV		-0.034 (0.741)	-0.253 (0.784)	-0.148 (0.762)

(continued)

Table 6.12: Within-Regression Results for Owner Identity Models (continued)

Dependent variable: Q	Controls only	Model 9.1	Model 9.2	Model 9.3
DEBT	0.331	0.366	0.370	0.396
	(0.325)	(0.311)	(0.311)	(0.286)
CAPX	0.739	0.655	0.628	0.645
	(0.629)	(0.627)	(0.626)	(0.633)
RDX	0.923	0.808	0.736	0.856
	(0.853)	(0.843)	(0.853)	(0.835)
GRO	0.002*	0.002**	0.002**	0.002**
	(0.001)	(0.001)	(0.001)	(0.001)
Constant	1.129***	1.041***	1.044***	1.038***
	(0.075)	(0.124)	(0.124)	(0.102)
R^2-within	0.158	0.173	0.177	0.183
R^2-between	0.043	0.006	0.002	0.001
R^2-overall	0.064	0.031	0.025	0.020
Sigma u (α)	0.888	0.907	0.914	0.924
Sigma e	0.452	0.449	0.449	0.447
Rho	0.794	0.803	0.806	0.811

Note. The analysis is based on 1,560 firm-year observations (452 firms). Asterisks denote statistical significance of the reported variables at the 0.01 (***), 0.05 (**) and 0.1 (*) level. Cluster-robust standard errors are in parentheses. All estimations include time dummies (estimated coefficients are not reported). The definition of variables can be found in Table 5.5.

In order to compare these results to alternative model specifications, random-effects estimations are also performed (results not displayed). The estimations confirm the results from the fixed-effects models and find positive effects of the control rights held by corporates (0.300, significant at the 0.05 level) and by financial institutions (0.261, significant at the 0.1 level). In order to provide supporting evidence of the appropriateness of the fixed-effects model as preferred estimation, several specification tests are applied (see Section 6.1.1.1 for a detailed explanation of the test procedures). The results are presented in Table 6.13.

First, the F-test for poolability examines the presence of individual effects and can be used to choose between the pooled model and the fixed-effects model. The null hypothesis is that there are no individual effects, that is, $\alpha_i = 0$. In this case, no panel models need to be specified as all individuals are sufficiently homogenous, and therefore the same coefficients apply across all individuals. As a result of the test, a p-value of 0.000 is obtained, which leads to a strong rejection of the null hypothesis, and hence the fixed-effects model is preferred over the pooled OLS model. The F-test thereby confirms the theoretically reasoned preference.

Second, the Lagrange Multiplier (LM) test examines the presence of random effects and can be used to choose between the pooled model and the random-effects model. The null hypothesis is that individual-specific error variance components are zero, that is, $\sigma_u^2 = 0$ or equivalently $Cor(\varepsilon_{it}, \varepsilon_{is}) = 0$ for $t \neq s$. In this case, no significant difference across individuals would exist (i.e., no panel effect). As a result of the test, a p-value of 0.000 is obtained, which leads to a strong rejection of the null hypothesis, and therefore the random-effects model is preferred over the pooled OLS model. Hence, both the F-test and the LM test reject the pooled OLS model. Instead, individual-effects models such as the fixed- and random-effects model are preferred.

Third, as the key consideration in choosing between a random- and a fixed-effects approach is whether α_i and $\boldsymbol{x}'_{it}$ are correlated, Hausman (1978) proposed a test for fixed effects based on the difference between the estimable coefficients of time-varying regressors in a random- and a fixed-effects model. Under the null hypothesis that individual effects are random, both estimators should be similar because both are consistent. Accordingly, as the fixed-effects approach is consistent when α_i and $\boldsymbol{x}'_{it}$ are correlated but the random-effects approach is inconsistent, a statistically significant difference is interpreted as evidence against the null hypothesis. The test of fixed effects against random effects yields significantly different coefficients for the owner identity variables, and the overall statistic therefore has a p-value of 0.000. This leads to a strong rejection of the null hypothesis, and hence the fixed-effects model is preferred over the random-effects model. In a fixed-effects model, the random-effects estimator cannot be used because only the within-estimator is consistent. As a consequence, the fixed-effects estimator is preferred for the analyses.

Table 6.13: Results from Model Specification Tests (OLS vs. FE vs. RE) – Owner Identity

Models	Specification test	Test statistic	Interpretation
OLS vs. FE	F-Test $H_0: \alpha_i = 0$	F(14, 451) = 16.630 Prob > F = 0.000	⇒ H_0 is rejected: FE preferred over OLS
OLS vs. RE	LM test $H_0: \sigma_u^2 = 0$	Chibar2(1) = 805.300 Prob > chibar2 = 0.000	⇒ H_0 is rejected: RE preferred over OLS
FE vs. RE	Hausman test H_0: Difference in coefficients is not systematic.	Chi2(14) = 35.450 Prob > chi2 = 0.000	⇒ H_0 is rejected: FE preferred over RE

Note. Tests are based on models using Tobin's Q as dependent variable and owner identity variables as regressors. Results are robust to the use of alternative measures of performance.

6.2.2 Summary

To summarize, the results from linear within-regressions provide evidence of a positive relation between the aggregated sum of shares in the hands of corporations (in particular, foreign corporations) and in the hands of financial institutions (in particular, domestic financial institutions) and performance measured as Tobin's Q. Accordingly, an increase of control rights held by corporations and financial institutions by 100 basis points results, on average, in an increase of firm performance by 0.315 and 0.408 basis points, respectively. Another finding is the negative relation between insider (in particular, managerial) holdings and capital market performance according to which an increase of control rights held by management by 100 basis points leads, on average, to a decrease of firm performance by 1.009 basis points. Banks and government agencies exhibit a negative but statistically insignificant influence on performance. The alternative use of ROA as performance measure generally confirms the positive relation between corporate and institutional ownership and performance but finds no statistical significance. A surprising finding is that the relation between insider (managerial) ownership and accounting performance turns out to be positive. When using ROE as performance measure, no significant ownership effects are detected.

6.3 Concentration and Identity Interaction Effects

After ownership concentration and owner identity have been examined separately, their effects are now conflated to an interaction model because it can be assumed that the shape of the effect of ownership concentration on performance crucially depends on the identity of owners. In a first step, the relation between the identity of the largest owner and performance is examined. This is followed by a further investigation of the effect shape depending on both the identity and the stake size of the largest owner.

6.3.1 Identity of the Largest Owner

In order to capture the performance effect of the largest owner as a function of his identity, five dummy variables are created, which reflect the identity of the largest owner (individual investor, insider, corporation, bank, government).[185]

Table 6.14 presents the within-regression results for owner identity models, using cluster-robust standard errors. Model 10.1 uses Tobin's Q as the dependent variable and five dummies for the identity of the largest owner as well as the control rights held by the largest owner as an additional control variable. The results find that the coefficient of the control rights held by the largest owner is positive (0.374, significant at the 0.05 level). This means that general ownership concentration is positively related to performance, that is, the slope of the regression is positive (for all owner identities). This compares well to the coefficient of 0.396 previously identified in the linear within-regression model of ownership concentration. In regard to the dummy variables, the results find that the coefficients of banks and government entities as largest owner are both negative (-0.418, significant at the 0.05 level; -0.133, significant at the 0.01 level). This implies that the regression intercept is lower, that is, average performance of firms with a bank or government as largest owner is lower than for firms with a financial institution as largest shareholder. The coefficients for insiders and corporations are negative, and the coefficient for private investors is positive, but these effects lack statistical significance.

Among the control variables, only growth has a significant, positive, albeit very small effect on performance. In regard to the explanatory power of the model, R-squared for the within-

[185] Institutional ownership is used as reference owner.

variation is 16.6% (15.8% in the controls-only model). When using ROA or ROE as the dependent variable (results not displayed), concentration is no longer statistically significant.

Model 10.2 focuses on corporations and financial institutions as largest owner and further distinguishes between domestic and foreign owners. The findings provide support for the results from Model 9.2 (superior performance of foreign corporations and domestic financial institutions), but the effects lack statistical significance.[186]

Model 10.3 investigates the negative effects identified for insiders as largest owner and further distinguishes between members of the management and members of the supervisory board.[187] An interesting finding is that the negative relation between insider ownership and performance, again, appears to be driven by the negative performance effect of managers as largest owner (-0.291, significant at the 0.1 level). In contrast, the coefficient of a board member as largest owner is positive but statistically insignificant. The findings are in line with the conclusions from Model 9.3.

---

[186] The general effect shape of domestic and foreign intercorporate ownership does not depend on whether financial institutions as a whole or only domestic financial investors are used as reference category. In both cases, effects are statistically insignificant, though. Further, these findings do no change when domestic intercorporate ownership is used as reference category in order to assess the effect of foreign intercorporate ownership (this reference identity is actually most appropriate; however, this would impede the comparability of regression coefficients across various models).

[187] The general effect shape is, again, not dependent on the reference category (see Footnote 186).

Table 6.14: Within-Regression Results for Concentration and Identity Interaction Models, Using Dummies for the Identity of the Largest Owner

Dependent variable: Q	Controls only	Model 10.1	Model 10.2	Model 10.3
OWN1		0.374**	0.367**	0.378***
		(0.165)	(0.163)	(0.164)
PRIVATE (dummy)		0.014	-0.022	0.046
		(0.130)	(0.138)	(0.120)
INSIDER (dummy)		-0.159	-0.201*	
		(0.110)	(0.119)	
MGMT (dummy)				-0.291*
				(0.162)
BOARD (dummy)				0.040
				(0.151)
CORP (dummy)		-0.002		-0.005
		(0.083)		(0.082)
DCORP (dummy)			-0.077	
			(0.134)	
FCORP (dummy)			0.002	
			(0.110)	
FINAN (dummy)		(omitted)		(omitted)
DFINAN (dummy)			(omitted)	
FFINAN (dummy)			-0.106	
			(0.078)	
BANK (dummy)		-0.418**	-0.457**	-0.420**
		(0.203)	(0.191)	(0.203)
GOV (dummy)		-0.133***	-0.243***	-0.134***
		(0.035)	(0.088)	(0.034)
DEBT	0.331	0.408	0.412	0.409
	(0.325)	(0.335)	(0.336)	(0.327)
CAPX	0.739	0.703	0.710	0.701
	(0.629)	(0.646)	(0.651)	(0.649)
RDX	0.923	0.897	0.821	0.915
	(0.853)	(0.927)	(0.928)	(0.919)
GRO	0.002*	0.002*	0.002*	0.002*
	(0.001)	(0.001)	(0.001)	(0.001)
Constant	1.129***	0.839**	0.879***	0.835***
	(0.075)	(0.115)	(0.119)	(0.112)

(continued)

Table 6.14: Within-Regression Results for Concentration and Identity Interaction Models, Using Dummies for the Identity of the Largest Owner (continued)

Dependent variable: Q	Controls only	Model 10.1	Model 10.2	Model 10.3
R^2-within	0.158	0.166	0.168	0.171
R^2-between	0.043	0.019	0.013	0.012
R^2-overall	0.064	0.045	0.039	0.039
Sigma u (α)	0.888	0.902	0.906	0.908
Sigma e	0.452	0.454	0.454	0.453
Rho	0.794	0.798	0.799	0.801

Note. The analysis is based on 1,560 firm-year observations (452 firms). Asterisks denote statistical significance of the reported variables at the 0.01 (***), 0.05 (**) and 0.1 (*) level. Cluster-robust standard errors are in parentheses. All estimations include time dummies (estimated coefficients are not reported). The definition of variables can be found in Table 5.5.

6.3.2 Identity and Stake Size of the Largest Owner

The dummies used in the previous analysis of the identity of the largest owner are designed to measure the average performance difference between owner groups, that is, they express a change in the intercept of the regression according to the identity groups (*intercept dummies*). In addition, interaction terms can be created in order to allow the slope of the regression to be different depending on whether the condition specified by the dummy is met (*slope dummies*). Interaction terms are obtained by multiplying the previously used intercept dummies by the slope variable, that is, the control rights held by the largest owner (e.g., *PRIVATE(dummy)* × *OWN1*). However, including only slope dummies (and omitting intercept dummies) could bias the slope by forcing it to explain more than it should as, for example, changes in the mean between groups – which, however, can be better explained by intercept dummies.[188] As a consequence, both slope and intercept dummies are included in the equation.

Table 6.15 presents the within-regression results for owner identity models, using cluster-robust standard errors; Figure 6.6 (Section 6.4) provides a graphical illustration of the regression results. Model 11.1 uses Tobin's Q as the dependent variable and five dummies for the identity of the largest owner as well as five interaction terms and the control rights held by the largest owner as an additional control variable. The results find a positive constant term (0.735, significant at the 0.01 level), which is used as the intercept of the regression for financial institutions (the reference owner identity) as largest owner. The coefficient of the control rights held by the largest owner is also positive (0.725, significant at the 0.01 level). This implies that an increase of ownership concentration in the hands of financial investors (the reference owner identity) as the largest owner is positively related to performance, that is, the slope of the regression is positive. This means that, for a given firm, an increase of the control rights held by a financial institution as largest owner by 100 basis points results, on average, in an increase of firm performance by 0.725 basis points.

For corporations as the largest owner, the coefficient of the intercept dummy is positive (0.282, significant at the 0.05 level). This indicates that performance is, per se, higher if the largest shareholder is a corporation (rather than a financial institution). The regression results further show that the interaction term of corporations as largest owner has a negative coefficient (-0.631, significant at the 0.001 level). This means that the slope of the regression for firms

188 See, for example, Studenmund (2001) for an in-depth examination of intercept and slope dummies.

with a corporation as largest owner is flatter than in the case of a financial institution as largest owner. However, the slope is still positive (0.725 - 0.631 = 0.094). This means that, for a given firm, an increase of the control rights held by a corporation as largest owner by 100 basis points results, on average, in an increase of firm performance by 0.094 basis points.

For private investors and insiders as largest owner, the coefficients for the intercept dummies are statistically insignificant. In contrast, the interaction terms are considerably negative, which results in negative regression slopes for private investors (0.725 - 0.939 = -0.214) and insiders (0.725 - 1.256 = -0.531). This means that, for a given firm, an increase of the control rights held by a private investor or an insider as largest owner by 100 basis points results, on average, in a decrease of firm performance by 0.214 or 0.531 basis points, respectively.

Dominant bank ownership is documented to produce a lower intercept (-0.483, significant at the 0.1 level) and a positive but statistically not significant coefficient of the interaction term. Hence, no strong conclusions can be drawn on the impact of bank ownership. For government entities as largest owner, the coefficient of the intercept moves around zero but is statistically not significant. The interaction term has a negative coefficient, which becomes significant if the group of domestic financial institutions (see Model 11.2) is used as reference category (-1.520, significant at the 0.01 level). There is hence some support for a negative relation between government ownership and performance.

Among the control variables, only growth has a significant, positive, albeit small coefficient. In regard to the explanatory power of the models, R-squared for the within-variation is 17.9% (15.8% in the controls-only model). When using ROA or ROE as the dependent variable (results not displayed), ownership concentration is no longer statistically significant.

Model 11.2 focuses on corporations and financial institutions and further distinguishes between domestic and foreign owners. In regard to corporations, domestic owners have a positive intercept dummy (0.459, significant at the 0.01 level), which is higher than the coefficient of foreign owners. This indicates that performance is, per se, higher if the largest shareholder is a domestic corporation rather than a foreign corporation (or a financial institution). However, the interaction term of domestic corporations is negative (-1.206, significant at the 0.01 level) and larger in absolute terms than the base slope (0.913). This means that an increase of the control rights held by a domestic corporation as largest owner results in a decrease of firm performance. In contrast, the slope of the regression for foreign corporations is positive (although flatter than in the case of a financial institution as largest owner) but the effect is statistically insignificant. These findings hence provide support for the results from Models 9.2 and 10.2, according to which foreign intercorporate ownership leads to higher performance than domestic intercorporate ownership (compared with institutional ownership, which is used as reference category).[189] In regard to financial institutions, foreign owners have a positive but statistically insignificant intercept dummy. This could indicate that performance is, per se, higher if the largest shareholder is a foreign rather than a domestic financial institution. The regression results further show that the interaction term of foreign institutions is negative (-0.700, significant at the 0.01 level) but smaller in absolute terms than the base slope (0.913). This means that an increase of the control rights held by a foreign financial institution as largest owner results in a increase of firm performance but the increase is smaller than in the case of a domestic financial institution. These findings hence provide support for the results from Models 9.2 and 10.2 according to which domestic institutional ownership leads to higher performance than foreign institutional ownership

Model 11.3 investigates the negative effects identified for insiders as largest owner and further distinguishes between members of the management and members of the supervisory board.[190] In regard to managers, the coefficient of the intercept dummy is positive but not statistically significant, and the coefficient of the slope dummy is negative (-1.850, significant at the 0.05 level) and larger in absolute terms than the base slope (0.693). This leads to a negative slope of the regression. In other words, an increase of the control rights held by a manager as largest owner results in a decrease of firm performance. This supports the evidence found in Models 9.3 and 10.3. In regard to board members, the coefficient of the intercept dummy is positive (0.379, significant at the 0.1 level), and the coefficient of the slope dummy is negative (-1.197, significant at the 0.01 level) and larger in absolute terms than the base slope (0.693). This leads to a negative slope of the regression and can be interpreted as a negative effect of increasing ownership in the hands of a board member as largest owner. This is in contrast to the findings from Models 9.3 and 10.3, which indicated a positive, although statistically not significant, effect of board ownership.

---

[189] The general effect shape of domestic and foreign intercorporate ownership does not depend on whether financial institutions as a whole or only domestic financial investors are used as reference category. Further, the findings do no change when domestic intercorporate ownership is used as reference category in order to assess the effect of foreign intercorporate ownership (this reference identity is actually most appropriate; however, this would impede the comparability of regression coefficients across various models).

[190] The general effect shape is, again, not dependent on the reference category (see Footnote 187).

Table 6.15: Within-Regression Results for Concentration and Identity Interaction Models, Using Interaction Terms

Dependent variable: Q	Controls only	Model 11.1	Model 11.2	Model 11.3
OWN1		0.725***	0.913***	0.693***
		(0.202)	(0.253)	(0.194)
PRIVATE (dummy)		0.260	0.308*	0.290*
		(0.159)	(0.173)	(0.152)
INSIDER (dummy)		0.199	0.235	
		(0.139)	(0.153)	
MGMT (dummy)				0.215
				(0.208)
BOARD (dummy)				0.379*
				(0.196)
CORP (dummy)		0.282**		0.271***
		(0.135)		(0.130)
DCORP (dummy)			0.459***	
			(0.209)	
FCORP (dummy)			0.128	
			(0.114)	
FINAN (dummy)		(omitted)		(omitted)
DFINAN (dummy)			(omitted)	
FFINAN (dummy)			0.112	
			(0.102)	
BANK (dummy)		-0.483*	-0.458*	-0.489*
		(0.294)	(0.276)	(0.294)
GOV (dummy)		-0.087	0.057	-0.084
		(0.060)	(0.122)	(0.059)
PRIVATE (dummy) × OWN1		-0.939**	-1.140***	-0.963***
		(0.383)	(0.422)	(0.343)
INSIDER (dummy) × OWN1		-1.256***	-1.431***	
		(0.443)	(0.457)	
MGMT (dummy) × OWN1				-1.850**
				(0.845)
BOARD (dummy) × OWN1				-1.197***
				(0.446)

(continued)

Table 6.15: Within-Regression Results for Concentration and Identity Interaction Models, Using Interaction Terms (continued)

Dependent variable: Q	Controls only	Model 11.1	Model 11.2	Model 11.3
CORP (dummy) × OWN1		-0.631* (0.243)		-0.587** (0.236)
DCORP (dummy) × OWN1			-1.206*** (0.370)	
FCORP (dummy) × OWN1			-0.360 (0.295)	
FINAN (dummy) × OWN1		(omitted)		(omitted)
DFINAN (dummy) × OWN1			(omitted)	
FFINAN (dummy) × OWN1			-0.700*** (0.255)	
BANK (dummy) × OWN1		0.178 (0.404)	0.015 (0.400)	0.206 (0.401)
GOV (dummy) × OWN1		-0.218 (0.549)	-1.520*** (0.577)	-0.256 (0.541)
DEBT	0.331 (0.325)	0.400 (0.329)	0.430 (0.323)	0.397 (0.320)
CAPX	0.739 (0.629)	0.606 (0.635)	0.546 (0.632)	0.537 (0.638)
RDX	0.923 (0.853)	0.892 (0.911)	0.807 (0.920)	0.924 (0.907)
GRO	0.002* (0.001)	0.002** (0.001)	0.002* (0.001)	0.002** (0.001)
Constant	1.129*** (0.075)	0.735*** (0.112)	0.695*** (0.124)	0.749*** (0.110)
R^2-within	0.158	0.179	0.187	0.185
R^2-between	0.043	0.004	0.001	0.002
R^2-overall	0.064	0.024	0.017	0.018
Sigma u (α)	0.888	0.920	0.932	0.931
Sigma e	0.452	0.452	0.451	0.451
Rho	0.794	0.805	0.810	0.810

Note. The analysis is based on 1,560 firm-year observations (452 firms). Asterisks denote statistical significance of the reported variables at the 0.01 (***), 0.05 (**) and 0.1 (*) level. Cluster-robust standard errors are in parentheses. All estimations include time dummies (estimated coefficients are not reported). The definition of variables can be found in Table 5.5.

6.3.3 Summary

In the final step of the empirical analyses, ownership concentration and owner identity effects have been conflated to an interaction model. First, the identity of the largest owner is examined. To summarize, the results from linear within-regressions confirm the positive effect of general ownership concentration. Accordingly, an increase of control rights held by the largest owner by 100 basis points results, on average, in an increase of firm performance measured by Tobin's Q by 0.374 basis points. The consideration of dummy variables for the identity of the largest owner yields that the coefficients for banks and government entities as largest investor are negative. Another finding is the negative effect of insiders (management) as largest owner. Compared with financial institutions as largest owner (dummy reference), the average performance effect is lower if the largest owner is a bank, governments or manager. The results are not fully robust to the alternation of the financial performance measure (ROA, ROE) as ownership concentration is no longer statistically significant.

Second, interaction terms are included in the model in order to allow the slope of the regression to be different depending on the identity of the largest owner. To summarize, the results from linear within-regressions find a constant term of 0.735 for financial institutions (the reference owner identity) as largest owner. In addition, the coefficient for the control rights held by the largest owner is 0.725, which implies that an increase of ownership concentration in the hands of financial investors (the reference owner identity) as largest owner is positively related to performance. This means that, for a given firm, an increase of the control rights held by a financial institution as largest owner by 100 basis points results, on average, in an increase of firm performance by 0.725 basis points. The positive performance effect is stronger for domestic than for foreign financial institutions. For corporations as largest owner, an increase of the control rights also leads to a positive performance effect; however, domestic corporations are found to decrease performance compared with foreign corporations. A negative performance effect is also revealed for private investor as largest owner as well as for insiders (both managers and board members). There is also weak evidence of a negative effect of government ownership. The effect of bank ownership is statistically not significant. Finally, the results are not robust to the alternation of the financial performance measure (ROA, ROE) as ownership concentration is no longer statistically significant. A graphical illustration of the results is provided in Figure 6.6 (Section 6.4).

6.4 Summary and Discussion of Results

The empirical analyses address the research question of whether and how ownership structure affects performance. The first part deals with the relation between ownership concentration and performance, and the second part examines the impact of owner identity. The final part of the analyses eventually conflates both effects to a combined model.

In order to assess the relation between ownership concentration and performance, a base case fixed-effects model is constructed. The within-estimation is generally superior to a pooled OLS estimation because it tackles the problem of unobserved heterogeneity. As a result of the estimations, a positive relation between ownership concentration and Tobin's Q is documented. A limitation of the within-estimation is that it does not address the problem of reverse causality. A commonly proposed solution is to identify instrumental variables (in this case, performance, firm size, firm risk and its squared measure) for the ownership variable and to use the fitted value in the second-stage fixed-effects regression. As a result of the estimations, a significant effect of ownership concentration on Tobin's Q cannot be confirmed. However, diagnostics on the instruments indicate that they are weak, which makes the estimates likely to be imprecise. Alternatively, lagged values of ownership concentration are used as instruments, which produce no weak-instruments problem, but estimations provide, again, no evidence of an effect of ownership concentration on performance. Nevertheless, contrary to the theoretically developed assumption of endogeneity of ownership, there is no econometric proof to support a reciprocal dependence of ownership and performance. This implies that there is no gain in endogenizing ownership concentration by means of an instrumental variable approach. The base case fixed-effects model is therefore preferred.

Having accepted the empirical evidence that a positive, one-way relation between ownership concentration and performance does exists, the question then arises whether this relation is linear across the entire range of ownership concentration. The use of restricted cubic splines confirms the generally positive relation but, indeed, reveals that the effect shape is better described as nonlinear with a negative effect at low levels of ownership concentration, a positive but bell-shaped effect at medium levels of ownership concentration, and a positive effect at high levels of ownership concentration. More precisely, performance is positively related to ownership concentration in the hands of the largest owner for ownership levels between 13.9% and 29.2% and beyond 44.1%. At the same time, performance is negatively related to ownership concentration in the hands of the largest owner for ownership levels below 13.9% and between 29.2% and 44.1%. The findings receive support from models estimating squared and piecewise-linear ownership concentration effects, which provide additional evidence of positive performance effects at high levels of ownership concentration. Figure 6.5 presents the shape of the relation between ownership concentration and performance graphically.

Figure 6.5: Empirically Identified Relation Between Ownership Concentration and Performance

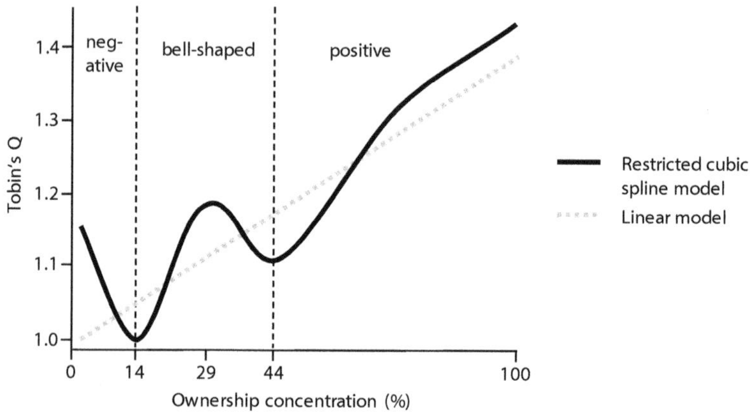

Note. Performance is measured as Tobin's Q. Ownership concentration is expressed as the size of shares owned by the largest shareholder (*OWN1*), although the general shape of the relation is robust to the use of alternative measures of ownership concentration. The definition of variables can be found in Table 5.5

The positive relation between ownership concentration and performance, especially for dominant share sizes above 44.1%, indicates that the positive effects of monitoring prevail at high levels of ownership concentration. The capital market hence appreciates if a shareholder holds majority control. The reason is that an increasing wealth commitment incentivizes the controlling shareholder to engage in monitoring. The incentive to take action is also spurred by the increasing cost-efficiency of monitoring. At the same time, and against theoretical predictions, there is no evidence of negative performance effects resulting from overmonitoring or from high costs of capital due to the liquidity reduction of the stock – or at least these effects are dominated by the positive monitoring effects.

In contrast, the negative relation between ownership concentration and performance at levels of ownership concentration below 13.9% can be interpreted as a result of the largest shareholder's noneffective monitoring role. Apparently, a dominant shareholder holding only a small stake does not possess enough power to control management and is probably also not willing to incur the costs of monitoring. Private benefits of control as a potential cause of negative performance do not seem to play a role because stakes are yet too small to give shareholders a substantial control.

At medium levels of ownership concentration, the relation between ownership concentration and performance appears to be positive but roof-shaped. For share sizes held by the largest owner between 13.9% and 29.2%, the relation is positive. The capital market apparently appreciates if a shareholder holds minority control (25%) or possesses at least enough power to bear responsibility for controlling management. In contrast, the relation turns negative for share sizes held by the largest owner between 29.2% and 44.1%. This could imply that a dominant shareholder owning a stake size that allows to exert a significant level of influence via minority control but that is too small to exercise a majority control (50%), feels trapped because there is no obvious benefit of owning additional shares. In this case, the controlling shareholder might prefer to increase his utility by private benefits rather than by monitoring. Another consideration arises from the German mandatory bid rule (§35 WpÜG) according to which an accumulation of 30% or more of a company's shares triggers a mandatory bid for all outstanding shares.[191] The capital market then expects the bidding shareholder to be able to collect a sufficient number of shares in order to build up a majority control (otherwise there would hardly be a reason to deliberately cross the 30%-threshold). Consequently, it can be reasoned that capital market performance decreases if the largest shareholder remains trapped between 30% and 50% as uncertainty arises regarding his intentions.

The empirical evidence is thus not in line with the originally formulated hypothesis of performance being a bell-shaped (first increasing, then decreasing) function of ownership concentration (except for medium levels of ownership). Hypothesis 1a is therefore rejected.

---

[191] The mandatory offer rule ensures that all owners of shares of the target company have the opportunity to sell their shares for adequate consideration in case of a change of control. The mandatory offer must be at a price equivalent to at least the highest consideration paid by the bidder for the target shares during the six months before the launch of the mandatory offer. In addition, the consideration offered must be at least equal to the weighted average stock price of the target shares during the three months prior to the announcement of the acquisition of control.

Moreover, there is also no empirical indication of a reverse or bidirectional effect of performance on ownership concentration. Ownership concentration should therefore be treated as exogenous. In other words, ownership concentration can be considered to have a significant impact on corporate performance, whereas causation does not run in the opposite direction. Hypothesis 1b is therefore also rejected. Table 6.16 contrasts the theoretically developed hypotheses (see Section 3.3.3) with the empirically identified relation between ownership concentration and performance.

Table 6.16: Hypothesized Effects of Ownership Concentration and Performance and Empirical Evidence

	Hypotheses		Empirical evidence
1a	Corporate performance is a bell-shaped (first increasing, then decreasing) function of ownership concentration.	×	No empirical support (except for medium levels of ownership concentration between 14% and 44%, with a maximum at 29%).
1b	Ownership concentration increases with corporate performance.	×	No empirical support.

Note. Performance is measured as capital market performance (Tobin's Q), and ownership concentration refers to the size of shares owned by the largest shareholder (*OWN1*), although the general empirical evidence is robust to the use of alternative measures of ownership concentration.

Having examined the generally positive, although nonlinear, effect of ownership concentration on performance, the question then arises whether this relation is robust to shareholder identity, that is, whether all owners can be treated as a homogenous group, or whether different motivations and abilities of shareholder identities result in their distinctive effectiveness to influence major corporate decisions and eventually performance. The second part of the empirical analyses therefore aggregates all shares owned by the same type of shareholders, assuming that there are no differences in the utility function and the behavior of shareholders with the same identity. As a result of the estimations, a positive relation between the aggregated sum of shares in the hands of corporations (in particular, foreign corporations) and in the hands of financial institutions (in particular, domestic financial institutions) and Tobin's Q is found. Another finding is the negative relation between managerial holdings and performance. The effect of ownership in the hands of board members, private investors, banks, and government agencies is not significant.

As a final step, the third part of the empirical analyses conflates the effects of ownership concentration and owner identity to a combined model. First, dummy variables for the identity of the largest owner are created in order to capture the performance effect of the largest owner as a function of his identity. Compared with firms with a financial institution as largest owner, firms with a bank or government entity as dominant shareholder are found to exhibit inferior performance. Another finding is the comparably negative effect of managers as largest shareholder. Second, interaction terms for the identity and stake size of the largest owner are created in order to capture the performance effect of the largest owner as a function of both his identity and his stake size. As a result of the estimations, a financial investor as largest shareholder is found to have a positive impact on performance. For a corporation as the largest owner, an increase of control rights also has a positive effect on performance, although this effect is smaller than in the case of a dominant financial investor. For private investors and insiders (both, managers and board members) as largest owner, ownership is negatively related to performance. Figure 6.6 illustrates the shape of the relation between the identity and the stake size of the largest owner and performance (Model 11.3).

Figure 6.6: Empirically Identified Relations Between Owner Identity and Performance (Model 11.3)

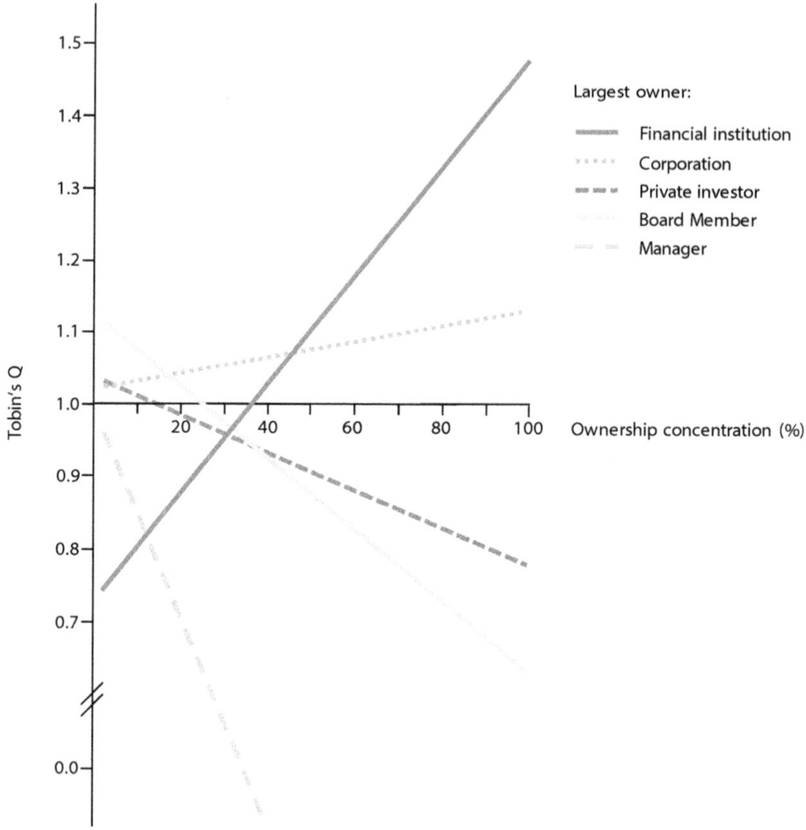

Note. Performance is measured as Tobin's Q. Ownership concentration is expressed as the size of shares owned by the largest shareholder (*OWN1*). The intercept coefficient of managerial ownership is not statistically significant so that the location (but not the slope) of the regression line might be biased.

The empirical evidence from the interaction model shows that an increase of shares in the hands of a dominant financial investor leads to a tremendous increase of firm performance. This provides support for the positive effects of active monitoring through financial investors who are assumed to be the most sophisticated and informed type of investor due to their professional occupation with capital markets, industries, and businesses. Industry knowledge and business insights also reduce the cost of acquiring information. Thus, financial investors have the ability to effectively engage in monitoring activities, thereby contributing to corporate performance. The empirical evidence is therefore in line with the originally proposed hypothesis of institutional ownership being positively related to corporate performance. Hypothesis 5 is therefore accepted. Table 6.17 contrasts the theoretically developed hypotheses with the empirically identified relation.

Firm value is created (based on the assumption that a value of Tobin's Q of greater than 1 reflects market optimism about the prospects of a company) if the commitment of a dominant financial investor exceeds 36.2%.[192] This threshold can be used to differentiate two types of financial investors: those holding comparably small stakes (thereby increasing performance but not necessarily creating excess value) and those holding large stakes (thereby increasing performance and creating value). This distinction might be attributed to the characterization of financial investors either as transient and quasi-indexing or as dedicated investors (see Section 3.4.4). Accordingly, transient and quasi-indexing financial investors hold relatively small ownership stakes and hence have few incentives to monitor the management. They intend to maximize short-term gains and focus on value proxies such as current earnings. They are therefore expected to be most sensitive to fluctuations in earnings, thereby creating incentives for myopic management behavior. As a consequence, it might be reasoned that the market value of firms with a dominant financial investor holding a comparably small stake is, on average, lower than the market value of firms with other types of largest owners (with the same size of ownership). However, an increase of control rights in the hands of financial investors increases their incentive to engage in monitoring, or, the other way round, increases the likelihood that the stakes are in the hands of dedicated financial investors. Compared with transient and quasi-indexing financial institutions, dedicated financial institutions hold relatively large positions in a few firms and trade infrequently. Their large, long-term oriented holdings provide incentives to monitor managers and to rely on information other than current earnings to assess the company's performance, thereby attenuating the pressure for myopic management behavior. As a consequence, managers have less reason to sacrifice long-term profits for short-term gains and instead focus on the long-term objective of making value-maximizing investment decisions. This is, in turn, appreciated by capital market

[192] The economic tuition beyond a Tobin's Q of greater than 1 is that if the market value of assets exceeds their replacement (or book) value, this excess part of the firm's value must reside in less tangible assets such as real options and investment opportunities, which are not recorded on the balance sheet but are expected to contribute to future cash flows. See Section 2.4.2.1 for a discussion on the limitations of Tobin's Q.

participants in terms of a high market valuation (and hence high values of Tobin's Q). There is no evidence of negative performance effects resulting from self-dealing – or at least these effects are dominated by the positive monitoring effects. Compared with other types of ownership, large institutional ownership produces the highest firm value.

Another interesting finding is the superiority of domestic over foreign financial institutions. While an increase of shares in the hands of both leads to an increase of firm performance, this effect is particularly stronger for domestic than for foreign financial institutions. The preference by investment managers for locally headquartered firms is a well documented phenomenon in literature, and explanations are associated with political and monetary boundaries as well as a preference for geographic proximity due to informational asymmetries (e.g., van Nieuwerburgh & Veldkamp, 2009). As a consequence, financial investors typically bias their portfolio towards domestic firms and invest abroad only to capture diversification effects rather than to improve governance – which hence results in low firm performance.

In regard to the impact of intercorporate ownership, the empirical evidence shows that an increase of shares in the hands of a dominant intercorporate owner leads to an increase of firm performance. The empirical evidence is therefore in line with the originally proposed hypothesis of intercorporate ownership being positively related to corporate performance. Hypothesis 4 is therefore accepted. The positive relation supports the view that corporations invest in other companies in the course of a general cash-management program and basically act as financial investors pushing firms in which they hold equity to increase performance. Their typically large stakes and long duration of ownership (see Section 3.4.3) make them comparable to dedicated financial institutions, which are positively associated with performance (as discussed above). At the same time, large stake sizes and long-term commitment may also indicate that corporations invest strategically in other companies in order to expand business opportunities. Intercorporate ownership then serves as an instrument to align incentives between firms to expand joint investment opportunities and to reduce the costs of generating business agreements and alliances. There is a risk that the advantages of strategic business ties come at the cost of deficient monitoring due to conflict-of-interest pressures or strategic alignments of interest between the business partners where the possible gain of active monitoring faces an opportunity loss in the business relation. However, there is no empirical evidence for negative performance effects resulting from undermonitoring as a consequence of strategic intercorporate investments.

A surprising finding is the superiority of foreign over domestic intercorporate owners. While an increase of shares in the hands of foreign corporations leads to an increase of firm performance, this effect turns even negative in the case of domestic corporations. In other words, the overall positive effect of intercorporate ownership appears to be driven by the beneficial role of foreign intercorporate owners. This is because international corporations typically invest in foreign firms for strategic reasons and often transfer new technology, organizational and financial resources or management expertise – and thereby actively contribute to firm performance. Moreover, as their resource commitment goes beyond solely financial contributions, management control is usually tighter than in case of other owners (Douma, George, & Kabir, 2006).

In regard to the role of private investors, the empirical evidence shows that an increase of shares in the hands of a dominant private owner leads to a decrease of firm value. The empirical evidence hence confirms the theoretically derived hypothesis of private ownership being negatively related to corporate performance. Hypothesis 2 is therefore accepted. Value is created (in terms of Tobin's Q being greater than 1) only if the commitment of this owner type is below 14.4% of the company's equity (with a negative marginal effect, though). This particular control threshold is almost identical to the average stake size held by private investors of 15.8% (see Section 5.2.3). As a consequence, it can be concluded that the average individual investor is not associated with superior market value. This provides support for the argument that private investors are bad monitors. Accordingly, individual investors typically have no adequate understanding or are relatively incompetent of using sophisticated valuation techniques and hence can hardly assess the financial performance of firms. In addition, they often lack adequate and relevant information (and acquisition thereof is costly) and are typically unfamiliar with the day-to-day-operations of the firm. As a consequence, individual owners are argued to have a serious disadvantage concerning their capability to engage in effective monitoring activities. This sleepy monitoring consequently leaves managers too much power to waste corporate resources on value-destroying activities. At the same time, individual investors are argued to be loyal owners who are beneficial for firm performance because they counter short-termism in the firm's investment decisions. However, there is no empirical support for this argument – or at least these effects are dominated by the negative effects resulting from undermonitoring.

The empirical investigation of insider ownership finds that an increase of shares in the hands of insiders decreases firm performance. The empirical evidence therefore disagrees with the theoretically predicted positive relation between insider ownership and performance. Hypothesis 3 is thus rejected. This has also important implications for the assessment of the role of family firms (as a special case of insiders), which are revealed to decrease firm value. A differentiation between managers and board members documents differences between the two types of insiders in so far as both are found to decrease firm value but the speed of destruction is significantly lower in case of board members as largest owners.

Board members create value (in terms of Tobin's Q being greater than 1) as long as their commitment is smaller than 25.4% of the company's equity. This might be interpreted as an indication that board ownership (initially) reduces potentially harming actions due to a convergence of interests between board members and general shareholders insofar as they engage in monitoring the management. Compared with other types of dominant owners with small stakes, board members produce the highest firm value. However, an increase of control rights in the hands of board members as largest owner leads to a deterioration of value. This is because at higher levels of ownership, board members might align with managers (and potentially exploit private benefits of control) rather than with general shareholders. This implies that family firms succeed against alternative forms of ownership only if the family is represented at the supervisory board and dominates the firm's equity with rather small ownership stakes.

In contrast, managerial shareholders are associated with a lower firm value than board members. However, the position of the regression line is statistically not significant and might be biased; therefore, no definitive conclusions can be drawn in regard to the performance difference compared with other owner types. Nevertheless, any increase of shares in the hands of a dominant manager leads to an enormous decrease of firm performance. This can be interpreted as an indication of entrenchment: As insider ownership reduces the power of controlling shareholders, it enables managers to extract perquisites from (other) shareholders at lower opportunity costs and, at the same time, to protect themselves against disciplining actions or reduce the degree of sanctions. Even if managers do not entrench themselves, capital market participants might find it difficult to assess the behavior of managers and, as a consequence, interpret managerial ownership as a potential for managers (and board members) to conduct wealth-destroying actions, which in turn leads to a lower demand for the company's shares and hence lower market valuation.

In regard to the role of dominant bank ownership, no definitive conclusions can be drawn because the relation is statistically not significant. Hypothesis 6 therefore remains unsolved. For government entities as largest owner, there is some (weak) evidence of a negative performance effect probably as a result of a focus on political goals instead of shareholder value, inefficient management and undermonitoring. However, the position of the regression line is statistically not significant; therefore, no definitive conclusions can be drawn in regard to the performance difference compared with other owner types. Hypothesis 7 therefore receives only limited support. A summary is provided in Table 6.17.

Table 6.17: Hypothesized Effects of Owner Identity on Performance and Empirical Evidence

Hypotheses: Corporate performance ...		Empirical evidence	
2	... decreases with ownership concentration in the hands of individuals.	✓	Supported. Individual investor ownership is in particular deleterious if an individual is the largest owner and controls medium to large stakes.
3	... increases with ownership concentration in the hands of insiders.	×	Rejected for both managers and board members. Board ownership is less deleterious if a board member controls small stakes, though.
4	... increases with ownership concentration in the hands of corporations.	✓	Supported. Intercorporate ownership is beneficial across all levels of ownership concentration.
5	... increases with ownership concentration in the hands of financial institutions.	✓	Supported. Institutional ownership is in particular beneficial if a financial institution is the largest shareholder and controls large stakes.
6	... decreases with ownership concentration in the hands of commercial banks.	?	No statistically significant relation.
7	... decreases with ownership concentration in the hands of government authorities.	✓	Supported, but evidence is weak.

Note. Performance is measured as capital market performance (Tobin's Q), and ownership concentration refers to the size of shares owned by the largest shareholder (*OWN1*).

An interesting finding evolving from the graphical presentation of the relations between owner identity and performance in Figure 6.6 is the intersection point between the regression lines of dominant institutional ownership and dominant intercorporate ownership at 46.2%. This implies that a dominant shareholder owning less than 46.2% is associated with higher performance if it is a corporation rather than a financial investor, while the opposite is true for ownership levels above 46.2%. At the same time, this intersection point relates very roughly to the average stake size of intercorporate owners of 38.4% (see Section 5.2.3). This means that if the average intercorporate owner is the largest shareholder in a firm, firm performance is almost comparable with a situation where a financial institution is the largest owner and holds the same amount of control rights. This can be interpreted as an indication of corporations being almost as sophisticated investors as financial institutions. Corporations appear indeed comparable with dedicated financial institutions (as reasoned above). As a consequence, this implies that firm performance can be expected to rise if (a) a dominant institutional owner with a share size of less than 46.2% sells his share package to a corporate owner or alternatively increases his ownership stake beyond this threshold, or (b) a dominant intercorporate owner with a share size of greater than 46.2% trades his block of shares with an institutional owner.

Another striking intersection point is that between the regression lines of dominant intercorporate ownership and dominant board ownership at 17.7%. This implies that firm performance can be increased if (a) a board member with a dominant stake of greater than 17.7% sells his share package to a corporate owner, or (b) a dominant corporate owner with a share size of less than 17.7% increases his ownership stake beyond this threshold or alternatively trades his shares with a board member (at an ownership level in the hands of board members of 11.5%, performance is comparable to a situation where either corporations or financial institutions hold a stake of 46.2%).

To summarize this aspect, for dominant ownership shares below 17.7%, the highest performance can be achieved if the largest owner is a board member. For dominant ownership stakes between 17.7% and 46.2%, corporations emerge as "best" owners. At high levels of ownership beyond 46.2%, dedicated financial investors are identified as value-maximizing dominant shareholders. Figure 6.7 illustrates the described interplay of effects by basically retracing the regression lines of the owner types with the highest performance.

Figure 6.7: Ideal Owner Types by Size of Dominant Shareholding

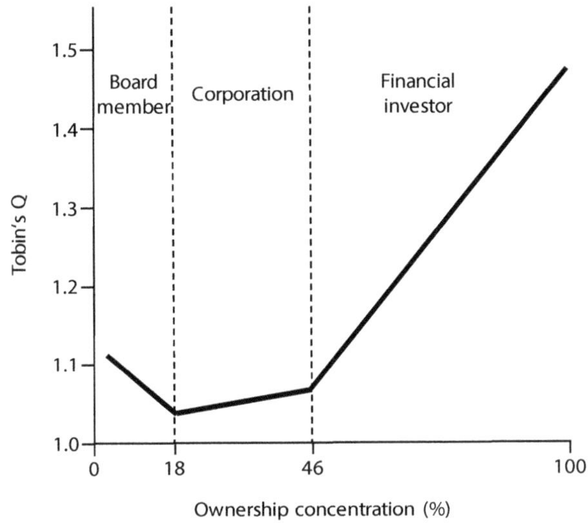

Note. Performance is measured as Tobin's Q. Ownership concentration refers to the size of shares owned by the largest shareholder (*OWN1*). The definition of variables can be found in Table 5.5

Finally, a major finding of the empirical analyses is the close link between the empirically identified relation between owner identity and performance (Figure 6.6) and ownership concentration and performance (Figure 6.5): As owner types have different implications for firm performance (as discussed above) and, at the same time, have different preferences for particular stake sizes (as discussed in Section 5.2.3), the evidence on ownership concentration and its impact on performance can actually to a large extent be explained by the presence of different owners at various levels of ownership concentration.

Most frequently, the largest owners are financial institutions, corporations and insiders (see Table 5.10 and Table 5.11). It is therefore assumed that the shape of the general ownership concentration effect can be interpreted as a function of the performance effects produced by these owners: At very low levels of ownership concentration (5.0-14.9%), insiders play an important role and because their influence on performance is very negative (as discussed above), it is reasonable to assume that this effect causes the overall relation between ownership concentration and performance to be negative. Financial institutions, which are generally found to be very beneficial for performance, are also dominant owners in this size bracket (they are found to be dominant owners across all stake sizes, though). This might cause the overall concentration effect to be less negative than it actually would be. Alternatively, it might be presumed that the relation between institutional ownership and performance is not consistent across the entire range of ownership concentration and that the relation is less positive or even negative at low levels of ownership concentration. The presumably negative effects of transient and quasi-indexing investors (as discussed above) as well as the finding that foreign financial investors (with typically small stakes) are deleterious to performance compared to large, domestic financial investors might underpin this argumentation.

At slightly higher levels of ownership concentration (15.0-24.9%), the relative importance of intercorporate owners doubles. Their positive effect on performance is likely to explain the positive relation between general concentration and performance. Likewise, at medium levels of ownership concentration (25.0-49.9%), the relative presence of insiders increases, and, at the same time, the presence of financial institutions decreases. This turns the relation between the overall ownership concentration and performance negative again.

Finally, at high levels of ownership concentration (greater than 50%), stakes are almost completely dominated by financial institutions and corporations, while insiders play no significant role. As a result, the positive performance impact of financial institutions and corporations produces the steep tail at high levels of ownership concentration. Figure 6.8 illustrates the discussed link between owner identity and ownership concentration graphically.

To conclude, while the analysis of ownership concentration effects on performance is based mainly on monitoring and private-benefits-of-control arguments but might not be fully able to explain the exact shape of the empirically identified relation, the investigation of owner identity reveals additional information on the type of relevant shareholders and their particular influence on performance. Conflating these two aspects of ownership illustrates that the relation between ownership concentration and corporate performance can be explained – to a large degree – by the distinction between various owner identities that have different implications for firm performance and, at the same time, diverge in their preferences for ownership in particular size brackets. This implies that ownership concentration effects should rather be interpreted as owner identity effects.

Figure 6.8: Link Between Owner Identity and Ownership Concentration Effects

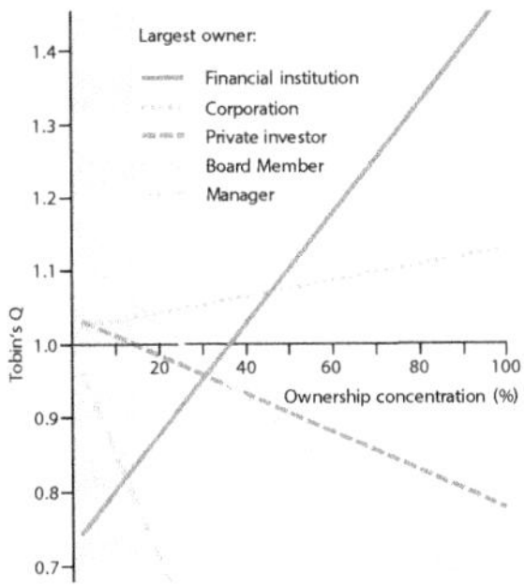

Low levels of ownership concentration (5.0-14.9%):

Owner types	Relevance in size bracket	Performance effect
Insiders	19.6%	-
Corporations	7.8%	+
Institutions	57.2%	+

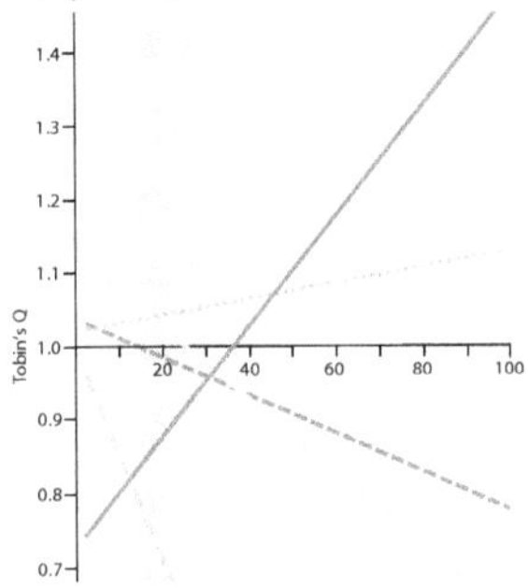

Low to medium levels of ownership concentration (15.0-24.9%):

Owner types	Relevance in size bracket	Performance effect
Insiders	21.1%	-
Corporations	15.5%	+
Institutions	49.7%	+

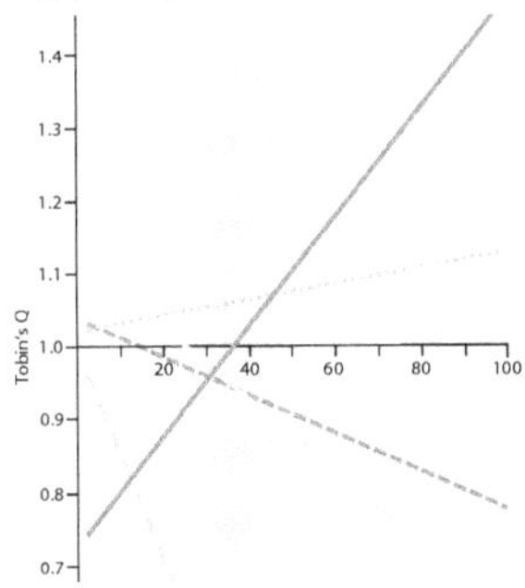

Medium levels of ownership concentration (25.0-49.9%):

Owner types	Relevance in size bracket	Performance effect
Insiders	28.1%	-
Corporations	16.7%	+
Institutions	44.7%	+

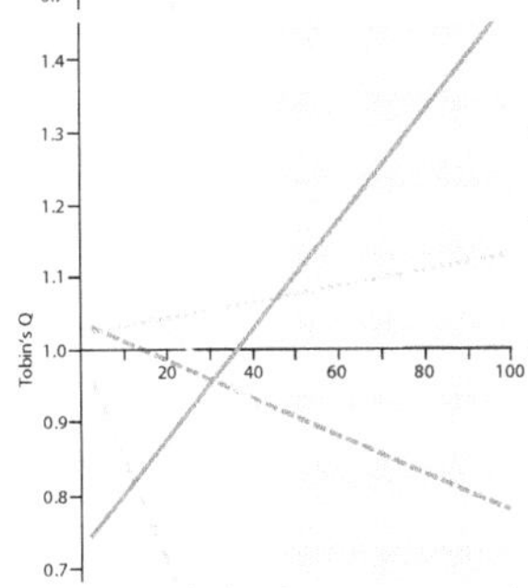

High levels of ownership concentration (50.0-74.9% / >75%):

Owner types	Relevance in size bracket	Performance effect
Insiders	25.1%/2.8%	-
Corporations	30.3%/45.6%	+
Institutions	38.7%/48.4%	+

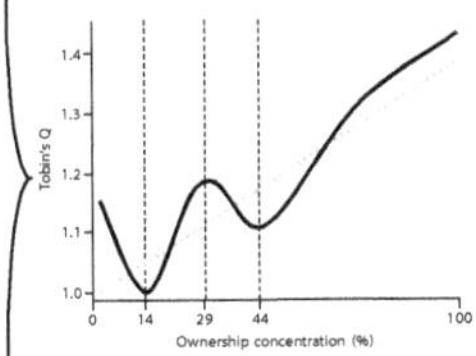

Note. Detailed information on the illustrations is provided in Figure 6.5, Figure 6.6 and Table 5.11.

7 Conclusion

A clear understanding of the relation between ownership structure and corporate performance is of great importance both to corporate decision makers who aim to create shareholder value (and other objectives) and to public policy. From a public policy perspective, ownership – more precisely, the quality of ownership engagement – plays a major role for effective capital allocation and monitoring of corporate performance (Çelik & Isaksson, 2014). A well-functioning market economy relies on shareholders to price and allocate capital among different business opportunities and to monitor these companies to make sure that they make the best possible use of the invested capital. It is in the self-interest of shareholders to gather information on the company's prospects and, whenever necessary, use this information to engage with the company and influence key decisions. This ownership engagement brings new and unique information to the economy. The new information will improve the allocation of productive resources and make better use of those resources that are already employed. Ownership engagement is therefore essential to value creation and economic growth. In order to assume this socially beneficial role, shareholders have also been given the legal rights to exercise it, which includes the transferability of shares, access to information, participation in key decisions concerning fundamental corporate changes, and the election of the board of directors. However, exercising these rights is always associated with certain costs, which some shareholders are motivated to bear and some are not. Shareholders who, for some reason, do not find it worthwhile to contribute to monitoring through any form of ownership engagement are obviously ill-equipped to serve the wider economic role of improving allocation and corporate performance. Instead, their role in the economy will be limited to providing risk capital. The observation that shareholders exhibit different degrees of ownership engagement makes it essential to understand how the structure of ownership, that is, the size of shareholdings and the identity of owners, influence shareholders' ability and willingness to serve as informed and engaged owners – and how public policy may encourage the economic contribution from share ownership.

From the perspective of corporate decision makers, equity ownership is a fundamental matter because companies rely on shareholders as primary suppliers of financial resources. Due to potential agency conflicts, however, equity cannot be procured on attractive terms without an accompanying grant of control rights. As shareholders use their power to influence key elements of corporate strategy (depending on the degree of engagement), it becomes important for any listed company to know who its owners are in order to connect with influential shareholders and build investor relations. A large survey of public company directors by PricewaterhouseCoopers (2014) reports that directors are very sensitive to shareholder support as 58% of the interviewed directors say that negative shareholder voting in the 11-25% range would cause them to be concerned about re-election. According to the same survey, 73% of directors believe that executive compensation has a top priority of the topics to be discussed with shareholders. Similarly, a majority of directors (56%) say it is appropriate to communicate with investors about strategy and changes in strategy or direction. The importance of shareholder interaction is also reflected by the ongoing trend worldwide to implement corporate board-shareholder engagement programs. However, in order to reach out to shareholders effectively, managers must have an understanding of the goals and objectives, risk perceptions and time preferences of their shareholders in order to establish a fit between corporate strategy (e.g., in regard to profit goals, dividends, capital structure, and growth rates) and ownership structure (Thomsen & Pedersen, 2000). Otherwise, corporate strategies are unlikely to be sustainable because they lack backing from the company's owners. The objectives of key owners can be made more precise by referring to the size of their shareholdings as well as their identity. There is hence a clear need for corporate decision makers to have an understanding of the company's shareholder base in terms of ownership concentration and the identity of key owners, their goals and characteristics, and their influence on corporate strategy as well as the consequences for performance.

There is an ongoing debate in academic literature as well as in the business world on the relation between ownership structure and corporate performance. However, the theoretical discussion has failed to reach any conclusions as to whether ownership does significantly affect performance. Empirical studies have produced different versions of the relation between ownership and performance and hence have also not resulted in consistent findings. Most of these studies focused on the effects of ownership concentration, thereby treating owners as a monolithic group. However, it is quite likely that there are differences in motives and behavior arising from differences in goals and objectives of owner groups. Ignoring this may fail to provide valuable insights into the relation between ownership and firm performance. A complimentary body of literature therefore suggests that the identity of owners is an equally important but often neglected dimension of ownership structure and investigates the performance effects of a major owner type (usually insiders). However, only few empirical studies sought to incorporate the entirety of owner identities into the empirical investigation of the effect of ownership structure on performance (Edwards & Nibler, 2000; Edwards & Weichenrieder, 2004; Lehmann & Weigand, 2000; Pedersen & Thomsen, 2003, and Thomsen & Pedersen, 2000). The objective of this dissertation was therefore to offer a rich theoretical and empirical examination of the role of ownership structure in explaining variations in corporate performance by including the identity of various parties of shareholders in the investigation. This fills a gap in literature and aims to contribute to a better understanding of the relation between ownership structure and corporate performance.

The empirical analyses in this dissertation document a significant, positive effect of ownership concentration on capital market performance, based on a fixed-effects regression model. The use of restricted cubic splines confirms the generally positive relation between ownership concentration and Tobin's Q but reveals that the effect shape is better described to be nonlinear with a negative effect at low levels at ownership concentration (<14%), a positive but bell-shaped effect at medium levels of ownership concentration (14-44%), and a positive effect at high levels of ownership concentration (>44%).

Evidence further reveals that the identity of owners matters for the relation between ownership concentration and performance. Owners differ in terms of wealth constraints, competence, preferences and nonownership ties to the firm. This affects the way they exercise their ownership rights and therefore has distinctive consequences for firm performance. Financial investors (particularly, domestic financial investors) are documented to have a positive impact on performance. For corporations, an increase of control rights also has a positive albeit smaller effect than in the case of financial investors (although this effect seems to be driven by the positive performance effect of foreign rather than domestic intercorporate owners). For private investors and insiders (board members and particularly managers), ownership is negatively related to performance. There is also weak evidence of a negative effect of government agencies as corporate owners. The impact of bank ownership is insignificant.

A major finding of the empirical analyses is the close link between the effect shapes of ownership concentration and owner identity. This is because owner identities have different implications for firm performance and, at the same time, have different preferences for ownership in particular size brackets. This implies that the evidence on ownership concentration and its impact on performance actually can be explained – to a large degree –on the basis of the relative importance of different owners in various size brackets of ownership concentration. At low levels of ownership concentration, the dominance of value-decreasing board members causes the overall relation between ownership concentration and performance to be negative. At slightly higher levels of ownership concentration, intercorporate owners contribute to a positive effect shape, and at medium levels of ownership, the increased presence of insiders turns the relation negative again. Finally, the positive performance impact of financial institutions and corporations produces a steep tail of the effect shape at high levels of ownership concentration. A significant conclusion to arise from this dissertation is therefore that ownership concentration effects should rather be interpreted as owner identity effects.

These findings have important implications for public policy, corporate decision-makers and shareholders who are concerned with the question: "*What type of large investors are best?*" The empirical analyses in this dissertation offer an answer on the basis of a comparison of the performance effects of various owner identities. Accordingly, evidence suggests that at small ownership levels, the highest performance can be achieved if the largest owner is a board member. For dominant ownership stakes between 18% and 46%, corporations emerge as "best" owners. At high levels of ownership beyond 46%, dedicated financial investors are identified as value-maximizing dominant shareholders.

Considering the fact that the largest owner holds an average ownership stake of 38%, it can be reasoned that German companies are generally well positioned – provided that the largest owner is another nonfinancial corporation. This is likely to be the case because the mean size of intercorporate ownership is 38% as well. Nevertheless, corporations can create additional value by stimulating a further increase of (foreign) intercorporate ownership or by attracting a dominant financial investor opting for majority control. In the used data set, financial investors are mainly identified as funds and insurance companies but, to a large degree, also as investment trusts whose business purpose is the acquisition and management of corporate and private investments. The group therewith also includes families who manage their (typically large) ownership stakes through investment trusts. This implies that the previously derived conclusions regarding a generally negative effect of family ownership (as a special case of insider ownership) have to be put into perspective as they presumably apply only to situations where family members hold small stakes and are directly invested. In contrast, family owners with larger stakes are typically observed to manage their shareholdings through family offices and can therefore be argued to behave more like financial institutions than like private investors. The superior role of domestic over foreign financial institutions in enhancing corporate performance might further underpin the argument of (typically locally investing) family trusts being beneficial to firm performance.

From a theoretical point of view, the largest gains from restructuring ownership could be achieved by attracting a financial institution who acquires nearly 100% of a firm's equity (Demsetz, 1983). In practice, however, this is not necessarily a universally desirable objective because owners as well as potential investors may weigh the anticipated gains in shareholder restructuring against other goals. For example, dominant shareholders may be aware that they could increase the price of the shares by (partly) selling out to other owner identities but nevertheless be reluctant to do so because of overpower concerns. Likewise, financial institutions may not wish to acquire large stakes or increase their existing exposure due to liquidity concerns and internally established ceilings on maximal ownership allowances, even though they know that a stronger pressure on managers would probably increase firm value. Nonetheless, the current low-interest phase in Continental Europe is expected to further spur (institutional) investments in corporate equity. In 2014, financial institutions invested €7bn in German companies, which is an increase of 40% compared with the previous year. For 2015, a further 10%-increase is expected ("Niedrigzins", 2015). With a solid understanding of the concept of ownership structure and its implications for firm value, corporate decision-makers and shareholders in German corporations should then benefit from the currently increased institutional investment appetite and bank on these equity participations to move up the value creation ladder. This is essential to secure the success and long-term survival of the firm.

These findings open up a variety of avenues for future research: First, one concern that should be addressed is the assumed linearity of owner identity effects. While the use of advanced econometric techniques identified a nonlinear effect shape of ownership concentration on performance (across all owners), this was not applicable to owner identity effects due to technical limitations given the large number of owner identity variables. However, it is quite reasonable to assume that the effects of ownership in the hands of large shareholders are a nonlinear function of their stake sizes. So far, the debate has concentrated on the shape of insider ownership effects (e.g., Morck et al., 1988), and evidence is scarce in regard to other owner identities. Further research could address this issue by focusing on other key shareholders such as corporations and financial institutions.

Another interesting area recommended for further investigation is the analysis of potential endogeneity of ownership in the hands of certain owner identities. As the theoretically derived arguments have demonstrated, it is reasonable to assume that large shareholders are influenced by firm performance, and the implication is that changes in performance may also lead to changes in ownership by certain identities. In the course of the empirical analyses, however, it seemed justifiable to assume exogeneity of owner identity because there was no econometric proof of endogeneity of ownership concentration – which turned out to be a reflection of owner identity effects. Nevertheless, the understanding of the concept of owner identity might significantly benefit from a further investigation of potential feedback effects (see Pedersen & Thomsen, 2003 for a practical approach on this topic).

A third field for future research is the analysis of tensions and potential interplays between shareholders. On the one hand, the question arises whether multiple large shareholders, as opposed to just one large shareholder, have a positive or negative effect on corporate performance, and whether this is affected by the identity of these shareholders. Maury and Pajuste (2005) and Sacristán-Navarro, Cabeza-García, and Gómez-Ansón (2015), for example, make an approach on this topic and find that large family owners are more prone to private benefit extraction if they are not monitored by another strong blockholder. The role of the various types of large shareholders hence appears to be an interesting topic for more research. On the other hand, it is also possible that small shareholders combine their ownership stakes and act in concert. Given the great power that the largest owner holds, on average, compared with other shareholders in the sample companies, voting coalitions among smaller shareholders might be highly relevant in the German market. More research on interaction effects between various types of shareholders and the implications for corporate performance is therefore needed.

Appendices

A.1 Previous Research on Ownership and Performance

Table A.1.1: Selected Academic Studies on Ownership Concentration and/or Owner Identity and Performance

Author(s)	Geographical focus	Sample description and study period	Methodology	Performance measure(s)	Main ownership concentration measure(s) and/or owner type(s)	Summary of main findings and conclusions
Agarwal and Elston (2001)	DE	100 large firms (public and private), 1970-86	FE regressions	ROS	Owner dummy: ▪ Bank ▪ Other	Bank ownership does not seem to enhance either firms' profitability or growth.
Alonso-Bonis and de Andrés-Alonso (2007)	ES	101 frequently traded nonfinancial firms, 1991-97	GMM regressions	Q	Concentration: ▪ VR(1)	Ownership concentration is found to increase performance.
Anderson and Reeb (2003a)	US	403 S&P 500 nonfinancial and nonutility firms, 1992-99	FE and FE-2SLS regressions	ROA, Q	Owner dummy: ▪ Family ▪ Other	Firm performance is first increasing and then decreasing as family ownership increases but is still better than in nonfamily firms.
Andres (2008)	DE	275 FSE-listed nonfinancial firms, 1998-2004	RE and IV regressions (not further specified)	ROA, Q	Owner dummy: ▪ Family ▪ Government ▪ Financial institution/bank ▪ Corporation ▪ Individual ▪ Other (e.g., management)	Family firms are not only more profitable than widely held firms but also outperform other types of blockholders.
Atkinson and Halvorsen (1986)	US	153 utility firms (public and private), 1970	ML estimations	Operating cost structure	Owner dummy : ▪ Government ▪ Other	There is no performance difference between publicly owned and privately owned firms as both types of firms are equally cost inefficient.

Beirne, Liu, and Sun (2013)	CN	1,184 companies that were (partially) privatized during the period 1997-2003	FE and FE-2SLS regressions	Debt ratio, investments, labor force growth, ROA, sales per employee	Owner dummy: ▪ Government ▪ Private (fully, partially) ▪ Private insiders (management and employees)	Partial privatization emerges as the best performing type of ownership model in terms of improved labor productivity after the reform.
Bhattacharya and Graham (2009)	FI	98 public firms with institutional ownership, 2004	3SLS regressions	Q	Concentration: ▪ HHI (institutions, both pressure sensitive and pressure resistant)	Institutional ownership concentration affects performance negatively. The effect is comparably larger for pressure sensitive institutions.
Boardman and Vining (1992)	CA	370 of the 500 largest nonfinancial firms (public and private), 1986	OLS regressions	Net income, ROA, ROS	Owner dummy: ▪ Government ▪ Mixed (government and private) ▪ Private	There is strong evidence of a superior performance of privately owned firms in competitive environments.
Cable (1985)	DE	48 of the largest 100 public industrial firms, 1970	OLS and WLS regressions	Income available to equity holders divided by total assets	Fraction of VR controlled by: ▪ Banks	There is a positive relation between the degree of bank ownership and corporate performance.
Chen, Hexter, and Hu (1993)	US	500 large public firms, 1976, 1980 and 1984	OLS regressions	Q	Fraction of VR controlled by: ▪ Insiders	Performance rises when managerial ownership is very low and falls as ownership increases.

Chirinko and Elston (2006)	DE	91 public industrial firms, 1966-88	OLS regressions	ROA	Concentration dummy: ▪ VR(1)>75% or VR(1-3)>75%, or VR(1)>50% ▪ Otherwise Owner dummy: ▪ Bank/insurer ▪ Other	Bank influence has negative but statistically insignificant effects on profitability.
Cho (1998)	US	326 Fortune 500 manufacturing firms, 1991	OLS and 3SLS regressions	Q	Fraction of VR controlled by: ▪ Insiders	Performance affects ownership structure but not vice versa.
Davies, Hillier, and McColgan (2005)	UK	802 public industrial firms, 1995	OLS and 2SLS regressions	Q	Fraction of VR controlled by: ▪ Insiders	Although managerial ownership levels are determined by corporate performance, performance itself is determined in part by managerial ownership.
Demsetz and Lehn (1985)	US	511 public firms, 1980/81; subsample: 406 manufacturing and mining firms, 1980/81	2SLS regressions	ROE	Concentration: ▪ VR(1-5), VR(1-20) ▪ HHI	No significant relation is found between ownership concentration and performance.
Demsetz and Villalonga (2001)	US	223 firms randomly sampled from the Demsetz and Lehn (1985) data	OLS and 2SLS regressions	Q	Concentration: ▪ VR(1-5) Fraction of VR controlled by: ▪ Insiders	Evidence supports the belief that (especially managerial) ownership is endogenous but not the belief that ownership systematically affects performance.

Dittmann, Maug and Schneider (2010)	DE	167 DAX 100 firms, 1994-2005	Granger causality tests, FE and Tobit regressions	ROA, Q	Fraction of VR controlled by: ▪ Banks	Bankers on the board cause a decline in the valuations of firms as there is little evidence that bankers represent their interests as shareholders.
D'Souz and Megginson (1999)	28 developing and industrialized countries (further specified in the paper)	85 firms that were (partially) privatized through public share offerings during the period 1990-96	Matched pairs	ROA, ROE, ROS	Owner dummy: ▪ Government ▪ Other	Both full and partial privatization yield significant improvements in financial and operating performance.
Edwards and Nibler (2000)	DE	156 of the 200 largest nonfinancial firms (public and private), 1992	OLS regressions	MTB	Concentration: ▪ VR(1-3) Owner dummy: ▪ Individual/family ▪ Big 3 bank ▪ Other bank ▪ Nonfinancial firm ▪ Public sector body ▪ Foreign firm	The performance effect is positive for the largest shareholder being an individual/family, one of the three biggest banks, or a foreign firm.
Edwards and Weichenrieder (2004)	DE	97 large public nonfinancial firms, 1992	OLS and IV regressions (not further specified)	MTB	Concentration: ▪ VR(1), VR(2) ▪ CFR(1) Owner dummy: ▪ Individual/family ▪ Bank ▪ Corporation ▪ Public sector body ▪ Foreign firm	For most types of largest shareholders (especially for family and foreign owners), the beneficial effects of increased ownership are at least as large as (and sometimes significantly larger than) the harmful effects.
Färe, Grosskopf, and Logan (1985)	US	Data used from Atkinson and Halvorsen (1986)	Linear programming	Six efficiency measures	Owner dummy: ▪ Government ▪ Other	Publicly owned firms are slightly more efficient than privately owned firms.

Gedajlovic and Shapiro (1998)	CA, DE, FR, UK, US	1,030 medium to large public firms with no government ownership, 1986-91	OLS regressions	ROA	Concentration: ▪ VR(1) ▪ Percentage of shares held in blocks of ≥5% ▪ HHI	The relation between ownership concentration and performance differs across countries: The effect of ownership concentration is first negative and then positive for U.S. and German firms, whereas it is negative but not significant for Canadian, French, and U.K. firms.
Gorton and Schmid (2000)	DE	283 large public nonfinancial firms and 82 of 100 largest nonfinancial firms (public and private), 1975; 280 large public nonfinancial firms and 56 of the 100 largest manufacturing firms (public and private), 1986	OLS regressions	MTB, ROE	Concentration: ▪ HHI Fraction of VR controlled by: ▪ Banks	Firm performance is positively influenced by ownership concentration and improves to the extent that banks have control rights from equity ownership.
Groß (2007)	DE	521 FSE-listed nonfinancial firms, 2000 and 2003	2SLS and 4SLS regressions	ROE, Q	Concentration: ▪ VR(1), VR(2-3) ▪ VR(1)/CFR(1) Fraction of VR controlled by: ▪ Institutions ▪ Insiders	The performance effect of general ownership concentration is first negative and turns positive above a certain level. Institutional and insider ownership both exhibit a negative effect on performance.

Gugler and Weigand (2003)	DE, US	167 public German firms, 1991-96; 491 public U.S. firms, 1989-97	FE and FE-IV regressions (not further specified)	ROA	Concentration: ▪ VR(1) Fraction of VR controlled by: ▪ Insiders	Insider ownership has no statistically significant effect on performance. The largest shareholder, however, affects performance first positive, then negative and positive again.
Hermalin and Weisbach (1991)	US	134 NYSE-listed firms, 1971, 1974, 1977, 1980 and 1983	OLS and IV regressions (not further specified)	EBIT, Q	Fraction of VR controlled by: ▪ Insiders	At very low levels of managerial ownership, performance improves with increases in ownership. Then, the relation turns negative.
Hill and Snell (1988)	US	92 Fortune 500 firms in research-intensive industries (public and private), 1980	OLS regressions	ROA	Concentration: ▪ Percentage of shares held in blocks of ≥0.2%	High ownership concentration (and hence great shareholder power) influences firm profitability positively through strategy choice in the interests of shareholders (innovation vs. diversification).
Himmelberg, Hubburd, and Palia (1999)	US	600 randomly sampled public firms, 1982-92	FE and 2SLS regressions	Q	Fraction of VR controlled by: ▪ Insiders	Changes in managerial stockholdings have no significant impact on performance.
Holderness and Sheehan (1988)	US	114 AMEX- or NYSE-listed firms with a majority shareholder, 1978-84	Matched pairs	ROE, Q	Concentration dummies: ▪ Majority ownership (50.1%≤VR(1)≤95%) ▪ Diffuse ownership control group (VR(1)≤20%) Owner dummy: ▪ Individual ▪ Corporation	Performance is statistically equivalent in majority-shareholder firms and firms with relatively diffuse ownership. Individual-majority firms tend to underperform their matched pairs, whereas corporate-majority firms do not, but the differences are insignificant.

Holderness, Kroszner, and Sheehan (1999)	US	1,236 large public firms, 1935; 3,759 large public firms, 1995	OLS regressions	Q	Fraction of VR controlled by: ▪ Insiders	The shape of the relation between insider ownership and performance is similar but weaker to what Morck et al. (1988) find.
Jaskiewicz (2006)	DE, ES, FR	785 public nonfinancial and nonutility firms, 2003	OLS regressions	ROA, ROE	Family ownership: ▪ Dummy ▪ PSC-value	Family influence has a positive effect on performance in Germany and France (no significant result is found for Spain). Within the group of family firms, performance is driven by family presence in management relative to its share in capital. Up to a ratio of 1, performance increases, and then decreases.
Kaserer and Moldenhauer (2008)	DE	358 CDAX nonfinancial firms, 1998; 290 CDAX nonfinancial firms, 2003	OLS and 2SLS regressions	MTB, ROA, stock return	Concentration: ▪ Percentage of shares held in outside blocks of ≥5% ▪ Number of outside blockholders Fraction of CFR controlled by: ▪ Insiders ▪ Outsiders	There is a significant positive relation between insider ownership and performance. Outside block ownership as well as more concentrated insider ownership are also found to have a positive impact on performance.

Kirchmaier and Grant (2005)	DE, ES, FR, IT, UK	473 of the sum of the largest 110 public nonfinancial firms in each country, 1992-2002	t-tests	Share price trend, stock return	Concentration dummy: ▪ Legal control: VR(1, 3)≥50% ▪ De-facto control: 49.9%≥VR(1, 3) ≥ 30% (in DE) ▪ Widely held firms: VR(1, 3)<30%	For the German sample, the best performing companies are widely held. Companies under de-facto control are the next best performing group, and legal control (although this is the dominant form of ownership) is performing worst. Results for the Spanish and French samples are similar. No conclusions can be drawn for firms in Italy and the UK.
Kole (1996)	US	Data used from Morck et al. (1988)	OLS regressions	ROA, Q	Fraction of VR controlled by: ▪ Insiders	Managerial shareholdings are determined by firm performance, rather than the reverse.
Kole and Mulherin (1997)	US	5 companies for which the U.S. government seized common stock during World War II (public and private), 1942 - date of disposition; 5 privately owned controls (public and private)	t-tests	ROA, ROS, sales per employee	Owner: ▪ Government (35-100% stockholding) ▪ Privately owned control group	The performance of government-owned corporations is not significantly different from that of private-sector firms in the same industry.
Konijn, Kräussl, and Lucas (2001)	US	3,722 firm-year observations for public firms (not further specified), 1996-2001	FE regressions	Q	Concentration: ▪ (scaled) HHI ▪ Number of blockholders ▪ Gini coefficient	There is a negative relation between firm value and blockholder dispersion as well as between firm value and the presence and total ownership stake of blockholders.

Leech and Leahy (1991)	UK	470 LSE-listed firms, 1983	OLS and probit regressions	Growth rate of sales and net assets, ROE, salary of highest-paid director, trading profit margin, valuation ratio	Concentration dummy: ▪ Owner-control if VR(1)>5%, 10%, 20%, alternatively if VR(1)>90%, 95%, 99% ▪ Management-control if no evidence of owner-control Concentration: ▪ HHI ▪ VR(1), VR(1-5), VR(1-10), VR(1-20)	Owner-controlled firms are profitable and fast growing. Independent of the control-type, greater dispersion of ownership influences performance positively.
Lehmann and Weigand (2000)	DE	361 mining and manufacturing firms (public and private), 1991-96	FE regressions	ROA, ROE	Concentration: ▪ HHI ▪ VR(1) Owner dummy: ▪ Institution/bank ▪ Corporation ▪ Individual/family ▪ Foreign owner ▪ Mixed	Ownership concentration affects profitability significantly negatively. The negative effect is mainly driven by firms owned by individuals/families and different large owners. In contrast, ownership concentration is beneficial to firms under the control of financial institutions/banks.
Loderer and Martin (1997)	US	867 acquisitions of public nonfinancial and nonutility firms, 1978-88	OLS and 2SLS regressions	Q	Fraction of VR controlled by: ▪ Insiders	Insider ownership fails to predict performance. In contrast, performance is a (negative) predictor of insider ownership.

Maury (2006)	AT, BE, CH, DE, ES, FI, FR, IE, IT, NO, PT, SE, UK	1,672 nonfinancial firms (public and private), 1998	OLS regressions	ROA, Q	Owner dummy: ▪ Family ▪ Other	Family ownership is associated with higher profitability and higher valuations. Efficiency gains result from active family control and do not vary with the level of shareholder protection. In contrast, value benefits (which are similar for active and passive family control) tend to disappear in countries where shareholder protection is low (such as in Germany).
McConaughy, Walker, Henderson, and Mishra (1998)	US	219 public firms whose CEOs are either the founder or a member of the founder's family, 1986-88	Matched pairs, OLS regressions	Asset turnover, cash flows per employee, MTB, sales growth, sales per employee, stock return, ROS	CEO status: ▪ Founder (or family member) ▪ Other	Founding-family controlled firms are more efficient and valuable than nonfamily controlled firms with comparable levels of managerial ownership.
McConnell and Servaes (1990)	US	1,173 AMEX- or NYSE-listed firms, 1976; 1,093 AMEX- or NYSE-listed firms, 1986	OLS regressions	ROA, Q	Concentration: ▪ VR(blockholder 1) ▪ Percentage of shares held in blocks of ≥5% ▪ Blockholder dummy Fraction of VR controlled by: ▪ Insiders ▪ Institutions	The performance effect of insider ownership increases and then slightly decreases. The performance effect of institutions is positive. Finally, when blockholder ownership is considered separately, no significant correlation with performance can be found.

Megginson, Nash, and van Randenborgh (1994)	18 developing and industrialized countries (not further specified)	61 firms from 32 industries that were (partially) privatized through public share offerings during the period 1961-90	Matched pairs	ROA, ROE, ROS	Owner dummy: ▪ Government ▪ Other	Financial and operating performance strongly improves after both full and partial privatization.
Meyer (1975)	US	30 randomly sampled utility firms each year (public and private), 1967-69	OLS regressions	Operating cost structure	Owner dummy: ▪ Government ▪ Other	Publicly owned firms operate at lower costs than privately held firms (differences in operating costs are interpreted as an indicator of the degree to which new technologies are adopted).
de Miguel, Pindado, and de la Torre (2004)	ES	135 MSE-listed nonfinancial firms, 1990-99	GMM regressions	Q	Concentration: ▪ Percentage of shares held in blocks of ≥5% Fraction of VR controlled by: ▪ Insiders	Performance increases with ownership concentration at low levels and decreases at high levels. The effect of insider ownership is first positive, turns negative, and is positive again.
Mínguez-Vera and Martín-Ugedo (2007)	ES	95 public nonfinancial firms, 1998-2000	FE and 2SLS regressions	Q	Concentration: ▪ VR(1) ▪ HHI ▪ Percentage of shares held in blocks of ≥5% Owner dummy: ▪ Individual ▪ Institution	The effect of ownership concentration on performance is not significant, but a positive effect is seen when the major shareholders are individuals. Endogenous treatment of ownership concentration reveals a positive performance impact.
Morck, Shleifer, and Vishny (1988)	US	371 of the largest 500 public industrial firms, 1980	OLS regressions	Q	Fraction of VR controlled by: ▪ Insiders	Performance first increases, then declines, and finally rises slightly as managerial ownership rises.

Morck, Nakamury, and Shivdasani (2000)	JP	373 TSE-listed manufacturing firms, 1986	OLS regressions	ROA, Q	Fraction of VR controlled by: ▪ Banks ▪ Management ▪ Corporate blockholders	At low levels of ownership by main banks, firm's valuation decreases as bank equity rises. At higher levels of bank ownership, this relation is mitigated and, in some specifications, even reversed. There is no evidence that banks increase their ownership stake as a response to poor firm performance. The performance effect of managerial and corporate blockholder ownership is positive and linear.
Mura (2007)	UK	672 randomly sampled public nonfinancial, nonbroadcasting, and nonutility firms, 1991-2001	GMM regressions	Q	Concentration: ▪ VR(outside blockholder 1) ▪ VR(institutional blockholder1) ▪ VR(noninstitutional blockholder 1) Fraction of VR controlled by: ▪ Insiders ▪ Executive directors ▪ Nonexecutive directors ▪ Outsiders ▪ Institutional outsiders ▪ Noninstitutional outsiders	The direction of causality runs from ownership to performance. The relation between ownership by executive directors and performance is cubic, whereas ownership in the hands of nonexecutive directors has no impact on performance (however, the proportion of nonexecutives on the board is positively related with performance). The effect of both institutional and noninstitutional ownership on performance is negative.

Pedersen and Thomsen (1997)	AT, BE, DE, DK, ES, FI, FR, IT, NL, NO, SE, UK	Sum of the largest 100 nonfinancial firms in each country (public and private), 1990	Multinominal logistic regressions	n/a	Concentration: ▪ VR(1)<50% ▪ VR(1)<20% ▪ 20%≤VR(1)≤50% ▪ VR(1)>50% ▪ Cooperative	National ownership structures differ, even after controlling for company size and industry. The nature of the nation effect can (partly) be explained by institutional differences.
Pedersen and Thomsen (1999)	AT, BE, DE, DK, ES, FI, FR, IT, NL, NO, SE, UK	518 of the sum of the largest 100 nonfinancial firms in each country (public and private), 1990-93	2SLS regressions	ROE	Concentration: ▪ VR(1)	Ownership concentration is found to have an insignificant effect on profitability.
Pedersen and Thomsen (2003)	AT, BE, DE, DK, ES, FI, FR, IT, NL, NO, SE	214 of the sum of the largest 100 nonfinancial firms in each country (public), 1992-95	3SLS regressions	MTB	Concentration: ▪ Percentage of shares held in blocks of ≥5% Fraction of VR controlled by: ▪ Individuals/families ▪ Financial institutions ▪ Corporations ▪ Government	Ownership concentration has a positive effect on firm value when the largest owner is a financial institution or another corporation. If the largest owner is an individual/family, concentration has no effect on firm value, and the effect is negative if the largest owner is a government organization.
Pescatrice and Trapani (1980)	US	56 utility firms (public and private), 1965 and 1970	IZEF regressions	Operating cost structure	Owner dummy: ▪ Government ▪ Other	Public firms perform better than their privately held counterparts as they benefit from lower production costs.
Picot and Kaulmann (1989)	Six Western industrial countries, excluding US and JP (not further specified)	Fortune's *The foreign 500* industrial companies (public and private), 1975-85	OLS regressions	ROA, ROE, ROS	Owner dummy: ▪ Government ▪ Other	Government-owned corporations are less profitable than privately-owned corporations.

Ruiz-Mallorquí and Santana-Martín (2011)	ES	111 public nonfinancial firms, 1996-2009	GMM regressions	Q	Fraction of VR controlled by: ▪ Banks ▪ Investment funds	The control exercised by a dominant owner has a negative effect on firm value if the dominant owner is a bank.
Seifert, Gonenc, and Wright (2005)	DE, JP, UK, US	4,206 public firms, 1997-99	OLS and 2SLS regressions	Q	Fraction of VR controlled by: ▪ Insiders ▪ Institutions ▪ Blockholders	For German firms, significant positive performance effects are found for ownership by insiders, institutions and blockholders. For firms in the other sample countries, findings are different.
Short and Keasey (1999)	UK	225 LSE-listed nonfinancial and nonutility firms, 1988-92	OLS regressions	MTB, ROE	Fraction of VR controlled by: ▪ Insiders	The study confirms Morck et al. (1988)'s findings but provides evidence that U.K. managers become entrenched at higher levels of ownership than their U.S. counterparts.
Thomsen and Pedersen (2000)	AT, BE, DE, DK, ES, FI, FR, IT, NL, NO, SE, UK	435 of the sum of the largest 100 nonfinancial firms in each country (public and private), 1990-95	OLS regressions	MTB, ROA, sales growth	Concentration: ▪ VR(1) Owner dummy: ▪ Institution ▪ Bank ▪ Corporation ▪ Family/individual ▪ Government	A positive effect of ownership concentration on performance is found, but the effect levels off for high ownership shares. Institutional investors are associated with higher shareholder value and profitability but lower sales growth relative to other owners. Ownership concentration is also associated with higher performance for institutional investors than for other owner types.

Thomsen, Pedersen, and Kvist (2006)	EU, US	876 of the largest public firms, 1988-98	RE regressions and Granger causality tests	ROA, Q	Concentration: ▪ Percentage of shares held in blocks of ≥5%	In Continental Europe, there is a negative association between ownership concentration and performance for companies with high levels of blockholder ownership. No effect is found for U.K. and U.S. firms.
Villalonga and Amit (2006)	US	508 Fortune 500 nonfinancial and nonutility firms (public and private), 1994-2000	OLS regressions	Q	Owner dummy: ▪ Family ▪ Other	Family ownership creates value only when the founder serves as the CEO.
Weiss and Hilger (2012)	BR, CA, DE, ES, FR, JP, UK, US	1,079 of the sum of the largest 150 public firms in each country, 2000	2SLS regressions	ROA, Q	Concentration: ▪ VR(1-5)	Evidence of a bell-shaped effect of ownership concentration on performance becomes insignificant after controlling for endogeneity.

Note. AT = Austria, BE = Belgium, BR = Brazil, CA = Canada, CH = Switzerland, CN = China, DE = Germany, DK = Denmark, ES = Spain, EU = European Union, FI = Finland, FR = France, IE = Ireland, IT = Italy, JP = Japan, NL = Netherlands, NO = Norway, PT= Portugal, SE = Sweden, UK = United Kingdom, US = United States.

AMEX = American Stock Exchange (acquired by NYSE Euronext in 2008), FSE = Frankfurt Stock Exchange, LSE = London Stock Exchange, MSE = Madrid Stock Exchange, NYSE = New York Stock Exchange, TSE = Tokyo Stock Exchange.

The *CDAX* is a German stock market index comprising all companies listed on the Frankfurt Stock Exchange. The *DAX 100* was a German stock market index of the top 100 companies by market capitalization (now succeeded by the *HDAX*, an index covering the top 110 companies). The *S&P 500* (*Standard & Poor's 500*) is an American stock market index based on the market capitalization of 500 large companies having common stock listed on the NYSE or NASDAQ. *Fortune 500* is an annual list compiled by the Fortune magazine that ranks the top 500 U.S. public and private corporations by gross revenue (as of 2014, top at the list are Wal-Mart Stores, Exxon Mobil, and Chevron).

The notations CFR(g) and VR(g) refer to the percentage of voting and cash flow rights, respectively, held by the g-th largest shareholder(s).

A.2 Pooled OLS Regression Results

Table A.2.1 and Table A.2.2 present the OLS regression results for ownership concentration models, using cluster-robust standard errors.[193] Models 2.1-2.6 use Tobin's Q as the dependent variable and apply six measures of ownership concentration. The results find all coefficients of the alternative ownership concentration variables to be significant, positive. Among the control variables, R&D has a significant, positive effect on firm performance, which provides support for the assumption that investors appreciate investments in R&D (see Section 5.2.2.3). The effect of sales growth is also statistically significant, albeit very small in size.

Models 2.7-2.12 are extended by the use of time-fixed effects because it appears reasonable to assume that there exist time-specific effects during the economic cycle in the sample period 2005-09 that affect all firms in the same way. Time effects are captured by including a dummy variable for each year. To verify the need for time-fixed effects, a Wald test on the time dummies is performed. The Wald statistic tests the joint significance of the time dummies in the model under the null hypothesis that the coefficients of all time dummies are zero. A p-value of less than or equal to 0.05 leads to a rejection of the null hypothesis, as desired (Cameron & Trivedi, 2010). For the models 2.7-2.12, the Wald-tests yield a p-value of 0.000, which justifies the inclusion of time dummies.

The results from models 2.7-2.12 confirm the positive relation between ownership concentration and performance as all ownership concentration variables are significant, positive. For example, the coefficient of the size of the largest shareholding is positive (0.457, significant at the 0.01 level) and means that, on average, an increase of the control rights held by the largest shareholder by 100 basis points results in an increase of firm performance measured by Tobin's Q by 0.457 basis points.

Among the control variables, sales growth has a significant, positive effect on performance, as expected. Investments in R&D are also found to have a significant, positive performance effect. This provides evidence for the argument that the capital market rewards managers for undertaking investments. In regard to the explanatory power of the models, the adjusted

---

[193] The OLS standard errors assume that the regressors are independent and identically distributed (i.i.d.). However, in panel data, the error u_{it} is likely to be correlated over time for a given individual. As a consequence, it is essential that the OLS standard errors are corrected for clustering on the individual firm (Cameron & Trivedi, 2010).

R-squared is around 21%.[194] Compared with the controls-only model, the adjusted R-squared increases by about one percentage point. The results are robust to the alternative use of industry- and market-adjusted Tobin's Q (instead of using industry dummies), although the adjusted R-squared decreases to around 11-13% (results not displayed).[195]

When using ROA as the dependent variable, the ownership concentration variables increase in size but turn out to be insignificant (results not displayed). In regard to the control variables, debt turns out to have a significant, negative effect on accounting performance. This seems to provide evidence of the theoretically argued underinvestment in projects with a positive net present value resulting from fixed interest payment obligations. It is surprising that capital expenditures have a significant, positive coefficient, whereas R&D expenditures, as expected, have a significant, negative effect on accounting performance. The effect of sales growth is statistically significant but has a small size. As expected, the effect size of growth on accounting performance is higher than on Tobin's Q. In regard to the explanatory power of the models based on ROA, the adjusted R-squared is 20%. Compared with the controls-only model, the adjusted R-squared remains relatively unchanged, which can be explained by the statistically insignificance of most ownership concentration variables. The results are robust to the alternative use of the industry- and market-adjusted ROA, although the adjusted R-squared decreases to around 14% (results not displayed).

When using ROE as the dependent variable (results not displayed), all ownership concentration variables turn out to be negative but statistically insignificant. The sign and significance level of the controls remains comparable to the results from the previous models based on ROA. The adjusted R-squared drops to around 12%. The results are robust to the alternative use of the industry- and market-adjusted ROE, although the adjusted R-squared

---

[194] The common use of an adjusted R-squared as a measure of model fit in regression analyses is an attempt to take account of the phenomenon of the R-squared automatically and spuriously increasing when extra explanatory variables are added to the model. The adjusted R-squared adjusts for the number of explanatory terms relative to the number of data points and increases when a new explanatory variable is included only if this improves the R-squared more than would be expected by chance. Its value will hence be less than or equal to that of R-squared.

[195] Industry-adjusted performance measures are calculated as a firm's Tobin's Q, ROA or ROE, respectively, minus the average performance in the relevant industry for each year of the sample, with industry defined by the first digit of the SIC code. In order to get market-adjusted performance measures, the average performance in the entire sample of firms is used as the benchmark.

decreases to around 9%. Due to the comparably low explanatory power of the models using ROE as the dependent variable, models based on Tobin's Q or ROA are preferred.

To summarize, results from the OLS equation estimates yield a first indication that there might be an economic rationale for firm value to be positively influenced by ownership concentration. Coefficients of ownership concentration variables are highly significant but small. Results are robust to alternative measures of ownership concentration. In contrast, the effect of ownership concentration on accounting performance is ambiguous. The Herfindahl-Hirschman-Index has a significant, positive effect on performance, but all other ownership concentration measures lack statistical significance. The results might indicate that investors value ownership concentration positive whilst this appears to be hardly justifiable in terms of increased accounting performance (at least for current period performance). Nevertheless, evidence from pooled OLS should be approached with care because OLS does not account for time-invariant firm-fixed effects and ignores a possible reverse causality running from performance to ownership concentration. As a consequence, results are possibly biased.

Table A.2.1: OLS Regression Results for Ownership Concentration Models, Excluding Time Dummies

Dependent variable: Q	Controls only	Model 2.1	Model 2.2	Model 2.3	Model 2.4	Model 2.5	Model 2.6
OWN1		0.436*** (0.149)					
OWN12			0.424*** (0.148)				
OWN123				0.386** (0.147)			
OWN1/OWN2					0.003** (0.001)		
BLOCK						0.309** (0.142)	
HHI							0.521*** (0.166)
DEBT	-0.157 (0.247)	-0.110 (0.248)	-0.121 (0.248)	-0.133 (0.248)	-0.126 (0.248)	-0.140 (0.248)	-0.107 (0.248)
CAPX	0.753 (0.774)	0.694 (0.771)	0.666 (0.769)	0.667 (0.768)	0.811 (0.777)	0.680 (0.768)	0.745 (0.774)
RDX	3.943*** (1.013)	4.156*** (1.015)	4.147*** (1.010)	4.093*** (1.007)	4.043*** (1.019)	4.017*** (1.004)	4.159*** (1.014)
GRO	0.005*** (0.001)	0.005*** (0.001)	0.005*** (0.001)	0.005*** (0.001)	0.005*** (0.001)	0.005*** (0.001)	0.005*** (0.001)
Constant	0.553*** (0.111)	0.303*** (0.141)	0.294*** (0.142)	0.310*** (0.141)	0.505*** (0.113)	0.361*** (0.136)	0.376*** (0.124)
R^2	0.197	0.210	0.208	0.206	0.204	0.203	0.213
R^2 adjusted	0.172	0.185	0.184	0.181	0.180	0.178	0.188

Note. The analysis is based on 1,560 firm-year observations (452 firms). Asterisks denote statistical significance of the reported variables at the 0.01 (***), 0.05 (**) and 0.1 (*) level. Cluster-robust standard errors are in parentheses. All estimations include industry dummies (estimated coefficients are not reported). The definition of variables can be found in Table 5.5. No F-statistic is reported so as not to be misleading not because there is something wrong with the model. The reason is that the variance-covariance matrix of the estimator is not of sufficient rank to perform the model test. This is the consequence of a few SIC dummies being nonzero for only one cluster in the sample when using the cluster-robust-covariance matrix. In such case the derivative of the sum-of-squares is zero for all observations. This implies that the outer-product-of-gradients variance matrix is singular, and hence the robust variance matrix is singular as well.

Table A.2.2: OLS Regression Results for Ownership Concentration Models, Including Time Dummies

Dependent variable: Q	Controls only	Model 2.7	Model 2.8	Model 2.9	Model 2.10	Model 2.11	Model 2.12
OWN1		0.457*** (0.150)					
OWN12			0.448*** (0.148)				
OWN123				0.415*** (0.148)			
OWN1/OWN2					0.003** (0.001)		
BLOCK						0.343** (0.143)	
HHI							0.545*** (0.166)
DEBT	-0.120 (0.246)	-0.070 (0.247)	-0.081 (0.247)	-0.093 (0.247)	-0.088 (0.247	-0.101 (0.247)	-0.067 (0.247)
CAPX	0.938 (0.782)	0.878 (0.779)	0.847 (0.775)	0.846 (0.774)	1.001 (0.785)	0.858 (0.775)	0.932 (0.781)
RDX	4.074*** (1.009)	4.301*** (1.010)	4.294*** (1.005)	4.240*** (1.001)	4.180*** (1.014)	4.161*** (0.998)	4.304*** (1.010)
GRO	0.005*** (0.001)	0.005*** (0.001)	0.005*** (0.001)	0.005*** (0.001)	0.005*** (0.001)	0.005*** (0.001)	0.005*** (0.001)
Constant	0.763*** (0.120)	0.509*** (0.145)	0.498*** (0.147)	0.511*** (0.146)	0.714*** (0.123)	0.560*** (0.140)	0.586*** (0.130)
R^2	0.226	0.240	0.239	0.237	0.234	0.234	0.243
R^2 adjusted	0.201	0.215	0.214	0.212	0.209	0.208	0.218

Note. The analysis is based on 1,560 firm-year observations (452 firms). Asterisks denote statistical significance of the reported variables at the 0.01 (***), 0.05 (**) and 0.1 (*) level. Cluster-robust standard errors are in parentheses. All estimations include industry and time dummies (estimated coefficients are not reported). The definition of variables can be found in Table 5.5. No F-statistic is reported so as not to be misleading not because there is something wrong with the model. The reason is that the variance-covariance matrix of the estimator is not of sufficient rank to perform the model test. This is the consequence of a few SIC dummies being nonzero for only one cluster in the sample when using the cluster-robust-covariance matrix. In such case the derivative of the sum-of-squares is zero for all observations. This implies that the outer-product-of-gradients variance matrix is singular, and hence the robust variance matrix is singular as well.

A.3 Random-Effects Regression Results

Table A.3.1 presents the random-effects regression results for ownership concentration models, using cluster-robust standard errors. Models 3.1-3.6 use Tobin's Q as the dependent variable and apply six measures of ownership concentration. The results find all coefficients for the alternative ownership concentration variables to be significant, positive. For example, the coefficient of the size of the largest shareholding is positive (0.396, significant at the 0.01 level) and states that, on average, an increase of the control rights held by the largest shareholder by 100 basis points results in an increase of firm performance measured by Tobin's Q by 0.396 basis points.

Among the control variables, investments in R&D, capital expenditures and sales growth have a significant, positive effect on performance, as expected. The R-squared (overall) is around 22%. Compared with the controls-only model, the R-squared increases only slightly.

When using ROA or ROE as the dependent variable, the ownership concentration variables increase in size but turn out to be insignificant (results not displayed). Among the control variables, capital expenditures and growth have significant, positive coefficients, whereas debt as well as investments in R&D turn out to have a significant, negative effect on performance. The R-squared (overall) remains at around 22% when ROA is the dependent variable and falls to 15% in the case of ROE.

To summarize, results from the random-effects regressions provide evidence of a positive effect of ownership concentration on capital market performance. Coefficients of ownership concentration variables are significant but small, and results are robust to the use of alternative measures of ownership concentration. Random-effects estimates hence support the results from the fixed-effects specifications. In contrast to the latter, coefficients of time-invariant regressors such as industry dummies are included in the random-effects regressions. However, these estimates are inconsistent if the fixed-effects model is appropriate.

Table A.3.1: Random-Effects Regression Results for Ownership Concentration Models

Dependent variable: Q	Controls only	Model 3.1	Model 3.2	Model 3.3	Model 3.4	Model 3.5	Model 3.6
OWN1		0.396*** (0.123)					
OWN12			0.377*** (0.135)				
OWN123				0.326** (0.143)*			
OWN1/OWN2					0.003*** (0.001)		
BLOCK						0.254* (0.138)	
HHI							0.448*** (0.122)
DEBT	0.077 (0.252)	0.113 (0.252)	0.101 (0.256)	0.088 (0.258)	0.095 (0.242)	0.086 (0.257)	0.110 (0.253)
CAPX	0.865 (0.558)	0.870 (0.556)	0.842 (0.551)	0.844 (0.552)	0.961* (0.561)	0.860 (0.552)	0.883 (0.556)
RDX	2.347*** (0.752)	2.396*** (0.761)	2.384*** (0.758)	2.367** (0.755)*	2.384*** (0.758)	2.340*** (0.753)	2.416*** (0.759)
GRO	0.002** (0.001)	0.002** (0.001)	0.002** (0.001)	0.002** (0.001)	0.002** (0.001)	0.002** (0.001)	0.002** (0.001)
Constant	0.501*** (0.057)	0.425*** (0.064)	0.392*** (0.071)	0.387** (0.077)*	0.492*** (0.058)	0.393*** (0.083)	0.466*** (0.059)
R^2-within	0.153	0.159	0.159	0.157	0.158	0.155	0.160
R^2-between	0.207	0.221	0.219	0.217	0.216	0.214	0.224
R^2-overall	0.209	0.221	0.220	0.218	0.217	0.216	0.225
Sigma u (α)	0.786	0.776	0.777	0.779	0.781	0.781	0.774
Sigma e	0.452	0.450	0.451	0.451	0.451	0.452	0.450
Rho	0.751	0.748	0.748	0.749	0.750	0.749	0.747

Note. The analysis is based on 1,560 firm-year observations (452 firms). Asterisks denote statistical significance of the reported variables at the 0.01 (***), 0.05 (**) and 0.1 (*) level. Cluster-robust standard errors are in parentheses. All estimations include industry and time dummies (estimated coefficients are not reported). The definition of variables can be found in Table 5.5.

A.4 Pooled 2SLS Regression Results

Table A.4.1 presents the pooled 2SLS regression results for ownership concentration models, using cluster-robust standard errors. Models 5.1-5.3 use Tobin's Q as a measure of performance and apply three alternative measures of ownership concentration. Results of the first-stage regressions to determine ownership concentration show that the coefficients of the instruments carry the expected signs, and all (with one exception) are statistically significant.

A commonly used diagnostic to investigate the weak-instrumental-variable problem is to obtain the R-squared from the regression of the endogenous variable on the several instruments and particularly the F-statistic for the joint significance of the instruments in the first-stage regression of the endogenous regressor on the instruments and the exogenous regressors. Low values of R-squared or F would be indicative of weak instruments. However, with an adjusted R-squared between 22.3% and 29.0% and an F-statistic for joint significance of the instruments between 94.720 and 608.270 (significant at the 0.01 level), there is no indication of weak instruments, and the used instruments seem to be adequate.

Then, the second-stage regression is performed to determine firm performance. Compared with the OLS estimation, the coefficients for the ownership concentration measures are smaller. For example, the control rights held by the largest owner have an estimated beta of 0.457 in the OLS regression, but this is 0.311 in the 2SLS regression. More important, however, in contrast to the OLS models, none of the ownership concentration measures is statistically significant. Hence, the analyses do not suggest a significant effect of ownership on performance when accounting for endogeneity by means of a pooled 2SLS regression.

Among the control variables, again, investments in R&D and sales growth have a significant, positive effect on firm performance. In regard to the explanatory power of the models, the pooled 2SLS regressions are able to explain around 21% of the variance (adjusted R-squared).

When using ROA as the dependent variable, results change considerably (results not displayed):[196] In contrast to OLS estimations, which yield positive although statistically insignificant coefficients for ownership concentration (when using ROA as the dependent variable), the effect now turns negative and is statistically significant.

[196] In the models with ROA as the dependent variable in the second-stage regression, Tobin's Q (instead of ROA) is included in the instrument set in the first-stage regression. The use of ROE as the dependent variable is omitted due to a low explanatory power of the model.

Table A.4.1: Pooled 2SLS Regression Results for Ownership Concentration Models

	Model 5.1		Model 5.2		Model 5.3	
	First stage	Second stage	First stage	Second stage	First stage	Second stage
Dependent variable:	OWN1	Q	OWN123	Q	HHI	Q
Exogenous variables:						
DEBT	-0.111** (0.058)	-0.090 (0.244)	-0.076 (0.055)	-0.107 (0.243)	-0.104** (0.052)	-0.093 (0.244)
CAPX	0.221 (0.257)	0.803 (0.770)	0.377 (0.244)	0.780 (0.771)	0.093 (0.234)	0.841 (0.773)
RDX	-0.367** (0.172)	4.236*** (1.028)	-0.318** (0.165)	4.186*** (1.014)	-0.299** (0.145)	4.213*** (1.024)
GRO	-0.001* (0.002)	0.005*** (0.001)	-0.001 (0.001)	0.005*** (0.001)	-0.001 (0.001)	0.005*** (0.001)
Instruments:						
ROA	0.003** (0.001)		0.002 (0.001)		0.002** (0.001)	
TA	-0.001** (0.001)		-0.001** (0.001)		-0.001*** (0.001)	
RISK2	-0.383*** (0.055)		-0.356*** (0.054)		-0.371*** (0.054)	
RISK2 (SQ)	0.112*** (0.037)		0.079* (0.042)		0.109*** (0.035)	
Instrumented variable:						
OWN1		0.311 (0.332)				
OWN123				0.255 (0.302)		
HHI						0.310 (0.348)
Constant	0.335*** (0.024)	0.577*** (0.090)	0.484*** (0.022)	0.545*** (0.124)	0.217*** (0.026)	0.612*** (0.069)
R^2	0.250	0.242	0.315	0.239	0.261	0.243
R^2 adjusted	0.223	0.216	0.290	0.213	0.234	0.218
F-statistic	127.140***		608.270***		94.720***	

Note. The analysis is based on 1,543 firm-year observations (452 firms). Asterisks denote statistical significance of the reported variables at the 0.01 (***), 0.05 (**) and 0.1 (*) level. Cluster-robust standard errors are in parentheses. All estimations include industry and time dummies (estimated coefficients are not reported). The definition of variables can be found in Table 5.5.

Following the estimations, more formal diagnostics for weak instruments are performed. Results are displayed in Table A.4.2. The first part is a summary table of key diagnostic statistics that are useful in identifying weak instruments: The first two statistics are the R-squared and the adjusted R-squared from the regression of the endogenous regressor *OWN1* on the instruments in the first-stage regression. The partial R-squared is that between *OWN1* and the instruments after controlling for the exogenous variables. The value of 14.2% signals a high explanatory power and flags no problem of weak instruments. The final statistic is an F-statistic of the joint significance of the instruments excluded from the structural model. With a value of 25.904, the F-statistic is considerably larger than the common rule-of-thumb value of 10; The instruments hence do not seem to be weak.

Further common post-estimation procedures are the two formal tests for weak instruments proposed by Stock and Yogo (2005). Both tests are built on the aforementioned F-statistic for joint significance in the first-stage regression but use different critical values based on different criteria. The first test addresses the concern that the estimation bias of the 2SLS estimator resulting from the use of weak instruments can be large, sometimes even exceeding the bias of OLS. To apply the test, the largest acceptable bias of the 2SLS estimator relative to OLS is chosen. The test statistics provide the critical value, which varies with the chosen relative bias toleration and with the number of endogenous regressors and the number of exclusion restrictions. If the F-statistic exceeds the critical value of the test, the null hypothesis of weak instruments is rejected. As a result of the test, a critical value of 16.850 is obtained for a 5% relative bias tolerance. As both the F-value of 25.904 and the minimum eigenvalue of 61.694 exceed the critical value of the test, the null hypothesis of weak instruments can be firmly rejected.

The second test addresses the concern that weak instruments can lead to size distortion of Wald tests on the parameters. The Wald test is a joint statistical significance of the endogenous regressors in the structural equation model [$\boldsymbol{\beta}_1 = 0$ in Equation 6] at a level of 0.05. To apply this test, a tolerance for the size distortion of the Wald test is chosen. The test statistics provide the critical value, which varies with the chosen relative bias toleration and with the number of endogenous regressors and the number of exclusion restrictions. If the F-statistic exceeds the critical value of the test, the null hypothesis of weak instruments is rejected. As a result of the test, a critical value of 24.580 is obtained if a distortion of a 5% Wald test based on the pooled 2SLS estimator is tolerated so that the true size can be at most 10%. As both the F-value of

25.904 and the minimum eigenvalue of 61.694 exceed the critical value of the test, the null hypothesis of weak instruments can be firmly rejected.

Table A.4.2: Weak Instruments Diagnostics (2SLS Without Fixed Effects)

Variable	R^2	R^2 adjusted	R^2 partial	Robust F(4, 451)
OWN1	0.250	0.223	0.142	25.904***
		Minimum eigenvalue statistic = 61.694		
Weak identification test H_0: Instruments are weak		Stock-Yogo weak identification test critical values for Number of endogenous regressors: 1 Number of excluded instruments: 4		
2SLS relative bias	5%	16.850	⇒ H_0 is rejected: Instruments are not weak	
	10%	10.270		
	20%	6.710		
	30%	5.340		
2SLS size of nominal 5% Wald test	10%	24.580	⇒ H_0 is rejected: Instruments are not weak	
	15%	13.960		
	20%	10.260		
	30%	8.310		

Note. The test is based on models using Tobin's Q as dependent variable and the control rights held by the largest shareholder (*OWN1*) as ownership concentration variable. Results are robust to the use of alternative measures of performance and ownership concentration.

Another common post-estimation procedure is the test for regressor endogeneity developed by Durbin (1954), Wu (1973) and Hausman (1978). The test requires the structural Equation 6 to be rewritten with an additional variable v_1, the error term from the first-stage Equation 7 for y_2:

$$y_{1it} = \boldsymbol{y}'_{2it}\boldsymbol{\beta}_1 + \boldsymbol{x}'_{1it}\boldsymbol{\beta}_2 + \rho v_{1it} + u_{it} \tag{14}$$

Under the null hypothesis that y_{2it} is exogenous, $E(v_{1it}\, u_{it} | y_{2it}, \boldsymbol{x}_{1it}) = 0$. If v_1 could be observed, then the test for exogeneity would be the test of H_0: $\rho = 0$ in the OLS regression of y_1 on y_2, $\boldsymbol{x}_1$ and v_1. Because v_1 is not directly observed, the fitted residual vector $\widehat{v_1}$ from the first-stage OLS regression Equation 7 is instead substituted. If the test statistics do not reject the hypothesis of exogeneity of the instrumented variable, then the 2SLS estimator is still consistent but can be much less efficient than the OLS estimator. As a result of the test, a

p-value of 0.647 is obtained, which indicates that the hypothesis of exogeneity of the ownership concentration variable cannot be rejected. Results are displayed in Table A.4.3. This means that, contrary to the theoretical arguments developed in Section 3.3.2, no reverse effects of ownership concentration on performance can be empirically detected. As a consequence, ownership concentration has to be treated as exogenous. This supports the findings from the model specification tests for the within-2SLS models, which also could not reject the null hypothesis of regressor exogeneity.

Table A.4.3: Results from Model Specification Tests (OLS vs. 2SLS Without Fixed Effects)

Models	Specification test	Test statistic	Interpretation
OLS vs. 2SLS	Durbin-Wu-Hausman test H_0: y_{2it} is exogenous.	$F(1, 451) = 0.210$ $p = 0.647$	⇒ H_0 is accepted: OLS preferred over 2SLS

Note. The test is based on models using Tobin's Q as dependent variable and the control rights held by the largest shareholder (*OWN1*) as ownership concentration variable. The instrument set includes performance, firm size, firm risk and its squared measure. Results are robust to the use of alternative measures of performance and ownership concentration as well as to the alternation of the instrument set.

To conclude, the chosen instruments are not weak, but the test of regressor endogeneity indicates that ownership concentration can be treated as exogenous. In this case, the pooled 2SLS estimator is still consistent but can be much less efficient than the OLS estimator. The results without instrumenting for ownership concentration are therefore more accurate.

References

Achleitner, A.-K., Kaserer, C., Kauf, T., Günther, N., & Ampenberger, M. (2009). *Börsennotierte Familienunternehmen in Deutschland.* Retrieved from Stiftung Familienunternehmen website: http://www.familienunternehmen.de/----2009-10-19-Stiftung-Familienunternehmen--Boersennotierte-Familienunternehmen-in-Deutschland------_site.site..ls_dir._siteid.31_entryid.46_likecms.html

Achleitner, A.-K., Kaserer, C., Kauf, T., & Volk, S. (2010). *DAXplus Family - Ein Aktienindex zur Darstellung der Performance von Familienunternehmen* (Working paper No. 2010-05). Technische Universität München, Germany. http://dx.doi.org/10.2139/ssrn.1651446

Admati, A. R., & Pfleiderer, P. (2009). The "Wall Street walk" and shareholder activism: Exit as a form of voice. *Review of Financial Studies, 22*(7), 2445–2485.

Admati, A. R., Pfleiderer, P., & Zechner, J. (1994). Large shareholder activism, risk sharing, and financial market equilibrium. *Journal of Political Economy, 102*(61), 1097–1130.

Agarwal, R., & Elston, J. A. (2001). Bank-firm relations, financing and firm performance in Germany. *Economic Letters, 72*(2), 225–232.

Akaike, H. (1998). Information theory and an extension of the maximum likelihood principle. In E. Parzen, K. Tanabe, & G. Kitagawa (Eds.): *Perspectives in statistics: Selected papers of Hirotugo Akaike* (pp. 199–213). New York, United States: Springer. (Reprinted from *Breakthroughs in statistics*, Vol. 1, pp. 610–6247, by S. Kotz & N. L. Johnson, Eds., 1992, New York, US: Springer. Originally published in *Proceeding of the second international symposium on information theory*, pp. 267–281, by B. N. Petrov & F. Caski, Eds., 1973, Budapest, Hungary: Akademiai Kiado).

Akerlof, G. A. (1970). The market for "lemons": Quality uncertainty and the market mechanism. *Quarterly Journal of Economics, 84*(3), 488–500.

Alchian, A. A. (1950). Uncertainty, evolution, and economic theory. *Journal of Political Economy, 58*(3), 211–221.

Alchian, A. A. (1996). Some econonomics of property rights. In G. Yarrow & P. Jasiński (Eds.), *Privatization: Critical perspectives on the world economy* (pp. 294–307). London, United Kingdom: Routledge. (Reprinted from *Economic forces at work*, pp. 127–149, by A. A.

Alchian & R. H. Coase, Eds., 1977, Indianapolis, United States: Liberty Press. Originally published 1965 in *Il Politico, 30*, 816–829).

Alich, H. (2009, January 28). Eigenhandel der Banken beerdigt. *Handelsblatt*. Retrieved from http://www.handelsblatt.com/unternehmen/banken/investment-banking-eigenhandel-der-banken-beerdigt/3098722.html

Allen, J. W., & Phillips, G. M. (1998). Corporate equity ownership, strategic alliances, and product market relations. *Journal of Finance, 55*(6), 2791–2815.

Alonso-Bonis, S., & de Andrés-Alonso, P. (2007). Ownership structure and performance in large Spanish companies: Empirical evidence in the context of an endogenous relation. *Corporate Ownership & Control, 4*(4), 206–216.

Alparslan, A. (2005). *Strukturalistische Prinzipal-Agent-Theorie: Eine Reformulierung der Hidden-Action-Modelle aus der Perspektive des Strukturalismus* (Doctoral dissertation, Universität Duisburg-Essen, Germany). Wiesbaden, Germany: Gabler.

Amihud, Y., & Mendelson, H. (2000). The liquidity route to a lower cost of capital. *Journal of Applied Corporate Finance, 12*(4), 8–25.

Anderson, R. C., & Reeb, D. M. (2003a). Founding-family ownership and firm performance: Evidence from the S&P 500. *Journal of Finance, 58*(3), 1301–1328.

Anderson, R. C., & Reeb, D. M. (2003b). Founding-family ownership, corporate diversification, and firm leverage. *Journal of Law and Economics, 46*(2), 653–684.

Andersson-Lindström, N., & Weber, L. J. (2011, June 4). Mit Loan-to-Own-Strategien aus der Krise. *Börsen-Zeitung*. Retrieved from https://www.boersen-zeitung.de/index.php?li=1&artid=2011107330&titel=Mit-Loan-to-Own-Strategien-aus-der-Krise

Andres, C. (2008). Large shareholders and firm performance: An empirical examination of founding-family ownership. *Journal of Corporate Finance, 14*(4), 431–445.

Arnott, R. J., & Stiglitz, J. E. (1988). The basic analytics of moral hazard. *Scandinavian Journal of Economics, 90*(3), 383–413.

Aspara, J. (2013). The role of product and brand perceptions in stock investing: Effects on investment considerations, optimism and confidence. *Journal of Behavioral Finance, 14*(3), 195–212.

Aspara, J., & Tikkanen, H. (2010). The role of company affect in stock investments: Towards blind, undemanding, noncomparative and committed love. *Journal of Behavioral Finance, 11*(2), 103–113.

Astrachan, J. H., Klein, S. B., & Smyrnios, K. X. (2002). The F-PEC scale of family influence: A proposal for solving the family business definition. *Family Business Review, 15*(1), 45–58.

Atkinson, S. E., & Halvorsen, R. (1986). The relative efficiency of public and private firms in a regulated environment: The case of U.S. electric utilities. *Journal of Public Economics, 29*(3), 281–294.

von Auer, L. (2007). *Ökonometrie: Eine Einführung* (4th ed.). Berlin, Germany: Springer.

Badrinath, S. G., Gay, G. D., & Kale, J. R. (1989). Patterns of institutional investment, prudence, and the managerial "safety-net" hypothesis. *Journal of Risk & Insurance, 56*(4), 605–629.

Baert, L., & Vennet, R. V. (2009). *Bank ownership, firm value and firm capital structure in Europe* (Working paper D.2.2). Ghent University, Belgium. Retrieved from Deutsches Institut für Wirtschaftsforschung website: http://diw.de/sixcms/detail.php?id=diw_02.c.236207.de

Bahng, J. S. (2002). *Nonlinear effects of insider ownership on corporate value: Korean evidence* (Working paper). Seoul National University, South Korea. http://dx.doi.org/10.2139/ssrn.438362

Baltagi, B. H. (2005). *Econometric analysis of panel data* (3rd ed.). Chichester, United Kingdom: John Wiley & Sons.

Bank for International Settlements, Committee on the Global Financial System. (2007). *Institutional investors, global savings and asset allocation* (CGFS paper No. 27). Retrieved from http://www.bis.org/publ/cgfs27.pdf

Barber, B. M., & Odean, T. (2013). The behavior of individual investors. In G. M. Constantinides, M. Harris, & R. M. Stulz (Eds.), *Handbook of the eEconomics of finance* (Vol. 2, Part B, pp. 1535–1570). http://dx.doi.org/10.1016/B978-0-44-459406-8.00022-6

Barberis, N., Boycko, M., Shleifer, A., & Tsukanova, N. (1996). How does privatization work? Evidence from the Russian shops. *Journal of Political Economy, 104*(4), 764–790.

Barclay, M. J., & Holderness, C. G. (1989). Private benefits from control of public corporations. *Journal of Financial Economics, 25*(2), 371–395.

Barontini, R., & Caprio, L. (2006). The effect of family control on firm value and performance: Evidence from Continental Europe. *European Financial Management, 12*(5), 689–723.

Barucci, E., & Mattesini, F. (2008). Bank shareholding and lending: Complementarity or substitution? Some evidence from a panel of large Italian firms. *Journal of Banking & Finance, 32*(10), 2237–2247.

Bascle, G. (2008). Controlling for endogeneity with instrumental variables in strategic management research. *Strategic Organization, 6*(3), 285–327.

Baum, C. F. (2006). *An introduction to modern econometrics using Stata.* College Station, United States: Stata Press.

Baum, C. F., Schaffer, M. E., & Stillman, S. (2003). Instrumental variables and GMM: Estimation and testing. *Stata Journal, 3*(1), 1–31.

Baum, C. F., Schaffer, M. E., & Stillman, S. (2007). Enhanced routines for instrumental variables/generalized method of moments estimation and testing. *Stata Journal, 7*(4), 465–506.

Baumol, W. J. (1959). *Business behavior, value and growth.* New York, United States: Macmillan.

Baums, T. (1992a). *Should banks own industrial firms? Remarks from the German perspective* (Working paper No. 3/92). Johann Wolfgang Goethe-Universität, Frankfurt, Germany. Retrieved from http://www.jura.uni-frankfurt.de/43029010/paper3.pdf

Baums, T. (1992b). *Verbindungen von Banken und Unternehmen im amerikanischen Wirtschaftsrecht.* Tübingen, Germany: J. C. B. Mohr (Paul Siebeck).

Baums, T., & von Randow, P. (1995). Der Markt für Stimmrechtsvertreter. Die Aktiengesellschaft, *40*(4), 145–163.

Beirne, J., Liu, G. S., & Sun, P. (2013). *The performance impact of firm ownership transformation in China* (Working paper Series No. 1598). Retrieved from European Central Bank website: http://www.ecb.europa.eu/pub/pdf/scpwps/ecbwp1598.pdf

Berger, P. G., & Hann, R. (2003). The impact of SFAS No. 131 on information and monitoring. *Journal of Accounting Research, 41*(2), 163–223.

Berle, A. A., & Means, G. C. (1932). *The modern corporation & private property.* New York, United States: Harcourt, Brace & World.

Beyer, J. (2002). *Deutschland AG a.D.: Deutsche Bank, Allianz und das Verflechtungszentrum großer deutscher Unternehmen* (Working paper No. 02/4). Retrieved from Max-Planck-Institut für Gesellschaftsforschung website: http://www.mpifg.de/pu/workpap/wp02-4/wp02-4.html

Bhattacharya, P. S., & Graham, M. A. (2009). On institutional ownership and firm performance: A disaggregated view. *Journal of Multinational Financial Management, 19*(5), 370–394.

Bhidé, A. V. (1994). Efficient markets, deficient governance. *Havard Business Review, 72*(6), 129–139.

Birley, S. (2001). Owner-manager attitudes to family and business issues: A 16 country study. *Entrepreneurship Theory and Practice, 26*(2), 63–76.

Björnberg, Å., & Nicholson, N. (2007). The family climate scales - Development of a new measure for use in family business research. *Family Business Review, 20*(3), 229–246.

BMW. (2014). *BMW Aktien: Aktionärsstruktur - Stammaktien* (as of June 2014). Retrieved from http://www.bmwgroup.com/d/0_0_www_bmwgroup_com/investor_relations/aktien/aktien/aktionaersstruktur.html

Boardman, A. E., & Vining, A. R. (1992). Ownership versus competition: Efficiency in public enterprises. *Public Choice, 73*(2), 205–239.

Bøhren, Ø., & Norli, Ø. (1997). Determinants of intercorporate shareholdings. *European Finance Review, 1*(2), 265-287.

Bøhren, Ø., & Ødegaard, B. A. (2006). Governance and performance revisited. In P. U. Ali and G. N. Gregoriou (Eds.), *International corporate governance after Sarbanes-Oxley* (pp. 27–64). Hoboken, United States: John Wiley & Sons.

Bøhren, Ø., Priestley, R., & Ødegaard, B. A. (2006). *The duration of equity ownership at the Oslo Stock Exchange 1989-1999* (Research report No. 2/2006). BI Norwegen Business

School, Oslo, Norway. Retrieved from http://web.bi.no/forskning/papers.nsf/0/6a2401bc7e321193c1257125004d7a59/$FILE/2006-02-bohren-priestley-odegaard.pdf

Bolton, P., & von Thadden, E.-L. (1998). Blocks, liquidity, and corporate control. *Journal of Finance, 53*(1), 1–25.

Boubakri, N., Cosset, J.-C., & Saffar, W. (2008). Political connections of newly privatized firms. *Journal of Corporate Finance, 14*(5), 654–673.

Bound, J., Jaeger, D. A., & Baker, R. (1993). *The cure can be worse than the disease: A cautionary tale regarding instrumental variables* (Working paper No. 137). Retrieved from National Bureau of Economic Research website: http://www.nber.org/papers/t0137.pdf

Bound, J., Jaeger, D. A., & Baker, R. (1995). Problems with instrumental variable estimation when the correlation between the instruments and the endogenous explanatory variable is weak. *Journal of the American Statistical Association, 90*(430), 443–450.

Bowsher, C. G. (2002). On testing overidentifying restrictions in dynamic panel data models. *Economic Letters, 77*(2), 211–220.

Breusch, T. S., & Pagan, A. R. (1980). The Lagrange Multiplier test and its applications to model specification in econometrics. *Review of Economic Studies, 47*(1), 239–253.

Brickley, J., Lease, R. C., & Smith, C. W. (1988). Ownership structure and voting on antitakeover amendments. *Journal of Financial Economics, 20*(January-March), 267–291.

Brickwell, D. M. (2001). *Zu den Einflusspotenzialen der Großbanken* (Doctoral dissertation, Freie Universität Berlin, Germany). Retrieved from http://www.diss.fu-berlin.de/diss/receive/ FUDISS_thesis_000000000625

Buis, M. L. (2008). "postrcspline": Stata module containing post-estimation commands for models using a restricted cubic spline (Statistical software component). Retrieved from RePEc IDEAS website: http://ideas. repec.org/c/boc/bocode/s456928.html

Bundesanstalt für Finanzdienstleistungsaufsicht. (2014). *Jahresbericht der BaFin 2013.* Retrieved from http://www.bafin.de/DE/DatenDokumente/Dokumentlisten/ListeJahresberichte/liste_jahresberichte_node.html

Bundesministerium der Finanzen. (2011). *Die Beteiligungen des Bundes: Beteiligunsbericht 2010.* Retrieved from http://www.bundesfinanzministerium.de/Content/DE/Standardarti

kel/Themen/Bundesvermoegen/Privatisierungs_und_Beteiligungspolitik/Beteiligungen_des_Bundes/beteiligungsberichte-archiv-anlage5.pdf?__blob=publicationFile&v=4

Bundesministerium der Finanzen. (2014a). *Bericht des Bundesministeriums der Finanzen zur "Verringerung von Beteiligungen des Bundes - Fortschreibung 2014": Grundlagen der Beteiligungspolitik*. Retrieved from http://www.bundesfinanzministerium.de/Web/DE/Themen/Bundesvermoegen/Privatisierungs_und_Beteiligungspolitik/Privatisierungspolitik/privatisierungspolitik.html

Bundesministerium der Finanzen. (2014b). *Die Beteiligungen des Bundes: Beteiligungsbericht 2013*. Retrieved from http://www.bundesfinanzministerium.de/Web/DE/Themen/Bundesvermoegen/Privatisierungs_und_Beteiligungspolitik/Beteiligungen_des_Bundes/beteiligungen_des_bundes.html

Burkart, M., Gromb, D., & Panunzi, F. (1997). Large shareholders, monitoring, and the value of the firm. *Quarterly Journal of Economics, 112*(3), 693–728.

Burnham, K. P., & Anderson, D. R. (2002). *Model selection and multimodel inference: A practical information-theoretic approach* (2nd ed.). New York, United States: Springer.

Bushee, B. J. (1998). The influence of institutional investors on myopic R&D investment behavior. *Accounting Review, 73*(3), 305–333.

Bushee, B. J. (2009). Identifying and attracting the "right" investors: Evidence on the behavior of institutional investors. In D. H. Chew & S. L. Gillan (Eds.), *U.S. Corporate Governance* (pp. 170–183). New York, United States: Columbia University Press.

Byrd, J., Parrino, R., & Pritsch, G. (1998). Stockholder-manager conflicts and firm value. *Financial Analysts Journal, 54*(3), 14–30.

Cable, J. (1985). Capital market information and industrial performance: The role of West German banks. *Economic Journal, 95*(1), 118–132.

Caillaud, B., & Hermalin, B. E. (2000). *Hidden action and incentives* (Working paper). École Nationale des Ponts et Chaussées, Champs-sur-Marne, France, and University of California-Berkeley, United States. Retrieved from http://faculty.haas.berkeley.edu/hermalin/agencyread.pdf

Cameron, A. C., & Trivedi, P. K. (2005). *Microeconometrics: Methods and applications.* Cambridge, United States: Cambridge University Press.

Cameron, A. C., & Trivedi, P. K. (2010). *Microeconometrics using Stata* (Rev. ed.). College Station, United States: Stata Press.

Campello, M. (2006). Debt financing: Does it boost or hurt firm performance in product markets? *Journal of Financial Economics, 82*(1), 135–172.

Çelik, S., & Isaksson, M. (2014). Institutional investors and ownership engagement. *OECD Journal - Financial Market Trends, 2013*(2), 93–114. Retrieved from Organisation for Economic Co-operation and Development website: http://www.oecd.org/daf/fin/financial-markets/Institutional-investors-ownership-engagement.pdf

Chaganti, R., & Damanpour, F. (1991). Institutional ownership, capital structure, and firm performance. *Strategic Management Journal, 12*(7), 479–491.

Chan, L. K. C., Jegadeesh, N., & Lakonishok, J. (1996). Momentum strategies. *Journal of Finance, 51*(5), 1681–1713.

Chen, H., Hexter, J. L., & Hu, M. Y. (1993). Management ownership and corporate value. *Managerial and Decision Economics, 14*(4), 335–346.

Chen, L. (2012). *The effect of ownership structure on firm performance: Evidence from non-financial listed companies in Scandinavia* (Master thesis). Aarhus University, Denmark. Retrieved from http://pure.au.dk/portal/files/48424135/The_Effect_of_Ownership_Structure_on_ Firm_Performance_Chen_Luzhen_2012.pdf

Chirinko, R. S., & Elston, J. A. (2006). Finance, control and profitability: The influence of German banks. *Journal of Economic Behavior and Organization, 59*(1), 69–88.

Cho, M.-H. (1998). Ownership structure, investment, and the corporate value: An empirical analysis. *Journal of Financial Economics, 47*(1), 103–121.

Chow, G. C. (1960). Tests of equality between sets of coefficients in two linear regressions. *Econometrica, 28*(3), 591–605.

Chrisman, J. J., Chua, J. H., & Sharma, P. (2005). Trends and directions in the development of a strategic management theory of the firm. *Entrepreneurship Theory and Practice, 29*(5), 555–575.

Chua, C. T., Eun, C. S., & Lai, S. (2007). Corporate valuation around the world: The effects of governance, growth, and openness. *Journal of Banking & Finance, 31*(1), 35–56.

Chua, J. H., Chrisman, J. J., & Sharma, P. (1999). Defining the family business by behavior. *Entrepreneurship Theory and Practice, 23*(4), 19–39.

Chung, R., Firth, M., & Kim, J.-B. (2002). Institutional monitoring and opportunistic earnings management. *Journal of Corporate Finance, 8*(1), 29–48.

Churchill, N. C., & Hatten, K. J. (1987). Non-market based transfers of wealth and power: A research framework for family businesses. *American Journal of Small Business, 11*(3), 51–64.

Çitak, L. (2007). The impact of ownership structure on company performance: A panel data analysis on Istanbul Stock Exchange listed (ISE-100) companies. *International Research Journal of Finance and Economics, 10,* 107–119.

Clark-Murphy, M., & Soutar, G. N. (2004). What individual investors value: Some Australian evidence. *Journal of Economic Psychology, 25*(4), 539–555.

Coase, R. H. (1937). The nature of the firm. *Economica, 4*(16), 386–405.

Comet, C., & Pizarro, N. (2011). The cohesion of intercorporate networks in France. *Procedia - Social and Behavioral Sciences, 10,* 52–61.

Conyon, M. J., Fernandes, N., Ferreira, M. A., Matos, P., & Murphy, K. J. (2013). The executive compensation controversy: A transatlantic analysis. In T. Boeri, C. Lucifora, and K. J. Murphy (Eds.), *Executive renumeration and employee-related pay: A transatlantic perspective* (pp. 11–122). Oxford, United Kingdom: Oxford University Press.

Cragg, J. G., & Donald, S. G. (1993). Testing identifiability and specification in instrumental variable models. *Econometric Theory, 9*(2), 222–240.

Daily, C. M., & Dollinger, M. J. (1992). An empirical examination of ownership structure in family and professionally managed firms. *Family Business Review, 5*(2), 117–136.

Damodaran, A. (n.d.). *Debt and value: Beyond Miller-Modigliani* (Presentation slides). New York University, United States. Retrieved from http://people.stern.nyu.edu/adamodar/pdfiles/country/levvalue.pdf

Damodaran, A. (2012). *Investment valuation: Tools and techniques for determining the value of any asset* (3rd ed.). Hoboken, United States: John Wiley & Sons.

Danielson, M. G., & Press, E. (2003). Accounting returns revisited: Evidence of their usefulness in estimating economic returns. *Review of Accounting Studies, 8*(4), 493–530.

Davies, J. R., Hillier, D., & McColgan, P. (2005). Ownership structure, managerial behavior and corporate value. *Journal of Corporate Finance, 11*(4), 645–660.

De Bondt, W. F. M. (1998). A portrait of the individual investor. *European Economic Review, 42*(3-5), 831–844.

Dechow, P. M., & Sloan, R. G. (1991). Executive incentives and the horizon problem: An empirical investigation. *Journal of Accounting and Economics, 14*(1), 51–89.

Deloitte. (2012). *Finanzierung im Mittelstand*. Retrieved from http://www.mitteldeutschland.com/uploads/media/Deloitte_Finanzierung_Mittelstand_Studie_2012_01.pdf

Demsetz, H. (1983). The structure of ownership and the theory of the firm. *Journal of Law and Economics, 26*(2), 375–390.

Demsetz, H., & Lehn, K. (1985). The structure of corporate ownership: Causes and consequences. *Journal of Political Economy, 93*(6), 1155–1177.

Demsetz, H., & Villalonga, B. (2001). Ownership structure and corporate performance. *Journal of Corporate Finance, 7*, 209–233.

Depken, C. A., II, Nguyen, G. X., & Sarkar, S. K. (n.d.). *Agency costs, executive compensation, bonding and monitoring: A stochastic frontier approach* (Working paper). University of Texas-Arlington, United States. Retrieved from LoPDF website: http://www.lopdf.net/d/Agency-Costs-ExecutiveCompensation-Bonding-and.pdf

Deutsche Börse. (2014). *Leitfaden zu den Aktienindizes der Deutschen Börse AG* (Version 6.29). Retrieved from http://www.dax-indices.com/DE/MediaLibrary/Document/Leitfaden_Aktienindizes.pdf

Deutsche Börse. (2010). *DAXplus family indices: Issuer data & analytics*. Retrieved from http://www.dax-indices.com/DE/MediaLibrary/Document/2010-01-11_Presentation_DAXplus_Family_de.pdf

Deutsche Bundesbank. (2013). *Bankendichte im Jahr 2012: Anzahl der Kreditinstitute nimmt weiter ab*. Retrieved from http://www.bundesbank.de/Redaktion/DE/Pressemitteilungen/BBK/2013/2013_05_17_bankendichte_2012.html

Deutsche Bundesbank. (2014a). *Beteiligungen an inländischen Unternehmen/Alle Bankengruppen, Kreditbanken, Großbanken* (Zeitreihen BBK01.OU8584, BBK01.OU8655, BBK01.OU8656). Retrieved from http://www.bundesbank.de/Navigation/DE/Statistiken/Zeitreihen_Datenbanken/Makrooekonomische_Zeitreihen/its_list_node.html?listId=www_s100_bh54_24

Deutsche Bundesbank. (2014b). *Ownership structure in the German equity market: General trends and changes in the financial crisis* (Monthly report: September 2014). Retrieved from https://www.bundesbank.de/Redaktion/EN/Downloads/Publications/Monthly_Report_Articles/2014/2014_09_equity_market.pdf?__blob=publicationFile

Deutsches Aktieninstitut. (2015). *Aktionärszahlen des Deutschen Aktieninstituts 2014*. Retrieved from https://www.dai.de/files/dai_usercontent/dokumente/studien/2015-02-12%20DAI%20Aktionaerszahlen%202014.pdf

Dharwadkar, R., Goranova, M., Brandes, P., & Khan, R. (2008). Institutional ownership and monitoring effectiveness: It's not just how much but what else you own. *Organization Science, 19*(3), 419–440.

Dittmann, I., Maug, E., & Schneider, C. (2010). Bankers on the boards of German firms: What they do, what they are worth, and why they are (still) there. *Review of Finance, 14*(1), 35–71.

Donckels, R., & Fröhlich, E. (1991). Are family businesses really different? European experience from STRATOS. *Family Business Review, 40*(2), 149–159.

Dougherty, C. (2011). *Introduction to econometrics* (4th ed.). Oxford, United Kingdom: Oxford University Press.

Douma, S., George, R., & Kabir, R. (2006). Foreign and domestic ownership, business groups, and firm performance: Evidence from a large emerging market. *Strategic Management Journal, 27*(7), 637–657.

Driffield, N., Mahambare, V., & Pal, S. (2007). How does ownership structure affect capital structure and firm value? *Economics of Transition, 15*(3), 535–573.

D'Souza, J., & Megginson, W. L. (1999). The financial and operating performance of privatized firms during the 1990s. *Journal of Finance, 54*(4), 1397–1438.

Dufey, G., & Hommel, U. (1997). Der Shareholder Value-Ansatz: U.S.-amerikanischer Kulturimport oder Diktat des globalen Marktes? Einige Überlegungen zur "Corporate Governance" in Deutschland. In J. Engelhard (Ed.), *Interkulturelles Management: Theoretische Fundierung und funktionsbereichsspezifische Konzepte* (pp. 183–211). Wiesbaden, Germany: Gabler.

Durbin, J. (1954). Errors in variables. *Review of the International Statistical Institute, 22*(1-3), 23–32.

Durrleman, S., & Simon, R. (1989). Flexible regression models with cubic splines. *Statistics in Medicine, 8*(5), 551–561.

Dymke, B. M., & Walter, A. (2008). Insider trading in Germany: Do corporate insiders exploit inside information? *Business Research, 1*(2), 188–205.

Eckbo, B. E. (1997). Comment on "Determinants of intercorporate shareholdings". *European Finance Review, 1*(2), 289–293.

Eckbo, B. E., & Smith, D. C. (1998). The conditional performance of insider trades. *Journal of Finance, 53*(2), 467–498.

Eckel, C. C., & Vermaelen, T. (1986). The effects of government ownership on the value of the firm. *Journal of Law and Economics, 29*(2), 381–403.

Edwards, F. R. (1995). Derivatives can be hazardous to your health: The case of Metallgesellschaft. *Derivatives Quarterly, Spring*, 8–17.

Edwards, J., & Nibler, M. (2000). Corporate governance in Germany: The role of banks and ownership concentration. *Economic Policy, 15*(31), 239–267.

Edwards, J., & Weichenrieder, A. J. (2004). Ownership concentration and share valuation. *German Economic Review, 5*(2), 143–171.

Eichel, H. (2000). Der Bund und seine Unternehmen: Perspektiven und Aufgaben im alten und neuen Jahrhundert. *Zeitschrift für das gesamte Kreditwesen, 53*, 274–277.

Eleswarapu, V. R. (1997). Cost of transacting and expected returns in the Nasdaq market. *Journal of Finance, 52*(5), 2113–2127.

European Central Bank. (2012). *Corporate indebtedness in the Euro area* (Monthly Bulletin, February 2012). Retrieved from https://www.ecb.europa.eu/pub/pdf/other/art2_mb201202en_pp87-103en.pdf

European Commission. (2014). *Statement by Vice-President Reding and Commissioner Barnier on European Parliament's vote to approve criminal sanctions for market abuse directive.* Retrieved from http://europa.eu/rapid/press-release_MEMO-14-77_en.htm?locale=en

Fama, E. F. (1980). Agency problems and the theory of the firm. *Journal of Political Economy, 88*(2), 288–307.

Fama, E. F., & Jensen, M. C. (1983). Separation of ownership and control. *Journal of Law and Economics, 26*(2), 301–325.

Färe, R., Grosskopf, S., & Logan J. (1985). The relative performance of publicly-owned and privately-owned electric utilities. *Journal of Public Economics, 26*(1), 89–106.

Fiss, P. C., & Zajac, E. J. (2004). The diffusion of ideas over contested terrain: The (non)adoption of a shareholder value orientation among German firms. *Administrative Science Quarterly, 49*, 501–534.

Fohlin, C. (2005). The history of corporate ownership and control in Germany. In R. K. Morck (Ed.), *A history of corporate governance around the world* (pp. 223–282). Chicago, United States: University of Chicago Press.

Fontrodona, J., & Sison, A. J. G. (2006). The nature of the firm, agency theory and shareholder theory: A critique from philosophical anthropology. *Journal of Business Ethics, 66*(1), 33–42.

Francke, H.-H., & Hudson, M. (2012). *Banking and finance in West Germany*. Abingdon, United Kingdom: Routledge.

Friedman, M. (1953). The methodology of positive economics. In M. Friedman (Ed.), *Essays in positive economics* (pp. 3–43). Chicago, United States: University of Chicago Press.

Friedman, M. (1962). *Capitalism and freedom*. Chicago, United States: University of Chicago Press.

Froot, K. A., Perold, A. F., & Stein, J. C. (1992). Shareholder trading practices and corporate investment horizons. *Journal of Applied Corporate Finance, 5*(2), 42–58.

Fußball-Aktien: Selten Erfolgsgeschichten (2011, August 17). *Frankfurter Allgemeine Zeitung*. Retrieved from http://www.faz.net/aktuell/sport/fussball/fussball-aktien-selten-erfolgsgeschichten-11114380.html

Gallo, M. A., & Sveen, J. (1991). Internationalizing the family business - Facilitating and restraining factors. *Family Business Review, 4*(2), 181–187.

Gallup. (2013). *U.S. stock ownership stays at record low* (Annual economy and finance survey). Retrieved from http://www.gallup.com/poll/162353/stock-ownership-stays-record-low.aspx

Gedajlovic, E. R., & Shapiro, D. M. (1998). Management and ownership effects: Evidence from five countries. *Strategic Management Journal, 19*(6), 533–553.

Gibson, S., Safieddine, A., & Sonti, R. (2004). Smart investments by smart money: Evidence from seasoned equity offerings, *Journal of Financial Economics, 72*(3), 581–604.

Giesselmann, M., & Windzio, M. (2012). *Regressionsmodelle zur Analyse von Paneldaten* (1st ed.). Wiesbaden, Germany: Springer.

González, V. M. (2013). Leverage and corporate performance: International evidence. *International Review of Economics and Finance, 25*(January), 169–184.

Gormley, T. A., & Matsa D. A. (2014a). Common errors: How to (and not to) control for unobserved heterogeneity. *Review of Financial Studies, 27*(2), 617–661.

Gormley, T. A. & Matsa D. A. (2014b). Implementing fixed effects estimation (Stata code related to Gormley and Matsa (2014a)). University of Pennsylvania, Philadelphia, United States. Retrieved from http://finance.wharton.upenn.edu/~tgormley/papers/fe.html

Gorton, G., & Schmid, F. A. (2000). Universal banking and the performance of German firms. *Journal of Financial Economics, 58*(1-2), 29–80.

Gosenheimer, S. (2013, April 10). Börse feiert bei BVB-Party nicht mit. *The Wall Street Journal Deutschland*. Retrieved from http://www.wsj.de/nachrichten/SB10001424127887323741004578414222846391876

Graham, J. R. (1999). Herding among investment newsletters: Theory and evidence. *Journal of Finance, 54*(1), 237–268.

Graham, J. R., Harvey, C. R., & Rajgopal, S. (2005). The economic implications of corporate financial reporting. *Journal of Accounting and Economics, 40*(1-3), 3–73.

Greene, W. H. (2012). *Econometric analysis* (7th ed.). Boston, United States: Pearson Education.

Groß, K. (2007). *Equity ownership and performance: An empirical study of German traded companies* (Doctoral dissertation, EBS Universität für Wirtschaft und Recht, Oestrich-Winkel/Wiesbaden, Germany). Heidelberg, Germany: Physica.

Grout, P. A., Megginson, W. L., & Zalewska, A. (2009). *One half-billion shareholders and continuing - Determinants of individual share ownership around the world* (Working paper). University of Bristol, United Kingdom, University of Oklahoma, Norman, United States, and University of Bath, United Kingdom. http://dx.doi.org/10.2139/ssrn.1364765

Grundfest, J. A. (1990). Subordination of American capital. *Journal of Financial Economics, 27*(1), 89–114.

Gugler, K., & Weigand, J. (2003). Is ownership really endogenous? *Applied Economics Letters, 10*(8), 483–486.

Guiso, L., Haliassos, M., & Jappelli, T. (2003). Household stockholding in Europe: Where do we stand and where do we go? *Economic Policy, 18*(36), 123–170.

Hadani, M., Goranova, M., & Khan, R. (2011). Institutional investors, shareholder activism, and earnings management. *Journal of Business Research, 64*(12), 1352–1360.

Halaby, C. N. (2004). Panel models in sociological research: Theory into practice. *Annual Review of Sociology, 30*, 507–544.

Hamilton, B. H., & Nickerson, J. A. (2003). Correcting for endogeneity in strategic management research. *Strategic Organization, 1*(1), 51–78.

Hand, J. R. M. (1990). A test of the extended functional fixation hypothesis. *Accounting Review, 65*(4), 740–763.

Handler, W. C. (1989). Methodological issues and considerations in studying family businesses. *Family Business Review, 2*(3), 257–276.

Hansen, L. P. (1982). Large sample properties of generalized method of moments estimators. *Econometrica, 50*(4), 1029–1054.

Hansmann, H. (1988). Ownership of the firm. *Journal of Law, Economics, & Organization, 4*(2), 267–304.

Harrell, F. E., Jr. (2001). *Regression modeling strategies: With applications to linear models, logistic regression, and survival analysis.* New York, United States: Springer.

Hart, O. D. (1983). The market mechanism as an incentive scheme. *Bell Journal of Economics, 14*(2), 366–382.

Hausman, J. A. (1978). Specification tests in econometrics. *Econometrica, 46*(6), 1251–1271.

Hermalin, B. E., & Weisbach, M. S. (1991). The effects of board composition and direct incentives on firm performance. *Financial Management, 20*(4), 101–112.

Hill, C. W. L., & Snell, S. A. (1988). External control, corporate strategy, and firm performance in research-intensive industries. *Strategic Management Journal, 9*(6), 577–590.

Himmelberg, C. P., Hubburd, R. G., & Palia, D. (1999). Understanding the determinants of managerial ownership and the link between ownership and performance. *Journal of Financial Economics, 53*(3), 353–384.

Holderness, C. G., Kroszner, R. S., & Sheehan, D. P. (1999). Were the good old days that good? Changes in managerial stock ownership since the great depression. *Journal of Finance, 54*(2), 435–469.

Holderness, C. G., & Sheehan, D. P. (1988). The role of majority shareholders in publicly held corporations: An explanatory analysis. *Journal of Financial Economics, 20*(January-March), 317–346.

Hommel, U. (1998). Regulating the market for corporate control: Lessons from Germany. *International Journal of Business, 3*(1), 101–122.

Hommel, U., & Wölfer, K. (2009). *Wertsteigerungsstrategien von Familienunternehmen - Eine empirische Analyse* (Unpublished manuscript). EBS Universität für Wirtschaft und Recht, Oestrich-Winkel/Wiesbaden, Germany.

Houmes, R., Boylan, R., & Dickins, D. (2009). Insider ownership and stock price performance: How greater concentrations of insider ownership affects returns of firms with various price-to-earnings ratios. *Journal of Technical Accounting Research, 4*(2), 72–92.

Howey, R. S. (1960). *The rise of the marginal utility school.* New York, United States: Columbia University Press.

Hsiao, C. (2007). Panel data analysis - Advantages and challenges. *TEST, 16*(1), 1–22.

Hsiao, C., Mountain, D. C., & Illman, K. H. (1995). A bayesian integration of end-use metering and conditional-demand analysis. *Journal of Business & Economic Statistics, 13*(3), 315–326.

Hu, Y., & Izumida, S. (2008). The relation between ownership and performance: A review of theory and evidence. *International Business Research, 1*(4), 72–81.

Huddart, S. (1993). The effect of a large shareholder on corporate value. *Management Science, 39*(11), 1407–1421.

Institut für Familienunternehmen. (2014). *Die 50 größten deutschen Familienunternehmen 2013 im Vergleich: Ende der Boomjahre?* Retrieved from http://www.institut-fuer-familien unternehmen.de/pdf/IFF_Presseinformation_140701.pdf

Institutional Shareholder Services (with Sherman & Sterling, & European Corporate Governance Institute). (2007). *Proportionality between ownership and control in EU listed companies* (External study commissioned by the European Commission). Retrieved from http://www.ecgi.org/osov/documents/ final_report_en.pdf

Jaskiewicz, P. (2006). *Performance-Studie börsennotierter Familienunternehmen in Deutschland, Frankreich und Spanien* (Doctoral dissertation, EBS Universität für Wirtschaft und Recht, Oestrich-Winkel/Wiesbaden, Germany). Lohmar, Germany: Josef Eul.

Jensen, M. C. (1986). Agency costs of free cash flow, corporate finance, and takeovers. *American Economic Review, 76*(2), 323–329.

Jensen, M. C., & Meckling, W. H. (1976). Theory of the firm: Managerial behavior, agency costs and ownership structure. *Journal of Financial Economics, 3*(4), 305–360.

Jensen, M. C., & Murphy, K. J. (1990). Performance pay and top-management incentives. *Journal of Political Economy, 98*(2), 225–264.

Jensen, M. C., & Ruback, R. S. (1983). The market for corporate control. *Journal of Financial Economics, 11*(April), 5–50.

Johnson, S., Boone, P., Breach, A., & Friedman, E. (2000). Corporate governance in the Asian financial crisis. *Journal of Financial Economics, 58*(1-2), 141–186.

Judge, W. Q., & Zeithaml, C. P. (1992). Institutional and strategic choice perspectives on board involvement in the strategic decicion process. *Academy of Management Journal, 35*(4), 766–794.

Kane, E. J. (1999). *The limits of stockholder privatization* (Working paper No. 9908). Deakin University, Melbourne, Australia. Retrieved from CiteSeerX website: http://citeseerx.ist.psu.edu/viewdoc/download?doi=10.1.1.198.3143&rep=rep1&type=pdf

Kang, J.-K., Shivdasani, A., & Yamada, T. (2000). The effect of bank relations on investment decisions: An investigation of Japanese takeover bids. *Journal of Finance, 55*(5), 2197–2218.

Kaserer, C., Fey, G., & Kuhn, N. (2011). *Kapitalmarktorientierung und Finanzierung mittelständischer Unternehmen.* Retrieved from Deutsches Aktieninstitut website: https://www.dai.de/files/dai_usercontent/dokumente/studien/2011-11%20Studie%20Kapitalmarktorientierung%20Mittelstand.pdf

Kaserer, C., & Moldenhauer, B. (2008). Insider ownership and corporate performance: Evidence from Germany. *Review of Managerial Science, 2*(1), 1–35.

Katz, S. P. (2009). Earnings quality and ownership structure: The role of private equity sponsors. *Accounting Review, 84*(3), 623–658.

Keele, L. (2008). *Semiparametric regression for the social sciences.* Chichester, United Kingdom: John Wiley & Sons.

Kester, W. C. (1992). Industrial groups as systems of contractual governance. *Oxford Review of Economic Policy, 8*(3), 24–44.

Kim, J.-B., Krinsky, I., & Lee, J. (1997). Institutional holdings and trading volume reactions to quarterly earnings announcements. *Journal of Accounting, Auditing & Finance, 12*(1), 1–14.

Kirchmaier, T., & Grant, J. (2005). Corporate ownership structure and performance in Europe. *European Management Review, 2*(3), 231–245.

Kleibergen, F., & Paap, R. (2006). Generalized reduced rank tests using the singular value decomposition. *Journal of Econometrics, 133*(1), 97–126.

Klein, G. (1998, July 8). The trouble with S.I.C. codes (Online forum post). Retrieved from Montague Institute website: http://www.montague.com/review/klein.html

Klein, S. B. (2000). Family businesses in Germany: Significance and structure. *Family Business Review, 13*(3), 157–181.

Kochhar, R., & David, P. (1996). Institutional investors and firm innovation: A test of competing hypotheses. *Strategic Management Journal, 17*(1), 73–84.

Köke, J. (2004). The market for corporate control in a bank-based economy: A governance device? *Journal of Corporate Finance, 10*(1), 53–80.

Kole, S. R., & Lehn, K. (1997). Deregulation, the evolution of corporate governance structure, and survival. *American Economic Review, 87*(2), 421–425.

Kole, S. R. (1995). Measuring managerial equity ownership: A comparison of sources of ownership data. *Journal of Corporate Finance, 1*(3-4), 413–435.

Kole, S. R. (1996). Managerial ownership and firm performance: Incentives or rewards? *Advances in Financial Economics, 2,* 119–149.

Kole, S. R., & Mulherin, J. H. (1997). The government as a shareholder: A case from the United States. *Journal of Law and Economics, 40*(1), 1–22.

Konijn, S. J. J., Kräussl, R., & Lucas, A. (2001). Blockholder dispersion and firm value. *Journal of Corporate Finance, 17*(5), 1330–1339.

Kosnik, R. D. (1990). Effects of board demography and director's incentives on corporate greenmail decisions. *Academy of Management Journal, 33*(1), 129–150.

Kummer, D. R., & Hoffmeister, J. R. (1978). Valuation consequences of cash tender offers. *Journal of Finance, 33*(2), 505–516.

La Porta, R., Lopez-de-Silanes, F., & Shleifer, A. (1999). Corporate ownership around the world. *Journal of Finance, 54*(2), 471–517.

La Porta, R., Lopez-de-Silanes, F., Shleifer, A., & Vishny, R. (2000). Investor protection and corporate governance. *Journal of Financial Economics, 58*(1-2), 3–27.

La Rocca, M., & La Rocca, T. (2007). *Capital structure and corporate strategy: An overview* (Working paper). Università della Calabria, Arcavacata, Italy. http://dx.doi.org/10.2139/ssrn.1023461

Lang, L. H. P., & Stulz, R. M. (1994). Tobin's q, corporate diversification, and firm performance. *Journal of Political Economy, 102*(6), 1248–1280.

Lansberg, I., Perrow E. L., & Rogolsky, S. (1988). Family business as an emerging field. *Family Business Review, 1*(1), 1–8.

Larcker, D. F., & Rusticus, T. O. (2010). On the use of instrumental variables in accounting research. *Journal of Accounting and Economics, 49*(3), 186–205.

Larner, R. (1966). Ownership and control in the 200 largest nonfinancial corporations, 1929 and 1963. *American Economic Review, 56*(4), 777–787.

Lazarus, D. (2013, January 25). An emotional investment in Apple. *Los Angeles Times.* Retrieved from http://articles.latimes.com/2013/jan/25/business/la-fi-lazarus-20130125

Learmount, S., & Roberts, J. (2006). Meanings of ownership of the firm. *Journal of Interdisciplinary Economics, 17*(1), 139–162.

Leech, D., & Leahy, J. (1991). Ownership structure, control type classifications and the performance of large British companies. *Economic Journal, 101*(409), 1418–1437.

Lehmann, E., & Weigand, J. (2000). Does the governed corporation perform better? Governance structures and corporate performance in Germany. *European Finance Review, 4*(2), 157–195.

Lemmon, M. L., & Lins, K. V. (2003). Ownership structure, corporate governance, and firm value: Evidence from the East Asian financial crisis. *Journal of Finance, 58*(4), 1445–1468.

Lev, B., & Sougiannis, T. (1998). The capitalization, amortization, and value-relevance of R&D. In D. Neef, A. Siesfeld, & J. Cefola (Eds.), *The economic impact of knowledge* (pp. 243–272). Boston, United States: Butterworth-Heinemann.

Lewis, W. A. (1949). *The principles of economic planning.* Abingdon, United Kingdom: Routledge.

Lin, J. Y., Cai, F., & Li, Z. (1998). Competition, policy burdens, and state-owned enterprise reform. *American Economic Review, 88*(2), 422–427.

Loderer, C., & Martin, K. (1997). Executive stock ownership and performance: Tracking faint traces. *Journal of Financial Economics, 45*(2), 223–255.

Löhr, J., & Schwenn, K. (2013, January 9). Politiker im Aufsichtsrat: Das Schweigen der Kontrolleure. *Frankfurter Allgemeine Zeitung*. Retrieved from http://www.faz.net/aktuell/politik/inland/politiker-im-aufsichtsrat-das-schweigen-der-kontrolleure-12018573.html?printPagedArticle=true#pageIndex_2

Maddala, G. S. (1977). *Econometrics* (4th ed.). New York, United States: McGraw-Hill.

Maier, A. (2009, July 22). Debt-equity-swap: Das Pokerspiel für klamme Firmen. *Financial Times Deutschland*. Online archive no longer available.

Mann, S. V., & Sicherman, N. W. (1991). The agency costs of free cash flow: Acquisition activity and equity issuances. *Journal of Business, 64*(2), 213–227.

Manne, H. G. (1965). Mergers and the market for corporate control. *Journal of Political Economy, 73*(2), 110–120.

Marchica, M.-T. (2008). *On the relevance of ownership structure in determining the maturity of debt*. University of Manchester, United Kingdom. Paper presented at the 2007 Eastern Finance Association annual meeting, New Orleans, United States. http://dx.doi.org/10.2139/ssrn.1101103

Marris, R. L. (1964). *The economic theory of managerial capitalism*. New York, United States: Free Press of Glencoe.

Marris, R. L., & Mueller, D. C. (1980). The corporation, competition, and the invisible hand. *Journal of Economic Literature, 18*(1), 32–63.

Maury, B. (2006). Family ownership and firm performance: Empirical evidence from Western European corporations. *Journal of Corporate Finance, 12*(2), 321–341.

Maury, B., & Pajuste, A. (2005). Multiple large shareholders and firm value. *Journal of Banking & Finance, 29*(7), 1813–1834.

McConaughy, D. L., Walker, M. C., Henderson, G. V., Jr., & Mishra, C. S. (1998). Founding family controlled firms: Efficiency and value. *Review of Financial Economics, 7*(1), 1–19.

McConnell, J. J., & Servaes, H. (1990). Additional evidence on equity ownership and corporate value. *Journal of Financial Economics, 27*(2), 595–612.

Megginson, W. L., Nash, R. C., & van Randenborgh, M. (1994). Financial and operating performance of newly privatized firms: An international empirical analysis. *Journal of Finance, 49*(2), 403–452.

Megginson, W. L., & Netter, J. M. (2001). From state to market: A survey of empirical studies on privatization. *Journal of Economic Literature, 39*(2), 321–389.

Mela, C. F., & Kopalle, P. K. (2002). The impact of collinearity on regression analysis: The asymmetric effect of negative and positive correlations. *Applied Economics, 34*(6), 667–677.

Meyer, R. A. (1975). Publicly owned versus privately owned utilities: A policy choice. *Review of Economics and Statistics, 57*(4), 391–399.

de Miguel, A., Pindado, J., & de la Torre, C. (2004). Ownership structure and firm value: New evidence from Spain. *Strategic Management Journal, 25*(12), 1199–1207.

Mikkelson, W. H., & Ruback, R. S. (1985). An empirical analysis of the interfirm equity investment process. *Journal of Financial Economics, 14*(4), 523–553.

Mínguez-Vera, A., & Martín-Ugedo, J. F. (2007). Does ownership structure affect value? A panel data analysis for the Spanish market. *International Review of Financial Analysis, 16*(1), 81–98.

Mishra, D. P., Heide, J. B., & Cort, S. G. (1998). Information asymmetry and levels of agency relations. *Journal of Marketing Research, 35*(3), 277–295.

Mitnick, B. M. (1975). The theory of agency: The policing "paradox" and regulatory behavior. *Public Choice, 24*(1), 27–42.

Monopolkommission. (2014). *Zwanzigstes Hauptgutachten der Monopolkommission: Eine Wettbewerbsordnung für die Finanzmärkte* (Unterrichtung durch die Bundesregierung). Retrieved from http://www.monopolkommission.de/images/PDF/HG/HG20/HG_XX_gesamt.pdf

Morck, R., Nakamura, M., & Shivdasani, A. (2000). Banks, ownership structure, and firm value in Japan. *Journal of Business, 73*(4), 539–567.

Morck, R., Shleifer, A., & Vishny, R. W. (1988). Management ownership and market valuation: An empirial analysis. *Journal of Financial Economics, 20*(January-March), 293–315.

Moulton, B. R. (1986). Random group effects and the precision of regression estimates. *Journal of Econometrics, 32*(3), 385–397.

Mura, R. (2007). Do non-executive directors and institutional investors have minds of their own? Evidence on performance of UK firms. *Financial Management, 36*(3), 81–112.

Myers, S. C. (1977). Determinants of corporate borrowing. *Journal of Financial Economics, 5*(2), 147–175.

Narayanan, M. P. (1985). Managerial incentives for short-term results. *Journal of Finance, 40*(5), 1469–1484.

Newson, R. B. (2012). Sensible paramters for univariate and multivariate splines. *Stata Journal, 12*(3), 479–504.

Ng, C. Y. M. (2005). An empirical study of the relation between ownership and performance in a family-based corporate environment. *Journal of Accounting, Auditing & Finance, 20*(2), 121–146.

Nickell, S., Nicolitsas, D., & Dryden, N. (1997). What makes firms perform well? *European Economic Review, 41*(3-5), 783–796.

Niedrigzins treibt Geschäft von Investoren in Deutschland (2015, February 23). *Handelsblatt.* Retrieved from http://www.handelsblatt.com/finanzen/maerkte/marktberichte/investitionen-steigen-niedrigzins-treibt-investoren-an/11411338.html

van Niewerburgh, S., & Veldkamp, L. (2009). Information immobility and the home bias puzzle. *Journal of Finance, 64*(3), 1187–1215.

Opler, T. C., & Titman, S. (1994). Financial distress and corporate performance. *Journal of Finance, 49*(3), 1015–1040.

Organisation for Economic Co-operation and Development. (2003). *Privatising state-owned enterprises: An overview of policies and practices in OECD countries.* Retrieved from http://www.oecd-ilibrary.org/governance/privatising-state-owned-enterprises_9789264104099-en

Organisation for Economic Co-operation and Development. (2013). *OECD institutional investors statistics 2013*. Retrieved from http://www.oecd-ilibrary.org/finance-and-investment/oecd-institutional-investors-statistics-2013_instinv-2013-en

Organisation for Economic Co-operation and Development. (2014). *Corporate governance factbook*. Retrieved from http://www.oecd.org/daf/ca/CorporateGovernanceFactbook.pdf

Orsini, N., & Greenland, S. (2011). A procedure to tabulate and plot results after flexible modeling of a quantitative covariate. *Stata Journal, 11*(1), 1–29.

Overland, C., Mavruk, T., & Sjögren, S. (2012). *Keeping it real or keeping it simple? Ownership concentration measures compared* (Working paper). University of Gothenburg, Sweden. Retrieved from http://www.gu.se/digitalAssets/1382/1382969_overland-mavruk-sjogren--120121-.pdf

Pagano, M., & Roell, A. (1998). The choice of stock ownership structure: Agency costs, monitoring, and the decision to go public. *Quarterly Journal of Economics, 113*(1), 187–225.

Palmer, J. (1973). The profit-performance effects of the separation of ownership from control in large U.S. industrial corporations. *Bell Journal of Economics, 4*(1), 293–303.

Pedersen, T., & Thomsen, S. (1997). European patterns of corporate performance: A twelve-country study. *Journal of International Business Studies, 28*(4), 759–778.

Pedersen, T., & Thomsen, S. (1999). Economic and systemic explanations of ownership concentration among Europe's largest companies. *International Journal of the Economics of Business, 6*(3), 367–381.

Pedersen, T., & Thomsen, S. (2003). Ownership structure and value of the largest European firms: The importance of owner identity. *Journal of Management and Governance, 7*(1), 27–55.

Pellens, B., & Schmidt, A. (2014). *Verhalten und Präferenzen Deutscher Aktionäre: Eine Befragung von privaten und institutionellen Anlegern zum Informationsverhalten, zur Dividendenpräferenz und zur Wahrnehmung von Stimmrechten*. Retrieved from Deutsches Aktieninstitut website: https://www.dai.de/files/dai_usercontent/dokumente/studien/2014-11-02%20Studie%20Aktionaersverhalten.pdf

Pescatrice, D. R., & Trapani, J. M., III (1980). The performance and objectives of public and private utilities operating in the United States. *Journal of Public Economics, 13*(2), 259–276.

Petersen, T. (2009). Analyzing panel data: Fixed- and random-effects models. In M. Hardy & A. Bryman (Eds.), *Handbook of data analysis* (pp. 331–345). London, United Kingdom: Sage.

Picot, A., & Kaulmann, T. (1989). Comparative performance of government-owned and privately-owned industrial corporations: Empirical results from six countries. *Journal of Institutional and Theoretical Economics, 145*(2), 298–316.

Picot, G. (2008). Familien- und Mittelstandsunternehmen im globalen Wandel von Wirtschaft und Gesellschaft. In G. Picot (Ed.), *Handbuch für Familien- und Mittelstandsunternehmen – Strategie, Gestaltung, Zukunftssicherung*. Stuttgart, Germany: Schäffer-Poeschel.

Pindado, J., & de la Torre, C. (2004). Why is ownership endogenous? *Applied Economics Letters, 11*(4), 901–904.

Pindado, J., & Requejo, I. (2012). *Data management and panel data models* (Course manuscript, July 9-13, 2012). Universidad de Salamanca, Spain.

Porter, M. E. (1992). Capital choices: Changing the way America invests in industry. *Journal of Applied Corporate Finance, 5*(2), 4–16.

Pound, J. (1988). Proxy contests and the efficiency of shareholder oversight. *Journal of Financial Economics, 20*(January-March), 237-265.

PricewaterhouseCoopers. (2014). *Trends shaping governance and the board of future: PwC's 2014 annual corporate directors survey*. Retrieved from http://www.pwc.com/us/en/corporate-governance/annual-corporate-directors-survey/assets/annual-corporate-directors-survey-full-report-pwc.pdf

Privatisation in China: Capitalism confined (2011, September 3). *The Economist*. Retrieved from http://www.economist.com/node/21528262

Prowse, S. D. (1992). The structure of corporate ownership in Japan. *Journal of Finance, 47*(3), 1121–1140.

Putterman, L. (1993). Ownership and the nature of the firm. *Journal of Comparative Economics, 17*(2), 243–263.

Radice, H. K. (1971). Control type, profitability and growth in large firms: An empirical study. *Economic Journal, 91*(323), 547–562.

Rajgopal, S., & Venkatachalam, M. (1997). *The role of institutional investors in corporate governance: An empirical investigation* (Working paper No. 1436). Stanford University, United States. Retrieved from http://www.gsb.stanford.edu/faculty-research/working-papers/role-institutional-investors-corporate-governance-empirical

Rapp, M. S., Schaller, P., & Wolff, M. (2011). Aktienbasierte Langfristanreize im Rahmen der Vorstandsvergütung: Evidenz auf Basis deutscher Prime Standard Unternehmen, *Betriebswirtschaft, 71*(4), 311–330.

Rappaport, A. (1986). *Creating shareholder value: A guide for managers and investors*. New York, United States: Free Press.

Rediker, K. J., & Seth, A. (1995). Boards of directors and substitution effects of alternative governance mechanisms. *Strategic Management Journal, 16*(2), 58–99.

Reed, W. R. (2015). On the practice of lagging variables to avoid simultaneity. *Oxford Bulletin of Economics and Statistics*. Advance online publication. Retrieved from Wiley online library: http://online library.wiley.com/journal/10.1111/(ISSN)1468-0084/issues

Reeder, J. R. (1975). Corporate ownership and control: A synthesis of recent findings. *Industrial Organization Review, 3*(1), 18–27.

Reiss, P. C., & Wolak, F. A. (2007). Structural econometrics modeling: Rationales and examples from industrial organization. In J. J. Heckman & E. E. Leamer (Eds.), *Handbook of econometrics* (1st ed., Vol. 6, Part A, pp. 4277–4415). Amsterdam, Netherlands: North-Holland.

Renneboog, L. (2000). Ownership, managerial control and the governance of companies listed on the Brussels Stock Exchange. *Journal of Banking & Finance, 24*(12), 1959–1995.

Richard, P. J., Devinney, T. M., Yip, G. S., & Johnson, G. (2009). Measuring organizational performance: Towards methodological best practice. *Journal of Management, 35*(3), 718–804.

Richter, A., & Weiss, C. (2013). Determinants of ownership concentration in public firms: The importance of firm-, industry- and country-level factors. *International Review of Law and Economics, 33*(March), 1–14.

Roe, M. J. (1993). Some differences in corporate governance in Germany, Japan and America. In T. Baums, R. M. Buxbaum, & K. J. Hopt (Eds.), *Institutional investors and corporate governance* (pp. 23–88). Berlin, Germany: De Gruyter.

Roll, R. (1988). R^2. *Journal of Finance, 43*(2), 541–566.

Roodman, D. (2009). A note on the theme of too many instruments. *Oxford Bulletin of Economics and Statistics, 71*(1), 135–158.

Ross, S. A. (1973). The economic theory of agency: The principal's problem. *American Economic Review, 63*(2), 134–139.

Rothschild, M., & Stiglitz, J. (1976). Equilibrium in competitive insurance markets: An essay on the economics of imperfect information. *Quarterly Journal of Economics, 90*(4), 629–649.

Rottwilm, C. (2015, April 10). ETFs - günstig, aber gefährlich. *Manager Magazin.* Retrieved from http://www.manager-magazin.de/finanzen/boerse/15-jahre-etfs-in-deutschland-die-macht-der-indexfonds-a-1027577.html

Ruiz-Mallorquí, M. V., & Santana-Martín, D. J. (2011). Dominant institutional owners and firm value. *Journal of Banking & Finance, 35*(1), 118–129.

Sáchez-Ballesta, J. P., & García-Meca, E. (2007). A meta-analytic vision of the effect of ownership structure on firm performance. *Corporate Governance: An International Review, 15*(5), 879–893.

Sacristán-Navarro, M., Cabeza-García, L., & Gómez-Ansón, S. (2015). The company you keep: The effect of other shareholders in family firms. *Corporate Governance: An International Review.* Advance online publication. Retrieved from Wiley online library: http://online library.wiley.com/journal/10.1111/(ISSN)1467-8683/accepted

Schäfer, U. (2010, May 17). Die Helden im Hintergrund. *Süddeutsche Zeitung.* Retrieved from http://www.sueddeutsche.de/wirtschaft/sz-serie-ueber-familienunternehmen-die-helden-im-hintergrund-1.791231

Schaffer, M. E. (2005). "xtivreg2": Stata module to perform extended IV/2SLS, GMM and AC/HAC, LIML and k-class regression for panel data models (Statistical software component). Retrieved from RePEc IDEAS website http://ideas.repec.org/c/boc/bocode/s456501.html

Schirwitz, B. (2007). Eine Chronik klassischer Konjunkturzyklen für Deutschland. *ifo Dresden berichtet, 14*(5), 3–11. Retrieved from CESifo website: https://www.cesifo-group.de/ifo Home/publications/docbase/details.html?docId=14575295

Seifert, B., Gonenc, H., & Wright, J. (2005). The international evidence on performance and equity ownership by insiders, blockholders, and institutions. *Journal of Multinational Financial Management, 15*(2), 171–191.

Semykina, A., & Wooldridge, J. M. (2010). Estimating panel data models in the presence of endogeneity and selection. *Journal of Financial Economics, 157*(2), 375–380.

ShareSoc UK Individual Shareholder Society. (n.d.). *UK stock market statistics: Some background information*. Retrieved from http://www.sharesoc.org/market_statistics.html

Sherman, H. C., & Kaen, F. R. (1997). Die deutschen Banken und ihr Einfluss auf Unternehmensentscheidungen. *ifo Schnelldienst, 23*, 3–20.

Shiller, R. J. (1981). Do stock prices move too much to be justified by subsequent changes in dividends? *American Economic Review, 71*(3), 421–436.

Shiller, R. J., & Pound, J. (1989). Survey evidence on diffusion of interest and information among investors. *Journal of Economic Behavior and Organization, 12*(1), 47–66.

Shirley, M. M., & Walsh, P. (2000). *Public vs. private ownership: The current state of the debate.* Retrieved from World Bank website: http://elibrary.worldbank.org/doi/book/10.1596/1813-9450-2420

Shleifer, A. (1998). State versus private ownership. *Journal of Economic Perspectives, 12*(4), 133–150.

Shleifer, A., & Vishny, R. W. (1986). Large shareholders and corporate control. *Journal of Political Economy, 94*(3), 461–189.

Shleifer, A., & Vishny, R. W. (1997). A survey of corporate governance. *Journal of Finance, 52*(2), 737–783.

Short, H. (1994). Ownership, control, financial structure and the performance of firms. *Journal of Economic Surveys, 8*(3), 203–249.

Short, H., & Keasey, K. (1999). Managerial ownership and the performance of firms: Evidence from the UK. *Journal of Corporate Finance, 5*(1), 79–101.

Siemens. (2014, September 22). *Bosch to acquire Siemens' stake in BSH Bosch und Siemens Hausgeräte GmbH.* Retrieved from http://www.siemens.com/press/en/pressrelease/?press=/en/pressrelease/2014/corporate/axx20140968.htm&content=CC&content=Corp

Slager, A. M. H. (2004). *Banking across borders* (Doctoral dissertation, Erasmus University Rotterdam, Netherlands). Retrieved from http://repub.eur.nl/pub/1301

Smith, P. L. (1979). Splines as a useful and convenient statistical tool. *American Statistician, 33*(2), 57–62.

Sorensen, R. (1974). The separation of ownership and control and firm performance: An empirical analysis. *Southern Economic Journal, 41*(1), 145–148.

Spence, M. (1987). Job market signaling. *Quarterly Journal of Economics, 73*(3), 355–374.

Spremann, K. (1990). Asymmetrische Information. *Zeitschrift für Betriebswirtschaft, 60*(5-6), 561–586.

Sribney, W., Wiggins, V., & Drukker, D. (1999, April). Negative and missing R-squared for 2SLS/IV (Online forum post). Retrieved from Stata website: http://www.stata.com/support/faqs/statistics/two-stage-least-squares/

Statistisches Bundesamt Deutschland. (2012). *Konjunkturindikatoren: Bruttoinlandsprodukt.* Retrieved from http://www.destatis.de/jetspeed/portal/cms/Sites/destatis/Internet/DE/Content/Statistiken/Zeitreihen/WirtschaftAktuell/VolkswirtschaftlicheGesamtrechnungen/Content75/vgr111ga,templateId=renderPrint.psml

Stein, J. C. (1989). Efficient capital markets, inefficient firms: A model of myopic corporate behavior. *Quarterly Journal of Economics, 104*(4), 655–669.

Stevens, D. E., & Thevaranjan, A. (2005). *Is there room within principal-agent theory for ethics?* (Working paper). Syracuse University, United States. http://dx.doi.org/10.2139/ ssrn.708524

Stice, J. D., & Stice, E. K. (2014). *Intermediate accounting* (19th ed.). Mason, United States: South-Western.

Stock, J. H., & Yogo, M. (2005). Testing for weak instruments in linear IV regression. In Andrews, D. W. K. & J. H. Stock (Eds.), *Identification and inference for econometric models - Essays in honor of Thomas Rothenberg* (pp. 80–108). Cambridge, United States: Cambridge University Press.

Studenmund, A. H. (2001). *Using econometrics: A practical guide* (4th ed.). Boston, United States: Addison-Wesley.

Stulz, R. M. (1988). Managerial control of voting rights: Financing policies and the market for corporate control. *Journal of Financial Economics, 20*(January-March), 25–54.

Stulz, R. M. (1990). Managerial discretion and optimal financing policies. *Journal of Financial Economics, 26*(1), 3–27.

Templin, B. A. (2010). The government shareholder: Regulating public ownership of private enterprise. *Administrative Law Review, 62*(4), 1127–1215.

Thomsen, S., & Pedersen, T. (2000). Ownership structure and economic performance in the largest European companies. *Strategic Management Journal, 21*(6), 689–705.

Thomsen, S., Pedersen, T., & Kvist, H. K. (2006). Blockholder ownership: Effects on firm value in market and control based governance systems. *Journal of Corporate Finance, 12*(2), 246–269.

TNS Infratest. (2002). *Differences in investor attitudes across Europe.* Retrieved from http://www.tns-infratest.com/presse/presseinformation.asp?prID=170

Tobin, J. (1969). A general equilibrium approach to monetary theory. *Journal of Money, Credit and Banking, 1*(1), 15–29.

Tovar, T., & Newbury, R. (2010). *Has director pay found its floor?* (Executive Compensation Bulletin). Retrieved from Towers Watson website: http://www.towerswatson.com/~/media/Pdf/Press/2010/09/Director-Pay-Bulletin-Aug-31-2010.pdf

U.S. Securities and Exchange Commission, Division of Corporation Finance. (n.d.). *Standard industrial classification (SIC) code list.* Retrieved from http://www.sec.gov/info/edgar/siccodes.htm

U.S. Securities and Exchange Commission. (2015). *Year-by-year SEC enforcement statistics.* Retrieved from http://www.sec.gov/news/newsroom/images/enfstats.pdf

Utete, G. (2008). *Institutional investor preferences and firm value.* Auburn University, United States. Paper presented at the 2009 Financial Management Association annual meeting, Reno, United States. Retrieved from http://www.fma.org/Reno/Papers/Institutional_Preferences.pdf

Venkatraman, N., & Ramanujam, V. (1986). Measurement of business performance in strategy research: A comparison of approaches. *Academy of Management Review, 11*(4), 801–814.

Verbeek, M. (2004). *A guide to modern econometrics* (2nd ed.). Chichester, United Kingdom: John Wiley & Sons.

Villalonga, B., & Amit, R. (2006). How do ownership, control and management affect firm value? *Journal of Financial Economics, 80*(2), 385–417.

Vittinghoff, E., Glidden, D. V., Shiboski, S. C., & McCulloch, C. E. (2012). *Regression methods in biostatistics: Linear, logistic, survival, and repeated measures models* (2nd ed.). New York, United States: Springer.

Volkswagen. (2014). *Aktionärsstruktur* (as of December 2013). Retrieved from http://www.volkswagenag.com/content/vwcorp/content/de/investor_relations/share/Shareholder_Structure.html

Voß, S., & Müller, A. (2011). *Die Wirtschafts- und Finanzkrise: Teil II* (Working paper No. 03-2011). Fachhochschule Hannover, Germany. Retrieved from: http://www.fakultaet4.fh-hannover.de/fileadmin/media/doc/f4/Aktivitaeten/Veroeffentlichungen/2011/gb-11-03-10a.pdf

Wahal, S., & McConnell, J. J. (2000). Do institutional investors exacerbate managerial myopia? *Journal of Corporate Finance, 6*(3), 307–329.

Walkling, R. A., & Long, M. S. (1984). Agency theory, managerial welfare, and takeover bid resistance. *RAND Journal of Economics, 15*(1), 54–68.

Wall, T. D., Michie, J., Patterson, M., Wood, S. J., Sheehan, M., Clegg, C. W., & West, M. (2004). On the validity of subjective measures of company performance. *Personnel Psychology, 57*(1), 95–118.

Weiss, C., & Hilger, S. (2012). Ownership concentration beyond good and evil: Is there an effect on corporate performance? *Journal of Management & Governance, 16*(4), 727–752.

Welch, E. (2003). The relation between ownership structure and performance in listed Australian companies. *Australian Journal of Management, 28*(3), 287–305.

Wenger, E., & Kaserer, C. (1998). The German system of corporate governance - A model that should not be imitated. In S. W. Black & M. Moersch (Eds.), *Advances in Finance, Investment and Banking* (Vol. 5: Competition and convergence in financial markets. The German and Anglo-Amercian models, pp. 41–78). Amsterdam, Netherlands: North-Holland.

Wildau, G. (2014, August 10). China kicks off second round of privatization. *Financial Times.* Retrieved from http://www.ft.com/intl/cms/s/0/ec28674c-13ac-11e4-84b7-00144feabdc0.html

Williams, R. (2015). *Outliers* (Technical note). University of Notre Dame, United States. Retrieved from https://www3.nd.edu/~rwilliam/xsoc63993/l24.pdf

Williamson, O. E. (1964). *The economics of discretionary behavior: Managerial objectives in a theory of the firm*. Englewood Cliffs, United States: Prentice-Hall.

Wintoki, M. B., Linck, J. S., & Netter, J. M. (2012). Endogeneity and the dynamics of internal corporate governance. *Journal of Financial Economics, 105*(3), 581–606.

Wölfer, K. (2010). Are family-owned businesses better innovators? In A. Gerybadze, U. Hommel, H. W. Reiners, & D. Thomaschewski (Eds.), *Innovation and international corporate growth* (pp. 393–415). Berlin, Germany: Springer.

Wooldridge, J. M. (2002). *Econometric analysis of cross section and panel data* (2nd ed.). Cambridge, United States: MIT Press.

Wooldridge, J. M. (2009). *Introductory econometrics - A modern approach* (4th ed.). Independence, United States: South-Western.

Woolridge, J. R., & Snow, C. C. (1990). Stock market reaction to strategic investment decisions. *Strategic Management Journal, 11*(5), 353–363.

Wu, D.-M. (1973). Alternative tests of independence between stochastic regressors and disturbances. *Econometrica, 41*(4), 733–750.

Zwiebel, J. (1995). Block investment and partial benefits of corporate control. *Review of Economic Studies, 62*(2), 161–185.

www.ingramcontent.com/pod-product-compliance
Ingram Content Group UK Ltd.
Pitfield, Milton Keynes, MK11 3LW, UK
UKHW021843100926
8556IPUK00019B/1015

9 783631 667156